4/03

Musical Landscapes in Color

Conversations with
Black American Composers

WILLIAM C. BANFIELD

The Scarecrow Press, Inc.
Lanham, Maryland, and Oxford
2003

SCARECROW PRESS, INC.

Published in the United States of America
by Scarecrow Press, Inc.
A Member of the Rowman & Littlefield Publishing Group
4720 Boston Way, Lanham, Maryland 20706
www.scarecrowpress.com

PO Box 317
Oxford
OX2 9RU, UK

Copyright © 2003 by William C. Banfield

British Library Cataloguing in Publication Information Available

Library of Congress Cataloging-in-Publication Data

Banfield, William C., 1961–
    Musical landscapes in color : conversations with Black American
composers / William C. Banfield.
        p.   cm.
    Includes index.
    ISBN 0-8108-3706-4 (alk. paper)
    1. African American composers—Interviews.   2. African Americans—
Music—History and criticism.   I. Title.
ML390 .B235 2003
780′.92′396073—dc21   2002005761

∞ ™ The paper used in this publication meets the minimum requirements of American
National Standard for Information Sciences—Permanence of Paper for Printed Library
Materials, ANSI/NISO Z39.48-1992.
Manufactured in the United States of America.

Contents

To Noel DaCosta, Tony Williams, and Jester Hairston

Foreword

Can you imagine American music without the work of black composers or without black music in general? Still, there is a refusal, a denial, of that reality. Through the work that I have done with the Black Repertory Ensemble, I have been able to see the entire panorama of American music as created by us, going back to Francis Johnson and coming down that long, tortuous road. Without these people, without their contributions, American music would be altogether different. This involves people from Louisiana and people from New York. This includes people like Will Marion Cook and Eubie Blake. American music would be radically different without what these people have done. And it is not only those who have dealt with nonpopular forms because, if you include the popular music, black music is what has given American music its identity. It is just the music itself; whether we can name two, three, a dozen, a hundred or a thousand black musicians and composers, it is the totality without which American music would be completely different. You can find traces of this stuff in Walter Piston. You can find traces of it in Charles Ives and certainly in Copland. It pervades American music to such an extent that it can be denied only by people who have blinders on or who cannot hear. The only real impact Chadwick has had on American music is that Chadwick taught William Grant Still. They were skilled, and all of that, but they didn't bring anything new; their work was just the rehashing of German Romanticism. I am saying that American music would be completely unrecognizable in terms of what we know now without the music of black composers. Somebody once said that without black music, American music would be Lawrence Welk.

Hale Smith, July 26, 1996

Acknowledgments

I must thank numerous well-wishers, helpful critics, scholars, consultants, and artists who have contributed to this quest to find meaning. Many thanks to Shirley Lambert and Norman Horrocks at Scarecrow Press, both of whom showed genuine interest and excitement and also gave me strong support and encouragement. Thanks to David Baker, my big brother, and to Lida Baker, both of whom were the primary consultants in this project. T. J. Anderson was and is my insightful, energetic mentor and critic. I am grateful for his input and enthusiasm. Crystal Keels is a friendly and combative editor who is responsible for all of the transcribing of "those exchanges." She listened to over two and a half years of conversations, fifty or more ninety-minute cassette tapes. This book is as much hers as anyone else's. Thank you, "Crystal with a C," for your patience, talks, insights, friendship, and unswerving belief in my work. My second editor was Leigh Linn, who began by helping me collate the composer's edits and organize all the various preliminary changes in the manuscript before the book went to press. Leigh, you saved our literary lives here! Thanxxxx!

My thanks to Linda Jean and the Department of Afro-American Studies, the Afro-American Arts Institute, and the Archives of African American Music and Culture at Indiana University for transcribing, telephone, and cataloging assistance. Thanks also to Indiana University RUGS (Research University Graduate School) for grant assistance. Many thanks to Laura Crane and Maysha Richardson for their care and archival expertise in organizing and maintaining the scores of the Undine Smith Moore Collection.

Maestro Bill Bolcolm deserves credit for his ideas, music, guidance, and the book *Reminiscing with Sissle and Blake* (R. Kimball and William Bolcolm, Viking Press, 1973). My gratitude goes to Olly Wilson, whose committed, critical reading and supportive discussions helped to clarify many issues that surfaced in the beginning stages of the writing. I would also like to thank Judith Anne Still for her tireless energies in upholding the work of her father and for encouraging me in my own. I am grateful to William Dargen and William Warfield for including me in their efforts with the Still Going On Projects. Philip Brunelle has encouraged me by championing my own music and that of many other black American composers. His contribution also includes providing books and scores from his own collection; he always bought one for himself and another for me. Thanks Philip. I also thank all my friends and colleagues at the American Composers Forum who have encouraged and supported my work.

Thanks to two great friends and incredible minds, Kevin Scott and Donal Fox, who were always there for those midnight technical questions like, "What year was Goercki born?" Also, and while their essays were not included here, I am very thankful to the critical comments made to me by composers Alvin Singleton and Tania Leon. Your stories and work are a great inspiration to me.

To composer Randall Davidson, for those long dinner talks about our future as creators; Mary Easter (daughter of Undine Smith Moore), who allowed me to examine the complete holdings of the Undine Smith Moore estate; composer Libby Larsen, a big sister who is always there to advise and counsel—many, many thanks.

To Hale Smith, who has fussed with me for several years about all this and offered one a most beautiful and insightful musical narratives on his life, a narrative that has become a great shaping element of this writing—thanks, Hale.

Thanks to Dean Willis Patterson for his encouragement and the gift of the Undine Smith Moore original manuscripts to my collection. Linda Jean (at IU), thanks for your "pushin' da paper." To Anthony Davis, I am appreciative for having been called out (at dinner over catfish and hot sauce at Fishbone's in Detroit) for the exclusivity in my language in regards to the wider spectrum of the work of historical Black composers like Louis Armstrong and Scott Joplin. Many thanks to friends like Guthrie Ramsey, Raelinda Brown, and Dwight Andrews, whose scholarly and precise thinking and critical reading of and suggestions on my work kept me reading my text over and over again for fear of their "friendly" scrutiny.

To Bobby McFerrin (the "walking note"), Herbie Hancock, Patrice Rushen, George Duke, Tony Williams, Michael Powell, and Ysaye Barnwell, in addition to your work as composers, your combined additional industry insights and the friendship you have extended are gifts beyond value. Ysaye Barnwell, your support of my work is greatly appreciated. I will write "your opera."

Most importantly, I wish to thank all the composers/creators who allowed me to tie up their dinner or composing time while we exchanged and shared in preparation for the publication of this book. Your ideas, music, and perspectives will greatly illuminate the meanings of your contributions for society as a whole and for all those who have the immediate privilege to "witness" your work. Thank you much, and be well. Hope you enjoy the journey.

Introduction

When one thinks of the avant-garde, one immediately thinks
of revolutionary composers, those with a new musical language, those who are involved in experimentation, or anything
outside the establishment. If we take this as definition, and
since we can already assume that all black composers have
always been outside the establishment, one logically reaches
the conclusion that all black composers are avant-garde.

—T. J. Anderson
Black Music in Our Culture, 1963

I thought about this book long before I could even imagine being able to under-
take such a project. The foundation upon which this endeavor rests is the 1978
book *The Black Composer Speaks,* by David Baker and Lida Belt Baker, a
landmark publication and a source of inspiration. It is a unique and forceful
document, providing potent, prophetic, and critical assessments and definitions
of what might be thought of as an elite group of black melody makers. As
Robert Klotman declares in the foreword, "*The Black Composer Speaks* is a
book for everyone!"

For the past four and a half years, I have conducted personal and intense
interviews with contemporary black American composers. Spanning a seventy-
year period, this book examines the evolution of the careers of some the most
influential contemporary black American artists. One result has been the collection of insightful, intriguing, and dynamic accounts of the philosophical elements involved in musical expression, the role of music in contemporary
culture, and the role of the contemporary artist from the perspective of a composer.

A shortage of documentation and sustained critical inquiry regarding
black American music and perspectives now impairs historical and contempo-

rary accounts of American musical culture. It is difficult to locate information pertaining to the contributions of African American composers, and it is harder still to find a body of collected writings expressing the ideas of black composers themselves.

As a composer looking at American musical culture, I have noted repeatedly the exclusion of both the music of black composers and the ideas of black musical thinkers from academic and historical discourse. While the contributions of contemporary popular, rap, and jazz artists are increasingly investigated in scholarly inquiries, the contributions of black American composers are often overlooked. *Landscapes in Color* reflects my passionate commitment to the documentation of the work of creative, innovative black American composers.

The Quest

Over the past few years, I have also embarked on a personal journey arising from my own academic, spiritual quest for meaning. The end result of this quest is the identification of a vast body of literature created by black composers in the United States. My intention here is not to suggest that black composers are questioning Western cultural hegemony (cultural domination), but rather to demonstrate that black American composers are an important part of the Western framework of composition. The composers themselves will discuss this in terms of musical conventions and practices, in concert as well as black American vernacular forms, all synthesized into what we have come to know as "American music."

Certain preliminary concepts of culture and aesthetics have helped to inform me of and sensitize me to the unique contributions these artists have made and continue to make in the contemporary world of music. The study of music involves a multidisciplinary approach; therefore, to extract meaning, understanding, and appreciation, many questions must be considered simultaneously. Discussions of the music of black American composers must consider not only the music itself but the personalities, lives, and perspectives of these artists as well. The music of black American composers should be viewed simultaneously through the lenses of American sociology, Western concepts of art and taste, and African and African American ideas of value and taste, including vernacular forms, from the spirituals to blues, jazz, and contemporary popular movements. Without a formal musicological or sociological analysis, in this text the composers themselves frame and address some of these issues, in their own unique ways.

Musical Landscapes in Color: Conversations with Black American Composers reflects, then, a quest to find meaning by examining the work and perspectives of nearly forty living African American composers of different generations, styles, and conceptual approaches. This project is also an attempt to identify creative and spiritual threads that may link these artists to common foundations. Equally important, this project includes dialogue with various artists who wear several hats—as composers, conductors, and performers, within diverse traditions.

Thus, *Landscapes* is constructed to provide a creative narrative that explores the experiences and ideologies of these composers in their own words. This project provides intimate and personal dialogue between composers speaking about common destinies, hopes, and triumphs. More importantly, perhaps, this quest will also illustrate the diversity among these creators in their perspectives, their stylistic approaches, and their backgrounds.

Certainly more needs to be written about earlier American composers like Francis Johnson (1792–1844), William Appo (1808–8?), Lawrence Freeman (1869–1954), Edmund Jenkins (1894–1926), Clarence Cameron White (1880–1960), Magaret Bonds (1913–72), and others. This particular project, however, focuses largely on the late-twentieth-century concert and symphonic music traditions, the heirs of William Grant Still, Florence Price, William Dawson, Undine Smith Moore, Ulysses Kay, and others. *Landscapes* looks at those who are taking up the torch to redefine canonic concert traditions, and it simultaneously examines historical, aesthetic and stylistic perspectives within black musical arts traditions. Ensuring the permanence of these contributions requires serious consideration of these artists who are taking up the burdens of the foundation builders.

These contemporary composers uphold certain traditions and forge personalized, profound voices while affecting American culture in powerful and unique ways. Thus this project examines individual creative processes as well as the possible links that exist as the result of shared historical realities within a largely written tradition that, as a discipline, is highly individualized. It should also be noted that black artistic traditions in American culture speak to and inform each other, and that therefore jazz and popular traditions are parts of the contemporary mix.

In their discourses the artists address questions pertaining to the direction of American contemporary art music in the twenty-first century; the role of tradition in shaping contemporary artists; the question of black cultural references in composed works; the cultural politics involved in recasting, or reshaping, the educational and repertoire canons; and the ongoing question of the definition and condition of contemporary black musical art.

The following journey is organized into two main sections. The opening discussions are my attempt to present issues in some of the history of the art music of black composers. The second section presents the insights of composers of various generations.

In my attempt to provide perspectives from living voices, I was faced with difficult choices in terms of which composers to include. Clearly, many have been left out. The intent of this project is to provide useful insights into the lives of some of the black composers in contemporary America as we begin the twenty-first century. Who, then, has something significant to say, and how do we measure significance?

The recasting of the American canon through performance, documentation, education, and public exposure by composers became the most important criterion. Even with this general criterion, some noteworthy friends have been left out, and for their exclusion I am sorry. Quite honestly, many volumes need to be written about black composers, more than could fit on the shelves. Composers included in this particular project are those who are documented as professional artists, contributing in established educational and research institutions, and whose work is performed by recognized concert venue organizations and symphony orchestras, heard and seen through recordings and radio broadcasts, and contributes to the musical life of our culture in various communities.

Differing opinions on the issues of race can be seen throughout four generations of the perspectives of American black composers, as early as James Reese Europe. I call this first generation "early nationalistic" (Harry T. Burleigh, Nathaniel Dett).

James Reese Europe (1881–1919) writes, "You see we colored people have our own music that is a part of us. It is a product of our souls. It has been created by the sufferings of our race." This is exactly what Duke Ellington, a member of the second generation, asserted in a 1931 article published in *Rhythm,* a British magazine. Ellington wrote, "My men and my race are the inspiration of my work. I try to catch the character and the mood and feeling of my people. The music of my race is more than just the American idiom. It is the result of our transplantation to American soil and was our reaction in plantation days to the life we lived. What we could not say openly we expressed in our music."

Adherents to this perspective were known as "race men," because their primary concern was focused on black communities. They were proud to assert themselves, to set themselves apart from the mainstream.

The second generation, the "African American composers" (Margaret Bonds, William Dawson, Undine Smith Moore), assert their perspectives as the first to move into recognized concert music circles. William Grant Still represents the concerns of the second generation in saying, "Negro music is infectious, memorable. Those who hear it will not soon forget it. It has developed from a dignified African folk art to a sophisticated, modern musical expression. It is often imitated, seldom acknowledged. But it is ever present, a vital, motivating force in a large part of contemporary music." Clearly, then, there was a feeling within which "we" wanted to be integrated, to be accepted. The second generation had to maintain a delicate balance on the line of cultural identity and in mainstream white concert venues.

The third generation of black American composers can be identified as "the Arrived and the Acknowledged" (George Walker, T. J. Anderson, David Baker, Dorothy Rudd Moore). It seems that the mainstream concert world was uncomfortable and unsure, but it did not matter. Once the doors had been opened by William Grant Still, Price, Dawson, and others, the following generation had a concert home. In a published interview Hale Smith (born 1925) said, "Don't place our music on all black programs. We can do that for ourselves, for our own people. Place our music on programs with Beethoven, Mozart, Schoenberg, Copland, and the contemporary avant-gardists. We don't even have to be called black. When we stand for our bows, the fact will become clear when it should. After the work has made its own impact."

There are two waves of this generation, which I have split into those born between 1925 and 1935 and those born between 1936 and 1945. Because of the mentoring relationships that developed and the similarities of their shared historical window, George Walker and Hale Smith represent the elders, while Tania Leon, Adolphus Hailstork, and Alvin Singleton are among the youngest of this group.

The fourth generation, "Generation X," or the twenty-first-century black composers (Anthony Davis, Donal Fox, Lettie Alston Beckon), are those born between 1950 and 1965; they will become senior figures during the first half of the twenty-first century. In addition to sharing some of the traditional sentiments and relating to an array of contemporary ideologies of previous generations, the fourth generation may also be energized by contemporary popular hip-hop or world-beat sensibilities as well as by Afro-centric academic philosophies. The fourth generation flirts more with Coltrane or George Clinton as opposed to Harry Burleigh, who was attracted to old Negro spirituals. Generation four seems to be interested in whatever musical explorations and hybrids it will take to challenge and change the old institutions and, more importantly, to provide new sound frameworks that were not available in 1950.

This group came of age in a post–civil rights era. Anthony Davis, for instance, argues, "We're warriors in a sense, we're out there and we have to bring this message that American classical music is something that is in the process of being defined. We're challenging in a sense the foundation of what would be described as, 'What is American culture?' There are high stakes in that."

The Questions

Artists have always maintained, at different points, some notion of where they, their discourses, their art, and their colleagues' works fit into their own society's contemporary mix. What follows are perspectives of and discussions with some of the leading composers in this country, legatees in many respects of some of the composers thought of as foundation layers and path builders. There are nine categories of questions, which were used to bring organization to the numerous issues presented and introduced by the composers. Categories are:

1. Personal evolution as a creator
2. Significant artistic influences
3. Philosophy of music/arts education
4. Composition process
5. Role as a creator in society
6. Issues and problems of ethnicity
7. Direction of art in American musical culture
8. Commentary on contemporary influences and movements
9. Most significant creations and achievements, and current and projected goals.

The questions that fell into these categories were:

1. What is your musical background? Talk about the influences of your church, geographical (southern/northern), or national associations. What is the developmental evolution of your music, or what are significant events that have shaped your career? What was the earliest, major, earthshaking artistic experience that awakened your creative instincts? Was this what drew you to being a composer?
2. Who was the composer, musician, or group that influenced you the most in your evolution as a creator? With which songwriting traditions

or personalities do you see yourself connected? Who do you see as the most important or influential American composer?

3. What is your philosophy of music, and how does it function in your mind? Are you a composer first, or a creative artist compelled to write? If you had one lesson to share with a young composer, what would you share? What steps do you see as necessary to address the problems of art education in this country? What is your opinion of Black History Month programs, concerts, or literature circulated currently? Do you see any commonalities between, for example, the Bach tradition (fugue theory) and Parker be-bop lines? Or between Ravel's orchestration and Ellingtonian traditions?

4. What is your process of composition or production? In which mediums or vehicles do you work most effectively (e.g., orchestral, chamber, jazz ensemble)? Why? Do you believe in extramusical influence, or are your works pure musical structure, made up solely of rhythm, harmony, or melody? Describe the process in choices made for a particular production—why Gregg Philangaines over Herbie Hancock? What advantage does the manipulation of jazz syntax or improvisation give you as a composer?

5. Do you think an artist has any particular role in our society? What is your opinion of the effect of popular music projections in shaping values or influencing youth, both good and bad?

6. Has your ethnicity served you or been a disservice to you the industry? Talk about your experience specifically as a black artist. In your education were you taught about black composers or artists? What were you taught? Do you see a problem in the way black creators have been educated? Do white artists and lay listeners understand what you are saying as a black artist? Do black people appreciate or understand what you create? Talk about your experiences as a black artist with established institutions (education, professional performance agencies). Is cultural reference an issue in qualifying, describing, or appreciating your art? Do you care to be, or prefer not to be, considered as or called a black composer?

7. Where do you see contemporary American music headed? Jazz? Popular? Concert? Can you foresee, or are you engaged in, any new aesthetic movements emerging in the near future (e.g., twelve tone and rap, orchestral hip-hop)?

8. In the last five years, what was the most shocking news, media, or cultural event, which you felt compelled to address creatively in a work? Are there any artists in contemporary America that really excite you? Has their work inspired you to the point of having a direct effect on your art or perspective? How would you describe your work stylistically and aesthetically? How has the public reacted to you as a composer? What have critics said? Where do you see yourself as a composer, in relation to, for example, Ellington, Copland, Mary Lou Williams?

9. In the end, what would you like to have done or said as an artist? That is, what is your ultimate goal? What is your most significant artistic achievement thus far?

Some of the common experiences and commonly expressed ideas among these composers are illuminating. First, one of the most commonly mentioned items was the value placed on the public school system as a training ground for many black American composers. In twenty-five of the composers' experiences, the most crucial training occurred in the public school system. Here, great impressions were made on composers by competent, inspiring, and dedicated music teachers in local communities and neighborhoods.

Another common linkage was musical training in church. While this is not a surprise, since the black church has traditionally provided an incredible base for all kinds of activities in black communities, what goes unspoken is that not only gospel and spiritual music traditions were common but the serious study of the "classic" literature.

A third important commonality was the playing experience, from which arranging interests arose. Many of the composers spoke about their experiences as players in ensembles where they were exposed to instrumental playing, and of developing their craft largely by arranging and creating "charts."

Another common thread was the notion of one's philosophy of music being a vessel for emotional expression or experiential reporting. While this is a very "romantic," and perhaps old-fashioned, idea, it was very much embraced by many of the composers interviewed. Also, while methods of composition ranged from serial to abstract conception, to "blowing over changes," many of the composers felt moved to compose for artistic expression, as well as linked to their prospective roles in society as reflective agents for inspiration and societal change.

While it can be argued that race, or racial politics, is a diminishing factor when it comes to the more universal ideas, such as professional competence and artistic quality, many black composers are acutely aware of the racial ingredient in the American concert music industry. Most, if not all, these artists suggested in their reflections that they would have felt all the more relieved and liberated as artists to reach their goals without the race issues they faced as black artists, particularly in concert music arenas.

Another linkage was the frequency with which black American composers used black cultural vernacular materials for their creations. Some works, while not exhibiting these materials in outwardly traditional ways, relied more abstractly on the conceptual and structural design of the blues, call and response, free improvisation, or rhythmic dynamism, reflecting aspects of African or African American musical sensibilities.

What we seem to see in the last five years of the twentieth century is a larger number of active black composers in the concert music arenas who consciously used, without compromise, apology, or incongruence, black musical principles, aesthetics, sonorities, and structural and formal principles (those found in jazz, improvisational and oral traditions, and popular materials) to create synthesized concert and orchestral works.

These works defy and move beyond the shallow definitions of third stream, fusion, or hybrid categorization. These works, which appear in much greater numbers than in the earlier parts of the century, are elevating concert music, redefining it, and providing new frameworks for what is meant by "American composer."

Another point of connection to the vernacular was the impression that major jazz figures had on most all of these composers. There is reverence for figures such as Duke Ellington and Miles Davis in particular; even composers who always maintained a concert music career saw in Ellington, especially, profound cultural and artistic significance. This is one example that suggests that there are many linkages that bind black American artists across class, stylistic, and aesthetic perspectives.

While this project is not intended to "shout down the system," the composers all agree that "serious" black music in America is excluded from the important places where culture gets critically viewed, heard, taught, and made available for the benefit of mainstream America. This point is made repeatedly throughout this text.

While most of these composers feel connected to what is going on with other artists and fields, the younger generation for the most part feel equally connected to popular culture and its artists. The main issue for many of us is the role and the responsibility of our younger rap and soul singing and performing artists. In every case, from Anthony Davis to Patrice Rushen, from Bobby McFerrin to Regina Harris Baiocchi, these composers feel intimately attached to the activity of the rapper, in terms of their cultural and musical importance. I think this is an important point. This connection to the "mostest" basic vernacular musical impulse remains crucial to black artistic survival in the future. Composers in the fourth generation are keeping a close watch on this part of the tradition.

I think it is important to keep in mind that what follows are transcriptions of conversations, sometimes heated exchanges. My concern here for the reader was to maintain the spontaneous and free-flowing character and energy of our conversations, which took place all across the country over a period of five years. These are not academic essays written by the composers. Some editing did take place, to help the flow of transitions as we moved from topic to topic. In some cases I inserted questions to reiterate for the reader what the issues were. In other cases I felt this was not necessary.

I first approached issues of artistic expression with relationship to the artist's cultural background and the artist's role in society during graduate studies at Boston University, Andover Newton, and Harvard Divinity School. My master's thesis, entitled "Composer/Theologian: A View of the Aesthetic," argued that music and theology were "inseparable disciplines" and further suggested the notion of the composer's role in the edification of the audience. I identified this type of expression as "theological music," a form of expression that has the potential to transform society. I concluded that the primary aesthetic stance of a creator should be didactic. The cultural example for this assertion was black music. Moving from its African root, black music was created in the context of a community in which people were concerned about the "souls of black folk." James Cone's *The Spirituals and the Blues* was the cultural manual for this endeavor.

A trip in 1988 to Dakar, Senegal, provided me with an important cultural justification for much of my argument. After reflecting on my own experience I realized that the cultural/aesthetic portions of the theory I had introduced at Boston University were in fact right on target. That is, within this specific cultural context, music served people in ways immediately connected with their "beingness" in the world, and the composer/creator was an integral part of that. During my stay in Dakar I was introduced to the old African proverb, "The spirit will descend with a good song."

Back home, to gain further insights into black aesthetic history from an academic perspective, I engaged in studies of both African and African American theologies and thus begin to recontextualize my Western concepts of art and creative expression. Still, I needed to find some European allies, to satisfy the concerns of the Euro-centric American academy. I found the nineteenth-century composer Richard Wagner, whose theories on the function of art in society had been accepted by the academy. An analytical probe into the theological/musical content of Wagner's operas as well as the writings of Nietzsche and Schopenhauer gave me an effective entry into the world of aesthetics and artistic reflection. The following year I completed a thesis entitled "Richard Wagner: Philosophical Perspective and Composition."

These findings and my interest in the subject carried over into later graduate work at the University of Michigan, where I pursued a doctorate in music composition. At Michigan I found both allies of and opponents to the concepts of culture I had begun to discover in my "Boston Daze." I then decided to focus on writing the best possible music I could and to make a concerted effort to research the lives, music, and perspectives of black composers. I found a "soul place" in the works and philosophies of black American composers as outlined in David and Lida Baker's *The Black Composer Speaks* (Scarecrow Press, 1978). I found here a group of creative thinkers who refused to accept the narrow thinking of an institutionalized school of music. For many of these black composers, black American music, social philosophy, and European structural principles coexisted in, were very much alive in, and were comfortably interwoven in, their music. It was through this group of composers that I was able to claim my intellectual and aesthetic musical heritages.

A Brief History of Cultural Exclusion

American concert music cannot be defined or adequately described without the inclusion of the background of the lives, perspectives, and music of African

American artists, primarily because so much of what has shaped this country aesthetically was done by black artists. Some of the rationale for exclusionary practices inherent in traditional studies of concert music may be borrowed European notions of the "cultural hero" and affectations associated with this concept. Bach, Mozart, Beethoven, and Wagner are all held up as examples of productivity and artistry, as cultural heroes, and well they should. Unfortunately, too much of the thinking about, and the values in, modern American "art music" was shaped early on by the desire in the United States to associate with the "best" of the modern Western world. Consequently "cultural product" and its preservation are somehow linked to exclusionary practices in education and in institutions where serious music is performed.

As a culture we have inherited some nasty, less than noble, ideas from a monarchical European cultural configuration. Concert music in the United States wears an elitist price tag. Social climbing and the symphony orchestra are often "joined at the hip"; symphony orchestras have been used as vehicles for social status. For example, the early music historian Thomas Kelly notes of concert music, "It is something of the bourgeoisie imitating the aristocratic of a generation before." Perhaps it is a nineteenth-century "thing." There is some evidence that it might have started in (the very proper) Boston. A publication called *Dwight's Musical Journal* in the mid-nineteenth century began to add a note of snobbery and class-consciousness to the idea of going to classical music concerts.[1]

The goal of *Musical Landscapes in Color* is not to place blame on educational and performance institutions but to aid in the efforts being undertaken in many circles to redefine and construct a cultural apparatus that documents and highlights the full history and the range of creations that contribute to American art culture. The need for such an endeavor is underscored in Eric Saltzman's *Twentieth Century Music: An Introduction.* Saltzman writes, "The history of culture can be thought of in many ways; as a succession of events, as the movement of great historical forces, or in terms of the creative personalities. . . . We think of the composer as a creative individual communicating personal, original and unique thoughts with a distinctive style and a particular point of view or expression."

This concept of the composer—derived from the Romantic idea of the artist as "cultural hero"—has led to greater emphasis than ever on creative individuality, originality, and freedom. The very notion of the avant-garde, as it is usually understood, is a nineteenth-century Romantic conception. Saltzman's view is an example of how certain culture biases are manifested in academic traditions of music. It is also useful as an insight into some of the motivations behind the documentation of the work of Western composers. The idea of a "cultural hero" is useful here: Saltzman's argument helps to identify one of the main issues relevant to the problems black composers often face. For example, in this historical configuration, what happens when the black artist intervenes in this discourse of concertizing, which has been traditionally defined by tight-knit rules that were established long ago and far away?

It is important to develop a broader understanding of "American cultural hero"—a powerful notion as it relates to education, research, and art in the public arena. This pervasive mental image must be expanded, especially when dealing with black artists. For instance, there is more to black cultural expression than Michael Jackson, a beautifully poised Michael Jordan, a rapper, or a gospel choir. Unfortunately, academia as well as other recognized institutions of cultural education (including the media, museums, symposia, intellectual research forums, magazines, periodicals and scholarly journals, arts academies, and symphony orchestras) often intentionally and systematically malign the significant artistic and intellectual accomplishments of black culture by engaging in exclusionary practices.

Western definitions of artistic and intellectual prowess are limited. Rarely do "other" or "minority" cultures receive thorough, legitimate, and systematic study in regard to contributions in science, language, or art. The corrective influence of black and other cultural studies helps to expand academic discourse and also challenges Western ideas of the closed canon. Models for the examination, appreciation, and assessment of the contributions of black art and the artists who create such work can be developed through such dialogue. *Musical Landscapes in Color,* therefore, by no means an attempt to tell the entire story of black composers, attempts to shed light upon particular major movements, persons, and ideas within the music of black composers.

In 1995, a *Time* magazine cover feature declared, "Black artists are now embarked on one of the most astonishing outbursts of creativity in the nation's history. Never before have black artists produced so much first-rate writing, music, painting and dance."[2] This "astonishing" news (actually no new news at all) strongly implies a lack of "first-rate" production by black artists until "just recently." While the article acknowledges the Harlem Renaissance of the twenties, there is no real indication for a first-time reader that black artists could be counted as a historical "presence" outside of these peculiar outbursts. Little consideration is given to the fact that generations of trained, creative thinkers have constantly, and fairly consistently, published and exchanged critical perspectives.

In the same issue of *Time* appeared a review of a recent book by literary critic Harold Bloom.[3] In it Bloom had written, "Shakespeare is the secular scripture; forerunners and legates alike are defined by him alone for canonical purposes. . . . Tradition is not only a handing-down or process of benign transmission; it is also a conflict between past genius and present aspiration, in which the prize is literary survival or canonical inclusion." This assertion reinforces a basic premise that the "prize," as Bloom calls it, given to art that is held up as "holy" is canonical inclusion. This mode of thought is strongly embedded in academic and literary traditions, and is inextricably bound with canonical considerations in art as well. Within this historical framework, black composers are invisible, considered not to have contributed work sufficiently significant to merit canonical inclusion, performance, or study.

Late-twentieth-century black American composers led a quiet but forceful revolution in twentieth-century art/concert music. This revolution, which continues into the twenty-first century, is neither "concocted, contrived or controlled" nor bound by a geographical boundary, but there is a connectedness of purpose among kindred creative spirits.

This revolution is occurring in part because of the emergence of unprecedented numbers of composers, their contact with each other, and their impact upon the concert music world. For instance, landmark symphonic recordings such as the Detroit Symphony orchestra's release of *Ellington/Still* (Chandos), offering interpretations that have raised new questions about the uniqueness of both men's creative vision; the release by the Bohuslav Martinu Philharmonic of symphonic works by David Baker, Adolphus Hailstork, and Gary Powell Nash, with Julius Williams contributing as composer and conductor (Albany); the Akron Symphony's *American Voices,* premiering works of Billy Childs, David Baker, William Banfield (TelArc); the Chicago Symphony Orchestra release of Hannibal Lokumbe's *African Portraits* (Teldec/Warner); Adolphus Hailstork's *Singing the Music of* (Albany); Tania Leon's *Indigena* (CRI); *The Focus of Blue Light,* by Jeffrey Mumford (CRI); the works of T. J. Anderson, Donal Fox, Olly Wilson, and David Baker (New World Records); works of Alvin Singleton, recorded by the Atlanta Symphony Orchestra (Elecktra/Nonesuch); Anthony Davis's *Opera X* (Gramavision); as well the recent London's Collins Classics four-part CD series on the works of black composers, performed by the Plymouth Music Series Chorus and Orchestra, conducted by Philip Brunelle. All these works were recorded by major orchestras, were widely distributed, and were released in mainstream international markets, another indication of the interest and scope of contemporary black American composers.

Of note as well are successful projects like Billy Taylor's trio recording *Homage,* with the Turtle Island String Quartet, and George Duke's *Muir Woods Suite* and Tony Williams's *Wilderness,* both with orchestra.

Simply by their presence and inclusion, and by the power and diversity of their music, these composers are perhaps shaping how concert audiences will redefine American concert music in the twenty-first century. This most recent surge is also evident in the numerous concerts, research materials, radio programs, critical reviews, symposiums and seminars, contests and national searches, and attempts by organizations like the ASOL (the American Symphony Orchestra League) to urge American orchestras once again to reconsider their often exclusionary practices in relation to the work of "minorities" and women.

The 1996 and 1997 Pulitzer Prizes in music were awarded to George Walker and Wynton Marsalis. This is clear evidence that the time has come for more significant public recognition of the artistic achievement of black composers. Although this recognition comes late in Walker's illustrious career, the award is monumental in a historical sense. Walker is the first black composer ever to receive the Pulitzer in composition; in the case of Marsalis, the prize was widened to accept "jazz as composition."

These are more than temporary, "affirmative action" gestures. In the early twenty-first century we are witnessing a revolution, a weakening of the artistic suppression that has historically hindered the work of black composers. There have been other such eruptions (James Reese Europe's Clef Club, the Harlem Renaissance, the Black Composer Series on Columbia Masterworks, London Symphony releases of 1974), but this contemporary emergence has more to do with the recognized presence of so many fine working composers. Whether or not the institutions can "deal" with this presence is another question.

These contemporary stirrings have for the first time created a real working "camp," one that has established an irrefutable and meaningful presence. Any noteworthy movement, group of artists, or style or set of conventions has meaning because it possesses a recognized history, a track record. The exclusion of black composers and their creations from the history, theory, and method books occurs not only because of conscious attempts to disregard these artists and their work but for lack of a constant stream of record keepers, generation to generation. *Musical Landscapes in Color* is an attempt by one creator and record keeper to document thoughts of a camp of American artists who are speaking significantly at the beginning of the twenty-first century.

Composers are creating and upholding important traditions. As T. J Anderson states,

> The duty of the composer is to document the culture as he or she sees it. Any composer that I think anything of is one who transforms the culture. Whatever things work to my advantage I use, jazz or whatever I want, because that's my duty, to transform musical language and culture. These traditions of the culture inspire, teach, tell a story, evoke images and "yell out" to society.

Black American composers have held unique positions as people whose work is on one hand the crystallization of black life in song and poetry, and on the other is synonymous with the Western European idea of the cultural hero (Saltzman), with Schopenhauer's model of composer as artist supreme. It is rarely recognized that the composer's work is one of the most important musical expressions of black cultural life in American society.

The exchange of ideas between the composer and the ensemble of musicians and a concert audience is an important dialogue that transcends the tall and heavy doors that have traditionally kept "others" out. Black composers can be seen as ushers at the door who invite "others" inside. This invitation is crucial. The composer is not just an elitist artist but an important and sensitive voice that speaks of the universality of musical expression from specific communities to broader audiences. In the changing and evolving definitions of art music, the inclusion of their voices, music, and perspectives is crucial to the direction of contemporary American concert music.

The issue of recasting the canon, enlightening the educational structure, and dusting off the old repertoires is a major concern as American institutions dealing in concert/art music face a general public that is becoming increasingly global, more sensitive, and more critical of past exclusionary practices. By preserving and researching the works of these composers, we are simultaneously enriching history and building a future, by expanding and gently challenging the institutional organizations and educational systems that perpetuate and inform American artistic culture. It is crucial for artists, scholars, and educators to take seriously the task of shaping the art of the twenty-first century, and black American composers have had an undeniably important voice in it.

The great visionary James Reese Europe once wrote, "We have created a kind of symphony music that, no matter what else you might, think is different and distinctive." This distinction underscores the necessity of examining what that art was and is, and what it will ultimately become in the twenty-first century.

The Issue of Racial Politics

Anton Dvorak was quoted on May 24, 1893, in the *New York Herald* as saying, "I am satisfied that the future music of this country, must be founded upon what are called the Negro melodies. . . . These can be the foundation of a serious and original school of composition, to be developed in the United States. They are American."

It is a peculiar thing that while few American composers were ready to accept these statements, Stravinsky, Ravel, Mihuad, and others were creating works that used the Negro aesthetic and are to this day clearly seen as European interpretations of American musical culture. Then came Gershwin, Copland, Bernstein, and others who also recognized the richness of this great artistic legacy, which had arisen at least two hundred years before, from the most desolate of human experiences. But it is not just the black slave melodies that have given inspiration to American composers; common, public, and well documented black melodies and musical methods were also employed in American music. As William Grant Still has noted, "Jazz (as one black form) has given one important thing to American music as a whole: great variety and charm in instrumental effects that were unknown to classic composers. An entirely new style of orchestration has developed, one that is not without dignity if employed intelligently and without discrimination."[4] Black American composers upheld many traditions simultaneously, including their use of traditional, nontraditional, and experimental languages and procedures. Those early decades, particularly in New York, were rich in all sorts of musical exchanges.

I once wrote a note to one of my music history professors, who taught the course "Music of the Twentieth Century" at Ann Arbor.

> Dear Professor:
> This little improvised periscope (though the story is true) really tells the story: There was a gentleman, George Gershwin, who went to hear another gentleman, Eubie Blake, and his band perform at a club in Harlem. There was this certain little melody that another gentleman played all the time, it was his little melody, or "lick." That gentleman was William Grant Still. He was the oboist in Blake's band. During warm ups Gershwin heard this little lick. We don't remember it as William Grant Still's little lick, but at least we know the lick. The unfortunate thing is that the little lick became known as George Gershwin's most popular "jazz lick" and tune, "I've Got Rhythm." (You can still hear this little lick in the principal oboe theme of the second movement of Still's first symphony 1931.)

(Gershwin acknowledged his debt to W. C. Handy [a noted black American composer] in an autographed score of his *Porgy and Bess* that he presented to Handy. In the inscription Gershwin thanked Handy for his music, which Gershwin recognized was a forerunner of his own). Composers and artists borrow all the time, but the proliferation of such exchanges between black and white artists can result in exploitation, commercialization, neglect, and the lack of due recognition. Aside from such well-documented borrowing and adaptations of black American musical materials into mainstream composition, there was a strange exchange between twenty-year-old Leonard Bernstein and mentor Aaron Copland in 1939, in which Bernstein addressed questions relative to his senior thesis in music at Harvard University.[5] The thesis tries to show that "the stuff that the old boys turned out" (by which he meant Chadwick, Converse, Shephard, Gilbert MacDowell, Cadman) had failed utterly to develop an American style or school of music, because their material (Negro, American Indian) was not common—"the old problem of America the melting pot."

"I will try and show," wrote Bernstein, "that there is something American in the newer music, which relies not on folk material but on a native spirit, or relies on a new American form. I am convinced that there is such a thing. . . . [W]hat music of what other composers in America would support my point? Would the music of Harris, Ives? or Schumann? or Piston? You see I know and hear so little American stuff." Copland replied, "Don't make the mistake of thinking that just because a Gilbert used Negro materials, there was therefore nothing American about it. There's always the chance it may have an American quality despite its materials (Negro)." This idea of Negro materials as apart from the conscious, "thinking and breathing Negro" is disturbing, and it further illustrates the exclusivity in the documentation of American composers during this period and beyond. The Negro composer, as widely circulated documents contend, was "invisible and nameless."

Note that in this extraordinary thesis Bernstein argued that the Negro had everything, including an aesthetic and a national basis upon which to build a indigenous composition tradition. Yet the Negro composer has no name. Bernstein argues for "a new and vital American nationalism" and claimed that by 1939 the Negro had Negro jazz, Negro music, Negro art, Negro melodic peculiarities, Negro scale variants, Negro poignancy, special Negro flavor, Negro timbre, the Negro (singing) voice, Negro character, Negro species of melodic syncopation, Negro syncopation, Negro rhythmic patterns, Negro tone color, Negro manner, Negro harmonies, and the Negro scale.

He further suggests that the "greatest single racial influence upon American music as a whole has been that of the Negro." On behalf of the "serious American composer," he further states, "Negro art and musical spirit, if the composer is a sensitive creator[,] . . . will become an integral part of [the composer's] pallet, whether or not he is aware of it." However, Bernstein insists that the serious composer must move beyond the Negro materials and mature an intrinsically "Negro spiritualism," therefore becoming indigenous and national. And yet, in all this, our Negro composers who have created all this still have no name and have made no contributions worthy of consideration at the conscious artistic level. This early Bernstein document is an example of how too much American art music is spoken of, constructed, and taught. Its traditional presentation is completely devoid of an African American presence or influence.

Then Bernstein moved to new level of exclusion and absurdity, arguing that unlike the banal and trite Negro creations, Aaron Copland's work stood "as a work of skill, structural merit, and great contrapuntal interest." Aaron Copland, according to the young Bernstein's estimate, had accomplished the "symphonization of jazz," by removing the banal Negro harmonic progressions, and achieved his own "American style" with "complete authenticity."

In Copland's use of the Negro material, "One finds Negro art . . . most clearly defined and fully outlined, and most consistently used." Why not simply go analyze Negro composers' output to document such clearly defined authentic American music? Living and creating not far away, in New York, were William Grant Still, Fletcher Henderson, and Duke Ellington. Additionally, voluminous accounts, recordings, and reviews of James P. Johnson's symphonic attempts and James Reese Europe's most amazing and successful Clef Club Orchestra were available. Yet in his thesis Bernstein relies heavily on Rupert Hughes's work *Contemporary American Composers,* which referred to blacks as "lazy and sensual slaves" and "imported Africs." This is America's frame of reference for serious art making by black people.

Despite Bernstein's appreciation of the music of the Negro, which certainly became apparent in his later years as he became a champion of jazz and social rights, there seems to be an implication in his early journey that the use of black materials was fine, but the creators of these materials were nonexistent and therefore nameless. Here again, our task is to challenge and change the exclusionary practices of American works about composers. Certainly Bernstein and Copland would have been aware of such strong traditions as those of Scott Joplin, James Reese Europe, and W. C. Handy. As one critic wrote, "James Reese Europe is one of the most remarkable men, not only of his race, but in the music world of this country . . . he is able to expend considerable energy upon the development of the Negro Symphony Orchestra. Unaided, he has been able to accomplish what white musicians said was impossible: the adaptation of Negro music and musicians to symphonic purposes."[6]

Black musicians were at work in the United States. As early as 1927, for example, Duke Ellington, under the management of Irving Mills, was promoted as a serious American composer and artist. Additionally, William Grant Still's *Afro-American Symphony* of 1931 was performed in 1935 at Carnegie Hall. After the premiere of Still's first symphony in New York, W. J. Henderson, critic for the *New York Sun,* wrote, "But one is tempted to ask whether the colored race must musically dominate the United States? If there is no other idiom native to the soil, it might be well to give over trying to be national in blackface." Black composers have received some mention. For example, the most influential Western music history text to this day, Donald Grout's *History of Western Music*, lists William Grant Still and Florence Price. Grout writes, "Likewise incorporating specifically American idioms (blues) is the Afro-American Symphony (1931) of William Grant Still. Florence Price (1887–53) adapted the anti-antebellum juba folk dance as well as melodic and harmonic elements . . . reflecting her black musical heritage."[7] Other notable American composers (nonblack) listed in Grout's work were George Gershwin, Aaron Copland, Roy Harris, Virgil Thompson, Walter Piston, Roger Sessions, and Howard Hanson. Eric Saltzman, in his 1974 publication *Twentieth Century Music,* adds Stephen Wolpe, Elliot Carter, William Flanagan, Arthur Berger, Irving Fine, Ernest Bloch, Ralph Shapey, and George Crumb, describing them collectively as creating an "American School."

Professor Glen Watkins lists as significant American composers Charles Ives, Henry Cowell, Carl Ruggles, Edgar Varèse, Wallingford Riegert, John Becker, Aaron Copland, Samuel Barber, Virgil Thompson, William Schuman, Roy Harris, Walter Piston, and Ross Lee Finney.[8] The author also lists Howard Hansen, Leonard Bernstein, and David Diamond, and recognizes black composers Ulysses Kay and William Grant Still. Brian Morton and Pamela Collins list five hundred contemporary composers.[9] Although they claim their work "is intended rather as a listener's guide to the broadest spectrum of contemporary composition," they name only three black composers, Roque Cordero, Alvin Singleton, and Olly Wilson. Furthermore, one cannot miss David Ewen or Harold C. Schoenberg.[10] Both of their books are extremely important to the discussion of composition traditions, but their inquiry stops at Cage and Peter Maxwell

Davies. What happened to the evolving notions of great art music as defined by the black presence in the West, particularly in the United States?

On a visit to Borders Books, among the 207 books dealing with the history, lives, memoirs, and letters, of composers and analysis of their works, not one single book examined the contributions of black American composers. Other contemporary examples of this methodical exclusion include Bryan R. Simms.[11] His book contains the most glaring omission, because although it mentions jazz and the blues, it does not deal with a single black composer. Unbelievable—black composers not named even in connection with jazz!

The authors of *New Voices: American Composers Talk about Their Music* state in the preface, "We never intended to paint the entire picture, however as our interests led us only to those whose music was in some way essentially American and not derived from or inspired by European models. . . . [F]or all their diversity of approach, [they] are linked by a fundamental desire to rediscover the essentials of shared musical experiences with little or no reference to European traditions."[12]

While the latter part of the objectives presented here is impossible (seeing that all these composers are linked to Western European–derived systems) the idea of "essentially American" with no black influence is also virtually impossible. The picture painted here is colorless. This is yet another contemporary example of racist absurdity. In contrast, Reid Badger and Geoffrey Self in their respective books provide an in-depth look at important black composers of the nineteenth and twentieth century.[13]

Of course, many names were excluded from all these lists besides those of black composers and women, but with so many scholars writing on the subject, why is there so little information regarding the contribution of black men and women, who often live and work in the same cities, university programs, and performance venues where these lists are compiled? To look at the problem on a larger scale, while many recognize the contributions of classical composers in shaping Western notions of taste and culture, few American writers, teachers, or critics make reference to the American composer either as a creator of cultural significance or as a bearer of tradition. America has never been able to break away from the notion that "great music" is strictly a European phenomenon; American creations of art have commonly been relegated to the entertainment realm. Even more difficult (as we could see in the Bernstein-Copland exchange) is the recognition of an American school of composition that is, and always has been, shaped by a prophetic and insightful group of African American composers who emerged at the end of the nineteenth century. Of course, today, some hundred years after Dvorak's prophetic comment, many are laying claim to the notion of upholding an American school, and "Negro materials" are clearly understood to be a part of the staple sound of "Americanisms."

The problems of inadequate historical documentation, exclusion, and the consequences of "closed and locked canons" are of concern in many fields as educational and artistic institutions address the furtherance of cultural product. How will the twenty-first century play out—as whole and complete, or fragmented and confused?

The Issue of Racial Politics

What profit has been gained by the establishment's sustained failure to acknowledge or appreciate this work for so long? What are the reasons behind this exclusion? One may have been Tolstoy's assertion that "the races of black men have not achieved or contributed anything significant to western culture." Another might have been our founding Father Thomas Jefferson's claim that "Blacks are inferior to whites in the endowments of both the mind and the body." Or perhaps it was Lincoln's seldom quoted assertion that "there remains two positions in America, one superior and one inferior, and I as much as any man would see the position of inferiority assigned to blacks." Thus there is a long literary tradition of exclusion centered on racial bigotry, and a tradition of distasteful art politics fueled by a literary tradition that clearly denies the existence and validity of significant artistic creation by black Americans.

Perhaps this is why Gilbert Seldes, in *The Seven Lively Arts* (1924) could write, "The one claim never made for the Negro shows is that they are artistic." Equally revealing is the politics of cultural exclusion from mainstream educational institutions. Dvorak writes, "The future music of America must be founded upon the Negro melodies. . . . In the Negro melodies of America I discover all that is needed for a great and noble school of music." The reactions to Dvorak's statement from white American composers and critics reflect distasteful art politics.

For example, G. W. Chadwick, a leading composer and one of the staple members of the New England school of composers, objected, "Such Negro melodies as I have heard however, I should be very sorry to see become the basis of an American school of musical composition." Composer Mrs. H. H. A. Beach responded, "I cannot help feeling justified in the belief that they (the melodies, nor the Negro) are not fully typical of our country. The African population of the United States . . . represent only one factor of the composition of our nation. Moreover, it is not native American; the Africans are no more native than the Italians, Swedes, or Russians." The American composer Jon Knowles Paine, then head of the music department at Harvard University, wrote, "Dr. Dvorak is probably unacquainted with what has already been accomplished in the higher forms of music by composers in America. In my estimation it is a preposterous idea to say that in the future American music will rest upon a shaky foundation as the melodies of yet a largely undeveloped race." (Little did Paine know that in fact America would be known artistically throughout the world almost primarily on the strength of those Negro melodies and their makers.)

Harold Cruse, in *The Crisis of the Negro Intellectual,* writes, "According to Seldes, Negro shows were not art. This peculiar and perverse tradition of cultural criticism, practiced by Gilbert and others, has severely distorted native American standards by overglorifying obsolete European standards. Such ignorant criticism and faulty documentation debased Negro creative arts by refusing to accept their originality as truly American. Selds rejected what was truly American because it was not European but African American. Thus by downgrading Negro musical originality he helped to undermine the only artistic base in the American culture in which the Negro could hold his own as an original artist." Herein lies a context out of which early American expression was to come. American literary and educational institutions and traditions have since perpetuated this distasteful politic of art and have deemed black creators "entertainers" rather than serious artists.

Despite the distasteful history of American art politics, from this milieu the music of black composers has emerged. One of the most fascinating aspects of this music and its creators is the fact that black composition for the most part was created in this distasteful soil, with little public support or critical acclaim. Yet the creators developed a resistant aesthetic base that refuted all claims of their inferiority and insignificance and fueled much of the greatest music heard in American history. It began to emerge strongly in the first three decades of the twentieth century. This matrix produced an incredibly provocative and prophetic group of composers, who, despite varying levels of mainstream exposure, provide a biting and telling perspective that plays an important role in the documentation of American art culture.

Once again I am reminded of James Reese Europe's 1912 reaction to a dissenting critic: "The result, of course, is that we have developed a kind of symphony music that, no matter what else you might think, it is different and distinctive and lends itself to the particular compositions of our race. . . . You see, we colored people have our own music that is a part of us."

Composers like Europe, Harry T. Burleigh, Florence Price, Will Marion Cook, and later William Grant Still created a black composition track that was sure to carve out a meaningful space in the history of American artistic expression. Although there is a powerful American popular art today created by blacks in America, the story of black composers who emerged early in the century is rarely told. Even in contemporary culture, more attention needs to be paid to the work of contemporary black composers and the questions and perspectives that come from their creative experiences.

For example, as noted earlier, in 1931 Howard Hanson, one of America's great composers, conducted the premiere of Still's *Afro American Symphony*. Performed by the Rochester Philharmonic, it was the first full-blown symphony using Negro themes and melodies and other black music materials to be created by a black composer. Still fulfilled Dvorak's prophetic notions by creating the first real American symphony. Then, in 1933, Florence Price's *Symphony in E* was premiered by the Chicago Symphony, a doubly important event since few women were ever recognized as significant composers, let alone black women.

In 1934, William Dawson's *Negro Folk Symphony* was performed by Leopold Stokowski and the Philadelphia Orchestra. This incredibly imaginative, well-crafted composition easily rivaled the best of the late Romantic German composers, who were being championed by American orchestras during this period. In 1935 (again, as noted) the New York Philharmonic performed Still's symphony at Carnegie Hall. These performances were not simply "Negro firsts." Florence Price, for example, entered a national competition in which her music dominated in quality and artistic merit alone.

Examining these black composers and the four generations that followed, one finds an extraordinary cast of characters in the redefinition of American music. Two of the crucial questions raised by the authors of *The Black Composer Speaks* were, "Do you consider yourself to be a black composer," and "What is black music?"

Despite contemporary projections of multicultural imagery and the emergence of commercial white/pop/urban crossover artists such as Sting, Michael Bolton, Kenny G., and Paul Simon, we are still asking these questions in art music. Is cultural reference an important issue for an African American composer? Does any sonic symbolization of blackness (a blues lick or jazz reference) disqualify notions of art or intellectualism?

With media coverage of the variety of black art as limited as it is, what images of black artistic presence come to mind when the terms "composer" or "cultural hero" are used? Are "traditions" significant, and is the black composer a cultural sellout if his or her music has no recognizable black component except for such abstractions as pervasive rhythmic cells? Clearly, with the emergence of the hip-hop generation and the projections of the media apparatus (MTV, BET, and CNN) the questions surrounding the blackness of artistic expression continue to impact our working lives. The rap group Public Enemy, for example, asks, "Who Stole the Soul?" and pushes the question further to illustrate some of the issues at stake when black composers are confronted with issues of authenticity and sincerity of cultural expressions of art.

In quite another spin on this issue, Cornel West, in *Keeping the Faith*, asks, "Has the commercialization of art rendered it a mere commodity in our market driven culture? Can the reception of the work of a black artist transcend mere documentary, social pleading, or exotic appeal?"

With the rise of American orchestras who sponsor black composer contests and such other programs as Black History Month concerts, these issues remain crucial in public support of new American music, curriculum development, and in public information forums such as conferences and seminars. NPR's 1993 program "Classical Music at the Crossroads" suggested that Jonathon Holland, born in 1974, stands among a new wave of voices yet to come.

No matter what the generation, however, the question of "to be or not to be" black in art music will not go away, mainly because the issue exists in the mind of the "gatekeepers." February remains the busiest month for many black American composers, and ASCAP and BMI performance points are the highest during January and February, because then it is "OK" to feature the music of a black American composer. Unfortunately, it seems that no matter what impact those premieres or first-time exposures have on concert audiences, the music is rarely included in a regular, repertoire concert season.

Programming of new works is, of course, always a problem, whether the composers are white, black, green, or in between. But it is fair to say that on a percentage basis, mainstream works by black composers, regardless of musical worth, accessibility, intrigue, or the composer's popularity, are underperformed because of cultural and racial politics rather than any other factors that would normally hinder a new work by a contemporary composer.

This game has caused identity problems among composers, who sometimes have had to decide when it is "OK" to be called a black composer, when it is insulting, and when stereotyped images or sounds become more important than the essence of the composer's work, purely in musical terms. For instance, when a composer receives a call from an interested orchestra, is the interest sincere, or by responding is the black composer casting his or her name and precious work in a "black book," never to be included in what should be a revolving file for new works? This duality—what W. E. B. Dubois called "twoness" of self, or double consciousness—is also seen in the academic realm, when the musical scope is split into jazz/popular versus serious concert music. What then becomes of the eclecticism that is a part of African American experience and identity?

We have been able to recognize Bach and Wagner as self-consciously German, and Ravel and Debussy as self-consciously French. Tchaikovsky and Stravinsky are recognized as self-consciously Russian. This has always been fair play in the classical music world. If this is a historically important and necessary cultural or aesthetic designation, there should be no problem in being known as an African American composer. The issue seems simple enough; the designation should not limit anyone. As a matter of fact, it should liberate the voice and provide further extension into multiple expressive modes. But for black American composers, unlike many of their white counterparts, the universal does not always get heard in their music, because ears and minds are too entangled in the American cultural color codes of black and white.

Samuel Coleridge Taylor, who lived from 1875 to 1912, was a black Englishman, living in Britain, who was described as "a musical genius of our times, the greatest musical sensation, . . . in a class with Beethoven, Brahms, and Wagner." After meeting the renowned African American poet Paul Lawrence Dunbar in London and reading Dubois's 1903 *The Souls of Black Folk,* Taylor became "a changed soul" and began composing several works that centered on themes more culturally relevant to blacks, musically and poetically. He got "in touch" with multiple traditions and was all the more appreciated for them. This transforming context, his connection with the black experience in America, became the transforming element in his career. He became a champion of black art and culture, toured the United States, and was invited to dine with Theodore Roosevelt at the White House. The point is that Taylor had become well known on the merit of his work. However, after Taylor's "coming to know himself" through encounters with black life and culture, his art took on expanded meaning.

It is bewildering that it has always been acceptable for any culture recorded in the West to be "culturally energized" (the Russian Five, les Seis, the American Five)—except for black artists. When they turn culturally inward, it is usually dismissed as insignificant and expected, downplayed, and recognized neither for artistic nor historical relevance.

The argument here is that most black composers—in fact, most black artists, writers, and poets—share, and have shared, a persistent anxiety about being black in American society. Furthermore, they create meaning for that blackness over and beyond making art for its own sake, and this is a crucial exercise in artistic expression. This is the "edge" that all black art has, on some level. It is this connectedness, this lineage, this blackness that despite aesthetic, social, and political perspectives makes this body of artists important for documentation. Despite the evils of the color game in American art politics, this sense, as the interviews will show, is a rallying point in many ways, and rallying points, conscious or not, have always been positive. In an address to the Indiana University School of Music on February 10, 1975, Undine Smith Moore remarked, "No matter how we have been separated, there is always some element of cohesiveness, some sense of supportedness. So that when one takes a look from the bridge, one may justly describe the black experience as a celebration of life." This celebration, this body of literature, applied to music and taken as a whole, is of marked significance. Poet Maya Angelou has also noted, "If the African poets have one theme, it is most assuredly the splendor of being 'Black like Me.' The poets revel in their Blackness."

Some composers argue, however, that cultural reference is not the identifying mark of their art. They simply suggest, "I am my music, it stands alone as personal expression conveying who I am apart from cultural connections." This is a most important and valid perspective, one that is held by many black American composers. But the majority of composers of African descent who have created music in America clearly identify themselves and their experiences as culturally relevant—or as the historian Eileen Southern says, as having created in the context of the black experience. Whether, as in rap and hip-hop culture, the issue of "authenticity," or being "real," is relevant in concert music or not, black artists continue to deal with these identifications, and they are at least important to mention, if not decisive. "Today a great many Negro composers, both serious and popular, working in the United States, cannot help but exemplify, to a certain extent, their African heritage." As William Grant Still further stated in 1938, "No matter how academic his training or how straight-laced his views, something of that exotic background will be heard in the music he writes." These issues are clearly on the table for the fourth generation, which is affected by hip-hop and urban contemporary aesthetics. Ultimately, if we hold to the notion of America as a melting pot—or better, a tossed salad, where many different ingredients define the flavor—then it is safe to suggest that being black, or being a significant cultural ingredient, is still important.

Contemporary Problems in Canonical Inclusion

Despite these claims for the importance of the recognition, study, and performance of significant concert music composed by black American composers, there is still great resistance throughout American symphony orchestras and teaching institutions. Some of the rationales are:

1. Concern in conservative circles about unwarranted and senseless attack on "tradition" and attempts to revamp the repertoire.
2. Suspicion of new music, in that it (whether black or other) lowers expectations of excellence and therefore presents art that is not challenging and has less artistic value than standard European or Euro-American works.
3. Disdain for a market-driven culture that perpetuates definitions of popular culture as "significant."
4. A feeling that African American and other cultural works, concerts, literature, and seminars are only products of affirmative action policies and therefore do not merit the respect and standing that they claim.
5. The incompatibility of new and challenging aesthetic conventions such as improvisation, foreign and challenging rhythmic conceptions, jazz language, and gospel and popular song traditions with Western European traditions.
6. Fear that the introduction of such artists and works will drive away the financial support provided by conservative boards of directors, commercial sponsors, and the subscription series patrons who constitute the core audience.

It is important to remember that concert music venues, orchestras, and art institutions are economics driven. Still, despite these eco-facts (bottom-line financial considerations) and resistance to cultural expansion and canonical revision, there has been a steady stream of new faces in strategically important places. Orchestras are in fact responding to these needs, by sponsoring contests, conferences, and concerts where audiences for the first time hear black composers of the past and as well new voices. While the objections listed above are in no way resolved, answers are arising that challenge old notions that have perpetuated exclusion.

The concert world is witnessing a great and powerful flood of talented black orchestral composers, as well as conductors, educational directors, and program directors whose passionate dedication to excellence and the evolution of music have gratifyingly undercut assumptions of artistic inferiority. One remarkable example was the 1995–2000 appointment of Bobby McFerrin as creative chair of the St. Paul Chamber Orchestra. His presence electrified a conservative institution, and his conducting as well as musical performance practice radically invigorated the musicians to new expressive heights.

There is still concern in most concert music circles that somehow the new aesthetics in popular culture (which include notions of multiculturalism, Afrocentrism, and feminism) will destroy the values of "our institutions," which are fighting for economic and cultural survival. What these institutions must recognize is that those who are asking for inclusion are members of the same profession; they have the same artistic concerns and standards. Few if any of the composers we are dealing with here want to see orchestras accompanying Michael Bolton ballads or performing background music for rap or break dancing.

While it goes unsaid, the feeling among the "gatekeepers" is that the work of "other composers" does not fit into the cultural scheme of the traditional orchestra. New, artistically challenging, or foreign tonalities, rhythms, and themes are sometimes seen as exotic, something to be "tolerated" for the moment.

The European masters who carved out these traditions would certainly question institutions about the lack of creative and visionary insight in programming today. Just this kind of progression is needed to keep art music traditions alive and forging ahead. American academic institutions of musical art—in particular, symphony orchestras, chamber groups, art agencies, and universities—must continue to take seriously their respective responsibilities to evolve, incorporate, and include the artistic contributions of other American cultural groups, women composers, and progressive music movements.

The detrimental effects of the marginalization of specific groups are already apparent and will become more pronounced as our society becomes more sensitized to exclusions. With the data available now on personalities, music, recordings, and writings, and our knowledge specifically of the African American artistic voice in the world, it seems incomprehensible that institutions maintain exclusionary practices.

We are now seeing in concert music circles a surge of cultural eruptions. Like waves that crash relentlessly against a rocky and unyielding shore, these current eruptions pummel the literal and figurative gates of the institution, vehemently demanding a place inside. This helps to explain the fears of the traditional institution. No one escapes such a confrontation unscathed. Established institutions increasingly experience shifts in the Western/American aesthetic mindset, in the fundamental definition of being, and in the canon.

On the other hand, the determined resistance of these camps (apart from appointed times, such as Black History Month) raises the question of whether even the sustained efforts of these artists, composers, and historians will keep them afloat. James Reese Europe's model of the "cultural design" serves as a paradigm that must be sustained simultaneously with determined efforts to pry open doors. (His Clef Club orchestra included black musicians performing music by black composers.) African American artists, institutions, composers, and entrepreneurs must have the commitment, endurance, and prophetic insight to create, as Europe did, ensembles of the new kinds necessary in the emerging cultural eruptions of African American composers.

This is not to suggest that composers abandon attempts to express their artistry through the traditional orchestra, but that confrontational struggles and ideological imbalances will be significantly reduced when there is greater respect for the validity of the emerging voices. This cannot be accomplished without the challenges from within and also from outside, through the creation of independent institutions. The efforts of Dr. Samuel Floyd at the Center for Black Music Research, Columbia College, in Chicago, is a fine example of commitment to this work. With the establishment of strong research endowments, publications, programs, archives, a new encyclopedia on black composers, and ensembles, the center is today one of the richest resources in the field. The work of the Department of Afro-American Studies at Indiana University, with its holdings at the Archives of African American Music and Culture, including the Undine Smith Moore Collection of Scores and Manuscripts by Black American Composers, should be mentioned.

Forging Foundations and Paths: The Perspectives

James Reese Europe observed in 1914, in the *Evening Post,*

> You see, we colored people have our own music that is a part of us. It's the product of our souls; it's been created by the sufferings and the miseries of our race. Some of the melodies we played Wednesday were made up by slaves of the old days and others were handed down from the days before we left Africa. Some would doubtless laugh heartily at the way our Negro symphony is organized, this distribution of pieces, and our methods of organization. . . . The result of course is that we have developed a kind of symphony music, that no matter what else you may think, is different and distinctive, and that lends itself to the playing of the peculiar compositions of our race.

Nathaniel Dett explained in *Musical America,* in 1916,

> In this country we are, musically, in much the same position as a man who owns a valuable mine. The fact that there are minerals in the ground, that he has that great supply of wealth stored up, will mean little to the owner unless he utilizes it. We have this wonderful store of folk materials, the melodies of an enslaved people, who poured out their longings, their griefs, and their aspirations in the one great, universal language. But this store will be of no value unless we utilize it, unless we treat it in such a manner that it can be presented in choral form, in lyric

and operatic works, in concertos and suites and salon music—unless our musical architects take the rough timbre of Negro themes and fashion from it music which will prove that we too have national feelings and characteristics, as have the European peoples whose forms we have zealously followed for so long.

These two composers' perspectives show that black artists and composers were very much involved and concerned with the shaping of American concert music at the beginning of the twentieth century. Europe and Dett were the first black composers to articulate formidable positions, thus documenting a "presence." However, there were many other perspectives as well: educators, writers, black historians, and historical publications.[14] The beginning of the track or historical path of the four generations of African American composers in the United States identified in this project begins with these two composers, who helped to codify two traditions within which most black American composers work.

Robert Nathaniel Dett was born in Drumsville, Ontario, in 1882 and died in 1943. In 1901 he trained at the Oliver Mills Halsted Conservatory of Music and went on to become the first black composer in the United States to receive a bachelor's degree in music composition. After completing studies at Oberlin College, Dett went on to the American Conservatory, Columbia, the University of Pennsylvania, and Harvard, finally studying under the famed "teacher of composers" Nadia Boulanger at the Conservatory of Paris at Foutainebleau. Dett received several honorary doctorates and held teaching positions in several colleges, most notably at Hampton University. His cantata *The Ordering of Moses* was performed in 1921 by the Cleveland Symphony and in 1937 by the Cincinnati Festival Orchestra. Dett's most important accomplishment with respect to our focus here was in laying the foundation for African American academic composers. Composers who are college and university trained and hold academic positions, conduct research, and perform and write about black contributions to American culture while working as professional composers within concert music circles are indebted to him. Dett was also one of the first composers to fuse traditional black materials into the Western idea of concert music.

James Reese Europe was for many reasons one of the most important black composers and musical voices in American history at the turn of the twentieth century. He established a nationalist stance that affirmed, in protest and practice, the importance of black music and musicians on black cultural/ aesthetic grounds. He did this by establishing one of the most unique and important ensembles in American history, the all-black Clef Club Orchestra. From 1912 to 1915 Europe produced concerts with his orchestra, 125 musicians strong, of works by black composers in the nation's leading concert venue, Carnegie Hall in New York City. Before Paul Whiteman, Gershwin, or Leonard Bernstein conducted a note, Europe received critical acclaim as a conductor and composer. The critics were "knocked out," and in those days of great musical ensembles, New York experienced one of the most unique and dynamic orchestras ever. While it is possible to describe the musical visionary Francis Johnson as a forerunner of James Reese Europe, and while Johnson actually established many of the "firsts" associated with Europe, Europe had a closer connection with the times and sensibilities of the "modern" black American composer. Europe is a more realistic model.

James Reese Europe was born in Mobile, Alabama, in 1881, to parents who were both musicians. As a student of the violin, at age fourteen he won second place in a sponsored composition contest. (The first prize was won by his younger sister, Mary Lorraine Europe.) As an older man, Europe volunteered to direct his band in World War I. He led what the *New York Post* called the "Best Military Band in Europe," Lt. Jim Europe and his famous 369th U.S. Infantry Jazz Band. After returning from the war, Europe settled again in New York and resumed his work on the scene as a writer/arranger. He composed music for such famous Broadway acts as the Williams and Walker Troupe, the Cole and Johnson Brothers, and the Vernon Castle dance team.

Europe began recording on Victor Records, making him one of the first "recognized" black American composers to be recorded on a mainstream label. Despite controversial comments on the hereditary qualities and abilities of black musicians, he believed in the strength, beauty, and majesty of black art. He took one of the first cultural and aesthetic stands on black music making in America, establishing models of thought and performance that were to inspire the likes of Paul Whiteman, Fletcher Henderson, Duke Ellington, Thomas Dorsey, and Count Basie.

The historical significance of Europe's and Dett's concert work, writing, and lectures cannot be overlooked. Their work helped to establish several things. The first was the theoretical assertion (for both nonacademic and academic traditions) of the importance and place of black musical expression in American musical literature. The second was reliance upon black aesthetics, procedures, structure, and musical materials and the extension of these ideas to the European ensemble and concert form, creating new hybrid forms. These dual perspectives allowed composers the freedom and expanse to be both "black" and Western. The third was the creation of the tradition of the black American composer as creative artists writing, expanding upon, and upholding black traditions.

These trailblazers and foundation layers used the news and print media of the times to disseminate their theories about the importance and relevance of black music. (Europe used the New York news media, trade magazines, and recordings. Dett used academic lecture and publishing forums and concert programs.) They also warned of the system's ability to exploit and dismiss. Their writings, articles, performances, lectures, and aggressive conversations with the press document this provocative and creative presence.

Despite what might be thought of as Nathaniel Dett's "Negro integrationalist conservatism" and James Reese Europe's "radical cultural-separatism," their combined perspectives and essays constitute a substantive arena of discourse regarding the problems of the American art music industry. These issues are strategically linked to the documentation of the work of contemporary black American composers. For example, both wrote on the importance of cultural considerations in industry practice, education, and on the Negro artist and their role in society. While these perspectives, excerpted below, in no way represent all that black artists were thinking (Florence Price and William Dawson may have articulated very different positions) on these or other issues, the discourse documented here profoundly touches our contemporary discussions.

On Cultural Considerations and Industry Practices

James Reese Europe, writing in the *New York Tribune* on Saturday, November 22, 1914:

> We Negroes are under a great handicap. For "The Castle Lame Duck" I receive only one cent a copy royalty and the phonograph royalties in proportion. A white man would receive from six to twelve times the royalty I receive, and for compositions far less popular than mine, but written by white men, gain for their composers vastly greater rewards. I have done my best to put a stop to this discrimination, but I have found that it is of no use. The music world is controlled by a trust, and the Negro must submit to the demands or fail to have his music produced.
>
> I am not bitter about it. It is after all, but a slight portion of the price my race must pay in its at times almost hopeless fight for a place in the sun. Some day it will be different and justice will prevail.

Nathaniel Dett, in his Bowdoin Literary Prize thesis, Harvard University, 1920:

> Why even more has not been accomplished by Negro musicians in the development of their own music will appear from a study of the following facts: There is general indifference, amounting almost to contempt, for the things of native origin, and a slavish admiration on the part of American composers, critics, and to some extent, publishers, for European ideals in music and art. . . . While it must be admitted as true that American composition so far has not materially advanced the art of music, the reason is not because there is nothing indigenous on which to build, but because the great store of native assets which might be used has been has been ignored by American musical architects.

On Education

James Reese Europe, again in the *New York Tribune* for November 22, 1914:

> No, the great improvements in higher education for the Negro has not yet developed music as you would think. The schools and colleges for the Negro are all of an industrial character. The artistic side has naturally been neglected as of less importance. . . . The great task ahead of us, as I see it is to teach the Negro to be careful, to make him understand the importance of painstaking effort in playing, and especially to develop his sense of orchestral unity.

Nathaniel Dett, in his "As the Negro School Sings," in the *Southern Workman* in 1927:

> It is in the Negro school (traditional black colleges) for the most part that the songs of the race have been most carefully preserved. It is in the Negro school that these folk songs, especially the spirituals have been used to create and intensify the atmosphere of religion, which is as their name implies, their best and most natural office. It is in the Negro school that music directors have led Negro songs with no idea other than to produce the effect of beauty and naturalness; so it is that now only in the Negro school is the ideal presentation of Negro music to be found.

Black Art and the Role of the Black Artist

James Reese Europe, in the same *New York Tribune:*

> In playing symphonic music we are careful to play only the work of our own composers. I know of no white man who has written Negro music that rings true. Indeed how could such a thing be possible? How could a white man feel in his heart the music that a black man feels? And in the same way, what white orchestra could render the music of Will Marion Cook, or Rosamond Johnson or the old plantation spiritual melodies, whose composers were workers in the fields?
>
> Music breathes the spirit of a race, and strictly speaking, it is a part only of the race which creates it. . . . I am striving at present to form an orchestra of Negroes which will be able to take its place among the serious musical organizations of the country. . . .
>
> I believe it is in the creation of an entirely new school of music, a school developed from the basic Negro rhythms and melodies. . . . These songs are the only folk music America possesses. There is indeed hope for the art product of our race.

Nathaniel Dett, in his entry entitled "Negro Music" in *The International Cyclopedia of Music and Musicians,* 1938:

> The Negro composer, rich in his heritage of song, reaches up for the canons of form, by which all music has been advanced; the white composer, schooled in the traditions of artistic development, reaches down for the inspiration that has ever sprung from the soul of those close to the soil. Eventually their hands must meet. It takes no prophet to foretell that from their union shall arise a spirit which shall sound the note of a new and representative art to the ears of the waiting world.

Notes

1. "Classical Music at the Crossroads," *All Things Considered,* National Public Radio, September 1993.

2. Jack E. White, "Black Renaissance: African American Artists Are Truly Free at Last," *Time* 144(15) (October 10, 1994): 66–73.

3. Paul Gnaz, "Hurrah for Dead White Males," review of *The Western Canon: The Books and School of the Ages,* by Harold Bloom, *Time,* 144(15) (October 10, 1994): 62–63.

4. William Grant Still, "Negro Music in the Americas," *Revue Internationale de Musique* (June 1939).

5. Leonard Bernstein, "The Absorption of Race Elements into American Music," reprinted in Leonard Bernstein, *Findings* (New York: Anchor, 1982).

6. *New York Evening Post,* March 14, 1914.

7. Donald Grout, *History of Western Music,* 4th ed. (New York: Norton, 1988), 825.

8. Glen Watkins, *Soundings: Music in the Twentieth Century* (New York: Schirmer Books, 1988), 457.

9. Brian Morton and Pamela Collins, eds., *Contemporary Composers* (Chicago: St. James Press, 1992).

10. David Ewen, *The World of Composers* (Englewood Cliffs, N.J.: Prentice Hall, 1962); and Harold C. Schoenberg, *The Lives of the Great Composers* (New York: W. W. Norton, 1981).

11. Bryan R. Simms, *Music of the Twentieth Century: Styles and Structure,* 2d ed. (New York: Schirmer, 1996).

12. Geoff Smith and Nicole Walker-Smith, *New Voices: American Composers Talk about Their Music* (Portland, Ore.: Amadeus, 1995).

13. Reid Badger, *A Life in Ragtime: A Biography of James Reese Europe* (New York: Oxford University Press); and Geoffrey Self, *The Hiawatha Man: The Life and Work of Samuel Coleridge Taylor* (Cambridge: Scolar Press).

14. Such as Martin Delaney, *The Condition, Elevation, Emigration, and Destiny of the Colored People of the United States,* 1852; James M. Trotter, *Music and Some Highly Musical People,* 1878; Sojourner Truth, *Narrative of Sojourner Truth,* 1878; and W. E. B. Dubois, *The Souls of Black Folks,* 1903.

H. Leslie Adams

H. Leslie Adams, one of a rare breed of successful composers in America who can claim they work as a "full time" composer, has created works in media from song cycles, opera, and ballet to symphony, concerto, and trombone quartet. A native of Cleveland and born in 1932, Dr. Adams obtained his undergraduate degree in music from Oberlin, a master's in music from the California State University in Long Beach, and a Ph.D. from Ohio State. He has held fellowships with the Rockefeller Foundation in Bellagio (Italy), Yaddo Artists Colony, Cleveland Foundation and Jennings Foundation, and the Cleveland Music School Settlement; he is also an awardee of the National Endowment of the Arts. His works have been sung by such distinguished vocalists as Martina Arroyo, Hilda Harris, Ben Holt, and Florence Quivar. His symphonic works have been performed by the orchestras of Cleveland, Buffalo, Indianapolis, Springfield, Detroit, Savannah, Ethiopia, Pontiac, and Oakland, as well as the Black Music Repertoire ensemble and the Ohio Chamber and Cleveland Chamber Symphonies. Dr. Adams lives and works in Cleveland, Ohio.

I was born and raised here through high school, returned in 1979, and have been in Cleveland ever since. My folks were not musical performers, but they loved music. They encouraged me to take piano lessons at the age of four. My first piano teacher was a neighbor who lived two houses away. My first books had some blank staves in them, and as I practiced my little Mozart and Bach pieces, I would start to imitate the style of those pieces I was working on, on those blank pages. I filled them up; I still have the book. It was just fascinating to see those staves, and I was thrilled with the idea of being able to put the notes down and play them over and have somebody hear those pieces. I didn't have any compositional training at that point.

When I was in junior high school, I was asked to play for the choral club, which I did. I started studying privately with another teacher who lived two streets away. When I went to high school, a teacher from Oberlin Conservatory of Music kept saying that he saw I had great ability and he wanted me to go to Oberlin. My teacher, in addition to a choral group, had a music appreciation class in which he would play many different kinds of music. One of the things I remember was this huge Bach *B-minor Mass* recording, with Robert Shaw conducting. He would also let the class bring in records and play them, things that they liked. It was a very fine time.

In the meantime, while I was still in high school, I went to the Cleveland Music School Settlement to take theory. Theory fascinated me, yet they said,

"Well, you can't take theory until you take Dalcroze Eurythmics." They put me in this class and I was very disappointed because I never did get to study theory. I don't know why they did that and to this day I don't know whether or not they had some quota to fill. Anyway, I started to study voice privately with my high school choral teacher, and I also continued my piano studies. I started composing and arranging, and my teacher encouraged me to go to Oberlin to audition. At that time there was a little military conflict going on—the Korean War was happening. This was 1951, and I was getting out of high school in early January. My dad was a volunteer at the draft board. He "saw the picture" and said I should try to get enrolled in college right away, not wait until the fall, because they were drafting young men. My parents drove me to Oberlin, and I got an audition. Part of the audition was to do dictation, to write down pitches and rhythms as I heard them. I had never been asked to do that before. My folks were there with me at the time; my mother said afterward she didn't think I could do it. I did the best I could, and it turned out that I passed the exam. That was without any theory training whatsoever.

I enrolled in Oberlin in January of 1951, and I was there for four years. I was a music education major with emphasis on piano, voice, and composition. The reason I went into education was to satisfy my parents' desire to get me into some kind of program that had a little bit of what they called "security." I participated in as many extracurricular activities as possible. I put a lot of energy into writing, composing, performing, conducting, singing in opera lab and opera theater productions (in baritone roles), singing with the Oberlin College Choir under Robert Fountain for four years, and studying privately as well. I really got immersed in voice, and, outside of piano, voice was very natural to me. I was able to empathize fully with singers.

The history of presence of African Americans at Oberlin wasn't emphasized much. I was just trying to get through it myself. I had those challenging courses, as well as all of the extracurricular activities that I was fascinated with. There was a production by a student group that put on original student works. I wrote a ballet that was performed there. I was conducting orchestras for some musicals, and I even directed a dramatic reading.

I would say that Johann Sebastian Bach has always been a "hero" of mine. I was in awe of him and still am. There is something about his work that is very special. However, I really liked all music. I didn't have any special favorites. I appreciated the guest artist series, the works that we performed in the college choir, the operas I was in, the repertoire that I was working on in voice and piano, and my composition work with Herbert Elwell. Elwell was at the time the music critic of the *Cleveland Plain Dealer*. He taught at Oberlin several days a week in a small-class situation, with about half a dozen of us. The next year I studied with Joseph Wood, who was very supportive. He gave me a lot of energy and a lot of encouragement to keep pursuing the challenges with which I was presented.

Some avant-garde music was played at Oberlin—the Julliard String Quartet came and played the complete six quartets of Bartók, for example—but the avant-garde was not really stressed. I was always very romantic in nature, and both Elwell and Wood understood, appreciated, and encouraged that tendency.

In Cleveland there was, of course, the Cleveland Symphony. George Szell was very much on the podium. Arthur Rodzinsky was there for a while. Metropolitan Opera productions were touring under the Lyndon B. Johnson administration; they would come to the Public Hall, which is one of the largest indoor auditoriums in the country. I would go each season and see a number of operas. One time I got a season subscription and saw all of them. They would present seven or eight major opera productions that were touring at the time. Each night there were big-name stars, of course; this was before television got so popular. Then there was a recital series at the Music Hall, which brought in such top-notch artists as Paul Robeson, Marian Anderson, and Hazel Scott, among others. Cleveland was very rich in culture. People seemed to appreciate fine music.

Right after Oberlin, I took off for New York City. I wanted to get some experience. This was in 1957, and I was there for about six years. I had a lot of experiences there. I studied composition with Robert Starer. He was a teacher at Julliard at the time, but I went to his home to study. Vittorio Giannini, who was at the Manhattan School of Music, also gave me lessons in his home. I produced a lot of compositions and got a lot of them performed at places like Town Hall, Carnegie Recital Hall, etc. Many different artists performed my works. I also had a couple of full evening programs, one at Steinway Hall and one at Jutson Hall, which was across from Carnegie. They were favorably reviewed in the *New York Times* and *New York Herald-Tribune*. Generally this was the beginning of my professional career as a composer.

I found the racial climate, from my standpoint, from my response to circumstances, quite positive. I felt I was accepted and received well in all kinds of cultural situations. I felt very comfortable in various settings. Artists of different cultural backgrounds seemed to take to my work very nicely. It was a good time for me. Oberlin had been the same way. I have always enjoyed a very healthy relationship with people of all ethnic backgrounds. I think one reason is because I grew up in a culturally diverse neighborhood in Cleveland. As far back as I can remember there were boys and girls of different backgrounds. My neighborhood was mostly Jewish, and the only reason I was aware of the fact was that on Jewish holidays at the elementary school, there were would be very few students in class. Actually, my mother told me, much later, that she and my dad had had a discussion about that subject. They didn't want to "dump" any possible negative "stuff" onto me. In other words, they just didn't say anything about such things; it just wasn't brought up. As a composer, ethnicity has never been a problem for me, not to my knowledge.

In my formative period there were probably some subconscious influences from Romantic music and jazz rhythms. I can't say that I was consciously trying to latch on to any particular trend or style. I appreciated certain works, like those of Gian Carlo Menotti, and I enjoyed Aaron Copland, among others—not that there was any special attraction. No special attraction to living composers was there. I was into my own thing.

I feel that music is a part of a larger context that is a creative expression. As human beings I feel that we are naturally creative and that we are to express ourselves in a very creative manner. Music is a means of expressing that which is within. Music is also a very mysterious kind of experience and always has been. Exactly what it is and what has been written about it is not music. Music is music. It is an experience of creativity, and it is difficult to verbalize what exactly it is, how it works, or how it functions. I feel that it is a spiritual thing, a cosmic endeavor.

With regard to my composition process, it really depends on what the commission is for. The most recent commission was a work for the educational division of the Cleveland Symphony Orchestra—a three-minute work in three parts. The main idea was that each part should be orchestrated differently, to demonstrate the different ways that instrumentation could affect the same musical materials. I began to imagine a growth of a certain energy, something being born, and one takes that energy and transforms it into actual notation. The conscious mind plots it out first, then the subconscious begins to take over, until it flows. At the same time one is consciously aware of a duration, with a beginning and an end. This work in particular turned out to be a work with a lot of fast notes. There is a discipline functioning within a given parameter; it turned out to be one minute of music orchestrated three different ways. Again, the process is conscious and subconscious, with many of the parameters set in the guidelines of the commission. I don't use any set theory, and I do work at the piano quite frequently. I begin with the parameters, then Leslie Adams takes over. That's my process.

In terms of younger composers, I would encourage them to listen to all kinds of music, to be flexible in considering different styles, and never to limit themselves to any small area. I would encourage them to write in the style of Mozart, Beethoven, or Chopin. This approach is very healthy; one can appreciate and get a feel for various approaches. I would not encourage twelve-tone writing until they experience traditional approaches first. It helps to free them up, because sometimes in the early stages one doesn't really know what to do. Some say this way leads to composers writing what they heard the night before in recital. I don't think that's necessarily bad. There is a point at which one's style will eventually evolve, and it matures with experience—the experience of living!

In terms of Black History Month, if one has an experience of black history to enrich their appreciation of this aspect of culture, great! Then it has fulfilled its purpose of enriching that individual's life.

If I had a main goal, I would say that I take one step and one day at a time. I try to express myself through my music, and I would like it always to be genuinely expressive. I'd like my music always to have a timelessness, a spirituality to it, something that can last and not be limited to a style, trend, or ideology.

Thomas J. Anderson

T. J. Anderson is recognized as one of the leading composers of his generation and as one of the most influential and innovative voices in American composition. Dr. Anderson works in various combinations, from orchestral to solo piano, chamber to soprano, and children's toys to chromatic pitch pipe. He is as well known for having first orchestrated Scott Joplin's opera, *Treemonisha*. Noted *New York Times* author and critic Harold C. Schoenberg has noted, "Anderson orchestrated the opera in a style that follows the one example of Joplin's orchestration that has come down to us." Born in Coatesville, Pennsylvania, in 1928, Dr. Anderson received his schooling from West Virginia State, Pennsylvania State, the Cincinnati Conservatory, and the Aspen School of Music; he received his doctorate in composition from the University of Iowa. He holds honorary degrees from the College of the Holy Cross, West Virginia State College, Northwestern University, and others. He taught at Morehouse College, Tennessee State, West Virginia State College, and Langston University. He was the chairman of the Music Department of Tufts University in Medford, Massachusetts, for ten years, teaching there for nineteen years before his retirement in 1990. He was the Rockefeller Foundation Composer in Residence with the Atlanta Symphony under Robert Shaw in 1969–71. Other awards include Danforth, Mellon, American Music Center, MacDowell Colony, and Yaddo Fellowships, and grants from the Fromm Foundation, Berkshire Music Center, and the National Endowment of the Arts. Dr. Anderson's works have been recorded by Nonesuch and Columbia and have been performed by various ensembles and orchestras throughout the country, including the London Philharmonic *(Squares for Orchestra)*. Dr. Anderson now lives and works in Chapel Hill, North Carolina.

I guess the major shift in my music has been toward sound platforms—I call them "orbiting ideas"—in which I have different performing stations in a chamber piece. Each voice is totally independent from the others, which means you have three, four, sometimes even five or six different pieces going on simultaneously. They are going on in different tempos, different interreactions, and things like that. I think that process was used in my *Orbiting Minstrels*. I used it in an intermezzo earlier in 1983. What that means to me is that on this planet there are lot of different voices speaking, and every voice is saying something that is meaningful to them, and we are not all saying the same thing. At the same time, there has to be a coexistence of the diversity of ideas. Just like this coexistence has to take place in society, it has to take place in music. In other words, I don't write things traditionally; there would be one piece, and there would be interaction between that piece as an ensemble.

Now I am working in terms of totally independent pieces going on at the same time. Seven cabaret songs that I did with the Mallarmé Chamber Group were written for an American jazz singer (Nnenna Freelon). I don't write for a jazz singer the same way I do for a classical singer. The abilities, the voice, the range, how the words are spoken, are all different. There are just so many nuances that you have to address in the music itself, if it is to fit. In other words, Nnenna Freelon and I had several sessions before I wrote the piece. I asked her to sing certain things, and she told me what she could do. We tried out things, and so in many ways that piece was tailored to her, and that accounts for the stylistic differences. But nobody would question whether or not it was my music. It *is* my music—in a different guise, a different genre, so to speak.

My mother was a pianist and my first teacher. My father taught at Howard University. In elementary school I studied the violin with one of his colleagues at Howard, Louis Von Jones. He had gone to Germany to study; he was a concert violinist who never had an opportunity to play a concert, and yet he was a marvelous violinist. In junior high school I sang in an Episcopal choir and studied with another violinist, Charles Keys, in Cincinnati, Ohio. My family moved from Washington, D.C., to Coatesville, Pennsylvania. Of course, that was my first experience in an integrated life. There I played trumpet and violin and also sang in the chorus. I did a lot of things while I was in high school.

One of the interesting things I taught myself to do was play saxophone, while I was in high school. There was a band at the Veteran's Hospital that needed a baritone saxophone player. I had never played sax in my life, so I got a student manual, cut out the fingers, and practiced on a stick. Of course I could read music; all I had to do was get a sound out of the thing. So I went up to audition, put the reed on the sax, blew it, and passed the audition—because I could read the music. The baritone sax wasn't that difficult, I just had to learn the fingering. That was a good experience. In college I picked up the bassoon and a number of other instruments, like French and baritone horns. I was being trained as a band leader, so to speak.

It wasn't until I got into graduate school that I decided to become a composer. I studied with George Ceiga, the university organist at Penn State. He was very tolerant. I wrote a terrible piece about a steel mill, but he was very nice and encouraging. He said I should go on in composition. I wasn't quite sure, so what I did was go to the Cincinnati Conservatory to study with T. Scott Huston. Basically what I wanted was a second opinion. I had a master's degree, but I really wanted to know whether I should go on in composition. Huston was very encouraging, and so I went out to Iowa, which was very rewarding. I did my doctorate with Philip Bezanson and Richard Hervig. After I finished under those two teachers, I went on to study with Darius Milhaud in Aspen.

Music requires an open mind; the things that I like now won't be things I like ten years from now, because I hope to change. The same thing is true of, say, Unitarianism; its basis is truth, which is constantly changing. That requires an open mind. Life is a continuous growing process, in which we are all involved. As a Unitarian as well as a composer, I bring the same sense of curiosity, the same search for truth, the same search for identity, the same search for those things that are meaningful to a compositional program as I do to religion.

Haydn, Mozart, Bach, and Beethoven are, of course, some of the composers who have influenced me in my evolution as a creator. There are a number of other composers, however, that nobody thinks of. There is a composer named Silvestre Revueltas, whom nobody talks about. He is a Mexican composer who wrote a piece called *Sensemayá* that I heard the Atlanta Symphony play in 1971. That piece was as important to me as Stravinsky's *Rite of Spring*. It is clearly from the New World—in other words, from this world. It is based on the Indians and the Aztec culture; it has that sense of repetition, that sense of ritual, that you don't often hear in music. (When I say "ritual," I mean ritual in the primitive sense.) It is a fantastic piece. I am also influenced by composers who I know personally—certainly Ulysses Kay [black American composer], Hale Smith, Olly Wilson, and George Walker—all of those composers with whom I have constantly looked at scores and with whom I have talked about other kinds of musics. I am "here" in one sense, but at the same time I am aware of what goes on in Europe with the avant-garde, and the musical experiences of Poland. My influences are just all over the place, and the reason is that I like to think that there are no boundaries in terms of what I want to find out and where I want to look. I don't take from everything that I hear, but I do catalog some things that I might like, and ten years from now I may come back to those things and use them as a resource.

Ivan Lins is a popular Brazilian singer whose work I admire. I was drawn to his work because of his use of the Portuguese language and the diversity of what he could sing. I hadn't heard a singer like that since Ella Fitzgerald, really. His harmonic vocabulary is far more interesting than American popular music—I mean, popular music in America is dead, as far as I am concerned. It died with rap, and rap died when public school music went out. It just got into rhythm. You can't have one-dimensional music and have great music. You have rhythm, yes, but you can't have great music. It takes more than a drumbeat to create something. The international experience in terms of scales and instruments and what they can do, all of that is part of our legacy. Certainly that has to be incorporated, and that is what I like to hear. That is why I was attracted to Ivan Lins.

I don't think about music, really. You can hear a cliché like, "I live to write and I write to live," all of those things. That's sophomoric, as far as I am concerned. Sure, all of us are driven by wanting to express ourselves, but at the same time, I can't say that I have some aesthetic that is going to change the world or make the world better. I don't believe that. I believe that what I do is the best I can do at this time and at this moment. That is all I am accountable for; the rest of it I can't be. An idea may be rooted in something ethereal, but that doesn't necessarily make it a better idea than something that is rooted in trash. The question is, how well does the composer use the idea? A lot of times people get caught up in profound abstractions, and to me that is not important at all.

I am ready to move off of the question about black music. I will tell you why. There was a time when we were insular, when we were basically segregated. Black composers reinforced each other because of the need to survive, and of course, we were closer to the culture. Now the second half of my life has been almost totally integrated. The question doesn't have the sense of urgency that it once had. I think for some people it does have a sense of meaning, but for me it doesn't. If you asked me what white music is, I couldn't tell you, any more than I can tell what black music is. I think that once you start trying to make these identifications and attempting to become specific, you are almost chasing a shadow. I mean, the classic example is to ask is, "Gershwin, white or black?" What about Ulysses Kay, is he black, or what? There is nothing in the music itself that depicts race. Everything in the music itself identifies with culture. Anybody can choose culture. I can be Italian if I went to Italy and stayed long enough. M. B. Tolson [black American poet] used to say if you took a black child and raised him in China, he would use chopsticks, and he would be Chinese. That is true. You draw on what you know best. I think in many ways as we move onward in the twenty-first century, the question of what a black composer is becomes almost obsolete. The questions now become what an American composer is, and how internationalism affects being an American composer. That is where we are headed.

We will never lose the identity of black culture. Leopold Senghor [famous West African poet and president of Senegal] was a student at the Sorbonne, in Paris. He got on the subway and saw a man from Africa, and said to himself, "What do I have in common, as a college student, with this man, who is a bum?" The answer was Negritude. In other words, there is a universal experience that black people have throughout the world. That will continue. I don't think for one minute that in my lifetime people are going to treat me any differently because I am a black man than I have been treated most of my life. That ties me to a set of experiences that make me unique. I am not running away from that, that is part of my baggage. I use the word "baggage" as a metaphor—I am carrying it, I am carrying European music, I am carrying folk traditions, I am carrying Asian music, I am carrying a whole lot of bags. I think that is the beauty of life, that you don't try to escape what you are. You try to look into that experience and bring it forth as best you can in terms of something that is meaningful.

I would tell a group of composers to be tough. I think that is the one thing that you have to be. You have to be tough, and you have to be patient. Nobody wants a composer, white or black; that is the reality of this society. Of course, you just have to build your career around people who have faith in what you do and are interested in your music. You have to be patient because since the society doesn't really want you, there is a constant feeling of rejection, yet you do form an audience. You do have a set of fans, a set of people who want you to do things. I have a patron in Richard Hunt, and I have an intellectual colleague in Leon Forrest. So you can have enough to sustain you against the pressures of being ignored and ostracized. That is not unique to black composers, either.

I had a talk with Philip Levine, the Pulitzer Prize winner, who is a good friend of mine, a very successful poet. He told me that when he writes a book, he can depend upon five hundred readers. By that he means that when he writes a book, he knows there will be five hundred people who will purchase the book, read it, and will be in touch with what he is doing as an artist. I said to myself, "My God! He is one of the most successful poets in America and he is only talking about a readership of five hundred?" What is that going to say to me? I am tickled to death to have a hundred. I don't know what I've got, but I know I am satisfied that I have enough to sustain me. If Phil says he has five hundred, you can imagine what the other poets should feel. They should feel like they shouldn't write at all, but it doesn't work that way. I would suspect that a poet who has fifty readers or twenty-five is just as active as Phil Levine with five hundred steady readers. That is very powerful, and it is a lesson for all of us.

The first thing I would do about the situation of contemporary arts education is fire most of the teachers. I will tell you why we have a problem. First, we have allowed them—the administrative structures of the public school system—to deemphasize music and art to the point where we are almost crippled. That is the only way I can describe it. When you take out Band, when you take out Orchestra, when you take out choruses, and you take out all of the things that are supportive of what we do, it is no wonder that musical illiterates are running around. It is no wonder that there is no musical taste to which one can appeal. The answer is to really look at the culture. In other words look at who we are as a people. Now, I talk about the tragedy of music in public or private education; you can also multiply that by other fields. In other words, what happened to languages in schools? They are gone.

How can we exist when in the ten biggest banks in the world, there is not an American bank among them? Of the ten biggest banks in the world, eight of them are Japanese. At least half of the American people ought to be learning how to speak Japanese now, because that is the new country of the future. Somebody ought to be teaching Chinese too, but we are not doing that.

Latin has disappeared from many high schools and colleges. Of course, we have had some members of society move toward technology and computers, but the masses of people aren't there. So what you are going to see in the future is an elite class educated in the new technology, and a lot of people being dragged behind. The only way this system can ever be corrected is for the federal government to assume responsibility, but it keeps talking about "no taxes, no taxes"; meanwhile, look at Japan, look at Sweden, look at the Asian countries that have really developed. Those countries tax to the hilt. Look at Germany, it taxes like mad. Why? Because it takes tax money to protect citizens in terms of moving toward an international goal.

What we need is a Franklin D. Roosevelt or Harry Truman, somebody who says "the buck stops here," this is what we have to do; the American people would have to swallow the pill. Not one of the candidates [Anderson was speaking in the midst of a presidential campaign in which Bill Clinton defeated Bob Dole and won a second term] is talking about us becoming a second-rate nation. If you look at the national debt, that tells you we are a second-rate nation, but nobody explains that to you. Nobody talks about it. The belief is that we are number one, we can do this, we can go on forever, when in reality we can't. We are going to be second or third rate, and of course when that happens, everyone is going to say, "How did we get there?" Look at Greece. Look at Egypt. Look at Rome. Civilizations have always come and gone, and we are going down too, but nobody is explaining that.

I think anything that lifts the human spirit is important and that holds for Black History Month celebrations. The real tragedy is that we have never seen a move beyond that. That is the real tragedy. Each generation thinks they are going to move into the mainstream, and they don't. That is what we mean by racism. That is a pathological sickness. It hasn't changed much. Chester Pierce, a psychiatrist at the Harvard Medical School, talks about racism as a pathological illness. Regardless of how you explain it to a person, and regardless of the facts that they are confronted with, they still come to the same conclusion, that blacks, Asians, and women are inferior—those kinds of clichés. As long as you have that illness, the country can never fulfill its dreams.

That is one side of the coin. The other side is that the demographics of the country are changing. We have many people coming in from south of the border, and I cheer that. In other words, the history of the country is, "Give me your tired and your poor." That is on the Statue of Liberty. I cheer when anybody comes to America—Haitians, Polish immigrants, people from Bosnia. In other words, I think the richness of the country is its ability to absorb immigrants, put them to work, and come up with geniuses. That is what made America. We have got the European Jews who came from Russia, we had the Germans who came to this country at the time of the rise of Hitler. We have always had Asians coming, and that continues.

I don't think in terms of identifying monumental pieces by black composers. That is a pyramid concept, and a pyramid concept is the product of industrialization. If you go into the Boston Symphony and look up at the roof, you see Beethoven in the center. Then you see Haydn and Mozart, and then it drops down to the second order, with Verdi and so on. That is the product of industrialized society. I think of a ball, a ball that is turning all of the time—there are times when Beethoven rolls over and Tartini, or Bellini, or somebody else comes to the top. Among black composers the ball is always circulating. Ulysses Kay comes up. So does William Grant Still. So does Herbert Mells. So does Noel DaCosta. The ball is constantly turning, and we have to think of it that way. For example, George Walker got the Pulitzer Prize when he was seventy-three years old.

George was writing beautiful music long before he wrote his piece for the Boston Symphony. The fact that pieces have not been recognized does not make them any less valuable, and the fact that he has the award doesn't make the music any more valuable. In other words, it is the same music. There may be a few more performances than before, but the music exists regardless, and it existed before that award. No African American composer of concert music has ever received a MacArthur, which is the usual standard for young geniuses; we don't have any young geniuses, according to the MacArthur committee. But that is ridiculous. What I am saying is regardless of what may happen, the ball is constantly turning over, and even in the case of a composer of Beethoven, Mozart, or Haydn's stature, there is still room for other composers to come to the forefront and be meaningful.

Dawson [black American composer], Florence Price [American concert singer], and certainly Howard Swanson [black American composer] come up. All of them come up, because I am not looking at a pyramid, I am looking at a ball. I am looking at a ball that is constantly turning on an axis that is being exposed to different kinds of music, different periods, and it is part of a continuum that is always there. It is not mine or any black composer's job to be part of the canon. Why should I have to compete with Charles Ives? That is ridiculous. All I have to be is T. J. Anderson. That is enough for me. They can recognize my music or not recognize it. The point is if I write the music, I will have done what I am supposed to do, and that is all that I am interested in.

I think we have to develop an appreciation for the pluralities that exist, not the sense of me trying to make a be-bop run by Charlie Parker equal to an invention by Bach. That is not the point. The point is that Parker is as valid as

Bach. If you ask why, it is because you believe in instruction. I would say your instruction has been limited if it hasn't included Parker, because Parker is a product of his age. You can't listen to Parker and try to find out what he is doing in relation to Bach. That is not the point. The point is that Parker is Parker, Thelonious Monk is Thelonious Monk, and Cecil Taylor is Cecil Taylor. Now Cecil Taylor isn't Bartók, nor should he want to be Bartók.

What I am talking about is the acceptance of plurality. For example, people are always talking about American Indian music, saying that it's not vital. American Indian music is vital to American Indians, and therefore it is vital music. Now if I don't understand what they are getting out of it, I need to understand. In other words I can't judge it on the basis of the fact that it doesn't have the rhythm of African music. No, it doesn't have the rhythm of African music, but there is more than one way to look at rhythm, and I have to adapt to that if I want to enjoy it. I can't say African music is superior to American Indian music. That is the most ridiculous thing in the world. All musics are products of culture. They are nothing more than that. They are the expression of the folk. When the folk speak, they speak in different tongues. We have to have an appreciation and understanding for that.

When I create music, it depends on what it is for. I study scores and see what I like and what I don't like. I also start sketching, and I think about it for a long time. I eventually evolve the whole piece in my mind. Once I have done that, I go on and write. I make sketches of what I am thinking—it depends upon whether I want to use source material. I may make a note to myself about David Murray's bass clarinet; that may be a sound that I want to use. I write myself little notes, reminders, but they are no more than just reminders.

I use my own system to generate music, one that Bruce Thompson talked about in his dissertation. It has expanded, but that is the system that I use. It is a series of related tones; it's not twelve-tone, it's just a series of related tones that exist as sets. These sets are manipulated and exist in varying environments. I stack them for sonorities, I do all kinds of things, but it is never numerical. That is why I am not a twelve-tone composer.

I would have been a twelve-tone composer if I were interested in that, but I am not. I wouldn't say there is an emotional component; there is a *sound* quality about it, the ear. All composers compose by ear, whether they admit it or not, because you have to hear what you are doing, and you have to like it, otherwise you wouldn't write. I just assume composers like their music because they put their names on it; I have to assume that, I can't assume anything else. I can't assume they don't like it, that is presumptuous of me. That is a value judgment I can't make.

Composers have a role in society; we have a voice that is trying to be heard. Everybody has a voice that is trying to be heard; it is not unique to composers. Tap dancers have voices and want to be heard, barbershop quartets want to be heard. My teacher, Bezanson used to say, "The only difference between you and anybody else is that you can take the tune out of the bathtub, put it together and bring some sense of order to it. But that idea, everybody else has got it. Everybody is singing in the tub. You are not unique." That's true, none of us are unique. We are unique in that we can organize it, but we are not unique in thinking it up. Someone else has thought of it before.

Internationalism—basically the walls are down and CDs are made available everywhere. I have a publisher in Berlin. I never dreamed that would happen. My music is played in Japan. Things are happening so fast that you just have to think in terms of everything becoming global. Now people think that a global perspective means that you have to have a global identity. You can't have any more identity than you have got. In other words, you are what you are. The fact that we are moving toward a global perspective doesn't mean we are moving toward a global music; that is something different altogether.

My experience with Robert Shaw [American conductor] and the Atlanta Symphony was great. The thing I learned most was a respect for the score. I had had that from Iowa but it developed further by going to rehearsals and seeing how Shaw put pieces together. It was marvelous to witness that. How I got the opportunity I have no idea, they just asked me to be in residence with the orchestra. I went for one year and then stayed for three. I learned a lot, and I got a chance to do a lot, too. I wrote a lot of music while I was there. We had a very good relationship. I had contact with Still, I had contact with Ulysses Kay—more with Kay than Still. My two major mentors were Ulysses and Hale Smith. They were both influential in my development.

I don't know how I would describe my work stylistically and aesthetically. That's not my job. I am referred to as an eclectic composer. In other words, there is a mix that doesn't ordinarily exist when people hear others' music. That is what Nicholas Slonimsky [writer and musicologist] said about my music, that I draw from a lot of diverse sources and that all of these things come together. They come together, and they make sense to me. They may not make sense to other people, but they make sense to me. That is what I try to do and what my music will continue to do; my life is always changing, because the influences are constantly shifting. Bill Bolcolm [American composer] once said that my music is like an arrow that goes in a straight line. What he means is that there is a continuum in my music that is recognizable; there is a style that you might be able to find in my work. I don't think too much about it, because I don't want to be trapped one way or another.

It's not a matter of what I would like, it is what everybody else likes. Whatever meaning my music has, it will have. If it has meaning, it will live. If it doesn't have meaning, it will die. Some things die and come back later; nobody knows. Nor should a composer care.

I could not care less what my music would do in this life. There is no ultimate goal. The ultimate goal in life is freedom, and you can't have an ultimate goal of freedom with strings attached to it. Freedom is the ability for the living to do whatever they want to do. And it is that way, whether we like it or not.

David Baker

David Nathaniel Baker is one of the most eclectic composers in American music. His output spans the vocabulary of notated musical forms from symphony, jazz quintet, gospel choral, serial, funk, experimental, chamber, string quartet, soul, art song, solo instrumental, and musical theater. Born on December 21, 1931, a native of Indianapolis, Mr. Baker is recognized as one the premiere scholars dealing with pedagogical approaches to jazz education, having written over a hundred books and articles on the subject. One of the most significant books was the 1978 *The Black Composer Speaks,* from Scarecrow Press. This work was the first comprehensive book documenting the works and perspectives of black American composers. Currently, a distinguished professor of music at Indiana University, he is founding chairman of the school's jazz studies program, which was initiated in 1966. His education includes both undergraduate and graduate degrees from Indiana University. As a performer, David Baker has worked with such greats as Quincy Jones, Lionel Hampton, Stan Kenton, Maynard Ferguson, and Wes Montgomery. A 1973 Pulitzer Prize nominee, a Grammy nominee, he has been honored several times by *Downbeat* magazine and is an inductee of its Jazz Educators Hall of Fame. Mr. Baker was appointed to the National Council of the Arts by President Ronald Reagan, served as the president of the National Jazz Service Organization, and was elected president of the International Association of Jazz Educators in 2002. He is currently the music director of the Smithsonian Jazz Masterworks Orchestra. He has been commissioned and performed by leading orchestras including the Boston, Indianapolis, Detroit, Houston, New York Philharmonic, Akron, Louisville, and Oakland Symphony Orchestras. His recording output of close to a hundred works includes concerti, string ensembles, small jazz ensembles, symphonic poems and suites, and pieces for solo piano and big band. Mr. Baker currently lives and works in Bloomington, Indiana.

We live in a global village now, and everything is available to anybody, even in the most remote areas, in pockets like the Georgia Sea Islands, where before people didn't have access to such information. When you have that happening, it seems to me, it is very, very difficult to delineate and talk about the defini-

tion of an American composer. I would say an American composer is, most obviously, someone who is American. What else are they going to be? I don't care if they write from the Second Viennese School of Music, or whatever. I would basically say somebody who is American, whether American born or an immigrant, tends to use those things that belong to the American experience, however broad that experience might be. It might be anything from Appalachian folk songs to jazz, to spirituals, to the music of Copland and Roy Harris, or whatever.

I grew up in the Midwest, specifically in Indianapolis. My whole life has centered around Indianapolis and Bloomington, Indiana. I was in Indianapolis during my formative years. In my professional life, however far-reaching and however far-flung it has been around the globe, Bloomington has been the nexus, the center. I grew up in Indianapolis in anything but bilingual circumstances. I grew up listening to Louis Jordan, Lester Young, Jimmie Lunceford, Coleman Hawkins, Mahalia Jackson, and all those people. I grew up listening to the Golden Gate Jubilee Quartet. That is the music I heard. I didn't know about any other kind of music, but I knew about all of the other vernacular musics of the time. Certainly there was Vaughn Monroe, "Racing with the Moon," and Bing Crosby and Doris Day, because their music was omnipresent. That is what the radio fare was at the time, unless you had a Randy's Record Shop from Gallatin, Tennessee. I grew up mainly listening to vernacular music. I came to classical music very late. What I got in high school was versions of that music in the concert band and marching band. That is hardly representative of what the music is, but at that time it titillated my senses and got me thinking, "Hey, that's pretty nice music."

It was only when I got to college that I got seriously interested in anything other than music from the vernacular. One reason for that, and for a practical reason, was that there was no foreseeable circumstance that I could imagine that would allow me to be a participant in any other music except the music that was set aside for black people—gospel music, jazz music, rhythm and blues music, and blues music. So I listened to jazz, assuming that was the kind of job I would get.

I was not always musical. Nobody in my family even played music. I guess my dad at one time or another played alto saxophone when he was going to Hampton Institute, but from what I am told—and these are his words, not mine—he "didn't play very well." He did sing in the choir under R. Nathaniel Dett, so he was aware of that tradition of music. I began messing around with our piano, which had a piano roll. I would go to the piano and worry people to death with that. I would pump away at the peddles that activated the player rolls. I tried to pick out pieces. I think my stepmother didn't think it was appropriate, or that I would be interested, so my sister got piano lessons, but I did not.

When I got to junior high school, I was discouraged by a piano teacher who said I had absolutely no talent. I didn't start again playing piano until the next year, and then the only instrument they had for me was an E-flat tuba. I played tuba well into high school. At some point in high school, I suspect about my senior year, my band director, Russell Brown, switched me to trombone. He thought the trombone would be more challenging. I went through bad times, because I learned the instrument wrong, in terms of what it was about, and had to start all over again when I came to Indiana University. Ultimately, I became a bass trombone player.

I had a lot of influences in Indianapolis. I played in the Hampton Family Band, which included, among others, Slide, Maceo, and Lucky, and we learned to play by taking things off records. When a gig would come up, everyone would say, "We are going to learn 'Eager Beaver' by Stan Kenton, and you are playing third trombone, so you take the record home tonight and learn your part." Then everyone else would learn their respective parts for the next day. It was a wonderful experience, quite unlike anything that happened in the academy. I learned that way. I also had a teacher who was very serious about teaching me to read music, because he understood that once I was in college I would be measured in terms of how literate I was.

It was not until much later that I decided to become a composer. I had no inclination even to try to write tunes. I can remember my first arrangement, a piece called "God Child," by George Wallington. My idea of arrangement was to take the piano sheet and simply write it out for everybody—in wrong transpositions, in my case, and with instruments playing completely out of their ranges. But I don't think I had any real interest in composition as such; I took a composition course, but I really wasn't serious about it. I began to write jazz pieces when I had my own jazz band. I think I was married by then and had taught down at Lincoln University, so I would have been in my late twenties. I taught Julius Hemphill [jazz musician and composer for saxophone] and Carl Soloman [trumpet] and those guys. But I wasn't really interested in composition. I did arrangements while we were down there at Lincoln, but I can't remember doing any real writing until after I left there. I put a big band together around 1958, when I came back to do graduate work. I had to create music for the band, so I started to write then. A lot of it was probably not much more than warmed-over pieces stolen from other sources.

I don't think it ever clicked for me all at once that I would be a composer. I think it was gradual and an evolutionary process. It was out of necessity. I needed music for the band, so I wrote it. When my father died in 1964, the theological seminary in Indianapolis commissioned me to write an oratorio. I don't think I had any notion of what I wanted to do. The oratoria was a hodgepodge; it was an oratorio only in the loose sense of the word. Gradually, I began to write. At first I was very prolific, because I was also very uncritical. Then I thought for a long time that I was drying up as a writer, because I wasn't writing as much as I had before. Then I realized that what was happening was that I was becoming more critical of what I was writing, and consequently was writing less. I wrote a lot of stuff that I am actually mortified to hear today. Unfortunately, some of it even got published, and I hate it. I hate it with a passion, because it's bad music.

Writing became a consuming passion somewhere along the way, probably by the time I came back to Indiana University to teach in 1966. By that time I was very serious about what I wrote. I didn't write well, because I hadn't had the opportunity to write and hear the music that I wrote in the classical tradition. At one point my work became exclusively nonjazz, nonvernacular music. I had to go through that stage when I was learning about counterpoint and all that stuff. I had to write music that taught me the craft. The notion that I could draw from sources that reflect my background in order to make music came to me much later. If I go back and listen to those pieces, for instance, under the title *The Black Experience,* one piece in there, "Early in the Morning," by Mari Evans—all of them are Mari Evans's poems—shows a big jazz influence and is the most viable. The rest of them were twelve-tone essays; when I listen to them now, I realize that at that time my head was in a different place.

My music is rarely ever programmatic, except in commissions where I am writing using words. If somebody asks for something, that is the stimulus, that is the impetus, that is the reason for writing the piece. I rarely ever write in the abstract. I learned something from a friend of mine named Howie Smith [tenor saxophone composer], who works out of Cleveland. I told him that whenever I started to write again after not writing for a month or two, the first week I would throw away everything I wrote, because it was just exercise to get the juices flowing. He said, "Have you ever thought about this? Instead of doing that, think about how easy it is for you to write jazz music and pop music." I said, "That's my language, I can write that in my sleep." He said, "Instead of throwing everything away, why don't you write three or four big-band arrangements to get your juices flowing?" If you give me three or four notes, or even if I don't have any notes, I can sit down and write jazz and pop tunes as fast as I can write my name. I can sit down now—it is five minutes to three—and by four o'clock I could write you ten good tunes, well-crafted pop tunes that I wouldn't have to do anything else with. When those sixteen or thirty-two measures are done, they are done.

Now, when it moves to the next level, where I have got to make that piece last twenty minutes without the benefit of a rhythm section to carry it forward, and without the benefit of improvisation to take up twelve minutes, that is a different thing. What happened for me, where the epiphany took place, was when I realized those were two different processes.

There was a time, maybe a year or two ago, when I probably would have said that there was a difference between music students now and those in the past. I saw the difference in terms of the sheer physical facility that I had as a college student and the facility that my players have now. Basically, the musicians, whether they are particularly gifted or not, are almost always more technically advanced now than they were then. The question has arisen in the last few years in various panels. I think *we* have not moved; the only thing that has changed is what we have to say. I have to confess that it is six of one and half a dozen of the other. There was a time when we were less formulaic in conceptual things, simply because we learned from records if we were players, and we learned by imitation if we were writers. There tended to be a more orderly approach when one was working one on one with a teacher, even though there was a much neater approach when one was working as part of a class in which everyone was trying to write in the same way, trying to learn through the same process. It is a kind of dichotomy for me. There is a greater quantity of players, now because there are more venues. As far as the quality, I really think—and I never thought I would say this—that the quality of players was higher then, simply because people found their voices much faster. There were no aids to help them. When Jerry Coker [jazz author, educator] and I wrote our first books, we could not have known that we were not only opening the door to a path that would allow everybody to participate but also laying down impediments that made them take longer to find out who they were.

I am absolutely devastated by the lack of young black musicians participating in college jazz programs around the country. It isn't just here at Indiana University, and not just in America, but in Europe as well. I heard people say just a few weeks ago that blacks weren't interested in cutting-edge music, that blacks were the "retros." We know who are the models for people who say blacks are retros. I was upset, because they were trying to tell me that if you go to New York, black musicians aren't doing breakthrough music, like the European players, meaning players of European extraction. I resent that, and I tried to tell them, "You know, you are looking at a very small slice of what this music is about."

I began to tell them about the World Saxophone Quartet. I began to tell them about the youngsters who are trying, in a lot of ways, to find their original voices. A lot of people have assumed that the fact that the white students outnumber us considerably somehow automatically confers on them the creative mantle. So I am very disturbed when I don't see any black faces. It is only recently that we have begun to draw quite a few black kids to the Aebersold Camps. But if you look at Indiana University, look at the makeup of the music school, out of 1,500 or 1,600 students, maybe twenty-five are black. Fifteen of those, maybe ten, are instrumentalists, and out of those maybe five are in jazz and five are in classical. So what do you do there? When I was up at Sandpoint—it had been in existence six or seven years—one student said to me, "I have been here several years, and you are the first black person I have ever seen here." I don't know how to account for it. Our kids don't seem to be terribly interested in music or in the arts. I don't know why that should be. I think that it is very specific to black students, maybe because we are in such a minority. When we don't have anybody out there, it shows up even more. If only 5 percent of white people showed up to do jazz, that would still be a big number. If you say 5 percent of black folks, then you have almost nobody.

Black History Month is like bad luck. Some people say if they didn't have bad luck, they wouldn't have any luck at all. Remember, I have been around long enough to see that it has moved from Black History Day to Black History Week to Black History Month. Now I am not sure where those parameters lead to—but I resented not having my pieces on programs of subscription concerts. I don't have that problem any more, and neither do some of the other black composers. A lot of us do get our music performed. But there is still this glut of people trying to do those works in February, because it is the proper thing to do. I would love for it no longer to be necessary to put all of our music on a single program. I think Hale Smith's manifesto is still one of the greatest yet— "Here I Stand." He says, the only time it is important for you to know what color I am is when you see me stand up to take my bow at the end of the piece. That should be the first time that you know I am colored, or that it is even important. But I am not sure that we will ever see that—certainly not in my lifetime.

I think there is no question that there are commonalities in the traditions that we talk about. Otherwise we wouldn't be able to classify them as American music, or post-Romantic music, or what have you. Make no mistake—jazz, rhythm and blues, and these things are basically Romantic musics. They tend to be more passionate than some other music, but I can find incredible passion in Rachmaninoff, for example. I think there are more commonalities than there are differences. For instance, when people tell me that they have problems learning jazz, I try to tell them, "Look, the language of jazz is a lot closer to the language of Brahms and Beethoven than is the language of Boulez or the language of Milton Babbitt." My flute piece was done at a flute convention in New York where there were three thousand flautists. One of the things they did there was profile each of the composers. I remember being amused when my wife read it, because she cracked up.

It said something like, Milton Babbitt, born "whenever, a degree from Yale or wherever, a BFA from some other Ivy League school," and then it said, "Fifty years later he received his doctorate because it was the first time they found a panel that could understand his doctoral work."

Unfortunately, very often that has been the case. It is easier for someone who understands Bach, Brahms, and Beethoven to learn to play jazz than it is for them to learn to play the music of Milton Babbitt. I see so much in common, which is another reason why I think jazz is starting to get a foothold in all kinds of music, not just because it draws people to the pops concerts but because maybe it saves somebody's season.

I think the first composer of real note, from the standpoint of pure composition, was, of course, Jelly Roll Morton. Without the groundwork that he laid in the 1920s with the Red Hot Peppers, there probably could not have been a Duke Ellington. If there had not been a Duke Ellington, then there probably would not have been a John Lewis [jazz musican and composer], or a George Russell, or a Gil Evans, or a Tadd Dameron. Duke Ellington, in my mind, was the one who took the mantle of Jelly Roll and began to bring together all the disparate parts of the Afro-American experience—the blues on the one hand, and on the other hand the use of extended forms, where he had to try to develop things, starting with "Reminiscing in Tempo." Ellington had the ears to understand how to record music in a way that nobody else thought about, in jazz or anything else. When you hear Ellington, even as early as 1933 with "Daybreak Express," you hear somebody who placed the microphones and the players in a way that gave a sonic picture that was correct. Ellington brought that to the table. Because he was able to stay above the fray, in a lot of ways, Ellington was able to try a lot of experimental things.

He could work in a way that Charles Ives, for instance, couldn't. Charles Ives didn't get to hear much of his music until many years later. Ives started writing in about 1912 or 1913, and the first performances of some of his works were as late as 1945. You can't grow when you don't hear the music that you are writing. Only Ellington kept his band through thick and thin. There was never a time when he made it smaller; even Basie for a long time had a septet.

Ellington subsidized his band to keep it together until he died. He was able to do that primarily because he was a successful composer. He was using royalties from his compositions to support the band so he could write more compositions—something that Basie could not have done, because Basie was not so prodigious a composer. This was something that Jimmie Lunceford [jazz musician and bandleader] could not have done, because he was dependent on Sy Oliver [jazz musician and arranger] and others to keep his band going. Ellington was unique in the sense that he was the main writer for his band, long before this was fashionable, the main writer as well as the conductor and the leader. Ellington, it seems to me, opened up a lot of doors. People seem to like to think that his most prolific and important years were from 1938 to, say, the [Ben] Webster [saxonphonist]-[Jimmy] Blanton [bass] years. More and more we see that that is absolutely false. From the very beginning, with pieces like "Choo-Choo," when he was finding his own voice, all the way up to the "Far East Suite" and his "Sacred Services," Ellington was a man of Promethean talent. The music grew and became strong. We are only now discovering that his compatriot, Billy Strayhorn, was damn near as strong—but Ellington was singular.

I think the most obvious reason for the lack of attention to the work of black American men and women in the concert arena is that they are black. That is still a given. They used to say that if you were black, you had to be twice as good. That hasn't changed. First of all, there is no level playing field. People extol the virtues of a system that will still tell Tiger Woods—and here is a prodigy in golf like we have not seen in years, never as a black person, and just signed a forty-million-dollar contract to play golf—that there are still places he can't play. So it is not a level playing field, and the color thing is very important. Secondly, we don't have access to the various media that allow us to do what we do, because people want to hear what they think we should write. They want to tell us that what we write has got to have jazz in it. Jazz is going to show up in my writing, because it is part of who I am, but nobody has the right to *tell* me that jazz has to be a part of what I do.

We have been circumscribed in that way. Then there is also the fact that people don't play our music except on special occasions. Here at Indiana University, during the thirty-plus years, I've been here, I bet we have played five, maybe six compositions by black composers. Probably two or three of those compositions were played because Herman Hudson [first dean of black studies at Indiana University] was a champion for me, and a couple when composers would say, "It's not right." Basically, however, those doors are closed to us.

One of the ways that people get into the classical world as composers is by performing in orchestras. There is a double benefit there, because when you are performing in an orchestra, you are also learning how an orchestra works. When you sit there in the middle of the violin section for twenty years as a player, you start to hear what makes it work. You learn how things work, what makes a good piece, what makes a bad piece. We don't have that experience, because we don't get to sit in the orchestra. It is obviously speculation, but I would bet there are not twenty blacks in the top ten orchestras. So where do we get our experience? Where do we find out how to do this? Then when they do play our music, it is all during a concert where they bring in a black conductor; he has got to learn seven pieces in one rehearsal, and then he plays one movement of this piece, five minutes of that piece, four minutes of another, and that is the end of it.

Then too, they say, "One of the reasons why we don't play this music, and why you are not in the orchestra, is because we don't see you in the audience." Then they say, "One reason why we don't see you in the audience is because there isn't anybody in the orchestra." So now we have the chicken and the egg—and all of it is subterfuge, as far as I am concerned.

Being director of the Smithsonian Jazz Masterworks Orchestra is not the main part of my creative activity. I had to recognize and reconcile that. I was in the repertory movement a long time before the Smithsonian Jazz Masterworks

Orchestra came into being. As an educator, first of all I see that I have to wear the Janus mask—I have to look forward and backward simultaneously.

I think that people who are only interested in preservation are in as weak a position as people who are interested only in nurturing new things. I think we have to be able to look forward and backward simultaneously. The Smithsonian Orchestra gave me the chance to play music that had not been heard live in years. Gunther Schuller [American composer and author], my colleague at that time, said, "Any music that is not heard live is doomed to extinction." Consequently it meant going back and playing pieces like "Daybreak Express," which was only recorded one time, I think in 1933. Inexplicably, Duke recorded it only one time. It is a great piece, but you didn't get to hear it played, and consequently it lost its importance and impact. That is one thing we are able to do.

The other thing we are able to do, is to do things in an authentic way. For instance, for years when you heard Duke Ellington playing Billy Strayhorn's "Take the A-Train," you heard somebody's arrangement of it. You heard it in a concert band, you heard it in Phil Spitalny and his All-Girl Orchestra, you heard it in any way but the way the composer intended it. Suppose you only heard the Bartók *Fourth Quartet* played by an accordion orchestra, or an arrangement that somebody had done for a woodwind ensemble. That would be unthinkable. We went years without hearing this particular music authentically played. We try to re-create the music in the way the composer intended. You would never think we would have to do that, because it is jazz, but we do.

We are going to do some new Billy Strayhorn pieces in a concert with a small group. When I tried to score these pieces for four horns, I realized that some of the magic disappeared. I asked myself, "Why isn't this working?" Then I knew why—the orchestration that he envisioned was missing. You can't image *Les Preludes* with a different orchestration than Liszt put there. You just can't imagine it. I can't imagine hearing the Brahms *First,* with that climbing string passage in the beginning, in the trumpet.

There are several other things that make this work important for me. First, we are able to restore things that were not done the way the composers wanted them. We get the original scores sometimes; we will see that a whole section has been cut out because the piece had to fit on a three-minute record. We can restore that, and people will hear it for the first time. We sometimes find a score that is correct, but the recording is just fraught with mistakes, because there was only so much time to record. We can repair that, and that is important.

Something else that I have tried to do with the orchestra that I think is important is widen its parameters. We started out by having the music that orchestras play stop at about 1940. It occurred to me, however, that if you have twenty or twenty-five years of temporal distance between you and the music, you can make judgments about whether it is worthy of being a part of the classic repertoire. If a piece has been around for twenty years and you haven't figured out if it is important or not, then it probably isn't. So, unlike classical music, where the repertoire is maybe 75 or 80 percent written in Europe before 1940, jazz, remember, has material dating only from about 1917. I figure we can go up to 1975 and still call it repertory music, and that is what we are doing. I have a concert coming up called "Big Band Renaissance." I can do the music of George Russell, John Lewis, and Thad Jones, because much of their earlier work is by now repertory music. Now, what makes it possible for me to do repertory in good conscience is that it is just a slice of what I do. The other part is working with my college youngsters and helping them deal with what has happened in music since John Coltrane, Julius Hemphill, and Jimmy Hendrix. I have the best of both worlds, because I can look forward and look backward and know that I am discharging my duties faithfully.

Sometimes I successfully incorporate my duties as a scholar, composer, and administrator, but often I am not so successful. A performer and writer often has to choose one or the other for a period of time. Maybe it was Donald Erb [composer] who once told me that at some point in your career, you have to choose—between performing and composing. I have not yet reached that point, and I hope I don't. But it is a juggling act. and it has made me think a lot about retirement. You can't write five minutes at a time, then go somewhere else, and then come back and write for five more minutes. Composition is a very singular and lonely occupation that demands a lot of uninterrupted time.

I organized my life into some specific cycles. Maybe twelve years ago, I decided I had to give back something to the field, so I accepted seats on various boards. I accepted the presidency of the National Jazz Service organization and a Reagan appointment to the National Council of the National Endowment for the Arts. I said, "All right, this is going to be my service, period." I know I am not going to be as prolific as usual. I probably will not play as much as I would normally play, and more importantly, I won't have the same degree of financial assistance. Because I am sitting on all of these boards of directors, there is a conflict of interest if I ask for financial help, and besides, I am not eligible. I can't ask the NEA for money while I am making decisions about who gets its money.

What I have tried to do—now, and at any given time—is to concentrate on one thing or the other, perform or compose. I have developed a mechanism, mentally, that allows me to shift gears. When I am writing, I am not thinking about my playing. When I am playing, the writing is completely out of my mind. That doesn't mean that it doesn't encroach and make me say, "Go away, when I get done with this I'll get to you." The concept of the Renaissance man is a wonderful one, but in practical terms, eventually you have to be able to segregate and concentrate on specific things. I wouldn't advise anyone to do what I have been doing, to try to be a jack-of-all-trades.

I am aspiring to a period when I can spend more time as a composer. I haven't gotten there yet. I have written books, and I am now trying to get more books written. All of a sudden I am starting to play and record more. I am going to have to find a way to spend more time composing, either by retiring or by simply setting aside blocks of a month or two and one thing exclusively. Of course, you have to keep the flow going, whether writing little ditties or practicing for one hour every day. But I wouldn't wish this notion of the Renaissance person on anybody. If all I had to do was play and write, I think I could manage that. I have friends who are jazz writers; that is all they do. They travel with a band, and they write. I envy them, because they don't have to deal with a twenty-one-hour-a-week teaching schedule. They don't have to deal with meetings in different cities. They don't have to fly back and forth to Washington, D.C., to conduct another orchestra concert. I see people who are very successful at that. Gunther Schuller does all of those things, but he doesn't have to play too. He is also not dealing with school.

I am not sure I am as successful as I would like to be. I'm probably productive, but that does not always mean that I am successful, because success, it seems to me, has to do with an inner peace, an inner fulfillment. As long as I have those loose ends, I am not getting that inner fulfillment.

My creative process runs the gamut. There was a time when I would just sit down at the piano and wait for something to happen. I write at the piano most of the time. When I approach the development, the scoring, and the orchestration of a work, I don't go to the piano, because by that time I know what I want. I do sketches. I went through a period of two or three years when I wrote mainly dodecaphonic music. I wish I could get that music back. Now most of the decisions are made before I sit down to write.

I have been very fortunate to write almost entirely upon commission. The more information given me when I get ready to write, the easier it is to write the piece. If somebody calls and says, "Look, I am a tuba player, and I need a concerto," they have already given me two of the parameters. He wants it to be for orchestra, he wants a band, and he tells me that it is for tuba. Then he says, "I would like it to be approximately fifteen minutes long." Now he has already closed another option. Then he says, "I'd like it to be three movements. Could the middle movement be slow?" Every time they add another constraint, another restriction, the easier it is for me to write. Once I have all of those things, then—I'm sure that it's fright that causes this—I go and research what other people have done. When I wrote my two-piano concerto, I must have spent months just listening. In retrospect, I think I was doing that so that I wouldn't have to start writing. When I wrote my first violin concerto, I spent hours listening to violin concertos. I did the same thing with the cello concerto, and all of my other works.

When I get ready to write, I go basically to the piano—usually early in the morning, because that is when my mind works best—and I begin to search for themes. Sometimes I don't have any notion of which movement I am working on; I am just writing. Once I get something going, I might find that it's the second movement. I find that slow movements are easier to write. So slow movements almost always get done with some speed; then it gets to those movements when you have to create. I can't tell you how many times I have had jazz people say, "Man, how can you keep the piece going? There isn't any rhythm section." I say, "Ah, that is where the creative mind works, and craft comes into it."

I can look in a score and I can tell you if it is moving, if it has development; I can see what is happening. I sat on the Pulitzer Prize committee for two years; I would look at the first two pages of a score and then turn to page eight, and if the same thing was still happening, I wanted to know why. I want see the piece evolving; I don't want to see repeat signs. My own writing, then, becomes a chess game. What do I move here? I try to imagine what I would like to hear if I were sitting in a hall listening to this piece—one of my teachers told me about that. Another thing that I learned from teachers was to lay out all my materials so I can see everything that I have already done. The last thing that is very important; I always try to end creative sessions while the juices are still flowing. I am in the middle of an idea that has me so excited that I can't contain myself, and I stop; I have to make myself go to bed. Then I can't wait to get up the next morning and start there. I don't write until I run out of ideas, because then the next morning I have to figure out where I was going and what I was doing.

One of the hardest things for me to learn as a composer—and I am sure that this is common to every composer—is that not every piece is going to be a masterpiece. I have a tendency with my books and with my pieces to constantly be rethinking and reworking. You have to edit; you do it with both books and music. There comes a point, however, where you have to say, "This is where it is going to be," and then leave it alone. If at some other point in your life you come back and do something else with it, that's fine. I would get stuck forever and not finish a work, because I wanted to keep reworking it. I found out that most composers whose work I really liked come back and rethink their work, even after it's published if necessary. One of the things that enables me to move forward with some speed when I am working on a book or some music is realizing that I am not writing Tolstoy's *War and Peace.* What I am writing is functional, it serves a purpose. I want it to be good, I want it to be professional, but I don't put the burden on myself of thinking that I have to write Milton's *Paradise Lost.*

I think what we did with the *American Voices* project is important (*American Voices,* Akron Symphony, CD 80409, TelArc). One of the reasons is that there were three composers, and there was a generational gap between me and the other two. Yet that gap did not impose any limitations upon what we wrote. *American Voices* was packaged in a way that showed a depth and breadth that I think very few other recordings show. I can't talk about the marketing, because I don't know what they are doing with it, but I have not seen as much activity with the CD as I would like. I would love to be able to see widespread publicity and more reviews. But the concept is a very good concept. I think the recording is much stronger as a result of these three diverse voices, all of whom I judge to be vital, rather than just a single composer. There is much to be said for single-composer albums, but we are trying to make a statement at this moment as black people. We still do have to make statements; I don't care what anybody tells you, we still have to keep proving who we are.

I am glad they said *American* voices, rather than black voices. The fact that we are black voices is of secondary importance at this moment, because if the voice is vital and meaningful, the color isn't going to make any difference. It just happens that it is us. My question is how one gets it out there, so people will understand what we are about and what we are trying to do, and realize that we are multivoiced. We have no one, single voice. It bothers me in the jazz field when the media designates a person as synonymous with jazz. I think it hurts us all, because people start to think, "Well look, that's all there is." That is what they tried to do with us politically, identifying one person as our spokesperson. That has never really happened since Dr. King, and even then you had polarity, Malcolm X on one side and Dr. King on the other. I think the importance of *American Voices* is that it starts to show that we are all not William Grant Still, George Walker, or Olly Wilson. We are individual voices who happen to have a common thread that binds us together. We pay all the same dues, as long as we wear this particular hue that God gave us.

I think artists have a role in society. Music is one of those nonrepresentational kinds of art. There are no "religious notes," for example; you have to put words with them. There are no jazz notes, there are no notes that belong only to classical music. It seems to me that as writers and players we have to tap into the universality of the human experience. The experience that I have as a black man is certainly unique, but when you get past man's inhumanity to man and the fact that there are still people who can't handle us, who don't want a level playing field, you see that there are universal feelings that are captured in music. We have to find a way to tap into those sources. The things that move people when they hear the *Victims of Hiroshima,* or the last movement of the Beethoven's *Ninth,* or the final movement of the Schoenberg's *D-minor*, when the singer sings, "I feel the breath of a new planet"—those are universal feelings. The things that make me cry in a movie, when I pretend I am dropping something so I can wipe a tear away before anybody sees it, I see everybody else crying about too—whites, blacks, all of them. We have more things in common than not. If you look at *Homo sapiens,* we can define "male" as a category, and it doesn't make any difference where that male is—in Australia, whether he is an Australian white or a native; or in New Zealand and happens to be a Maori. There are certain things that belong to males that don't belong to females, and it doesn't make any difference where on the globe you are. Things like hate, most of the time, are learned things.

But people learn about love, too. I think it is our role, more than anything else, to project accurately what that universal feeling is. As a conductor, as a writer, as a performer, I try to say in the most meaningful way what my vision of the world is at that moment and hope that it communicates in the same way. People make up stories. Duke Ellington use to talk about the "Harlem Airshaft," about what the piece meant—and then we find out he originally had a different title. I don't find this dishonest, this is the way we do business. The main thing is a universal kind of thing; people will draw their own conclusions, they will make up stories about what they are hearing, and I don't care. Titles are evocative and provocative. Sometimes I wish I could just title something, "Song"; then it could be wide open for everybody to interpret whatever they want. But to tap into whatever it is that is universal and what communicates from one human being to another is our role as artists.

Now, other people say we should take an active role politically with our music. I think that can be valid, but that can also be dangerous. Look at what happened back in 1938 and 1939, after the *Kristallnacht;* Richard Wagner became the standard bearer for all that hatred and Aryan nonsense. They tried to do that to Coltrane and others, talking about their music as "angry." How in the hell can a note be angry? I don't understand any of those imposed things. I think the main thing is clarity of vision.

There is no question, because we move from the specific to the general, that cultural issues and references are valid and can still be seen as universal. You start with a feeling, you start with a concept. Shakespeare, for example, is just as valid to the black person as to the white. But it started with Shakespeare and his experience. That is the reason why we laugh when we see Sinbad, that is why we laugh when we see Bob Hope, that is why we laugh when we see Red Buttons, because what they do is transcendent. That is why we can deal with Bill Cosby or Richard Pryor; those experiences are universal; even if you did them in pantomime, they would still strike you. It doesn't have anything to do with what color you are. But there are certain things, it seems to me, that have a specific reference, because of who we are. There is "inside" stuff that blacks can talk about that I can't talk about with my colleagues at Indiana University, and there are things that they can talk about that have no relevance to me at all. Black people can say things that are meaningful to each other, because we share a common culture that is not just American but is black culture. When we start talking about "conks" and "belly rolls" or say, "Turn out the lights and call the law," that is another whole experience.

Most white folks don't know about those things. When we caricature white folks, and when white folks caricature us, they blow particular things out of proportion. I think there is an area that is very specifically black music, but it isn't necessarily by black people. It is people who use all of the things that make up that aesthetic, whether they are white or black. Who more than Bernstein tapped into black culture? I can't imagine what *West Side Story* would sound like if you took away all of the things that came from us. What would George Gershwin's *Porgy and Bess,* or the *Piano Concerto,* or *Rhapsody in Blue* sound like? We have an inside track to it, but with this "global village" concept, it is available. I can write in the style of the Second Viennese School, I can also write in a style that is reminiscent of Brahms, because that belongs to everybody.

I would be at a loss to project where American music is headed. To make an educated guess, we have been and will continue to be in what Leonard Meyer calls a "period of stasis," where all the things that have ever happened and are going to happen will be in a peaceful, or perhaps not peaceful, coexistence. Everything that has ever happened in music is being done right now somewhere on Earth, and sometimes whole academic departments are dedicated to it. Indiana University, for example, has an early music department specializing in all the music that used to be. We have a new music department that, on occasion, truly is new music. Other places, like Wesleyan, or the University of Massachusetts, have world-culture music. With these areas of specialization, it becomes very important to realize that we will never go back to a time when only one music holds sway. There are people who try to maintain the superiority of a kind of music, just like people who would like to maintain the superiority of WASPs. Forget it! By the turn of the twenty-first century, people of color will outnumber white folks by some astronomical figure. So the notion that another John Coltrane will hold sway over jazz music, in the way that Charlie Parker or Louis Armstrong did, is nonsense. There will never be another time when a single person like Schoenberg holds such a preeminent position. That is just like I think the whole concept of minimalist music dissipated very quickly. Philip Glass, Terry Riley, John Adams, all of those guys are just part of a fabric. For good or bad, I don't think we will ever see another monolithic music scene. I think that is healthy.

On a personal level, one thing I have done that is monumental is raise a daughter who turned out to be a good musician, a good human being. Musically, one of the biggest leaps for me was coming back from sheer disaster, when I had to quit playing trombone and start an instrument at age thirty-four. To have entered the world of academia as late as I did and to combine that with a career as a composer when every obstacle in the world was thrown in front of me and to be able to survive—those are the things that stand out as important in my life.

Then there is the constant assurance that there is a God, for whom justice is a way of life. Sometimes I let my own pettiness take over, I get jealous of somebody, and I have to say to myself, "Now, what are you doing that for, why are you jealous? That person has got whatever it is, and that doesn't take anything away from you." Or when I am angry with somebody because of what I perceive to be a slight—then I remember that the greatest gift that I have is good health, and a benevolent God who doesn't care what I do, because no matter how ugly it is, forgiveness is in sight. There isn't an evening that I don't go to bed without remembering to say, "Thank you for everything I have got. Thank you for the health of my loved ones and please take care of Magic Johnson," or somebody who I know is in trouble. That's a gyroscope that will keep you in line. For one thing, you can never get arrogant, because you understand that somebody has as much talent and ability who just didn't get the break that you did. I can't ever let myself get caught up in the notion that I am something special. Everyone is something special. What did that song say? "God didn't make no mistakes." When I see arrogant cats, telling me who they are and how much they have done, I give them a bemused look that says, "You had better wake up because, if you aren't careful, it is going to be rude awakening."

Noel DaCosta

Noel DaCosta, a true voice of the Diaspora, was born in Lagos, Nigeria, in 1929, of Jamaican parents. He lived as a youngster first in the Caribbean, then in New York City's Harlem in the early 1940s. At the age of eleven he began to study violin with Hungarian violinist Barnabus Istok, and English with Countee Cullen, in junior high school. DaCosta remembers Cullen as the one who taught him to appreciate the lyrical nature of words. This DaCosta points to as his first "composition lesson." He received his formal training at Queens College, City University of New York (B.A., music, 1952), and an M.A. in theory and composition from Colombia University (1956). As a Fulbright Scholar he studied for two and a half years with Luigi Dallapiccola in Florence, Italy. DaCosta's works represent a wide range of cultural influences—African American, African, and Caribbean folk traditions, as well as abstract compositional thought. His works have been performed by the Symphony of the New World. His *Primal Rites,* for Max Roach and orchestra, was performed by the Boston Esplanade Orchestra and the Memphis Symphony. His works also include chamber compositions, a one-act opera, theater works, and documentary films. Noel DaCosta served as a professor of music at Rutgers University from 1970 until his passing in the summer of 2002.

In the Caribbean, where I lived—places like Trinidad, Barbados, Antigua, and Jamaica—I remember that each island had its own speech inflection and musical lilt. In Antigua, for example, in our backyard, it was quite natural for me to hear musicians drumming and singing in preparation for carnival. That was a very rich surrounding that I absorbed.

Arriving in New York City when I was eleven, in 1941, we settled in Harlem in a brownstone on 135th Street, between Lenox and Fifth Avenues. I heard new kinds of speech and was exposed to a different musical experience, listening to the radio. Harlem for me was extremely special, although we were warned that it was a dangerous place and that the public schools were inferior. Despite these warnings, I ended up at Junior High School 139 (located on 139th Street between Lenox and Seventh Avenues), where the distinguished Harlem Renaissance poet Countee Cullen was teaching English and French. Having a teacher like Cullen really stimulated me to do well; he was dedicated and had very high expectations of all of his students. I specifically remember he had us

read poetry, then create our own limericks and short poems. That helped us to understand the writing process. Thinking back upon those early exercises, I consider them to be my first composition lessons. From that point on, I was tuned into the idea of creating something beautiful out of words organized in a structured way.

One of my other vivid Harlem memories is the Sunday afternoon church concert. This was a rich and wonderful new cultural experience; I heard black singers sing art songs in inflected German, French, and Italian. Many of these singers would go "downtown" to learn vocal production ("voice culture," as they called it) to facilitate their performance of European art songs. However, despite all the layers of "studied" vocal production, when they sang spirituals and folk-derived songs, their natural voices would emerge.

I have often thought about the versatility and aesthetic shifts that a performer has to consider. In fact, after hearing a black soprano sing "My Lovely Celia" (by George Monro), a work that adored the image of a young white ("Heav'nly fair") female, I wondered why these singers sang songs that weren't about their own experiences. Many years later, in the 1970s, I recalled "My Lovely Celia" after reading George Bass's poem "Julie-Ju," praising his "lovely" little black goddaughter. So, out came a wonderful impulse that conditioned, inspired me to set this poem to music. It requires singers to extend their vocal styles to include an inflected, rhythmic, "earthy" sound.

For me, composing "Julie-Ju" served an important creative need. I could reflect back on those Sunday afternoon Harlem concerts, when I listened to black singers performing a range of expressive songs set to poetic texts that were not about their own cultural backgrounds. In my setting I offered black singers an opportunity to celebrate and acknowledge their cultural identity. As a composer, and especially as a black person, I am sensitive to the texts I work with, and I have often selected works reflecting my cultural history and heritage. In fact, I am sure that deep within I have always been conscious of embracing the cultures I come from—Caribbean and African American—and I believe that this is evident in many of my compositions. Although I use the formal techniques and procedures of a Western musical practice, tempered by seemingly contradictory interjections, I am attuned to the inflections of traditional African American musics—from the church, blues, and jazz. Much from these traditions finds a home in my memory.

I value the experience of getting involved with singers through conducting, in my evolution as a musician. From my early college days I had opportunities to work with choral groups. I taught those groups Renaissance motets and madrigals, works from classical and Romantic periods, as well as folksong arrangements and spirituals reflecting a very broad range of musical styles. Throughout my musical career, I can say, I have always kept in touch with the human voice.

As far as my influences go, I studied violin and played the standard works of Beethoven, Mozart, and unaccompanied Bach, as well as shorter pieces by other European composers. At the same time, I was also listening to black composers, like William Grant Still, R. Nathaniel Dett [black American composers], and Howard Swanson. Dett and Swanson spoke in very specific voices coming out of the African American experience.

Many of my compositions come from requests of performers for specific concerts. For example, *Time Patterns,* for bassoon and harpsichord, I composed for David Miller, a bassoonist who was attracted to the sound of the harpsichord and thought that the combination of that with the bassoon timbre would be wonderful for an art museum concert. I wrote for him an idiomatic work that featured rhythmic patterns weaving in and out between the two instruments. Over the years my music has circulated without an active promotional effort from me. Composing has been a fascinating way to solve things musically in ways that I hope bring pleasure to others.

Briefly, as far as my compositional process goes, if an idea is present, I can explore possibilities and develop it within a given structure. Some of my pieces from the late sixties were written in an abstract twelve-tone technique. Yet I insisted on a very personal rhythmic freedom, which can be heard in *Five Verses with Vamps,* for cello and piano. Works from the seventies showing a strong tonal orientation include pieces like *Spiritual Set,* for organ; *Jes' Grew,* for solo violin; *Four Preludes,* for trombone and piano; and *Ceremony of Spirituals,* for soprano soloist, saxophonist, chorus, and orchestra.

One of my compositions during the eighties—*Ukum Memory Songs,* for organ and percussion—explores an element of Nigerian rhythm, together with a contrapuntal organ style. *Primal Rites,* for solo drummer and symphony orchestra, commissioned by Elma Lewis [educator] in Boston and performed by Max Roach as solo drummer with the Boston Esplanade Orchestra, reflects a continuation of the ideas from *Ukom Memory Songs.*

In the late eighties I collaborated with my wife, Patricia DaCosta, and wrote music for theater pieces such as "Generations" for narrator, dancers, and percussion ensemble; and "The Dreamer behind the Garden Gate," for actress, vocal ensemble, dancer, and percussion. Both works were dramatic poetic narratives written by Patricia, and they brought me back to my primary love of the human voice.

Q: Where do you believe musical traditions are headed, in the twenty-first century?

A: Over the years, I have simply used my ears and intellect to arrive at my compositional focus—making use of what I have learned about harmonic and contrapuntal invention. These days I see people staying home more and enjoying music from high-technology systems. Sitting in the concert halls listening to music will probably diminish. In the 1950s, as a younger concertgoer, I would hear concerts every week in Town Hall or Carnegie Hall. The singers and instrumentalists would enthusiastically perform debut recitals to receptive audiences. In the last fifteen years the debut recital has diminished in favor of group performances. There is less of an opportunity for younger artists to develop their art, because of the high costs of financing a career (even after winning major competitions). It will be a major challenge to develop concert audiences for nonpopular performances. I see a shift in musical taste and preferences in the culture and also a great influence and expansion of the television medium and other technological means of reproducing sound. As a composer I can envision being asked to write works specifically for television. Perhaps television can be used as a means, on certain channels for artistic work, as an option, in search of an audience. This could provide possibilities for mixed-media work, to include dance, mime, speech, and song in staged visual concepts.

Q: As a composer are you intrigued or moved by the current rap and hip-hop movements so prevalent in New York?

A: I am intrigued by how the black contribution to this genre has emerged as a dominant voice in the culture, one with a universal impact. In fact, I am reminded of the predecessors of rap, such as Moms Mabley [comedian], Pigmeat Markham [comedian], and The Last Poets [spoken-word artists]. There were also wonderful gospel and soul singers, who always introduced their songs with a timely and evocative "rap." It's "black noise," screaming at the top of its lungs in highly charged rhythms. It's political, involving their experiences, observations, expressions, and interpretations of alienation, anger, and the confusion in their lives and within the culture at large. At times they use vulgar language that jolts because it is quite rough and objectionable, but I understand it as a defiant expression challenging the entire society. In its boasting at times it denigrates everybody. But the entire body of rap is full of energy; it is alive, a part of our times.

Q: What do you think about the notion of challenging the canon? Is that something that black composers should be in the business of doing?

A: For me it's a necessary challenge to expand the meaning of "the canon" to include the cultural influences that define someone like myself. I believe we must expand upon the traditional idea of canon, because it has been limited to a narrow Western or Western-derived aesthetic. I would alter the canonical perimeters to be more inclusive. For me, the canon expansion is inevitable. All I feel I have to do is to continue writing music and being true to who I am.

Q: After the many things that you have done, what stands out as an ultimate goal?

A: Musically, as a ultimate goal, I would want to write a body of music that is expressive and well crafted, based on ideas coming from my background as a Caribbean/African American composer born in Africa.

George Russell

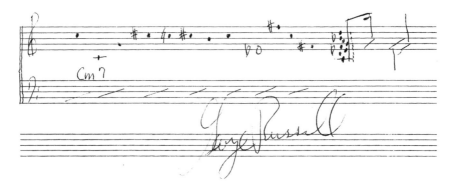

George Russell, born 1923 in Cincinnati, remains one of the most important theorist/composers still producing. He is also known as the man who taught Miles Davis how to "compose music." Mr. Russell is a major figure among the theorist/composers in New York (among them Gil Evans) who carved out much of the intellectual support that gave rise to the revolutionary be-bop and post–be-bop—figures such as Monk, Dizzy Gillespie, Eric Dolphy, Ornette Coleman, and others. Russell's first recorded work, "Cubana Be/Cubana Bop," commissioned by Dizzy Gillespie and premiered at Carnegie Hall 1947, was the first work to fuse jazz and Afro-Cuban rhythms; it became a model. Russell's revolutionary book *The Lydian Chromatic Concept of Tonal Organization,* first published in 1953, was a forward-looking approach for composers and performers working with sonorities, chord changes, and melodic manipulation. He searched for a congruent chord-scale unity; his systematic approach would later surface in the landmark modal recording "Kind of Blue," by Miles Davis, and in streams of post-bop composition from the sixties until today. A music major at Wilberforce University, he began arranging there among fellow and former students, including Coleman Hawkins, Benny Carter, and Ernie Wilkins. Currently professor of music at the New England Conservatory of Music, he has been teaching theory and leading ensembles for over twenty-five years. His discography includes some twenty-four recordings for Blue Note, Columbia, Milestone, RCA/Victor, and Label Bleu, among others. As a conductor, with his Living Time Orchestra, he regularly performs and conducts residencies in Europe and Japan. Among Mr. Russell's awards are a MacArthur Foundation Fellowship (1989), the National Endowment for the Arts American Jazz Master (1990), two Guggenheim fellowships (1969 and 1972), the National Music Award (1976), the British Jazz Award (1989), the Oscar du Disque de Jazz (1962), and three Grammy Award nominations. Mr. Russell lives and works in Boston.

I was natural-born loner, an adopted child with a rampant imagination that, in retrospect, appears to have been dominated by two urges. The first was a compelling need to know the why of things, and the second was the need to experiment freely and on my own, exploring a hunger that was above all else the intuitive faculty. A quiet radicalism aimed at evolution, rather than revolution, was already in motion. The incessant fascination with the why of things inevita-

bly led to the question, Why my life? What do I want to be recognized as having accomplished in my life?

I love innovation. I always have, I always will. What art form really evolves without innovation? No true art form has evolved without innovators to give it new impulses. I came through Bird [Charles Parker], Dizzy, Miles, and Coltrane. I came through a time when innovation was absolutely primary. What everyone was striving for then was not just to reach that goal but to perpetuate and constantly reinvent themselves.

Early on in life I had a very strong impression that my goal should be to contribute something different to humanity, some fragment of knowledge that had been left unexplored. I discovered I was not alone in that aim; I've never known a true innovator in any style of music who didn't have the aim to break through the barrier of the possible. Louis Armstrong, Charlie Parker, Miles, Coltrane, Ornette, Lester Young, Monk, Ellington, Roy Eldridge, Max Roach, Gil Evans, Arts Tatum, Jimi Hendrix, Mary Lou Williams, Sly Stone, Bud Powell, Jimmy Blanton, Albert Ayler, Jaki Byard, Don Cherry, Wayne Shorter, Gunther Schuller, Jan Garbarek, Dorothy Donegan, Jimmy Giuffre, Chalres Mingus, Marvin Gaye, Eric Dolphy, David Baker, Michael McDonald, Steely Dan, Sonny Murray, Nadi Quamar, Elvin Jones, Herbie Hancock, Tony Williams, Ray Nance, Harry Edison, J. J. Johnson, Ed Blackwell, Billy Higgins, Charlie Haden, Bill Evans, Terje Rypdal, Edgar Varèse, Toru Takemitsu, John Lewis, Kenny Dorham, Palle Mikkelborg, Bosse Broberg—all these people and countless more of generations past and present possessed something of that Olympian spirit to break through the barrier of the known to the unknown. It is that spirit, reaching for the impossible, that Gil Evans encouraged in all of us who were members of his 55th Street enclave. It is that spirit that is absent in jazz as currently defined by the "retrograders."

It was in this spirit that I began work on the theory in which I was to be involved for the rest of my life. In 1945, I had a conversation with Miles Davis that would ultimately give both of us a new direction. We would often go to his modest apartment to talk about music, trade chords, and gossip. One night I asked him, "What's your musical aim?" He answered, "To learn all the changes." This seemed like a strange answer, because at that time Miles was famous for knowing all the chords. But his answer served as a seed that ultimately led me to the development of the Lydian chromatic concept of tonal organization. I reasoned that since Miles already knew how to arpeggiate each chord in an interesting manner (sometimes expanding the chord with nonchordal tones), what he really meant was that he wanted to find a new and broader way to relate to chords. One night, about four years after my first publication of the concept, I convinced Miles that all definable chords have a parent scale, the scale that more than any other blends with the chord in the most complete state of chord/scale unity. I had been consciously using modes since 1947, when I wrote "Cubano Be/Cubano Bop" for Dizzy's orchestra.

Soon after the first publication of the concept, I began to apply its fundamentals to rhythm, form, and the other elements of music. In the early 1960s, I became interested in finding ways of scoring jazz that would give musicians a freer role in interpreting the music. I was impressed with the aleatory methods of scoring employed, and I was enriched by Stockhausen, Henri Pousseur, Penderecki, Ligetti, Varèse, and others. For these and a number of other reasons, I stayed in Scandinavia after a 1965 tour with George Wein's Newport All-Stars. In Oslo, the very gifted composer Kore Kolberg tutored me in the basics of aleatory scoring. I wrote a number of pieces fusing aleatory and mensural [barred] scoring in what I termed "vertical form." All my works from 1966 to the present have been, to a greater or lesser degree, vertical-form pieces.

When I left New York in 1965, the building housing the radio and television divisions of the Columbia Broadcasting System was on Madison Avenue, while CBS Records was on Sixth Avenue. The church/studio used for recording was on 27th Street, and the CBS Distribution Division was over on Tenth or Eleventh Avenue. When I returned in 1969, there was one big building, a monolith, on the corner of 52d Street and Sixth Avenue. Columbia and everything affiliated with it was in there—TV, radio, the record business, the electronic business, all of it. I stood in front of the building, looked up, and thought to myself, "This is a cannon aimed at individuality. . . . [T]he media is going to take creativity away from contemporary musicians." And that's exactly what happened. The music industry now controls the jazz aesthetic. This is evidenced by what the record companies are releasing and by the music being played by the majority of jazz DJs. As a result, the state of jazz as an art form has diminished to the level of what Keith Jarrett aptly call "virtual jazz," in a stinging critique of the retro-jazz movement (in *Musician Magazine,* March 1996).

The only obligation that I can see that we as composers all have is to protect the spirit of music. I stayed in Brooklyn for nine months with Max Roach, who graciously invited me into his home after I came out of the hospital, and I met a lot of guys in the neighborhood. Jimmy Gittens owned a little soda stand where we all gathered, Freddie Brathwaite and all the cats on the street. Those people could sing Bird solos. They walked around singing Bird, and they weren't musicians. And where I grew up, in Cincinnati, guys on the street could sing Lester Young solos—this in an area similar to the Bed-Sty [Bedford-Stuyvesant] section in Brooklyn. Show me anyone on the street now who sings that way—Bird and 'Trane solos! The level of the music used to be quite high. For as long as I have been involved with jazz, people expected to hear something new, to get a shock from the music and be uplifted by someone who expressed their unique identity. People were excited by an artist who did not have a club mentality.

I think it was during the eighties that things started to die, attitudes froze, a dark cloud descended over all things. Banality is beautiful and very much "in." Cutting the National Endowment for the Arts and the state arts council is in. Even the French conservatives defeated the late champion of the arts, François Mitterand. In jazz, the Olympian spirit, which for generations had been the driving force for innovators, withered away, creating an atmosphere ripe for a jazz movement in Armani suits and Gucci ties with an attitude to match, giving the evil eye to any innovation after 1950.

The technical feat of an African-American jazz musician playing Mozart didn't hurt, either; it was highly acclaimed by people who otherwise wouldn't be moved by a technical feat of this nature if color had not been involved. It may have occurred to the cost-effective overseer of the plantation to ensure that the instrumentally gifted slaves were well tutored in the classics as well as the jigs. Indeed, the plantation appears to be exactly were jazz is headed. The retro-jazz publicity blitz is giving it a big push in that direction, as well as the reissuing of decades of old recordings from the vaults. The cost to the companies is negligible, the original composer is asked to take less than his full share of royalties, and no recording fees are due to the musicians.

Artists should do all they can to preserve their own integrity. All of us who do that have taken a kind of silent oath that we would never lower our standards, that we would always search for new ideas, for a rich future that would allow us to leave our marks. We wanted to always preserve our identity. I, personally, for example, never looked for a style. When Coltrane did *My Favorite Things,* his record company wanted him to continue doing the same kind of music. I talked with him about it, and he didn't know what to do. He was afraid if he changed his style, he'd lose all of the things he'd never before had, like his house, his car. But I said, "You're 'Trane." That's all I said. I don't know how much that comment influenced him, but a short time after that he made *Ascension,* with Archie Schepp [jazz saxophonist] and the others. 'Trane took that music "out" and lost all of his audience, but he gained another audience, and another status as a god within the black movement, which was attracted to the avant-garde. There is a certain path that all of us who believe in the spirit of music have taken. We are dedicated to it, and that is all we can do.

It was indeed wonderful to receive the MacArthur Fellowship; it made me feel that after many years of striving very, very hard for a kind of crystallization in my work and my being, there was this huge confirmation of both from the MacArthur Foundation.

My international big band, the Living Time Orchestra, continues to perform and record in Europe, as we've done for the last ten years. We're doing primarily special projects and arts festivals, which require a very high level of performance. We were the first jazz orchestra to be invited to give a concert in the Theatre Champs-Elysées as part of the Festival d'Automne in Paris. We also opened the Great Hall of the Cité de la Musique in Paris and often play venues like Queen Elizabeth Hall in London, the Glasgow Arts Festival, and the Pori, Finland, and Swedish Jazz Festivals. Many of the tours are sponsored by the British Council and others.

All this recognition has, again, been a positive confirmation not of academic credentials but of my identity as a theorist and composer with, I hope, something new to say.

As an artist, you make your own opportunity. You make it by taking an oath and aiming for a level that is so high it might cause you to have to make some sacrifices. You show in that sacrifice that you are loyal to your aim. There are forces out there, and music is one of them. Music is alive. That's what I learned from the Lydian concept—the ideas in music tie in with ancient ideas of all and everything. If you live in a time when the very spirit of music is being downsized, it is not healthy for people in general, nor for the people who are doing the downsizing. The downsizers, in particular, might appear to be well off, but they are interacting with forces they don't understand. Eventually, they will have to deal with what they have done.

If you can be consistently loyal to your goals, set your aim high, and when necessary, sacrifice those lower wants and needs, and you'll make it.

Hale Smith

Hale Smith, who considers himself the "father of many musical children" and an elder statesman, is one of the few black American composers to have reached mainstream success and notoriety. He began studies at the piano early, and after a restless time in school as a youth he earned both the B.M. (1950) and M.M. (1952) degrees, with postgraduate work following. Mr. Smith settled into New York in the late fifties, establishing himself as a formidable presence in many music circles, including publishing. Known to have "one of the best hands in the business," he served as editor for E. B. Marks Company, as editor and general music advisor for Frank Music Company, and later did editing work for C. F. Peters. His works have been performed and recorded by such orchestras as the Louisville, Detroit, and New York Philharmonic Symphonies, as well as by performers Natalie Hinderas, Hilda Harris, and others. Among his many awards is the BMI Composition Award, of which he was the first recipient (1952). He has also received the Outstanding Achievement Award from the Black Music Caucus of the Music Educators National Conference, and he was an appointee to the New York Council of the Arts. Mr. Smith taught from 1970 to 1984 at the University of Connecticut. He served as the principal arranger/orchestrator for the Columbia College Black Repertoire Ensemble, which tours the country performing concert works of past and present black composers. He has been a leading consultant and serves on the board of directors of the American Music Center. Mr. Smith lives and works in Freeport, New York.

It ain't over until it's over, and I don't know how soon it is going to be over. But I am not ready for it to be over yet. I have learned a lot of things, but whether that comes from being a musician or just from growing older, I can't really say. I do think that being a musician has sharpened my sensitivities and perceptions where people are concerned. But a part of that has to do with the fact that even though I never became a very well known performer, I have been a performer all of my life. Even as a child I started learning how to relate to people, especially audiences, and from that I learned how to deal with individuals. I have learned to give things their own time, because they are going to *do* what they are going to do. They are going to develop and grow at their own pace, no matter what the situation. I have learned to develop that type of patience, although I am not naturally a patient person. I find myself very often having to exercise restraint, and there are those who have been around when I have exceeded the bounds of my patience.

I have done what I wanted to do. I guess about the only thing I might have wanted to do and deliberately didn't try was architecture. I have a great love for architecture, but then, I have a great love for a lot of things.

When I was seven years old, an announcement was made at the elementary school I attended that a young lady was going to come in and give piano lessons. I went home and asked if I could take piano lessons. My parents agreed, but that whole first year I had to go around the corner to a family friend's home and practice, because we did not have a piano. A year later, when my father did bring a piano in, it was an old player piano, the innards of which he had ripped out before I even saw it, because he didn't want me to depend on the player mechanism. That piano stayed with me until 1949, when I bought one of the early Baldwin Acrosonic studio pianos. I still have that Baldwin in my study, but the keyboard is piled so high with books and tapes and stuff that I can't even use it.

But when I was first learning to play, I would go around to this friend's home and do my lessons. When I finished my lesson and went through it, I would start experimenting. My neighbor, like most other adults at that time, would interrupt me when I did that, saying I was supposed to practice, not to fiddle around. But that is where I was discovering myself, I think.

I was eight years old when I realized that what I wanted to do was create my own music. I didn't know how I was going to do it, but I realized that was what I wanted. My family never interfered with anything I did, and it might be because they didn't know enough about music. They knew other things. For example, my father had a very small but very fine library. He had the Harvard Classics, he had the eleventh edition of the *Encyclopedia Britannica,* and a few other collections like that. He started me reading in *The Odyssey* from the Harvard Classics when I was eight years old. He also had combined a barbershop and a printing shop in one room; they were divided by a partition in the center. When I was eight he put me in the barbershop cleaning, sweeping the floor, cleaning the spittoon, and shining shoes. I started getting exposed to the public then, through shining shoes, because I had to quibble with these grown men over the price of a shoeshine. They were doing it in fun for the most part, I imagine. Then my father put me in the printing shop, dealing with the compositor's stick and the printer's type.

I think one of my main musical influences was my first piano teacher, Margaret Heller, who died when I was in my forties. Margaret Heller was a very fine young woman who took a lifelong interest in me. After I first started studying with her, she recommended to my parents that I be brought to her home on Sunday mornings for private lessons. She thought that I had a talent that went beyond the kind of piano lessons she was giving at the school. So every Sunday morning, I would go out there to her home and take lessons. She is the one who introduced me to Mozart, Schubert, and Muzio Clementi. Margaret Heller was a wonderful lady. I had lost contact with her for years; then, when I was at the Cleveland Institute, one of the faculty members there told me that Margaret Heller was a close friend of hers. I discovered that my first teacher had been keeping up with me all that time.

After the score of *Contours* was published (when Lewis Lane conducted it with the Cleveland Orchestra), a reporter with the *Cleveland Plain Dealer* asked me if I would mind doing an interview with my original teacher. That was a great thing for me. We went out to Margaret Heller's home. She and I sat on the sofa together, holding the score, while we were interviewed.

My second piano teacher is still living, out in Los Angeles. She is an

African American whose name is Evelyn Freeman Roberts. Evelyn is the oldest of three siblings, and her younger brother, Ernie Freeman [composer], was one of the greatest arrangers in the business, bar none. Ernie died out in Los Angeles a few years ago, but he was the one who did that arrangement of "Strangers in the Night" for Frank Sinatra. I remember when I was out in L.A. in 1974, I visited Ernie Freeman's office up on Sunset Boulevard, and every wall in that place was so loaded with platinum, gold, and silver records that it was like wallpaper.

I went to Evelyn for lessons when I was between ten and eleven years old, but when I was fourteen, she and Ernie brought me into their jazz group. Evelyn, who was young then herself, conducted a chamber music group they called the Freeman Ensemble. I played horn in that group. Ernie at that time was about seventeen. When I went into the seventh grade at the age of fourteen, I started playing French horn, and then the Freemans brought me into the jazz ensemble, playing piano, when I was fourteen. Evelyn had some other things to do, and she had been the pianist in the group. I remember them giving me a crash course in reading chord symbols and learning to hear how things moved.

I was a lousy horn player and pianist, but that band had some extraordinary musicians in it. One of those musicians is still a friend of mine—who doesn't want me including his name everywhere, so I will do him a favor and I won't. He was a brilliant trumpet player and then became a brilliant singer and choral conductor. He has conducted a number of shows like *Raisin in the Sun, Guys and Dolls,* and things like that. Then another friend, Brenton Banks [musician], who is out in L.A. now, is the one who put the string sounds in *Nashville.* We were both offered teaching jobs at Tennessee State, but I didn't want to go back to the South, so I wouldn't go. He went. Banks is a brilliant player, a hell of a pianist too. It wasn't that these musicians tried to influence me in any particular way, but I was the youngest.

There was a group of us who grew up there in Cleveland, most of whom had great talent. In fact, the people I grew up with had so much talent, people like Branton and Ernie, that I couldn't start growing until they left. It was just that heavy. But Brenton and I went through the Cleveland Institute together. We took the same courses all the way through.

I started playing jazz when I was fourteen, when Evelyn and Ernie decided to put me in their jazz group. One of the bass players was Aaron Bell, who later played with Duke Ellington. One of the trombonists—who later was part of the first James Moody Group, a sextet—was William Shepherd, who played as much on trombone, nearly as much as J. J. Johnson. Shepherd learned that by playing cello parts in the chamber ensemble, because we didn't have a cello. I just soaked this stuff up. I just soaked it up and went my way.

I had a disastrous public school career. I got out of sync very early; I think I was already out of synchronization by the time I was seven. The fact that I had latched onto music did not help things. Actually, my interest in music made things worse, because I had no interest in doing many of the things that were prescribed in school, especially through elementary and junior high. My mind was elsewhere. I was kicked out of elementary school at the age of fourteen, because I was too old to stay there. A nice little sideline to that is that Juanita, my wife, and I got to junior high school in the same year, and she is two years younger than I am. She left me behind in junior high. I just had a terrible time all the way through those years, because I just didn't fit. My contemporaries who remember those days recall me being dragged up the stairs to the principal's office. There would be a teacher at the side of the stairs giving them directions, and I would be held by three or four other students who would drag me up to the principal's office. Oh, man, that was something!

Then I got over into senior high school. I went to Central High School, the same school that Langston Hughes had gone to, and before Langston's time John D. Rockefeller had gone there. Central High had been a very famous school, but by the time I got there it was almost all black. I spent that one year there, that one tenth grade in high school, and it was during that school year when I met Langston Hughes. I was seventeen when I met him. I finished that school year on probation. I turned eighteen over that summer [1943] and was drafted, so right there was the end of my public school career. I have told that story about my education to students over several student generations. They see me, this so-called dignified professor with a beard telling them, "Look, don't try to pull anything on me and think you can get away with it because I have done it all."

Yet I was always a reader. I read, and I still read. When I got out of the army in 1945 I didn't have any intentions about higher education; that wasn't part of my thought process. I tried summer school, but it was just terrible. It didn't mesh with me. So one Friday, less than halfway through my summer-school career, I read an article in the newspaper about the Board of Education offering a comprehensive examination for veterans. That turned out to be one of the first high school equivalency exams. I read about this thing on Friday, went down to the Board of Education on Monday, and registered to take the two-and-a-half-day exams the following Monday. My father saw me about halfway through that week and said, "Well son, aren't you supposed to take an examination next week?" I said, "Yes." He said, "Well I haven't seen you open a book! When are you going to study?" I said, "Well, the way I figure it, if I don't know it now, it's too late to learn." That is the attitude I carried all the way through school. I never took notes, I never crammed. If I passed it, I passed it. If I failed it, I failed it. I figured that if I learned as I was supposed to learn it, I would have it. But if I crammed, I would have it long enough to pass an exam, and that would be the end of it. That is one reason why I have what I think is a fair accumulation of knowledge, because I don't easily forget those things that are important to me.

When I got out of the army, a group of fellows had a sextet that consisted of three saxophones and a rhythm section. They asked me to take over as the leader. I had been writing ever since I was a kid. I was lucky—I got a chance to write for my peers. Some of it made sense, some of it didn't, but I was writing for my peers who would play this stuff, so I was able to hear back what I wrote. I wrote some things for Ernie's band too, but those cats could swing whole notes; I didn't know a thing about syncopation. When I was in the army, I got stuck arranging music, songs that one of the soldiers down at this base in Florida, who was white, had written. Somebody at command level decided to build an army show around this fellow's tunes. He wrote some very nice tunes, one of which I can remember most of today. But they wanted me to do the orchestrations of everything, and I had to do it fast. I didn't have enough experience to sync quickly with E-flat transpositions, so I wrote it all for clarinets and tenor saxophones, plus a rhythm section. I wrote, "da-da-da-da-da-da," and that is the way this band, which was all white, played it. I said, "No, man, it is not supposed to go like that! It's supposed to go, DA-DADADA-DA!" They said, "If that's the way you want it, write it that way!" So I had to take all of that stuff back, go through it, and learn just how I wanted it to sound—whether I wanted to go before the beat or behind the beat, and precisely how much before or behind. I had to learn that on the spot. I learned most of the things I learned on the spot. By the time I got out of the army, I was a good arranger.

I was stationed first in Venice, Florida, and then I went back up to Augusta, Georgia, to Daniel Field, where I came in contact with one of the very greatest influences of my life, a wonderful arranger and saxophonist named William Randall. Randall was from Chicago and had been with Earl Hines with his Grand Terrace Bands. He had also played with Fletcher and Horace Henderson. Randall was known as a wonderful musician, and he is the cat who made me into a man. He didn't play around. He put the heat on! I know what some of the heat can be. But when I got this band in Cleveland, I got the grand idea of writing a major composition. I was going to write a big composition for three saxophones and rhythm section. I went down to the Lyon and Healy Music Store and got a manuscript pad, and I started putting tunes in there.

This was in 1945, right after the war, in the late fall. I got this pad, a booklet, of manuscript paper. I filled maybe two-thirds of it with my own tunes. I could write a tune. But I had this thing two-thirds of the way filled, and then all of a sudden it hit me. See, I had been scratching, trying to create my own stuff, ever since I was eight years old, and here I was twenty. It hit me that I didn't know how to compose. To this day, I make a distinction between a songwriter and a composer. I came face to face with it, because I had all of this material and didn't know what to do with it.

I went down to the Cleveland Institute of Music, a very small school, and told the registrar that I wanted to study form. That turned out to be one of the smartest things I ever did in my life. That was my first awareness that I can remember of the musical connotations of that word—"form." The registrar started questioning me and found out that I was a veteran. She said, "Well, have you finished high school?" I told her about me taking that test, and that I hadn't gotten my diploma yet, because I refused to go to the school to pick it up during the commencement exercise. But I told her that I had passed the exam. She said she would check that out, and if it were true I should think about registering full-time, with a major in composition. That way I would have access to the GI Bill. She told me the GI Bill would not only pay my tuition but pay me some money on the side. I think it was about twenty-eight dollars a month. I thought for a long time—what they call a nanosecond—and said, "Sure, it's a good deal." I think that was one of the best bargains the U.S. government ever gave itself, that GI Bill back then.

I started at the institute in January of 1946. I tested into the third semester. I never did get the first two semesters of school, but there were a couple of courses, like keyboard harmony, that I had to start at the freshman level. I had solfège [vocal sight-reading], and the very first thing I saw in solfège was the tenor clef. When I did my sight-reading exam, I just did the do-da-dat stuff. When I got in the class we used English syllables rather than Italian [the "solfa" syllables], but since I had never gone through that kind of discipline and had never seen those C clefs, I flunked that first semester.

The same thing happened in keyboard harmony. I flunked that first semester. I failed Spanish, and then at the end of my bachelor's I had to take French, which I squeezed through by the barest margin, and I flunked piano. I had to make that up, but then I went in and did my master's work. For the theoretical subjects, I averaged between B and A+. I got ear training and solfège, and I caught on to it. I had five years of solfège, five years of ear training, and four years of keyboard harmony. The three last exams in keyboard harmony called for me to improvise in order a minuet, a rondo, and a sonata form. A few years ago (maybe ten), I gave a recital out here in Freeport, which was the last time I did any improvising like that. I improvised the entire recital, including a three-movement sonata. The piano playing was lousy, but the thinking was good.

I was still working on my master's when the first BMI Student Composers' Award was announced. I entered that, and Don Martino, Yehudi Weiner [American composers], and I were the first winners of the Award. At that time I never saw the money, none of us did I guess. When I got it, I used the money to work with Marcel Dick [American composer]; that is what I consider my true postgraduate work, studying with him for another year or so at the Cleveland Institute of Music. I remember Dick telling me in my first postgraduate lesson, "Well, you have done everything this school has to offer. You have earned your bachelor's degree, and now you are a master." He was speaking ironically in terms of my degree, because then he said, "Now you can begin to learn something about music." That is when he gave me the stuff that I know about music and that most other people out here don't know. That might be cold to say, but it is true.

I had to make a living, so I got a job about this same time, around 1951 or 1952. It was the only time in my life when I ever looked for a job. I got a job as a file clerk, at the very bottom of the scale, working in the disbursement office for the Navy in Cleveland. At the same time I was given a job at a printing place called the House of Kennedy.

I worked in their music division under a man named Robert Nelson, who was head of the division. It was the first company to come out with this green-tinted paper called K-lith paper. The K stood for Kennedy; there was a father and his two sons who ran it. They did a photographic process instead of actually engraving musical plates. I was hired to do what they called "page finishing." I had to draw slurs and stems, and I had to learn to draw slurs freehand. The first two days on the job, all I did was draw slurs freehand with a crow quill pen. To this day, I can draw a slur with the proper gradation from thin to somewhat thicker in the middle and back to thin again. Robert Nelson is the one who actually trained my hand.

I used to buy Esterbrook fountain pens when I graduated from the dip pens. I started out using just the plain dip pens and ink, but then I got these Esterbrooks. I didn't know anything about the stub points and those so-called music pens. I never did like music pens and don't like them to this day. I think they are awful, especially those three-pronged monsters. They just never made sense to me. I would get a plain old secretarial point, because I didn't know anything else, and I would shape it on a stone. I would shape it until I got the proper shape for my hand and the proper degree of smoothness, and then I would work. That gave me a sensitivity to pens that I obviously still have, but my hand was really refined after I got to New York and started working in the publishing business.

I went to New York in 1958, because I had gone as far as I could go in Cleveland. There were no openings then for anybody like me. I also wanted to be sure that I could cope with things, and going to New York was a brand new education. There were a lot of fine points, especially in regard to the preparation of music, that I did not know and could not have learned in Cleveland.

When I first got here, there were still rough edges in terms of the mechanics, but now there are things in print, like the song cycle *Beyond the Rim of Day* and a choral piece called "Two Kids," which I wrote when I was an undergraduate student. There is another set of four songs, called *The Valley Wind.* The second two were written as part of my master's requirement. I am amused when articles that deal with those songs, especially *Beyond the Rim of Day,* speak of the sophistication of the setting and so on. They're just direct responses to poetry that I liked. My reputation as a composer started growing while I was in Cleveland. When I did my very first set of art songs, I really didn't know what I was doing. I used Langston Hughes's *Dream Variation and Prayer.* In between those songs was a another one, based on *From the Delta's Unmarked Graves,* by a Cleveland poet, Harvey Williamson. I set it to music on September 7, 1949. My teacher thought to the end of his life that those were among the best things I ever did. At the same time I had written a set of variations for flute and piano that I loved, but they were nothing but imitation, watered-down, second-rate, fourth-hand Debussy. I got in trouble over those variations, but interestingly enough, Marcel arranged for them to be performed. The songs were sung by Helen Cartmel, a Nordic blonde, as part of a student recital there at the institute. Howard Whittaker, who was the director of the Cleveland Music School Settlement, arranged for Helen Cartmel to do them at his school. He then brought me to the attention of Russell and Rowena Jellife, who were the directors of the Karamu Theater, and my reputation just spread.

Langston Hughes had graduated in the early twenties, but when he came back to Cleveland he would usually go by the school and give readings for the students. Hughes was one of the early participants in the Karamu program and even wrote his first plays for it. Mrs. Jellife used to help him write plays back then; the Karamu program gave a lot of us a lot of help.

When the cast was put together for *Porgy and Bess* around 1950 (the cast that included Leontyne Price, Cab Calloway, and Bill Warfield), many actors in it came out of Karamu Theater. It was a remarkable thing. Dorothy Dandridge and Ruby Dee were among them, all in Cleveland. I never knew them there, but they were all part of Karamu. Howard Swanson was not a part of the circle, he was older. He had gone to the Cleveland Institute before I did and had gotten out in the thirties. Everett Lee [black American conductor] and Raul Abdul [writer] were part of that, and of course Ernie and Evelyn Freeman, Howard Roberts [composer and singer], Aaron Bell [jazz bassist], and Brenton Banks were as well. There were a number of brilliant people in Cleveland, Ohio, at Karamu, who went on to brilliant careers.

When I went to New York I was thirty-three. My family's business was not doing too well, and I was not much help, to tell you the truth. I wanted to make music. I'll put it this way—I was going to be the great out-of-town genius who would go to New York, stay for two weeks, go back home, and commute whenever they wanted my services in New York. I figured they were going to be desperate for me. That hasn't happened yet. I stayed at one of the YMCAs in New York, and during that first week Jim Hall, the guitarist, stopped over. Jim had been a younger schoolmate of mine at the Cleveland Institute. He said, "Man, if you stay here, you will be a fool. I've got this apartment I have sublet over in Brooklyn Heights, and you can stay there as long as you want. Don't worry about rent." That is where I spent the rest of the time. I stayed almost three months in New York, and of course nothing happened, except that some roots were put in the ground.

When I went back home it was spring, and during the summer I got a couple of letters. One of them was from Oliver Daniel, who was director of Contemporary Music at BMI and also the founder of the BMI Student Composers Awards. Oliver wrote to say that I had been chosen to be part of a series of concerts by the Composers Forum in New York. I was on the first program, which I shared with a composer named Sergius Kagen, who had written a very useful book called *Music for the Voice*. That is where I met Carlos Salzedo, the great harpist. Salzedo told me that he and Varèse were close friends; he was the first person I had come in contact with who knew Varèse. (But I did not meet him myself until a few years later.) I came in contact with Samuel Dushkin, whom I had met just before I came to New York. He was the violinist who had commissioned Stravinsky's violin concerto, among other things. I met Felix Greissle, who had been Schoenberg's son-in-law. When I told Felix that I had studied with Marcel Dick, he just put his arm around me, and that was it. Through Felix I met a number of other people, like Edward Steurman [pianist].

I left the Brooklyn Heights apartment and stayed at a New York hotel that no longer exists (because of the expansion of the Rockefeller Center), a place called the Flanders. I picked this out of the phone book. The original movie version of *The Odd Couple,* with Jack Lemmon, opens with Lemmon, very distraught, checking into the same hotel. I found out that a lot of musicians stayed there at the Flanders. It was cheap, and it was decent. I stayed there for two years before Juanita came up. This is getting ahead, to 1961, when she came to New York for a visit. Ron Carter [bassist] had just joined Miles Davis, who was going on an extended tour to the West Coast. Ron told me, "Look man, Juanita is coming up here, why don't you folks stay at my apartment?" He was taking his wife Janet with him on tour.

Juanita and I stayed in Ron's apartment, in Harlem, and while we were there a childhood friend of ours who was living in New York came by and told Juanita he was going to apply for a job as a translator at the United Nations, because he was fluent in French and Spanish, and he wanted Juanita to keep him company. So they went over to the United Nations. He was a plain-looking colored fellow, highly literate, from the street where I grew up in Cleveland. He had not studied languages in school but living in the countries. Because he didn't have a degree in either Spanish or French, he didn't get the job. Since Juanita was there, she decided to fill out the forms. They asked her to start the next day, though they ended up giving her a month. That was the fall when the bigwigs came to New York raising hell. Fidel Castro came up and moved into the Teresa Hotel, up in Harlem. Nikita Khrushchev came—that is when he became notorious for banging his shoe on the desk at the UN. That was the time she came, and we lived together at the Flanders Hotel, in Harlem.

Interestingly, I got behind in rent. The folks at the hotel let me go a long time. Then a woman asked me to do some arrangements for a Puerto Rican singer whom she was going to manage. I told the woman to give me a down payment, but instead of that she paid me in full, about three hundred dollars for four arrangements for two horns, a rhythm section, plus the singer. She gave me the check, I cashed it at the hotel desk, and it bounced. I never did get the money from her. I ended up promising the manager of the hotel that if he would go along with me, I would pay every penny, including twenty dollars the hotel had to pay to a lawyer, who refused to sue the woman without suing me, because I was the one who had passed the bad check to the hotel. By the time we paid the last bill, we had already made arrangements to lease a house from one of Juanita's coworkers who was being sent to Korea for two years. That is what got us out here on Long Island. We stayed in that house for two years, and then in 1963 we got a house in Freeport, on Independence Avenue. We are now in the second house we have been had since we have been out here.

I just drifted into civic activism. I became involved with a neighborhood organization and eventually became president of it. I was one of the people who broke up the racial thing here. When we moved into Freeport we could not have moved into this neighborhood, and now anyone can move where he or she can afford to be.

Oliver Daniel, who at that time (1960), was the head of the Contemporary Music Department at BMI, commissioned me to write an orchestral piece. I was one of twenty composers, here and in Europe, who were commissioned in honor of the twentieth birthday of BMI. BMI had been formed in 1940. I was the least known of all of the composers involved—people like Roger Sessions, Gunther Schuller, and a number of others who had major reputations and belonged to BMI. I understand that a number of rather well-known composers were indignant because I had gotten this commission, but I got it simply because Oliver Daniel believed in me. It was announced in the newspaper; somebody told me that they had seen it; I called Oliver and asked him about it. He told me that he had been trying to catch up with me for several days but that I was always away. He said he figured I wouldn't turn it down, so he had just announced that I won it. I rushed home and started scratching some junk on paper, because I saw myself getting this money. What I was writing was rubbish. I stopped after two or three days and told myself, "You damned fool, this might prove to be the biggest opportunity you have ever had in your life, and here you are throwing it away on this garbage." So I threw the stuff away and went through a purification process for a whole year, just to clear my mind of all the stuff I had been doing trying to make a living. Of course, the result of this was *Contours*. It was done in 1961.

Oliver Daniel was a very powerful man. He was one of the most powerful men in the entire field of music. He could call conductors wherever they were, from the most famous conductors in the world on down, tell them what he wanted, and they would give it to him. Now he called Robert Whitney, who was the head of the Louisville Orchestra at that time, and said that he wanted Whitney to program this new piece by me. Then he called Walter Hinrischen, who was the president of C. F. Peters, and told him that he wanted this piece to be published. Then he also told Whitney that he wanted this piece to be recorded as part of the Louisville Series; that was not a Louisville Orchestra commission, it came directly from Oliver Daniel, through BMI.

I have never had a problem working with the New York Philharmonic. The first thing it played of mine was *Contours,* with James DePreist. I went up on the stage during rehearsal at one point. I called for the percussionists to use a stiff hairbrush at one spot. A lot of the percussionists used their regular wire brushes, but it is a completely different thing. You can't even make the strokes I call for with the regular wire brushes. I had gotten into the habit of carrying a hair brush with me, so I went up on stage during the period when DePreist was explaining something to someone else. As I walked between the desks, I heard several people comment, "Well, he certainly knows his way around an orchestra." Then I just handed the hair brush to the drummer, the principal percussionist, and said, "Try this, if you don't mind." Like all of the rest of them, he went out and bought a hair brush to use for that piece. But what I found out was that the musicians, when they were really notorious, would test anybody who got involved with them, whether it was the conductor, soloist, or composer. They just took for granted that living composers didn't know their craft. Oscar Wiener, the principal second violinist at that time, told me plainly, "Man, when a new piece comes up there, we will just play whatever we want to play. Most of the times these composers just sit there with idiotic grins on their faces not knowing what is happening."

Unfortunately, far too many would-be composers either were intimidated by being played by an orchestra like that or really did not know any different. In some cases the errors weren't theirs; they could have been copying errors. If the composers didn't comment or get the news to the conductor or somebody, the players would then just go berserk and mess the stuff up. To avoid things like that, my rule has always been to turn in impeccable material. The material is always straight when I turn it over to an orchestra. Then, when they play it, even if the piece is difficult, they learn that the difficulties fall within the natural range of the instrument. I don't expect the violin to play passages that would be better written for piano. Everything is precisely heard, so musicians don't have any problems. The good orchestras have always done their best for me, but I have had a couple of lousy orchestras.

I have had no personal problems with orchestras, especially not based on race. But at the same time I know full well that for a musician of my caliber, if I were white, many things would happen that do not happen. I am well aware of that nuance, but that is another reason why I am absolutely adamant about having my materials correct. No player, nobody who knows me, can say that I am inadequate as a technician. The players seem to like it, but there have been snide comments. In fact, Malcolm Breda [organist] dug up a review of *Contours* when Everett Lee conducted it with the Cincinnati Symphony. The review was in the *Cincinnati Enquirer,* but when Breda contacted the paper for a copy of the review, they told him that it must not have been reviewed, because they had no record of it in their files. But Malcolm found it in the Library of Congress. What this review had said—and I memorized it—was that he would have liked to have ended the review on a pleasant note, but since Hale Smith's concert for orchestra was on the program, unfortunately he could not. He went on to say that the piece was unbelievably tasteless and inept, and had as much business on a program of serious concert music as a chimpanzee in the last act of *King Lear.* Now I can't help but think that has something to do with my color. I will be generous and say I am not sure, but just the mention of a chimpanzee in this context makes me lean toward this other thing. I do think, though, had I been white, I would have gotten a lot more recognition, especially by authors who write books about modern, or American, music, in most of which there is no mention of my name. They do mention the names of younger white composers, some of whom have benefited from me, composers whom I have helped. What else can I say?

In 1961 or 1962, I was sitting up in bed working out my plans for the day, and Juanita had already gone into New York. I got a call from Ulysses Kay, who was second to Oliver Daniel. (Until he got so ill that he couldn't handle it, Kay was also always in charge of these student composers awards. I guess his official title was "Consultant of Contemporary Music"; it was a high-powered job there at BMI.) He said BMI had received a call from the Edward B. Marks Company, which was looking for somebody to be a proofreader and editor. They had a list of requirements.

Now, this list can be found in my article in Dominique DeLerma's [musicologist] first book, *Black Music in Our Culture,* a panel discussion dealing with music publishing. What it boiled down to was that there was nobody that they could think of who had those particular skills and background but me. The requirements for that job were completely unrealistic, but there was only one of them that I could not fulfill—they had asked for a Negro woman, if possible. We were still Negroes back then.

I worked directly under Felix Greissle, Schoenberg's former son-in-law. I came in contact with a man named Arnold Shaw, a man who did a number of books on popular music and who died just a few years ago. Shaw did a book on Janis Joplin, one on Sinatra, and several others on popular music in this country. Shaw was one of the editors of the Schillinger system. He had been one of Schillinger's students; when Schillinger died, his widow asked Shaw to edit one of the very famous composition books that Schillinger had done. That was interesting to me, because later, before he retired, Shaw started doing collections of piano pieces, especially for younger people. He would always call me to do his editing. Even when he moved out to Las Vegas he would send stuff to me to edit for him. I thought that was curious, but nice.

There was one very interesting incident that you might find delightful. There was a young man there named Jerry Landis, who worked under Arnold Shaw in the pop division. He was a brash man, and I took an instant dislike to him. One day a lady named Francia Luban, who was head of the Latin American Department there, spoke to me about this young man. I told her that I didn't care for him, and she told me, "Well, I think if you take the trouble of meeting with him and talking to him you might find you are wrong, that he is really a delightful person and that he has a lot of talent."

That Christmas, for the office Christmas party, I was asked to play. I asked Major Holly [bassist] to play. (He refused to take money, as always. He never took a nickel from me all of the times we played together.) Then there was a fellow working in the stockroom, wrapping packages, named Eddie Dougherty, who had played on Billie Holiday records—and he was there wrapping up packages. So we had this trio: me, Major Holly, and Eddie Dougherty. Then this young fellow, Jerry Landis, came on to do his thing. He played guitar and sang some really lovely songs. They really were. In fact, I transcribed two or three of those things, and I still have the original manuscripts. During the following year this young man got caught breaking one of the cardinal rules for anyone working for that company, which was, when you are on company time, you take care of company business and do not try to push your own stuff. He got caught, and he got fired instantly. Before that year was out, this cat became world famous as Paul Simon, which is his real name. He was Paul Simon, from Simon and Garfunkel. I did grow to like him, very much; his brashness was a front.

I had started playing jazz back in clubs in 1939, so by the time I went into the army, at the age of eighteen, I already had several years of actual playing experience. I met Duke Ellington the year before I met Langston Hughes. I went to hear Ellington's band at the Palace Theater in Cleveland. The Palace Theater was one of a string of movie theaters around the country that had both films and big bands. All of the bands at that time played in places like the Palace Theater. I had become aware of Duke by that time, and when I was fourteen, I became really aware of his music.

I knew jazz was around and all of that, but I hadn't tuned my ears into it for the first seven years of my study. It was a quick-study process that threw me into playing in clubs. On the day I met Duke, I went to the first show, and afterward I went backstage to the stage door. I was about fifteen or sixteen years old then. I asked if I could speak to Mr. Ellington; the fellow at the stage door called Duke in his room and said that there was a Mr. Smith down there and he wanted to say something. Duke told him to send me on up. I don't know, I must have caught him at a rare point in his life. I spent the entire day with Duke up in his dressing room. When the band was on stage, I was in the wings looking out at the band. That was an experience I have never forgotten in my life. Duke showed me some little things, and we discussed little points. I had one of the things that I had written with me; it was sloppy, as all young folks' work is, I guess. That was when Duke had what I think of as his greatest band. Jimmy Blanton had just died, and the bass player, Junior Raglin, who took his place, was a very nice man. We became friends and saw each other several times after that, but then he died also. This band also had people like Ben Webster and Tricky Sam Nanton in it.

Every single time I met Duke, he never remembered me from the time previous. This included once at the UN when the band was playing there. Aaron Bell was playing bass with him, and Aaron reminded me that we had played bass together as youngsters with Ernie Freeman. I had to be introduced to Duke twice, once at the beginning of the evening and again at the end of it. He didn't remember me from one time to the next. So people who tell me that Duke never forgot anybody are really letting me know—he was telling me something. I only had a few, very brief, conversations with him after that. The last one was at a concert that Ellington did at Lincoln Center. We were together at rehearsals for a couple of his orchestral pieces.

Using jazz elements in orchestral music has never been my aim. I generally keep the two idioms separate, even though I know that elements spill over from one to the other. But unless I am writing jazz, I don't intend for the music to swing, as a jazz element should. For me there is more than one language, even though they share the same alphabet. It has only been in recent years that

I have combined elements. I suppose I did something like that when I was writing for Chico Hamilton, but that was a special case. That was for the original groups that he had, starting with Jim Hall and Buddy Collette and then later with Eric Dolphy. But I just don't think of either area in academic terms. If I am going to do a jazz piece, I just think in jazz terms. That is one reason I can sit up there and swing a rhythm section, because that has never become past tense to me.

When I first played with Dizzy Gillespie, there was no score anywhere in sight. The only person now living out of that group who can tell the story is Charlie Persip [drummer]. He remembers how I went in there cold and played tunes that I was hearing for the first time (for example, "Tour de Force" and "Con Alma"). There was only one piece that threw me, a blues piece ("The Champ"). The thing that threw me was that it was going by so fast, I couldn't keep up with it. I did four gigs with Dizzy, a matinee and an evening, on a Saturday and on a Sunday. He told me after that Saturday night performance that I should pat my feet on quarter notes, not half notes. I told him I was coming in the next day and not pat my feet at all. I went home that night and practiced with the metronome until I could play the piece faster than I knew Dizzy was playing it. That next evening, when we got to this particular piece, we took off; Dizzy looked at me and smiled. I think that is really where our friendship started. But I did have that facility. I could hear chords, the whole stream, and pick up the implications of them. I played with Dizzy in 1952 or 1953. I loved him very much.

There are, of course, commonalities in these traditions. Let's just start this way. A correctly notated jazz piece will look just about like any other correctly notated music. About the only points of distinction would be perhaps the instrumentation and the space left for improvisation. The differences come through the inflections, as the music is played. But if we take just the basic materials, the rhythms are all there, available for anybody—at least the notated rhythms. The harmonic structure, with very, very few exceptions, comes straight out of tonality. With regard to the harmonic structures I see no difference. When somebody tells me he wants to learn something about jazz harmony, I tell him I don't know what it is. I am serious. Even that so-called minor seventh with the flatted fifth that Dizzy and Monk talked about is a half-diminished-seventh chord; there is a half-diminished-seventh chord, in C-sharp, in the first string quartet Mozart wrote as a kid. He arrived at it through voice leading, which is how all of these chords developed; they all came about originally through convergence of individual voice lines. So, whether we are using the seven-tone scale or the twelve-tone chromatic scale, it is all the same stuff. It is just a question of inflection.

First of all, I don't use systems when I create music. Secondly, I don't particularly decide ahead of time what I am going to do. I like to have a piece talk to me. Unless the piece talks to me, I can't really do anything with it, which leaves me vulnerable to such things as writer's cramp or writer's block. Unless I hear the piece, I really cannot do it. If I do hear the piece, of course, it is a direct process. If I make an arrangement of something, like a spiritual, I just start thinking about the piece. I might not think about it very long; the treatment, or the setting of that particular piece, seems to be in my mind. How it gets there, I don't know. I arranged some hymns for orchestra that Paul Freeman recorded before he did the spiritual album with Bill Brown [concert singer]. One of these was "Nearer My God to Thee," the very last of these hymns that I arranged. I had a time problem, in that I had to take the music into New York to a copyist, who was waiting for it. I had sat up all night doing two or three others and then I settled down to "Nearer My God to Thee." It is an almost empty score but it sounds rich. But the whole thing, from the first stroke of the pen to the end, was done in twenty minutes. It just fell into my head like that.

Now, to me, composing is a much different proposition from arranging, on just about every level. First of all, the structural problems are different, but even there I have to hear the thing. One process that I follow most of the time—and the bigger the piece the more I do this—is to start writing almost blindly and then, perhaps twenty-five, thirty, to forty measures into it, sometimes not that much, stop. Then I will dissect everything that I have written. I will separate the rhythms. I will put the rhythms on a sheet of paper. Then I will put the harmonic structures on paper. Then I will put the melodic lines on another sheet of paper. I analyze these things. I call this process "becoming acquainted with the biographies of my ideas." What I do is become thoroughly acquainted with these various elements. I study them in terms of their potential for growth.

Nearly every time, when I start writing, this material starts dictating to me. If I am writing serially, for instance, I use it as a method—and there is a vast difference between the two approaches. I will think in terms of a precise period of time—be it five minutes, ten minutes, twenty-five minutes, thirty minutes, or whatever. Sometimes I will think in terms of seconds. Of course, if I am writing for film or television, I think in terms of tenths of seconds. All of this becomes part of the conception. I think of that block of time as the musical equivalent of a piece of marble or stone that a sculptor would use. The piece grows naturally to fit into this block of time, with its own set of proportions and everything. That is one reason why I say I don't think academically, that I don't think in terms of the traditional academic forms.

I didn't decide to teach, I was talked into it by a composer at C. W. Post College. His name is Raul Pleskow. I ran into Raul in New York one day, I think it was 1969; we had both been members of the board of the American Composers Alliance. He stopped me and said that he was the head of the music department at C. W. Post, which he still is, all of these years later. He said he would like me to teach a couple of music appreciation courses, introductory courses to music for nonmajors. I told him frankly that I didn't have any interest in teaching. In fact, I had avoided any idea, when I was going through school, that I might come anywhere near music education, teaching music, or teaching, period. I had always been a professional in terms of playing, writing, or publishing. I told him that I didn't feel I had any teaching ability and that I wasn't interested. He said, "On the contrary, I feel that you can communicate." There on the street, in the middle of the summer, he talked me—tentatively, at any rate—into accepting this thing. There were to be two classes that would meet two times during the week. I spent all the rest of that summer trying to figure a way out; I just wasn't interested in teaching, and C. W. Post College was on the northern part of the island. North-south travel on Long Island is almost impossible without your own vehicle, and I didn't know how to drive then.

I finally had to give in, though, because I couldn't think of a reasonable excuse. So I went up there at the beginning of the semester, and Pleskow said, "You know, you have to have a rank here. I know what I will do, I will make you an adjunct associate professor." I didn't know what any of those words meant. I also told him I was not going to teach in the conventional way, because I didn't care for music education or music-appreciation kinds of things. To me it was just a crock. So I used a book by Ernest Toch called *The Shaping Forces of Music,* which to this day, I think is one of the best books on how music is put together. I started with classes on the rudiments of musical notation, on the ground that any discipline that is worth study has its own vocabulary and language, which has to be understood before the subject itself can be dealt with adequately.

Then I got a call over the Christmas vacation in 1969 from a fellow named James Eversole [composer and teacher], who became one of my best friends; he was then on the faculty at the University of Connecticut. He invited me up to give a talk. He had just started a new course called "The Black Experience in the Arts." I went when the spring semester began; I was the third speaker that they had come up there. It turned out to be one of those typical academic ploys. They had me up there giving this talk, but really I was under observation. When I finished, a group of us went out for refreshments, and I was asked if I would be interested in coming back to talk with them about joining the faculty, which I did. When I went up there I figured that since I didn't ask for the job, I could make certain demands. The first thing I told them was that I did not have a doctorate and didn't have any intention of getting one.

The dean made the point that it would be silly to insist that I have a doctoral degree, because of my professional life and my reputation. I wouldn't have taken the job if they had said I had to get a doctorate. I haven't earned a doctorate yet. The one I have is honorary. But I have taught at the postgraduate level there; I have taught a lot of doctoral candidates.

I also told them I would have to be there only Tuesday, Wednesday, and Thursday, so I would have time for other things. Then I said my first class should not be scheduled earlier than noon, because I needed time to drive up there. My last class on Thursday would have to end no later than 3:30, to give me time to get back to New York; at that time I was on the Parks Commission out here in Freeport, and it met every other Thursday evening. They went along with everything. They would insist only that I teach no place but there. I told them they didn't have to worry about that because teaching was never my major interest in life. I was hired there to teach composition, starting at the beginning level all the way through the higher levels, to whomever had the ability to deal with them. I found very few students like that. I also taught graduate and postgraduate level orchestration, and on occasion I did some form and analysis and counterpoint. Just before I started teaching, in the fall of 1970, I got a call from the head of the Music Department, a wonderful pianist named Louis Crowder. He asked me if I would have any objections to taking on an improvisation course; he and some others on the faculty thought it would be good to take advantage of my experience in that area. I said okay. I was, I suppose, a rather free type of teacher, in the sense that I didn't follow any strict regimen. I have never done a lesson plan in my life. To this day I wouldn't know what to do with one.

Can you imagine American music without the work of black composers, or without black music in general? Still, there is a refusal, a denial of that reality. Through the work that I have done with the Black Music Repertory Ensemble and Sam Floyd [its founder], I have been able to see the entire panorama of American music as created by us, going back to Francis Johnson [black American composer and bandleader] and coming down that long, tortuous road. Without these people, without their contributions, American music would be altogether different. This involves people from Louisiana and people from New York. This includes people like Will Marion Cook [black American composer] and Eubie Blake [black American composer and songwriter]. American music would be radically different without what these people have done. And it is not only those who have dealt with nonpopular forms, because if you include the popular music, black music is what has given American music its identity. It is just the music itself. Whether we can name two, three, a dozen, a hundred, or a thousand black musicians and composers, it is a totality without which American music would be completely different. You can find traces of this in Walter Piston. You can find traces of it in Charles Ives and certainly in Copland. It pervades American music to such an extent that it can be denied only by people who have blinders on, or people who cannot hear. Edward McDowell [American composer] got upset over Dvorak's comment about an American school of music being derived from the African American and Native American sources. McDowell thought that was a lot of poppycock. But his own music is so strongly Germanic that except for his little set of pieces called *Woodland Sketches for Piano,* which includes a piece called "To a Wild Rose," McDowell would be completely irrelevant, just like Payne and Chadwick [American composers]. The only real impact Chadwick has had on American music is that he taught William Grant Still. They were skilled and all of that, but they didn't bring anything new; their work was just a rehashing of German Romanticism. I am saying that American music would be completely unrecognizable, in terms of what we know now, without the music of black composers. Somebody once said that without black music, American music would be Lawrence Welk.

Frederick C. Tillis

Frederick C. Tillis is certainly one of the Renaissance people of his generation. Born in Galveston, Texas, in 1930, Dr. Tillis is a composer, saxophonist, poet, educator, author, and arts administrator. A graduate of Wiley College, he went on to earn his master's and doctoral degrees in composition from the University of Iowa. Known as a composer of multiple palettes, among his commissioned works is *A Festival Journey* for percussion and orchestra, written for Max Roach and performed by the Atlanta Symphony. His *Concerto for Piano and Jazz Trio* was performed by Dr. Billy Taylor and the Springfield Symphony, with additional works performed by the Atlanta and Hartford Symphonies and the University of Massachusetts and Howard University ensembles. For many years Dr. Tillis has served as director of the Fine Arts Center, professor of music composition (since 1970), director of the Afro-American Music and Jazz Program (including direction of the "Jazz in July" Workshops in Improvisation program), and associate chancellor at the University of Massachusetts at Amherst. He has also held positions at Wiley College, Grambling University, and Kentucky State University. Dr. Tillis has published five books of poetry and has written scholarly articles, and the book *Jazz Theory and Improvisation.* Also known as a saxophonist, Dr. Tillis has performed abroad, leading ensembles to Australia, China, Japan, New Zealand, the former Soviet Union, and Poland. His awards include the Commonwealth Award (Massachusetts), Rockefeller Foundation Grant, National Endowment for the Arts and United Negro College Fund Awards, and a Danforth Associate fellowship. Frederick Tillis lives in Amherst, Massachusetts.

I was born on January 5, 1930, in Galveston, Texas. I went to preschool at age three. This was a very different era. It was a period when segregation based on race was the law in southern states and de facto in other regions of the nation. I'm part of the national Depression era. Fortunately for me, the adversity I experienced in society has turned out to be an asset rather than a liability. I learned to observe and appreciate differences between racial and ethnic groups, in spite of the hostile social environment. Ironically, as I reflect on my elementary and secondary education, because of the nourishment I got from the AME [African Methodist Episcopal] Church, my parents, and my teachers in segregated schools, I was blessed by being encouraged in everything I can remember pursuing as a young student.

My mother played piano and sang as a soprano soloist in the church choir. I can remember her voice in that context. She tried to teach me piano somewhere between the ages of six and eight. Unfortunately, I rebelled and failed to take advantage of this opportunity. However, by the time I got to the fifth grade at George Washington Carver Elementary School, my attitude had changed. Dr. Carver had been a very important scientist. My mother encouraged me to read an inspiring biography of him. Carver Elementary had a drum and bugle corps, and I was taken in by all the glamor of those gold-plated instruments and the drums. I played the bugle in the fifth grade. That was the beginning of my involvement in playing music, and a lifelong journey in the pursuit and discovery of arts and culture.

In the 1930s and '40s secondary schools were divided between grades seven and eight and grades nine through twelve. At age eleven, I joined the high school band. I transferred from the bugle to trumpet. I studied trumpet (and later saxophone) with Fleming Huff. He was the director of the high school band, and a chemistry major in college. The man loved music, and he was an excellent teacher. I took lessons the summer before I entered high school on the trumpet. I worked awfully hard and was able to make the band in three months.

By the time I was twelve, which was in 1942, I was playing trumpet and performing at a serviceman's club (this was in World War II) seven nights a week from 8 P.M. to midnight. I was performing with people who were either too old to be drafted into military service or who had disabilities. That was a great training ground, because here I was, playing with people who were more mature in music and other worldly experiences. The only reason I had the opportunity was because I worked awfully hard; I was really driven to succeed. In addition, some of the other musicians probably had been called into military service. I was lucky I was too young to be drafted for military service but proficient enough to be utilized in this civilian jazz band. My band director said, "Hey, if you want somebody who can do it, he can do it," meaning me. People complained, and I wondered why. A twelve-year old working 8 P.M. to midnight seven nights a week and still going to high school? It was no problem. I was enjoying the work. It was very good experience for me, and I received compensation for my employment as a musician.

In about another year my band director, Mr. Huff, suggested that I study the saxophone. I said, "Well, it's possible." Again, I used models. I listened to records all of the time. My mother would send me off to the grocery store. If there was any money left over, I came home with a music recording or two. I was acquainted with Benny Carter, who was another influence and role model for me. He played trumpet, saxophone, and clarinet. I thought, "If he can do it, I can do it." I started the saxophone. At age thirteen, I was allowed to audition with the Benny Carter Jazz Orchestra. The major jazz orchestras made the circuit down south every year. Joining the ensemble was vetoed by my parents, because there was no way that their thirteen-year-old son was going on the road! I can appreciate their point of view now. It took me some time to develop an embouchure [a lip] for both the trumpet and saxophone. I think for two or three years I kept a gig playing both of them.

Later, Professor Huff, as band director, encouraged me to take up the violin. I briefly studied the violin but did not have the success I enjoyed on the trumpet and the saxophone. My high school days continued with my performing professionally with local jazz bands and other high school ensembles. At age sixteen, I won a music scholarship and entered Wiley College as a music major in a bachelor of arts degree program. Wiley College is a small AME Church–related institution in Marshall, Texas. There, sometimes I was playing trumpet, and at other times I was playing saxophone. I played in the marching band and the concert band and sang in the choir. If you got a music scholarship, you did it all. I am grateful for the opportunity. As a composer, I work now writing for voice and chorus with no intimidation. In fact, vocal composition becomes part of your vocabulary, and you develop the ear for it. But I trace these aesthetic sensitivities back to these experiences.

Q: At what point did the impulse come that made you decide to be the person behind the pen doing the creating as well as composing?

A: I entered college at age sixteen and graduated at age nineteen. During my sophomore or junior year in college, I became interested in the piano. My piano teacher, Mrs. Lucile Tyson, introduced me to Bach, the preludes and fugues and the *Well-Tempered Clavier*. I became very enamored with Bach's craft. By practicing Bach's contrapuntal works slowly, I actually savored the harmonic structure, which I found very close to the jazz vocabulary of be-bop. In fantasy and improvisatory passages, Bach uses many suspensions, major sevenths, and even flatted fifths. I was delighted to discover these connections between the European classical music tradition and jazz. In the senior year, it was a requirement of music majors at Wiley College to study some of the Mozart, Haydn, and Beethoven sonatas and to write an original composition. During my junior and senior years in high school I had been composing and arranging music. I was also transcribing Charlie Parker themes and solos from music recordings, without a lot of formal composition study. It was just a normal course of development for me to write music, because of my interest in music in all of its dimensions.

My earliest influences in wanting to write music probably came from Duke Ellington and the unique sound of his jazz orchestra. The college thing was just another medium, because I considered jazz a classical music of America. I know people don't like to hear that, but I'll stand by it. My early influences in performing and arranging were inspired by the jazz orchestras and soloists of Duke Ellington, Jimmy Lunceford, and Count Basie. I was practicing very diligently so that I could be in one of those ensembles, because they were the three most distinct in terms of jazz styles and images. As a result of these driving forces, I was interested in performing, arranging, and composition in music.

Well, of course, now I can speak to you about music in a much more mature voice than in my first twenty years. I was doing music earlier because I loved it—for the joy of it. It meant something to me. It had become an important part of my life, and it is still that way. I never dreamed of becoming wealthy doing music. That didn't worry me, though. It is a matter of self-expression. It is a critical matter. I don't try to merge or fuse art. I write poetry now about as much as I did music. It is just another medium. I have to do it. I don't have an option. I perform, write music, and write poetry. Those are the three spheres in which I have a certain level of confidence and that mean something to me personally.

I make a distinction between art and trying to use art as a means of politics. Does it mean that I don't believe in politics? Of course I do. You can't successfully lead in an administrative position without an awareness of politics and all the other social and cultural aspects that surround it. But I prefer to use art as a refuge from some of the more mundane things in life. I live and dwell in the realm of the spiritual facets of human relationships. That is where my interest is, and music is one of those facets. So are poetry and all of the arts. In fact, I believe the arts are a reflection of human expression in matters of the spirit and flesh. Some people might say this is an amorphous, or political, definition. However, it does recognize the importance of the multidimensional aspects of art that have been a part of human communication from the Stone Age to the present.

Q: With all the political problems and all the cuts that are being made, how should we address this in terms of the lack of education?

A: Broadly speaking, I think the country itself has not addressed the issue in the way that it should. We don't place enough emphasis on education, period, for all people. We have lost the way. Schools and their environment are so different. You don't have the triangle that you once had—that is, parents, church, and the school—working together to hone an individual who has not only some technical and literary development but also some sense of civic, moral, or ethical responsibility. They all have to be blended. We have lost that because in some fashion we have allowed the social system itself, which has always had a capacity for instability, decadence, and so forth, to triumph. This is an inevitable cycle, which all great civilizations have had to encounter.

Now we have a legalistic system that puts ethical and moral issues somewhere on the back burner. Unfortunately, we have deemed these values to be excess baggage. In fact, however, they must be a part of a comprehensive education. When you separate those things you get a distortion of what humanity is about. That is just one among many problems. I think in education we need to realize that the social environment now is very different from the time when I grew up. Education should be addressed much more radically, aggressively, and vigorously than our current institutions do—including universities. We do not now use sufficiently the arts or new technology. We thought all students should have schoolbooks when we grew up; how does one teach without them? I think the question should be asked, "How do you really teach and engage students now without computers?" If utilized effectively, computers can enable a student to learn at his or her own pace. There are so many programs. But we are not there. At the wealthier schools there is computer literacy, right? But that is not universal by any means. We have all these divergent views, all these students who are somewhere else and you can't even get to them. A human being alone won't get to them—not in the present context and influences of mass media and marketing practices.

Q: What do you think about Black History Month and Black History Month programs?

A: Well, I will rephrase your question, because I would approach it differently. For some people, these limited celebrations are effective and positive, and for some they aren't. I grew up with an appreciation of African American culture. I knew what the Negro national anthem was. We were not prohibited from singing "Lift Every Voice and Sing." Some people are teaching some unfortunate aspects of integration and the losses that occurred as a result of that. I don't want to go back that far, but the truth of the matter is, there was a loss of the nurturing that we had experienced earlier. You are not going to receive the sensitivities needed in this kind of context. Black History Month programs are a kind of substitute to try to give young people a sense of their own history, which, if they had been brought up in a more homogenous environment, they would already know, because of contacts with influential teachers who had related cultural and educational experiences.

You should have that pride. I told you I was proud to go to George Washington Carver School. I don't know how young I was when I was inspired by this scientist who could do so much with peanuts—George Washington Carver. That's pride. That's racial pride. Now we are trying to institutionalize it by having a month of it in February. I run into too many students who don't know the culture we come from. That is unfortunate. I'm not against these programs at all, but some people believe Black History Month is about affirmative action. There are some African Americans now who believe that it is time to get away from affirmative action. They are saying it is time for African Americans to stand on their own two feet. I disagree. Nobody stands on their own two feet in this country. The wealthy stand on the shoulders of those who have less money.

Q: How do you put your music together?

A: I compose in a lot of ways, but a commission is sufficient impetus and stimulation for me to begin to write a work. But even if I don't get a commission and I have something that I am interested in, I will compose something of personal interest. The first thing that I consider is the medium. Am I writing for orchestra? Am I writing for piano, or piano and voice? The medium is a frame of reference from which I begin to explore possibilities for musical adventures. Therefore, idiomatic expression of the medium becomes a primary factor. I have enough skill. I've been doing this long enough to know how to approach the process. I have often used a medium or moderate-sized orchestra for practical purposes.

I can say as much as I need to express with an orchestra of strings, with three trumpets, three trombones, tuba, percussion, and woodwinds in pairs. I have also been commissioned to compose for chamber orchestra. Unfortunately, I don't think most orchestras have enough time to rehearse new music. I think that also, even as an administrator, not many words are necessary. Say what you have to say and make your points. An economy of means is one way to express my point of view in composition.

I start thinking about what I am going to do, whether the people that commissioned the piece have something specific in mind. I remember one of the Atlanta Symphony commissions was for mixed chorus and orchestra. Maestro Robert Shaw wanted to know if the composition might include some reference to the African American gospel music tradition. Yes, I told him that was possible. The gospel reference was made by including a jazz trio of drums, bass, and piano, which served like a baroque continuo to underpin what I wrote, strictly in the European orchestral tradition. I wrote idiomatically for the orchestra and for the chorus, because voices have their own personality and nuances. Indeed, if a text is involved, that influences the color of the entire composition. If there is no text involved, I think of the instrumental timbres of the ensemble.

I've written about seventeen spiritual fantasies, because I want to keep the African American spiritual tradition alive. In many of the pieces there is some reference to spirituals or blues in the texture. Sometimes the reference is literal.

I call them "spiritual fantasies" because they can be very abstract as they develop in certain regions of the composition.

A part of my compositional palette includes cultural references to various music traditions of the world. In the 1960s it was less so, but after 1968, when Martin Luther King, Jr., was killed, a broader perspective was invariably expressed. I thought, who am I, anyway? Why am I writing this music that reflects so heavily the European aesthetic, with so little reference to other music idioms and cultures? Now I think of idioms and stylistic techniques as colors and textures. I use those things when I want to get certain kinds of tensions and drama in music I am writing or performing. It is like painting and like poetry.

Q: Do you think that the artist has any particular role in society, particularly today, given the tenor of the times?

A: Yes, I think artists have a particular role in society. If you have a commitment and a dedication to something and gain a reasonable amount of success, along with that success comes a certain amount of influence. An artist should speak his mind on subjects or questions he is asked. In some ways, I don't mix art with politics. But ask me a political question, and I will respond. I don't try to have my art serve that purpose. That is the difference. I want art to communicate the things that it communicates best, and those are things in a spiritual realm, outside of politics. Art has its own ambiance and nuances.

Q: Has your ethnicity served you as a composer, either informing your music or in terms of the way people have appreciated what you are doing as an artist?

A: I don't know how precisely I can deal with that question. I have been at the University of Massachusetts since 1970. I know why I am here and why I was recruited here—to teach music composition and theory. Based upon my portfolio and references, they thought I had sufficient intellectual ability and music craftsmanship to compete with the faculty here. Otherwise, research universities can be pretty brutal, and I would be out of here. The administration of the university believed that I could make a valuable contribution to the diversity of the institution. If I didn't have enough confidence, I would not have come. I don't think that was the question—how much my ethnicity helped me to get a faculty position. It was a combination of two things. One, the fact that there were more than twenty faculty members in the Music Department before they had any blacks suggests that it is not a completely separate issue, but if they had any incentives to bring in a black musician, they wanted to make sure that person was competent. Two, they asked me for scores and examples of my music. I know the political climate in the predominantly white prestigious research institutions. Without special administrative incentives, I wouldn't have been recruited to the institution. In some sense, yes, my ethnicity has something to do with my having an equal opportunity to compete and make a contribution to the university.

Since 1968 I have made a point of making sure that somehow or another, this voice was not another carbon copy of traditional academic music. I have done that; I don't wish to do it any more. How do I inform that attitude? Musically, I have a spiritual reference or melodic or rhythmic elements that reflect other music traditions. I put in program notes that this piece has some Asian influence or that this scale has this or that reference. It is not just African American. I am inspired by many things, including poetry, art, drama, and architecture. Every piece that I have written for orchestra has had, in my own mind, a relationship with the rhythmic genius of the continent of Africa. Sometimes I put it in strings—it doesn't matter. It is implied sometimes in the way the percussion is used. There are different ways. It is what I think is an expression of my own voice, after a period of writing, what I want to project as a composer. It is not hindering my will to continue.

Q: Where do you see American music going?

A: There are some trends that I can observe. Jazz will be still strong in the twenty-first century. There is no question about that, because it is a classical music of America. Travel anywhere in the world and hear it, and you know what country or culture it reflects. That means something. However, jazz and also the European classical tradition both have more serious applications in life. There is jazz that is very popular, but there is some jazz that appeals mostly to people who understand the language and its idiom. Classical jazz is no longer a popular music. It was in the 1930s. It's not a popular music anymore, and the economic barometers are only one of the indicators. European classical music is about 4 to 5 percent of sales of music recordings, and jazz about 4 to 5 percent. The remaining 90 percent of recordings sold is in the vast number of popular music styles. But jazz and European classical music will remain important music in the twenty-first century.

There have been some interesting exchanges and mixtures. Jazz has influenced European classical music considerably. Copland, Stravinsky, and Debussy and scores of contemporary American composers are good examples of that. Many composers have found out that the style of music that was the benchmark in the academy in the 1960s and perhaps the 1970s is no longer the predominant language. In the 1980s many composers began to recognize a sharply dwindling audience for rigidly academic styles of music composition. It is a matter of aesthetic taste, time, and judgment as to why a composer chooses to communicate in a given musical language or style. I made a conscious choice. I am not writing for other composers. In the past, I have done that. Now, I am writing to communicate with a broader and more diverse audience. The young composers who are winning Pulitzer Prizes now are returning to "Neoromanticism" and all sorts of eclectic styles and idioms, because they need to reconnect with a broader audience. This is particularly true for the symphony orchestra, with increased tendencies to perform primarily established masters of the past. This, coupled with very limited time for the rehearsal of new music scores, contributes to a constant erosion of a loyal core of new listeners for the symphonic literature.

Composers have a right to address the issues. One of the most significant ones was the death of Martin Luther King, Jr. One of the best pieces of music that I have ever written is called "Freedom," and it is right out of that. It is almost a stream-of-consciousness work. It was not hard—it just flowed out. I played a recording of the work while I was in Detroit with some students at Cass Technical High School. I asked them what they thought about the piece. They said the work had seriousness in its expression. It is not a spiritual, but there was an intensity about it which was strongly communicated to them. That is fine.

The text of the composition only uses about seventeen words— "freedom," "degradation," "poverty," "anger," etc. I don't know whether earlier I overstated the case by saying politics is not involved. I didn't do "Freedom" for a political reason. I did it as a result of a political assassination that happened, but it was my response, my way of coping and dealing with the shock of that tragedy. I didn't march in the streets, but I wrote the work. It also comes out in my poetry. I have several poems that address political figures. Among them are Malcolm X, Jessie Helms, Clarence Thomas, and Adam Clayton Powell. So it's there through poetry, in an artistic expression.

Whenever I read interesting poems or hear interesting music, I enjoy them. I am beyond the stage where it is an impetus for me to do something. It is just a question of recognition of the intellectual nuances, craftsmanship, the ability of an artist to communicate in whatever the medium may be. That is about the extent of it.

I don't know enough hip-hop to have too strong an opinion about it. I have not heard a lot of it that interested me. I have listened on a few occasions, off and on. The best way for me to really develop and cultivate a taste for hip-hop (because there is so much of it out there) is for me to hear somebody whom I respect as a musician make a reference to a particularly strong performance. Much hip-hop has too much repetition, rhythmic dance elements, and insufficient variety of music content to hold my interest. Some of the text I don't like, particularly those that denigrate women and other respected values of our society. I do recognize that some hip-hop deals with positive texts with useful social messages. So I can't categorically make blanket statements that it shouldn't exist. I think it serves a purpose, incidentally, and it sometimes is useful. However, much of this genre is so commercial; I question its value, and I am certain most of it won't have lasting value—just like much rock music, most of which had little lasting value.

Q: If you had to graph yourself into a line from your first influence, let's say Bach, on up through Ellington, on up to the present, what stream or group of composers would Frederick Tillis graph himself into?

A: Right now I am in the stream of any kind of music that I have heard that is interesting to me. Mine is an international concept; it is not just American. There is no way that international influences will be absent in my music. In so many subtle ways, compositions that I have written have an African influence. Several works that I have written contain a bell motif that I associate with a West African piece that I heard years ago. My influences and inspirations are all over the place. What is challenging for me to do is to combine seemingly disparate music traditions and idioms and still speak in a language that musicians and other listeners find interesting. It is not a severe language, but it can be turned into poetry. Turning music into poetry and vice versa can be both dramatic and lyrical.

My primary influences were from my culture; the marvels of Ellington, Jimmy Lunceford, and Basie were my inspirations. However, many other sources of inspiration spring from diverse cultures of the world. So one of the pieces I have written recently was based on an old folk tune that I heard when traveling in Japan in 1984. I relate to, and enjoy, sounds of supposedly unrelated music styles, traditions, and cultures. I am very enamored of some great classical music of India. I am an internationalist in that sense.

Q: What would be the goal that you want to have as an artist, as a composer, particularly? What impact do you want your music to make in the American canon?

A: I want it to be a music that reflects who I am as an individual voice. This is impossible without some recognition of the cultural and social milieu from which I have come. That is why I use certain themes and write the way that I do. Nobody else is doing it exactly like that. There are some African American composers who do some of that. William Grant Still did that. By the way, you know that William Grant Still studied with Varèse. Why did he not imitate Varèse? He certainly had the intellectual ability, but I think he made a decision to express another ideal. His music reflects who he was and where he came from. That is what I expect my music to do, whether it is heard while I am here or some other time later. Cultural identity and references are important to me.

George Walker

George Walker has long been considered one the leading American composers working today. Born in 1922 in Washington D.C., he earned a B.M. in piano from Oberlin (1945), an artist diploma from Curtis Institute (1945), a piano diploma from the American Conservatory at Fontainebleau, and a doctorate in musical arts from the Eastman School (1957). Dr. Walker began his long, distinguished career as a concert pianist touring the United States and Europe beginning in 1985. Upon his father's suggestion, and with encouragement from Nadia Boulanger, he decided to make a career as a composer and in teaching. Dr. Walker has held posts at the University of Delaware, Dillard, Smith College, Peabody Conservatory, and Rutgers University. In 1996, George Walker received the Pulitzer Prize in composition for his work "Lilacs," making him the first black American to have received the coveted award. In his almost fifty years in American music he has been awarded Fulbright, Guggenheim, Yaddo, and Rockefeller fellowships. Dr. Walker has been performed by many major orchestras throughout the United States and abroad, including the New York Philharmonic, Boston, Detroit, Philadelphia, and Cleveland Orchestras, his most performed work being his well known *Lyric for Strings*. His works can be heard on Columbia and Albany recordings. Dr. Walker's output includes works for orchestra, concerti, song cycles, solo piano pieces, and a variety of chamber combinations from brass quintets to sonati for cello and piano. George Walker currently works and lives in Mt. Clair, New Jersey.

The Pulitzer Prize–winning work *Lilacs*, for voice and orchestra, was commissioned by the Boston Symphony in 1995 after the orchestra had requested scores of my vocal works from my publisher, MMB Music, in St. Louis. The terms of the commission specified that the work should be for tenor and full orchestra, eight minutes in duration. The commissioned work would be performed on a concert honoring the tenor Roland Hayes, who had made his American debut with the Boston Symphony.

Unfortunately, the tenor, Vinson Cole, found the score too demanding. A soprano, Faye Robinson, was selected to sing the solo part. The completed score was virtually twice as long as the contract required. Four stanzas were chosen by me from the Walt Whitman poem "When Lilacs Last in the Dooryard

Bloom'd." The entire poem, which has been set by Hindemith and Sessions, among other, consists of sixteen stanzas. The settings by the aforementioned composers utilize a chorus.

In my setting, there are motifs that recur throughout the work. It is essentially atonal. There is a cyclic aspect to its conclusion. There are three symbols in Whitman's poem—the lilac, the star, and the bird. There is a musical representation for two of them, the lilac and the bird. The vocal part is occasionally melismatic. The large orchestra is employed carefully to avoid, within reason, covering the vocal part.

My first attempts at composition began when I had private lessons with Normand Lockwood at the Oberlin Conservatory of Music. Since the first assignments in writing melodic lines without a text, I have continued to explore the relationship of music to poetry. The independence of the accompaniment that is found in many of Schubert's *lieder* is even more in evidence in my textural settings.

There hardly seems to be sufficient justification for spending as much time as I have in honing the details in a miniature form, the song for voice and piano. The absence of a significant body of American classical songs is, however, a reason to attempt to make a contribution to this genre. There is almost no expectation that singers will be curious to discover works beyond the predictable repertoire that they learn. In fact, it appears that there were more black singers thirty years ago, who sang a few songs by black composers, than the current crop of operatic divas.

It is gratifying to observe that more black composers are having their music recorded on CDs. Optimism is tempered by the realization that record companies have saturated the market with reissues of old recordings while maintaining the high prices of early digital releases. The slump in CD sales, the restrictive use of advertising for new products, and the retrenchment of newspaper and magazine coverage for classical music contribute to the invisibility of releases. There does not seem to be any solution in sight to this dilemma. When the president of Sony Classical Records and his underlings state that the only viable music is the music that "sells," Western culture is perilously close to extinction.

This myopic rhetoric is not the only factor in an unbalanced equation. There are, of course, the philistines in government, elected federal and state employees. There are the concert reviewers, writing their fictionalized and woefully ignorant accounts in the major dailies in this country. One would be hard pressed to find anything as asinine as a statement made by a professor of Catholic University, Glenn Dillard Gunn, in a review that appeared fifty years ago in the *Washington Times-Herald.* He referred to Schubert and Schumann as "lesser lights of the nineteenth century. As composers for the piano either of these heroes of German romanticism may be described as an amateur and lacking in those technical skills that make the expert." In comparison to that insightful comment, any observation about a contemporary score may well seem less egregious. Certain well-known mavens, nevertheless, have managed to illuminate their intellectual deficiencies.

Harold C. Schoenberg, a piano guru writing in the *New York Times* about my *Piano Concerto,* stated, "It never made up its mind where it was going to." One doesn't expect such an exhibition of a limited attention span from even a modestly endowed critic, especially since my program notes clearly discussed the formal structure of the work. More recently, Donald Rosenberg of the *Cleveland Plain Dealer,* in a highly controversial and jaundiced review, had the audacity to demean a superb performance of my *Poeme for Violin and Orchestra,* by my son, Gregory Walker. This is a work that has been rapturously received since its premiere in 1984.

Contemporary classical music needs advocates, not detractors who intentionally seek to subvert and undermine the progress that has been made in creating awareness of the high standards of musical excellence that can be found in different stratas of the world culture. In New Jersey, Michael Redmond and Paul Somers *(Newark Star-Ledger),* offer a sharp contrast in style and content to some of the more readily identifiable names.

The works of black composers whose music is not overtly jazz oriented or does not conjure up in its title some exotic connection to Africa do not conform to the ideas held by many whites, both musically literate and musically illiterate, about what is unique or individual. There is often a hostility—no longer latent but frequently expressed—as to what is viewed as an encroachment on musical territory that has been regarded as the highest expression of emotional and intellectual achievement, Western music. White composers are admired for the nuggets that they extract and exploit from black ghettos. When black composers distill the oftimes doctrinaire techniques of twentieth-century icons, their music is labeled derivative. When there are critics who still idolize the Beatles (shades of their adolescent years), or who feel that the crudities of rock musicals offer a salutary example for contemporary symphonic music, or who are galvanized by the mindless and countless repetitions in the music of Phillip Glass and similar minimalists, a new tribalism has emerged.

It is still incumbent upon black music students in colleges and conservatories to discover and perform the music of black composers. One cannot expect white and Asian students as a group to have the same vested interest in this music. Several years ago, a black student at the Juilliard School of Music (which has never had a black instructor in its major instrumental or theory studies program) had to inform the president, Joseph Polisi, that the music library had virtually no scores by black composers. This is a sad commentary on the leadership and perspective of an institution that had attracted so many black students for so many years.

Fifty years ago, it would have been impossible to predict that there would be a score of well-trained black conductors who had had the opportunity of conducting community ensembles, metropolitan as well as major orchestras. Some of these orchestras, those of Philadelphia, Chicago, Boston, and Los Angeles, are still swathed in a nineteenth-century perspective. Their music administrators, myopic and market oriented, perpetuate the elitism for which they are known. It is hard to fault their foreign-born conductors without some qualification, but American-born conductors are guilty of neglect.

Forty years ago, when Eileen Southern's epoch-making book *The Music of Black Americans* appeared, I wrote in a review for the *Music Educator's Journal* that I hoped that this work would serve as a basis for detailed studies of the material. This has not happened for the classical composers. What are the recent graduates with doctorates in theory and history doing to illuminate the complexities of black classical music? The cataloguing of composers hitherto unknown is commendable, up to a point. But what is needed is scholarship analyzing and comprehending works in far greater detail than a cursory summary permits. This complaint can, of course, be lodged at white historians as well. The popularity of certain works of Aaron Copland continues to be reinforced by weekly broadcasts of his music on FM radio. No one risks a criticism of his simplistic style, the stultifying repetitions, or the annoying use of the unresolved leading tone. (Nadia Boulanger would not in principle have approved of this. But who can quibble with success?) The flabby proportions of Mahler symphonies or the lack of any distinguishing melodic or harmonic interest in the symphonies of Bruckner are never scrutinized, either. The Tin Pan Alley aspects in Leonard Bernstein's music are accepted as manifestations of New York machismo. Myths are created out of the necessity to establish a hierarchy. As Americans, we are not different from the French, the Viennese, or the Greeks.

3

The Arrived and the Acknowledged, Part 2 (1937–1945)

Adolphus Hailstork

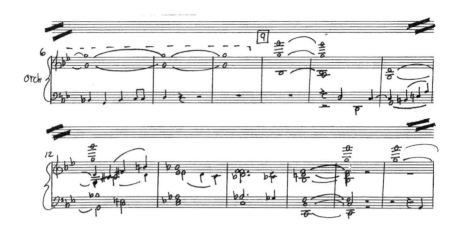

Adolphus Hailstork, born 1941, has established himself as one of the most performed composers of his generation, having had works performed by the New York, Virginia, Louisville, Richmond, Baltimore, Phoenix, Rochester, Detroit, Roanoke, and Savannah Symphonies and dozens of leading choral and chamber organizations around the country. His works include symphonies, cantatas, operas, and chamber and choral works of numerous combinations. A commission by a five-orchestra consortium led to a piano concerto that was premiered by Leon Bates in 1992. His *Celebration: An Overture for Orchestra, Done Made My Vow,* and *American Port of Call* remain among his most requested works. His symphonic and choral works have been recorded by several labels, including Columbia and Albany Records. Dr. Hailstork is presently teaching and a professor of music and eminent scholar at Old Dominion University. His studies include work with Mark Fax, Nadia Boulanger (at the American Institute at Fontainebleau), and David Diamond. Dr. Hailstork received his undergraduate degree from Howard University, a master's in music from the Manhattan School of Music, and a Ph.D. from Michigan State University. His awards and commissions include the Ernest Bloch Award, Belwin-Mills/Max Winkler, Boys Choir of Harlem, and the Barlow Endowment of Music. Dr. Hailstork was proclaimed a cultural laureate of the state of Virginia, where he works and resides.

My first instrument was the violin. After that, in junior high school, I became involved in the choir. Before that I had already joined a cathedral choir. Truly one of the most important influences was the Episcopal Cathedral of All Saints in Albany, New York. The cathedral choir and the public school system were the most important influences in my early life.

I stayed in the choir until I got out of high school, and I went from being a treble to being a bass. I then went to Howard University for college, and that was another major influence, because after that I became very intimately exposed to the black music traditions. Then I went on to the Manhattan School of Music. I was conscious of being a composer in 1956, when I was fifteen years old. By the time I entered high school, I had done everything. I had sung in

choirs, I had played in a junior high school orchestra, I had taken piano lessons and organ lessons, and I had conducted the choir at both the cathedral and in junior high. The only thing I hadn't tried was composition, and so I decided to do that. I enjoyed it, so I stayed with it.

I just liked classical music. That is what I wanted to do, but I didn't know any composers. When I was coming along, Stravinsky, Aaron Copland, and Samuel Barber were big names; everyone knew those three composers. Samuel Barber was big. Leonard Bernstein was the rage when I was coming along. I certainly liked their music more than most of the stuff I heard by Schoenberg. Serialism had become dominant, and everyone was into that. Another one was Paul Hindemith. But I liked the American School. That's looking at the classical side. But in our home we had the blues, rhythm and blues, Duke Ellington, Count Basie, and all those guys. There was the whole black side, which was not classical but was also important.

I can't really say that Howard discouraged gospel music, but they encouraged the great classics like Beethoven's *Ninth,* Carl Orff's *Carmina Burana,* Giuseppe Verdi, and the Brahms' *Requiem.* There was none of the black consciousness thing. There were no required courses in black music or black history—there was no such animal at that time. Eileen Southern had not written her book. And certainly there was no ethnomusicology or the study of African music. At Howard University they didn't have a composition major, but they did have a theory major. I studied with Mark Fax from 1959 to 1963. Then I studied at the Manhattan School of Music from 1963 to 1966, two years in the army, 1966–68, and then worked on my doctorate from 1968 to '71 at Michigan State University.

During the summer of 1963, I studied with Nadia Boulanger. She was very nice and a fascinating person. It was very exciting to see the high intensity and the high level of excellence she insisted upon. But I wasn't overly awed, because they insisted on a high level at Howard also. The Howard program was very interesting, because its theory program was modeled after the European model, complete with fixed "do." So when I arrived in France, it seemed very familiar. All this was prior to the black revolution.

Howard taught the classics. It was very European oriented. At the time, they didn't have any gospel. It was frowned upon. We were told not to play any gospel music in the practice rooms. I got my first job in Youngstown, Ohio, stayed there for six years, then I came to Norfolk State University, and I've been here for twenty years.

I think I became more actively racially conscious after I got out of the army. With the death of Dr. Martin Luther King, I became very sensitized to all this, and in fact that influenced my decision to get a doctorate. All the newspaper articles were calling him Dr. King—and here I was with a master's degree in music and not having the slightest idea what I was going to do for a living. I then decided to get my doctorate at Michigan State.

I just enjoy music. I leave all the deep thinking to people who want to write books. I prefer to write music, and I'm a pragmatist. I write music to get performed. I don't write esoteric, ivory-tower stuff to be played by a few people in a loft for an audience of a few people. That's just not me. If I'm anything, I'm a populist. But so was Verdi. I don't mind that. I've never liked the "off the wall" school of music composition that doesn't communicate with people. I've never been a great fan of Elliot Carter. That's all there is to it.

I just sing. My whole fundamental approach to music is lyrical, because I came up as a singer. I've been in choral music for forty-six years. The vocal line, the singing line, is absolutely fundamental to my artistry.

As far as my process is concerned, I begin looking for materials from goo-gobs of themes. I've got a couple of boxes filled with ideas that were outtakes from other compositions or ideas that were not ready to be used yet. So I just start growing new works from there. I have a very organic approach to it. I take a cell and grow a composition from the cell. That's what I do.

About Black History Month programs, I've got a couple of feelings about them. It's worked for me. I get played now twelve months out of the year, so rather than calling January and February "ghetto months," I call them "show-case months." For two months of the year, we get to showcase our works, and if some conductor begins to champion them, they will take these works to other orchestras during other months of the year, and from that your performance base grows and grows. It's a good opening, and it's practical, considering the fact that we are a minority of a minority. I mean, there are not that many classical composers in the world. There are certainly not that many of us, and we need the opportunities. There's no harm in writing something relating to black culture. Since that is the two months that orchestras do programming with an eye toward black people coming into the hall, that's a time we black composers can write something for our people to relate to. It didn't hurt Bach to use German chorales or Haydn to use German folk dances. Cultural nationalism has existed throughout history, and some of the strongest music grows out of that. So when someone writes things for a particular constituency, wonderful things can happen that transcend any particular month.

When we listen to the *German Requiem,* we don't say, "Well, the *German Requiem* should only be played in Germany." We say, "Oh boy, there's the Brahms' *Requiem.*" But Brahms was thinking about writing a work for German people. Writing a work for national interests does not necessarily have to be limited only to it. The only thing that bothers me about the January–February thing is that orchestras are starting to do this on the cheap. They ask black conductors to do this one rehearsal, a potpourri of little bits of this and that, instead of presenting a substantial composition. This is a dangerous trend.

I think there are a hell of a lot of things in traditional black music that are exciting. I just listened to a couple of new recordings by Sweet Honey in the Rock. That stuff, that folk, black-flavored stuff drives me crazy. I love it! Its earthiness, its directness, its rhythmic and harmonic power is great stuff. Now when we use the word "great" in classical music, we usually mean monumental. You get into some grand thing like Beethoven's *Ninth* or Sibelius's *Second.* One has to ask how many of our works have been used in a monumental, big-form way. I've always been interested in creating an amalgam between European structural principles and African American rhythmic and melodic materials.

I think we as composers have more of a role to play in society than the people who only write for the ivory tower. The ivory-tower people think their job is absolutely to challenge. But this challenging only brings people into a back room somewhere. Then there are other people, like Henryk Gorecki, who think we have to do something to reflect the spiritual depth of human people.

We've got a bunch of different roles that composers can assume. For the past twenty years I've wanted to use African American materials in monumental ways for our people, because I wanted our people to have a reason to go to the concert hall. I used to say, "African American culture does not have to stop at the doors of the symphony hall." I thought it would be a good idea for me to create works in which black people listening to it would hear something of their own musical experience reflected. They could still say, "Hey, I've heard that lick in church before. There is something there that is a reflection of my experience as a black person in this country." Now, that's cultural nationalism. For quite a few years, I used to advocate that. Now, I'm into more of a world-music thing, because that's the future.

I don't know much about rap. I have not been following pop music for several years. I'm really not into it. I hear little bits of it as I flip the dial. I'm into concert hall music. That's what I do.

I was taught nothing about black classical composers. Nothing! Nothing! There's been a very big hole, and that's what I've been interested in filling. I don't think there is a black repertoire. What I'm thinking about is the monumental types of concert works—piano sonatas, chamber works, and symphonies. We still have all of that to fill in. That's why I do not think it was wise to go chasing after the majority culture as they went into twelve-tone oblivion and all their pounding on the piano, the screeching-and-scratching approach to making music—especially since we hadn't developed our own repertoire. Instead of spitting or sneering at the nineteenth-century achievements, we need to create our own repertoire.

We need to create our own repertoire, and after we've created our sonatas, tone poems, symphonies, and whatever else we may invent, then perhaps we'll be called old fogies, but we would have created a black canon. I want to help establish a black canon, so that after I have gone away, I would have left a few symphonies, piano sonatas that black and white conductors will want to do. And they will say, "Hey, this is great music." But there will be a hint of African American experience in it. You see, we were left out of the American school of composition in the twenties, or forties of Copland, and all that, we were left out of it. Now, it's our time to make our own impact and to add to the American repertoire, and that should include us.

The black masses will probably never be crazy about concert music. But I believe there will be more for us one day. They will say, "Oh, they're playing a piece by Bill Banfield tonight. That man writes music I can really appreciate." Then there will be more black faces in the audience, and that's what I hope for.

I like pluralism. I hope it never happens that there will be one dominant aesthetic again where someone holds a gun to your head and says, "Thou must write this or else we will ignore you." Well, I say the heck with that! American composers are independent enough to say, "There are enough outlets for everybody's music. No one or two people in New York City can hold a gun to the rest of the country." When I was a student, it used to be that way. You can have a fine career being played all over the country, even if the New York critics are not standing on their hands and doing cartwheels for you. I don't believe in genuflecting in the direction of New York every day. The thing that's wonderful about what's going on is that anybody can write the way they want to write. And the critics are finally wising up to evaluating a piece, whether or not it's the latest thing. I was shocked that there could be something that was called "postmodern." I always thought "modern" already meant the latest thing. Now they've come up with postmodern. We were all sniffing after the hind parts of Krzysztov Pendereski when I was working on my doctorate. Then, he turns around and writes a symphony that sounds like Dvorak. That's when I'd made up my mind that I wasn't going to follow after anybody. What I believe in is called "authenticity." That is, I've got brains, ears, viscera, and I'm going to blend everything I've got together to create music that I want to hear. It's going to be authentically me.

I call my work "evolving." I found a term in the *New York Times* used to describe the work of James Macmillan, a hot Scottish composer. They said he was a "postmodern pluralist." That's a nice way of saying he's an eclectic. My work is always lyrical, always tonal, it sings. I can't help it. Singing is to me as natural as anything.

The line to me is a new Americanism, harking back to the early forties based on folk patterns of the African American. It's like, I want to rewrite that period of time and be a participant in it. I go along with the folk composers, like the whole Slavic school, Dvorak, Bartók. Anybody's music that is based on the folk element, I'm a fan of. That's probably why I love Sibelius. Sibelius wrote these great tone poems and great symphonies, but his melodic materials were very folksy. I've always liked that.

I'd like to leave a life's work that would still be performed. I don't think that's so hard any more, because there are so many recordings. It's especially possible now, because we are turning out so many great black virtuosos from the University of Michigan, Julliard, and Curtis. But these kids are coming up now saying, "I've got all this fabulous ability as a pianist, a violinist, a singer, so, where are the black composers?" That's what I began to see, and that's one of the reasons I decided to become a composer.

The more we're in the public eye, the better its going to be for everybody. I happen to think we have seen the last bastion of the country club mentality. We need to get our faces out there.

Wendell Logan

Wendell Logan, currently chairman of the Department of Jazz Studies at the Oberlin Conservatory, is another example of the varied collection of composers working successfully and comfortably in multiple camps. Born in 1940, he was educated at Florida A&M University, the American Conservatory, Southern Illinois University, and the University of Iowa. He is a composer whose works consistently reveal an equal interest in both written and improvised idioms. Dr. Logan works in a variety of mediums ranging from jazz to electronic, to symphony orchestras. His works have been performed by a diverse collection of ensembles reflecting these varied interests, including Boston Musica Viva, the Black Music Repertoire Ensemble, the St. Louis Symphony, the Thamyris New Music Ensemble, the Dallas Symphony, the Center for New Music/University of Iowa, and the Cleveland Chamber Symphony. His best-known work, *Runagate,* has received critical acclaim and was featured in Samuel Floyd's *The Power of Black Music.* Recordings of his work can be found on the Orion, Golden Crest, and Argo labels. Dr. Logan has received awards, from the National Endowment of the Arts, the Endowment of Humanities, ASCAP, the Martha Baird Rockefeller Fund, the Simon Guggenheim Foundation, and the Meet the Composers/*Reader's Digest* Fund. He currently lives and works in Oberlin, Ohio.

Is it a myth that black people have made significant contributions in American music? No, it is not a myth. That is factual. In terms of so-called vernacular music, the evidence is there, beginning with the blues, going through jazz, in religious music. It is everywhere, in terms of our contributions. I would go so far as to say there probably wouldn't be any real identifiable—from a world perspective—American music if it weren't for black music. In so-called concert music, that becomes a little bit more difficult to say. I think what we can do is look at the careers. This is probably going to happen many years from now, after the fact, and this is probably for theorists or analysts to do, of course, not the composers themselves, because perhaps we are too close to what we do. But someone needs to take a real, objective look and see what things black compos-

ers do creatively, in terms of concert music, that has an identifiable stamp. Maybe that will take years for someone to do that. I see various brothers doing things that nobody else does—that is, looking at the European art form and then molding it into something that is unique.

I am from Thompson, Georgia, which is between Atlanta and Augusta, probably closer to the South Carolina border. Obviously, we didn't have symphony orchestras and that type of thing at our disposal. Even if they had them there, I wouldn't have been able to hear them, and certainly not participate in them. I would say my evolution began in terms of rhythm and blues, the music that was around me. I certainly heard James Brown as a kid. My dad owned a community center, and all kinds of acts came through there, people like Fats Domino. I didn't know that at the time. None of these guys had any national reputation then—Little Richard, James Brown, the Jimmy Liggins band. These were the kinds of groups that came through there. The area was very rich in that type of music. I heard it and tried to play it. We sat in with those groups. Of course, my dad was a musician by avocation, not by vocation. My parents were both educators, and my father started a band there in the public schools. In fact, we had a band before the white school did, and I am always fond of saying that. We did have a band, and that is where my interest began.

At the age of eleven I started on trumpet. Then I started playing all the instruments; I learned something about all of them. I wanted to write very early. We would go to music stores, Snyder Music Store in Augusta, Georgia, and I would see various books. There would be transcriptions of Dizzie Gillespie solos. Be-bop was, of course, the reigning music then; the first thing I noticed about it was that it was rhythmically difficult and certainly more harmonically complex than other things I had heard. I realized these things right off.

Jimmy Liggin's band played there. They said they were from Los Angeles. They had arrangements, they had things like "Stardust" in their book and all that, and they let me play with them. I said, "Hey, I know that tune, 'Stardust.'" I told them that I played, and I went over and heard the pianist playing. He was playing these chords I had never heard before. I said, "What kind of chord is that?" He said, "That's a thirteenth chord." I said, "What's a thirteenth chord?" He told me what a thirteenth chord was—not that it helped but at least he explained it to me—and I asked him where he learned about thirteenth chords. He told me at the conservatory; I said, "What's a conservatory?" And it went from there.

I had an aunt who talked about Lester Young. She said he was from Mississippi, where my folks are originally from. Well, I didn't know where Lester Young was from, and I didn't even know who he was. But my aunt loved Lester Young, and I just remembered that name. I went into the record shop, which was right across the street from Snyder Record Shop in Augusta. I started looking around, and I saw this record, it was Lester Young. I also saw Dizzie Gillespie and Charlie Parker. What made me buy Charlie Parker and Dizzie Gillespie records I have no idea, but I bought all of them anyway. I remember I bought four records. The fourth one was Earl Bostick, the alto saxophonist from New Orleans. I even remember some of the tunes—"That's Earl's Brother," and things like that. I heard that kind of stuff and realized right off that that wasn't represented where I lived. I had to definitely leave there to learn something about this music. Also, in terms of books, I've mentioned things like transcriptions of

Dizzie Gillespie solos. There was also a book there by Spud Murphy about arranging. I remember having my dad buy that book for me. I started reading the book—you know, no theoretical studies, but you start to notice certain kinds of things, like how chords are constructed. I got as much material as I could and tried to do some writing for our school band, things like "You Ain't Nothin' but a Hound Dog." That is where it all started, at eleven years old, and I knew what I wanted to do with music. I knew right then, so high school was a continuation and confirmation of what I knew at eleven.

In high school I was a pretty good athlete. I got an athletic scholarship to Florida A&M, which at that time was a feat in itself, because A&M was a football powerhouse in terms of black schools. I went there, and of course I majored in music, which was considered to be unusual.

At that time, though, Florida A&M had some very good musicians. Olly Wilson was there for a couple of years of my education. There was a guy by the name of Lynn Bowden there who had been director of the Main Event in the Great Lakes Navy Band. There was a guy by the name of Bruce Hayden, who was a hell of a string player. There was also a lady by the name of Johnnie B. Lee; anybody my age and older and went to Florida A&M and did anything in music can tell you about her. James Lattimer who is a percussionist who teaches now in Madison, Wisconsin, was there, and Charlie Cox. We had some of the best black musicians in the country teaching there, simply because they couldn't teach anywhere else. The other interesting thing was that all of them still played jazz. Olly did only a little playing, but all of them played. We saw them operating in the clubs and on the concert stage. There was no distinction between classical and jazz. You just didn't hear that. You heard it only in the contexts. Something I remember Charlie Cox saying, "This is what Ravel and Debussy are doing, and it is closely related to our music." You heard those kinds of things, but there was no comparative sense, like, this is better than that, or this is more difficult than that. You just didn't have those kinds of things happening, and I am grateful for that to this day. They all respected the African American tradition. All of them participated in it in some way. They also knew a great deal about the Euro-American tradition.

I went from college to work for a year at Florida A&M, and then I went on to graduate school, because that was what a lot of my teachers did. But that was not what I had planned to do. What I wanted to do was go on the road for a while and play, because I definitely played at that time. The other thing I wanted was to do studio work, movie work, and that kind of thing. Oliver Nelson and Quincy Jones were certainly idols for the studio work that they were doing. That was the kind of thing that I was interested in. I pursued the education. It was going to school then working for a year, then going back to school, working, and then going to school. This is what I ended up doing, because I became more interested in composition. Then I started thinking about options in terms of composition, and it seems this is where we composers congregate, in schools. Obviously schools have the best resources for a lot of performances, because you have all of these players at these institutions; you can hear anything you write. It is a way of making an honorable living, without starving.

People didn't make jazz and European music a struggle for me, because I didn't let them, although they talked about it. They denigrated the jazz. Some of the things they had to say were absolutely ridiculous—not all of the teachers

I had, but most of them. The teacher I had at Iowa (Richard Hervig) certainly didn't. I remember him once saying, "You have a lot of resources that you can draw from and you should do that." I didn't know what he meant; I didn't pay very much attention to it. Later on, probably a couple of years or so, I had a chance to stand back and think, and what he said had just stuck with me. I decided he was right.

I don't remember formally studying composition with Olly Wilson, but we talked a lot. He gave me insight into things, and he also was writing music. I have been told by Sam Floyd that there is a book out, *Stepping the Blues* or something like that, that has to do with black dance. The book, he tells me, talks about the Florida A&M band and about our girl there, Beverly Hillsman, who was a choreographer and a dancer. She had a dance group there. Olly did two pieces for them; one of the pieces was "The Hunt," on which I played cello. The thing I remember about that piece was that it was very contemporary and had mixed meters, something we were not accustomed to playing. I remember asking him, "Did you write the music and re-bar it later?" He said, "No, I wrote all of that and the meters were there at the time." I said, "Well, how did you do that?" He said, "That is the way I heard it." We would talk about things like that. We talked a lot about things like how to get music reproduced. He told me places where you could get it done. There were these kinds of questions. We talked about the twelve-tone procedure. It was a very informal kind of thing, looking at scores. He looked at some of the things I did and heard some of them. I wrote for that same group, things for brass quintet and that kind of stuff. He heard what I did, and I got encouragement from him, as well as from other people.

I studied composition there with Mrs. Lee, the lady I talked about before. I remember talking to Mrs. Lee about the twelve-tone idiom. She had given me a book, and I started studying. I remember she would also give me scores. She gave me a lot of books and a lot of scores. She gave me a score to one of Stravinsky's ballets, the *Firebird Suite*. Listening to that and listening to the score, it just blew my mind that someone could comprehend something that complex. This was the start.

Music does a hell of a lot for me, but I don't have any philosophy about it. Music operates as a part of who I am; people say they can listen to pieces and tell that. I don't know what they mean by that; I don't have any philosophy. I do think that music is a way of interpreting life experiences. I think that for me that is what it is about. In some way music is something that reflects life experiences; you are in it, you have learned all these techniques, and then you just do it. I can't say any more than that. Certainly you know something about form, you know something about process, and all that. But in terms of philosophy, I don't know.

I really don't know the process I go through when I sit down to create music. My usual answer is that I am not sure that I even want to know. I don't know how I begin a piece, I just go there. Each piece has its own kind of vernacular. When you are writing for a woodwind quintet, you start asking yourself certain questions like, "What is it for? Who is it for?" It has to do with the players, whether you are writing for high school groups or professional players. Do you know something about the players? If you do, then you know something about the way they play, some of their strengths, some of the things that they do that are unique. You have some idea about the duration of it, these kinds of things.

This is a process that is both away from the keyboard and at the keyboard, probably about equally. Many times I stay away from the keyboard, because that slows you down. I do a lot of sketching, and then sometimes I will go back and put the details in at the keyboard. The sketches are musical, we did learn how to do that. The pitches are pretty accurate, but sometimes it is hard to hear vertical things, particularly in terms of this language. It is not about triadic harmony; that is a little bit easier. But when you start talking about the harmonic language that we are dealing with, that becomes a little bit more difficult in terms of the vertical things. The melodic things, you deal with those. In terms of process, people talk about things like twelve-tone. No, I don't deal with any system like twelve-tone. Do I know about it, have I done it? Yes, I can do that. I do work with cells, with pitch cells, trichords, tetrachords, and even scalar kinds of things. I would say it is primarily about the combination of various kinds of trichords, three-note kind of cells. That is how I deal with the pitch, and that allows me a lot of freedom when putting those things together. Some of it comes out sounding twelve-tone-ish and all of that, but there is no "tone row" [from twelve-tone theory] there. I don't have a matrix written out dictating that E-flat should follow D, and so forth; that is a little bit too restrictive. I have done that, but writing is not about that at all.

It is a very difficult to decide whether or not there is a way to define black music, or black art, or black creative activity. I know everybody is looking for an answer to it. I would like to just immediately say yes, but then I have to give some particulars. Getting back to the statement I made before about music being an interpretation, or reflection, of life experiences, we have to be true to the culture, that is, black culture—but what is black culture? That means knowing something about the blues, knowing something about the real church music, long-meter hymns and those kinds of things. We are talking in an artistic sense—how Charlie Parker's blues are different from Muddy Waters's. It is all about the same thing, but one is a city expression and the other is a country expression. It is knowing about and being close to that tradition, closer in the sense of really understanding it and respecting it. A lot of us have heard the term, and some of us aspire to get as far as we can away from that tradition. I don't. Does that make me better than anyone else? No, it doesn't. I am just simply saying that blues is a tradition that I truly respect, and, I hope, understand something about it.

Those traditions certainly influence my work in terms of feeling, sound, and, first of all, attitude. The blues for me is about everything. It means that you have got everything at your disposal. In fact, I consider myself to be a blues musician, that is what I am.

We are dealing with a different group of musicians right now, and I see it as a positive thing. I don't agree with everything that I see, but as I told Hale Smith, I've always heard this phrase that youth is right. I told him that I really don't understand that. He said, "It probably has something to do with the fact that there is nothing we can do about what they do anyway." In that sense I don't agree with some of the choices that they make, but they are certainly supertalented. They are sharp as hell. They have all kinds of things at their disposal. I told a kid once, "You guys should be farther ahead than you are, you should be doing all kinds of things, because you have so much more information than we had." They have scores; we didn't have scores, we had to go transcribe stuff. If you scratched up the records, you went back and bought another record, and they were expensive. We didn't have tape recorders, so we had to develop our ears and hear this stuff. He said, "Yes, but that is our problem. We have too much information at our disposal. The problem is knowing what to assimilate and what not to." I said, "You know, you have got a point and I never really thought about it like that." In any event, they are making different choices, and they are doing different things, but there are some talented youngsters out there, no question about it.

I have to listen to and study contemporary music, like hard-core rap. In terms of education you have to know what is going on, and I have to just for my own information. The attitude I like very much, but some of the language I find simply horrifying. The whole emphasis on hedonism and violence I cannot condone, but some of it I genuinely like, and I see possibilities for where it can be employed—not so much in terms of language but of the rhythmic things and using those things as an envelope where some other things can happen.

Black History Month is our busiest month. If you aren't working during that time then you don't have anything going for you. It's funny. We laugh. Obviously I wish that it were other than that, but I'll take that if the choice is Black History Month or nothing. Sure, I feel as if being solicited during this time is ghettoizing and minimizing, but it could be worse than that. I see it as an opportunity to knock the hell out of them. That is the thing. If you can just try to use that as a stepping-stone for something else. Right now I am going to put a positive spin on it and say if that is the choice we have, fine, but I am not going to sit back and fret about that either.

As I said, I was not taught about a lot of black composers. I was told that William Grant Still was an arranger, which he was, but he was also a hell of a composer. The others I came to on my own, because I started searching. I was thinking that there had to be other guys, and this is when I came upon people like Howard Swanson. I would just go to the library; every week I would be in there, just listening to all kinds of stuff, listening, trying to get scores, and checking things out. I came upon Howard Swanson pretty early on. I also came upon Hale Smith early on. Of course I knew about William Grant Still, I knew about Olly Wilson, and over at Tuskegee there was William Dawson.

In 1969 they had that famous conference at Indiana University ["Black Music in College and University Curricula," June 18–21 1969], and this is when a lot of things just opened up. There were a lot of composers there, and certainly that was an opportunity. I got a chance to meet William Grant Still, Hale Smith, a lot of people. By that time David Baker's name had come by me, and I knew who he was. And of course, he knew about guys like Quincy Jones and Oliver Nelson. Oliver Nelson I had learned about through talking with Olly. Both of them had studied composition at Washington University. They were there together. I found out that he did not only do so-called jazz stuff but he was also a very good composer of so-called concert works. That is where I started to pick up a few names and started talking with people, and then they would talk about other people. After a while I built a wider vocabulary and knowledge of black composers.

Some of the things black composers do are distinctive from what our white counterparts are doing. One of the first pieces I heard of Hale Smith's was *Contours,* for orchestra. To discern how he uses a twelve-tone row, there are some things that you have to see. In the middle of that piece there is a ostinato figure, and you get a kind of layering of rhythms. That suggested something to me—it was the same thing that happens in African music. The heavy use of the wind instruments that black composers are into is very distinctive. I can talk about Hale Smith and Olly Wilson and specific pieces in which you hear musical ideas that are specific to them. I can listen to some of their music without knowing what the piece is, I can tell who the composer is; that has happened on many occasions. That is not to say that I can always tell if the composer is black or not. Not at all—it depends upon what the piece is and upon its subject matter. If I hear that part in David Baker's piece, "now that he is safely dead," I start listening to the text. I would say, "Hey, why would white composers be writing with that attitude and use that particular text?" This tells me something in terms of who the composer probably is, and the probable ethnicity of the composer. It is like when people talk about spirituals; George Pullin Jackson says that spirituals are based on white hymns, but I ask, Why should white folks be singing things about "'sometimes I feel like a motherless child'?" I mean, come on. Just looking at the text and the subject matter tells you something. But getting back to abstract music, no, you can't do that all the time. A lot of times you just can't.

I can't describe my own music. I'm too close to it, and it is something I don't even stop to think about. I don't even try to connect my work with other composers, I just try to do the best that I possibly can in terms of making a musical statement. If it hits the mark, fine. If it misses the mark, maybe the next one is going to be better. I listen to my work and say that there are some things that are attractive but there are also some things I think can be improved. So none of them have really hit the mark. It's often painful to listen to my own work. I would say there are times when I hear something and decided I like certain things, certain licks, etc., that I can extend and use in other ways. This is what leads to something called style. Other than that, this stuff about hitting the mark doesn't work for me.

Let me tell you, this is the honest to God truth, I wrote *Runagate* [chamber symphony, 1990] and started to tear the damn thing up. I had finished the piece, it sat around, and I said, "Damn, what was that about?" I worked on it for a summer, put it down and forgot about it. I said, "Okay, that is that." It was only later on that I went back and said, "This is a piece that I can keep." That is what happened in terms of that particular piece. There are some things that I find attractive about it, but I am not going to sit down and claim that they are. Don't get me wrong, there are some things I find attractive about *Runagate,* and probably a couple of other pieces, but again there are some things that I know can be improved about the piece. I have an orchestral version of that piece, too. Bill Brown swears that the orchestral version is better than the other, but there are some balance problems I hear; I am not going to go back and correct them, but I know they are there. That is something I don't do, I don't go back. That's history; I go to the next thing, the next project. But I know that they are there. I chalk these things up to learning experiences that will be helpful in the future. It is that kind of thing. There are some things about it that are attractive.

There are things that I have done when I have said, "Oh, that works."

Dorothy Rudd Moore

Dorothy Rudd Moore remains one of the most prominent of the woman composers of color of her generation, having had symphonic works commissioned and premiered by the National Symphony, Opera Ebony, Buffalo Philharmonic, and throughout the United States, Europe, and Asia. Born in 1940, she received her bachelor of music from Howard University, with studies in composition with Mark Fax, and further studies with Nadia Boulanger at the American Conservatory at Fontainebleau, as well as with Chou Wen Chung at Columbia University. Ms. Moore has taught at the Harlem School of the Arts, New York University, and Bronx Community College. Along with her noted husband, the conductor and cellist/composer Kermit Moore, and others, she founded the important Society of Black Composers in 1968. She has been awarded fellowships and commissions from Meet the Composer, the American Music Center, as well as the New York State Council on the Arts. Ms. Moore has written symphonies, operas, and an impressive array of chamber combinations from string quartets, wind ensembles, and piano, cello and voice works to pieces for solo cello. Ms. Moore has for many years been a teacher and musical figure in New York concert circles. She has been called by the *New York Times* "a gifted and creative mind at work." She lives and works in New York City.

During the summer of 1963, I had private lessons with Nadia Boulanger in Fontainebleau. She had come to the States in 1962 during a tour here. I heard her speak, I think it was at the State Department Auditorium. That was when I first saw her, and I was very impressed. I was later awarded a Lucy Moten Fellowship from Howard, which I could use any way that I wanted. It wasn't that much money, my parents had to add to it, but I used that to go study with her. Of course, I had to apply and be accepted. I was lucky.

A lot of people say they studied with Nadia Boulanger, but they didn't study with her privately. She could only take so many composition students, and I was lucky enough to be one of her private students. She was very, very helpful. She looked at the music I had written, including my *Symphony Number One,* and she looked at my *Songs from The Rubaiyat,* which was for mezzo-soprano and oboe, no piano. She liked them. We had student concerts, and we also had regular concerts in the evening. She had the proctor come and tell me

that she wanted my songs done on an evening concert, which was quite an honor. *Songs* is a setting of twelve quatrains, and she said she wanted to do six of them. I told the proctor that he had to tell Mademoiselle that we had to do the entire work, or we couldn't do it at all. He took that message back, and she agreed. I had gone to a lot of trouble to choose twelve quatrains out of 103 from *The Rubaiyat.* They did the whole thing, and it was quite successful. Then I had a form and analysis class with her where she would play through compositions and discuss them, works of the masters. I was also in her madrigal choir, which was wonderful. She chose only about twenty some people for that choir. Of course, we had to audition for it, we gave concerts. Her sense of pitch and everything was so pristine that she wouldn't let us utter a tone until we were all perfectly tuned. That was a great experience.

She was very nice to me. She could be quite demanding sometimes, but I got along with her very well. She dealt with my music as music. She treated me as a human being who had come over to study with her, and she treated me with respect. She didn't put any racial or national tinge on it at all. When I went over to study with her, I didn't know who else had been to study with her. I had no idea.

When I went to the American Conservatory in Fontainebleau, all I knew about it was that it was an American Conservatory. I didn't yet know that Aaron Copland had been there, I really knew none of that. All I knew is that she came to the United States, I heard her speak, and I knew that she was this great teacher in Paris.

I was born in Delaware in 1940. I grew up in New Castle. My mother was a singer, and that is where the musical influence began. I never knew a time when I wasn't interested in music. I have been involved with music my whole life. I don't ever remember not knowing I was going to be a musician, because we had a piano, of course, and my mother started me with piano lessons. When I was about eight or nine she sent me to a piano teacher. After that private teacher I also studied piano at Wilmington School of Music. I had music all through elementary school on up. At Howard High School my music teacher started a music theory class for me and pianist Robert Jordan. That was a very lucky thing. Of course, I sang in the choir, and then when they decided to integrate the band, which means that they allowed female players, I became the first girl in the band. I also took clarinet lessons for a summer, then I played clarinet in the band, and I played it in the orchestra. I sang in our little Methodist Church, not gospel but hymns and anthems.

When I went to Howard University I graduated magna cum laude with a major in music theory and composition and a minor in voice and piano.

I have always been involved in music. When I was a little girl I used to make up songs, words, and music, and then sing them. I didn't even know that the word "composer" existed; I just used to do the music. Then when I was around sixteen years old, I realized that I might as well just major in composition. Bach and Duke Ellington were definitely some of the influences, and of course, I knew of other composers too. I was very fortunate, because New Castle was near Philadelphia, and I went to the Academy of Music to hear the Philadelphia Orchestra. I was spoiled because that is one of the best orchestras in the world. I was very influenced by that experience.

I was fascinated seeing all the people on the stage playing together, and I wondered how one person could write for all of those instruments. I wondered if I could do it too.

When I went to Howard University, I studied with Mark Fax, which was really great. Adolphus Hailstork and I were at Howard at the same time, and Adolphus also went to Fontainebleau the same time I did. The school of music at Howard had a symphonic wind ensemble contest, and I entered it, along with six males. I wrote a piece called "Reflections of Life." We all had to have pseudonyms, so they wouldn't know who wrote the pieces. I won the contest, which was a big boost. The prize was that the piece was played at a concert.

I wrote my *Symphony Number One* while I was at Howard. That was also for a contest. There were five universities in the Washington area, and the National Symphony Orchestra had this contest for area composition students. Again, pseudonyms were used. Ten compositions were chosen out of all the entries, and mine was one of them. Again, the prize was that the piece was to be played, and that is how it happened that the National Symphony played my *Symphony Number One.* That was my senior year, and after graduation I went to Fontainebleau. When I returned from France, I went home briefly and told my parents that I wanted to live in New York.

When I arrived in New York I didn't know anybody here, but eventually I met Kermit Moore, and I got married. I also met Howard Roberts and Hale Smith. They were doing a very big, fancy fund-raiser in Philharmonic Hall, as it was called then—now it is Avery Fisher Hall—for the Congress of Racial Equality (CORE). I had met the man who was the director of it, and he offered me a job as assistant director. Some of the people involved were Ruby Dee, Ossie Davis, Dick Gregory, Shelly Winters, Robert Ryan, and other black and white socially aware actors and performers in New York. The whole thing was called *The Ballad of the Winter Soldier,* which included readings from a script by John O'Killens, a well-known writer. People read from lecterns, and the Howard Roberts Choir sang. They needed a song, and the person who was supposed to write the song couldn't, so on a trip home to Delaware over Labor Day Weekend, I decided to just write the song.

I wrote the words and music to the song, and when I came back from Delaware, I showed it to the director and the writers, and they liked it very much. Hale Smith orchestrated it, and Howard Robert's Choir sang it with orchestra. I hadn't been in New York a year when I had had a piece played in Philharmonic Hall. It was at the very, very fancy reception afterward that I met Kermit Moore. He had not been at the concert, because he had been playing somewhere himself, but he came to the reception, which was at the home of Arthur and Mathilde Krim. Krim was the head of United Artists, the movie company that became Orion. This was in 1964.

Kermit once played as a guest artist for a concert with Selwart Clarke, a violist, in Town Hall. While they were practicing, I just wrote something for viola and cello, because I liked the combination. One day they saw it on the piano and they played it. They asked if they could play it for an encore on the concert, and that is what they did. Normally encores don't get reviews, but this piece got a really good review in the *New York Times.* It was luck. That piece eventually became the middle movement of *Moods,* for viola and cello—I later wrote a first movement and a third movement. After that I got commissions. That is really the basis of my career. I never really wrote anything unless it was commissioned, and I have never had any other job outside of music. I did teach one semester at New York University and one semester at Bronx Community College.

My husband and I were also two of the first teachers at Harlem School of the Arts. Dorothy Maynard, when she was starting the school, asked us if we would help in the fund-raising and teach at the school, which we did. That was in 1965 and 1966.

Steve Chambers, Carmen Moore, Benjamin Patterson, my husband, and I founded the Society of Black Composers. We had the meetings right here in our apartment. We got in touch with composers all around the country to make a network, because we didn't know each other. It was a very important organization from that point of view. We found out who the black composers were, and I built a file on everyone. We had correspondence and created a network, and we also put on concerts here in New York. As a matter of fact, Herbie Hancock once did a concert with us.

As a group, we felt that black composers didn't have any recognition, so we created the organization, which lasted for a quite a while, until we felt it was no longer necessary. People know we exist, so the organization served its purpose. People now know about many of the composers, and one of the reasons why people know is because of our organization. The Society for Black Composers was formed in 1968 and continued into the seventies. It spawned other things like, for example, the Center for Black Music Research, an organization that I am sure took a lot of what we did. The Symphony of the New World was also started here in New York. My husband is one of the founders; they started that symphony so that black musicians would have someplace to play. The Symphony of the New World didn't exclude anybody—it also had white musicians, Asian musicians, and women—but a lot of the musicians were black. They had a regular season, and their concerts were in Philharmonic Hall. The Symphony of the New World started in 1964 and lasted until the late seventies. It played a piece of mine, the orchestral version that I made of *From the Dark Tower.* Running the Symphony of the New World was a lot of work. It was a regular symphony orchestra, not a fly-by-night thing. Many people were involved in fund-raising, and the symphony did several concerts a season. There were guest artists and guest conductors. The orchestra also premiered the Joseph White *Violin Concerto* in this country, at a concert that my husband conducted.

Duke Ellington also did a concert with the Symphony of the New World. He provided his band to play with the orchestra free of charge when my husband asked if he could do something with the orchestra.

My husband has done a lot of orchestrations of Ellington's music. I first met Ellington when I was eighteen years old, after my freshman year at Howard. I was home for the summer, and Ellington was playing in Pennsylvania, at the Brandywine Music Box. I went to the concert, and I told him that I had written a piece called "Flight" that I wanted him to hear. He invited my friends and me back to his suite at the Hotel DuPont, which is in Wilmington, Delaware. We spent a fabulous evening with him. That was my first meeting with him. I told him I was majoring in composition. The others weren't musicians, so Duke and I talked mostly, but not only about music. The next time I saw him was when he played at Howard University. He remembered meeting me, which was very nice, and then in June he sent me this big Christmas card.

He sent his Christmas cards in June. They were cards that he designed himself, and they were like posters. After I came to New York and I got married, we met up again through his sister, Ruth Ellington, who is still living. We are still friends with Ruth to this day. My husband and I knew Duke from then on, but it was interesting that I knew Duke from before. Ellington was definitely encouraging, but he wasn't my teacher. I am not somebody who sits at somebody's knee. He didn't take me under his wing as a composer.

I think that like a lot of people, I got interested in music at a young age. I thought music was important and thought it would change the world. I had very traditional training. I thought Beethoven, Bach, Mozart, and Schubert were great, and I still think so. I just loved that music, but I wanted to create in my own way. I think writing music is fascinating. Growing up I heard rhythm and blues, jazz, and rock and roll. We didn't have gospel in our church, so I didn't know that much about that type of music, but I did know about spirituals, of course. I wasn't interested in writing rock and roll or rhythm and blues, or things like that, though. I was interested in writing symphonies, string quartets, chamber music, and song cycles. That doesn't mean other things didn't influence me, but I see these as different disciplines.

Weary Blues is a long poem by Langston Hughes for which I wrote a piece for baritone cello and piano. Given the text you can say that you can hear certain African American elements in it, because I am using that particular text. When I use text, there is an allusion to the black experience, because most of the poems I have set have been written by black poets. Of course, the first poet I set, in 1962, while I was at Howard, was Omar Khayyam who wrote *The Rubaiyat.* I wrote this piece for Dr. Evelyn White, one of the faculty members at Howard, but for some reason she was not able to do it, and that is why the piece was premiered at Fontainbleau, France. I later gave the American premiere here at Carnegie Recital Hall. But when I use black poets, depending upon what allusions they make to certain things in their poetry that pertain to African American life, I can use those elements.

When I am going to write a work, I think about things a lot first. It is a thought process. Then I get a theme or a germ, which is different in each piece; each piece is organically different. I don't use the piano to get an idea for a theme. That doesn't mean that you don't sit down at the piano and try things out after you get the idea, but it is not just one process. It all depends, but I have never seen a piano yet that can write music. Usually I begin in the sitting room, where the piano is not, just sitting there thinking with manuscript paper in front of me. But if you heard *Moods,* for viola and cello, for instance, you might say it has modern and angry dissonance. Then you hear my string quartet, and it is altogether different. I do have a twenty-minute piano work that is programmatic in a way; it is called *Dream and Variations.*

When I came to New York I was already into writing my own music. I had my own ideas. It is not that I heard some piece and said, "Oh, I want to write something like that." I do my own thing. I also write poetry, and I am also writing a novel at the moment. But poetry is poetry, and music is music. They only connect in that they come from the same person. When I am writing poetry I am not thinking of music, and vice versa. I have also never set my own poetry, though my husband has. He wrote a work for me called *Five Songs for DRM* [Dorothy Rudd Moore], and I performed them. Now of course when I wrote my opera, *Frederick Douglass*, the libretto was my own. It was commissioned by Opera Ebony, an organization that has been in existence since the early 1970s.

Singers from all over have performed with Opera Ebony. The organization has a connection with a Catholic nun who is from Louisiana. They commissioned me to write this opera, and I did, a full three-act opera that was premiered in 1985. They have since from it done scenes all over the world, in places like Switzerland, Germany, the Caribbean, and here in New York. It was quite a big deal, and it got very good reviews in the *New York Times,* in *Opera News,* and in *Amsterdam News,* so it was really quite something. I wrote the book, the libretto, and everything, so in that sense with that opera I have set my own words.

I was not particularly influenced by other people's work. When I came to New York, for example, a lot of people were doing this aleatoric music. I wasn't influenced by any of that. Now, I did know Margaret Bonds, and I had a great deal of respect for her. I met Julia Perry, too, when she came to Howard. I knew Hale Smith; it was he who introduced me to my husband. I was impressed by Hale Smith, certainly, and by Ulysses Kay and Margaret Bonds. I was very excited about knowing these people, because they were black composers, and I had the chance to hear their music. As I said at one of my very first lectures at the University of Connecticut—and this is my quote, anyone who says they said it first is lying—I told this sea of people at this lecture where they did my music, "The only composers I had known growing up were white, male, and dead." I said that. It wasn't an attack against the tradition. The point was that the only composers that I knew of when I was growing up were white, male, and dead. Beethoven was dead, Bach was dead, and they were both white and male. That is not an attack, it is just a fact. There were black composers, but I didn't yet know of them when I was growing up. All that is not to say that I didn't care about other composers, though, because people can influence you in a lot of different ways, just by their very existence.

Our culture of black composers here in New York was really fantastic. When I came to New York, almost every week somebody was giving a concert somewhere. It was really amazing. If I sound like I am turned off now, I am, because I really hate what has gone on in society when it comes to black creative people. The society has managed to ghettoize us. If somebody is shaking their behind, hopping, yelling, and singing gospel, they are the ones who get recognition. Or when people want to program something now, and I see this all the time, they don't necessarily program a black classical composer, but they will put on something like the Boys Choir of Harlem. They can then say, "Oh, we have got our black performers now."

I am not talking against any of these things, I am merely saying it is almost as though black people are ghettoized in the general culture to do only certain kinds of music. It is almost as if the black classical composer doesn't exist.

I have served on the board of the National Endowments of the Arts for three years, and I was also on New York State Council of the Arts for three years. In both situations I always talked about what happens when people program music by black composers. They think about us in February. Understand, this is not a person who is bitter talking, because I have been very lucky in terms of getting my music performed. I am talking realistically here, and I am not the only person who has said this; it happens to performers too. In February during Black History Month, organizations think of us. But performing the works of black composers across the board—that really is not done. It is almost as though all the work we did in the 1960s and 1970s didn't make much difference.

I don't think anything will change. Think of the whole fabric of our society, look at what is going on right now with the political mood. We know of everything that went on in the 1960s, when people were getting their heads banged for talking about civil rights. People had hope and were looking up, thinking things were going to change. Things are worse now than they were then. When women are worried about getting thrown off welfare and not being able to feed their kids, composers can hardly talk about anything, because there are issues that are bigger than that, but it all factors in the situation. Then there is the other thing, the commercial element. This is a society that judges things in terms of how much money it makes.

I remember when they used to give movie reviews on television but now they don't give reviews so much, they only talk about which one was the top box-office gross. This is what has happened to our society in general. This is a society where people in Congress want to cut off the teensy-weensy, piddling amount of money that they give to the arts. This is the society that we live in. In academia, though, whatever you are doing, you are going to keep on doing. You might be doing things and getting pieces played within that community, but people out here who are not in an academic situation; people in the larger world, in general, don't have the same opportunities. Forget about black composers for a moment—what do you see in the culture about any composers, black, white, green, or yellow? You certainly don't see it on the huge medium of television.

Bach made a living from writing his music; at some point as a composer you understand it is not romantic to write music. When we are younger we want to do something. We want to create. When Fontainbleau was over, for example, I told my parents I was going to stay in Paris. They sent all of my things over. I said I was going to get this little garret, work as a waitress by day, and write music by night. Ha, ha, ha! I didn't know any better. I wised up in time, and I brought my little self back home. I said, "Let me be poor and write music in close proximity to my parents." What happened was, I found out that in order to stay there I needed a job and a work permit. I didn't have either. Paris is a beautiful city, but it is a city. You have got poor people and rich people and everything in between, When school was over I stayed in Paris for a week and just walked around. *La Bohème* might sound romantic, but it is an opera. In real life those people were sick, starving, cold, and dying from consumption. Anyway, I certainly had a much more optimistic outlook when I first came to New York, because it just seemed more thriving in terms of the arts. Now what you have is commerce.

There is a reason for that. People have got to make money from what they do, so they have to have things like "Mostly Mozart," which has been going on during the summer for twenty some years at Avery Fisher Hall. Basically it is a gimmicky, commercial kind of thing.

You have symphony orchestras doing outreach things. Well, they are put in that type of position because, if you have ever served on any of these things, as I have, you know in order to get funding, it is mandated that you have to have minorities—which, by the way, is a term I don't use, as I told folks both at the

National Endowment for the Arts and the New York State Council. At the very first meeting, when they started talking about minorities, I said, "For the record, I want you to know that is a term that I don't use because I am not part of a minority. And besides it is a sociological term, it is not a numerical term."

I used to think that art could change things, I really did. I have many, many poems that I have written over the years, for example, and they are really excellent. They are not vernacular poems, and they are not poems that talk about "old, poor, black me" either, because I don't write poems like that and I don't think of myself in those terms. Yet, again, that ghettoization thing occurs. For example, I wrote a poem when they landed on the moon, I wrote a poem about the *Challenger* exploding. I have written on different subjects. I have three great Nixon poems; a lot of my other poems are political. Often I think a person creates things because they can't help it. Creating is an expression, it is an outlet.

When it comes to writing music, I don't just say, "Oh, I have this idea for a melody," like I did when I was a little girl. Writing music is too difficult for me just to dally at it. If I am writing something I have to be really writing it. The poems come from a different place. Writing is very hard. You can't just sit down and write a novel. There is a lot of thinking that goes into it.

Once upon a time, I grew up Methodist. I was not zealously religious; however, I used to believe a lot of what was taught. The day that I realized that no man could actually be born unless someone had sex with someone else, I put all of that stuff behind me. The thing of it is, I really used to believe that there were good people in the world, and I used to believe good would overcome evil. I don't believe that any more. I think the world is as it is. The world is the same way as it as always was. People are the same way as they always were.

There are some people who we call good and some we call bad, but what happens all over the world? We sit here, I am sitting here in a nice comfortable apartment, but there is so much hate and killing and horribleness going on right now all over world.

If Beethoven's *Ninth Symphony* couldn't do it, especially with the last movement, there ain't nothing I can do. You have got Schiller's poem, and you have got Beethoven's music, which both often talk about all men being brothers. So the fact is that art helps sometimes and to some extent, but not necessarily. I don't have any illusions about what the arts can do or what music can do. It only helps when it helps.

Art can do things for individual people at individual moments, but the sun is going to come out whether I kill somebody or not. The moon will be there, and this earth will be here. Now I am not advocating killing somebody. What I am saying is that you want to put out positive energies. For example, *From the Dark Tower* is a song cycle of eight poems by black poets. It was written for Hilda Harris and Kermit Moore, and it premiered in 1970. I called that work my "black power statement." With all the turmoil that was going on then, I knew that I wouldn't go out, pick up a gun, and kill somebody or anything like that even, though I was very sympathetic to groups like the Panthers—and that was not what they were about either, by the way. But what I am saying is that as a composer and artist, I made my statement in this way, and that work has been performed many times. I do therefore have a social consciousness, and I do not just write music in a vacuum, but I was thinking that communicating my ideas and emotions about the world would make a difference.

I am very lucky in my life as a composer; I have had many gratifying moments. One of the most memorable musical offerings and involvements was the premier and recording of my *From the Dark Tower,* for mezzo, cello, and piano.

I can say that the opera *Frederick Douglas*s was my biggest project, because it was eight years of my life. I have had some very gratifying moments overall, and such moments occur not when I hear a hall full of people applaud me but when I hear somebody do my work and I know I made a connection, in that the musicians did it the way I wanted, that there was that reaching out from me to the performer and then out to the audience, so the audience gets it. Every time that happens it is very gratifying. I don't need any big overall arching thing, because little moments, like a wonderful warm bath or watching the sunset, are some of the greatest things in life. Those might seem like ordinary things, but for me, if I create something and I like it, and if it is performed and the audience receives it well—I don't care how many times I hear the work done, if I am proud of it—I am very happy about the whole thing. I don't think in terms of, "Oh, I did this and I did that and I did this." When I write music I am very honest about it. I hate minimalism with a passion, for instance. I just feel like if you are going to do something you should give it your best effort. If you do that and the effort is realized, that's just wonderful. That is not to minimize anything, because when my husband did *Dirge and Deliverance,* my cello sonata, which premiered at Tully Hall, that was simply a wonderful experience for me. It was the first sonata of mine for cello and piano, and the work was reflective of the black existence and "experience" in this country, as the title suggests.

The opera was, first of all, a lot of work. It's in three acts and lasts three hours. The reward was to see all of those people on stage performing my work, and seeing all the people in the audience. Warren Wilson conducted the premiere of the opera. Everett Lee has conducted it in Sweden.

One thing I have not been happy with is that well-respected universities have very little information about black composers. If a black person is on a faculty of music at a university and that music department has no information on other black musicians, something is wrong. There is no excuse for this. I heard of Margaret Bonds and Julia Perry, and other black composers when I was in college. The information is available. There is just no excuse for this omission.

Olly Wilson

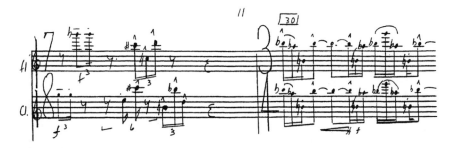

Olly Wilson remains one of the most prominent figures of his generation as a composer, arts educator, and scholar in black artistic thinking and work. Born in 1937, a native a St. Louis, he received his education from Washington University (B.M.), University of Illinois (Mus. M.), and the University of Iowa (Ph.D.). His teachers have included Robert Wykes, Robert Kelly, and Philip Bezanson, with further studies in electronic music at the University of Illinois. In addition to working as a pianist in jazz ensembles, Dr. Wilson was an orchestral player on double bass in the St. Louis Philharmonic, St. Louis Chamber Players, and Cedar Rapids Symphony. He has held faculty positions at Florida A&M University and Oberlin Conservatory. He served as a professor of music, holding the Jerry and Evelyn Hemming Chambers Distinguished Chair, and chair of the Music Department, University of California, Berkeley. Dr. Wilson holds further distinction as an elected member of the American Academy of Arts and Letters (1995). His works have been performed by the Boston, New York Philharmonic, Cleveland, Moscow Philharmonic, St. Louis, San Francisco, Baltimore, Houston, Atlanta, Louisville, Detroit, and Dallas Symphonies, and many others. His recordings include performances by the Boston Symphony and his *Akwan,* for orchestra, recorded on Columbia. He has received awards and commissions from the Dartmouth Arts Council, Fromm Foundation, the Guggenheim and Koussevitzky Foundations, Lila Wallace–*Reader's Digest,* National Endowment of the Arts, and the National Institute of Arts and Letters. In addition to Dr. Wilson's distinguished career he has had published several seminal articles on the theory and interpretation of black music and practitioners. Dr. Wilson currently lives and works in Berkeley, California.

I believe that certain aspects of a composer or a creative artist's work are not necessarily time dependent. I think human beings have a basic urge to express themselves. I think that fundamentally a composer expresses his or her experience in the best way that he or she knows how, by consciously reflecting upon that experience and recreating it and, in so doing, redefining the reality of that person's experience. I think that is a transcendent thing, and human beings in every culture do it in different ways. Of course, one learns certain things within the context of a specific culture, but attempting to express one's self is a basic human impulse. Having said that, I also think that there are certain individuals who, for whatever reason, have a greater propensity to want to express themselves and perhaps in some respects are probably better than others at doing that. I think those are the people we tend to call "artists," human beings who

have some insight into the process or the experience of living and thereby are able to communicate with others about that human experience. From this broad perspective, the imperative of a composer in the end of the twentieth century is not that dissimilar from the imperative of a composer at the end of the eighteenth century, or a composer in Western society, as opposed to a composer in an Asian society or an African society.

The imperative is that you as a human being have that impulse to create. From that broad perspective, I don't think it is that much different. I think, though, that each generation has its own dynamic, and one's sensitivity to those dynamics enables one to reflect that particular time in a particular way. Whether or not the person would be as sensitive and as effective or as insightful or perceptive in reflecting on that experience if they lived at a different time, I don't know. I think it might have to do with personality; certain personalities do better in certain kinds of situations than other personalities. Perhaps that is true, I don't know, but I think there is an inner urge to create, and that is the fundamental thing.

I think the experience of living, the dynamics and the sensibilities of the times, the things that people are concerned about and the opportunities available, vary from time to time. For example, the context of an African American composer writing music in 1965 is different from an African American composer writing music in 1995 in some respects. And yet in other respects it is not different. Still, the thing that makes the person compose is that fundamental urge to engage and try to reflect upon experience.

Now if you ask what specifically are the differences between 1995 and 1965, there are certain obvious things. For instance, the whole sociopolitical situation is different in '95 than it was in '65. While some of the same problems that existed in '65 still exist today, there are also opportunities that exist today which didn't exist to the same degree in 1965. For example, an African American composer who simply wanted to make a living as composer in 1965 had less of an opportunity to be successful in the commercial world than an African American composer has in 1995. There were very few black film composers, jingle composers, composers who wrote commercials, or that kind of thing in 1965. There certainly were African American composers in the popular world, as African American music has dominated the pop scene since its inception, but the opportunities for a composer, even in the pop world in 1965, were bracketed in ways that they are not as bracketed in 1995.

So I am saying that there are different options that a person had. If a composer aspired to write for a symphony orchestra in 1965, there were less opportunities than there are today. Actually '65 is a funny year, because 1965 was a period when there was considerable interest in contemporary music; so comparing '65 with '45, there were a lot more opportunities in '65 for a composer who was writing contemporary music in the United States. But in 1995, because there has been a tremendous growth in the number and quality of all orchestras—regional orchestras, provincial orchestras, major orchestras, and so forth—there are even more opportunities for a composer than there were before.

The notion of the black composer in the written tradition is a relatively new thing to the public. That is not to say that it hadn't existed, because this tradition goes back to the nineteenth century. But until recently there was no readily available body of research that identified, and therefore made a reading public aware of the existence of, African American composers. That body of research is certainly much larger in 1995 than it was in 1965. Eileen Southern's book *[The Music of Black Americans]* was published in 1971. Prior to that Maude Cuney-Hare had published her work, and there were earlier books, but these were published in the 1930s with limited distribution. They didn't have the impact that Eileen Southern's book had in 1971, at least in the scholarly world. Even though many scholars had never heard the music, they had at least heard of some of the composers that were active in the '30s, '40s and '50s. By 1995, there were several generations of African American composers that anyone who was seriously interested in American music could familiarize themselves with. Not that these composers had all of the performances that they should have had, but a portion of their work had been performed. Certainly, some of them had been recorded, and that was something that was extremely rare in 1965.

I became a musician in part because I grew up in a musical family. We lived in St. Louis, and my father was an amateur singer who literally mandated that all of his children learn how to read music. My father was a tenor and sang in amateur groups and in choral societies. I remember him going to choir rehearsals with the Harry T. Burleigh Choral Society. I didn't even know who Harry T. Burleigh was at the time.

My father valued music very much and wanted to make sure that his children learned music formally. He had studied music himself in both high school and college. He possessed a beautiful voice. As I have frequently said, he had the loudest and the best voice in the First Baptist Church Choir, the church in which I grew up. He was a very musical person who loved music and made sure that his children studied music. My father mandated that if you wanted to eat in his house you had to learn how to play the piano. There was a reason for that. Part of the reason was that he was literally raising accompanists; on Sundays when he would go sing at afternoon teas, he could go to child number one and say, "You are going to accompany me today," or child number two, or number three, or number four. I was number three.

We all had to learn piano at a very early age. We started taking lessons at a very good school of music in St. Louis called the Kroeger School of Music. I must have been seven or eight when I began my first piano lessons. I had two older sisters, both of whom had preceded me in studying at this school. I assumed that this type of music education was normal, and I didn't realize that everybody didn't do this. I also didn't realize that this school was a pretty good school. It was a private school in segregated St. Louis. It was one of those places that was integrated—that is, integrated in the sense that all of the teachers were white but some of the students were black. We were one of the few black families that went there. At the age of seven I didn't understand the significance of that. Nevertheless, I studied at the Kroeger School of Music for two or three years, and then I started taking music from a series of private piano teachers in the area, most of whom were black. That was the beginning of my formal music education.

I must have been about ten when I started playing the clarinet in grammar school. The school district introduced an instrumental music program in the elementary schools, and I wanted to play an instrument. The teacher came over, we looked at instruments, and I chose the clarinet. I remember my mother renting a clarinet and then subsequently buying one. I must have been ten or eleven by that time. The clarinet was my second instrument. I already knew how to read music because of my earlier piano lessons, so I made rapid progress playing the clarinet. For me, it was simply a matter of learning the technical side of producing sound.

Also, as I said, we were told that we would take piano lessons. After I had been doing it for two or three years, I realized I enjoyed it. When you are a little kid, you want to please your parents in any way. I enjoyed playing, and so, by the time I was a teenager, I had made good progress playing both instruments. In my early teenage years, I became interested in popular music and jazz. I was concerned about my image at that time, and I think my view of a little boy who played classical music on the piano had changed by my teenage years. I mean, it is great to get strokes for being a good little kid who can do something different, but by the time you reach age fourteen or fifteen, then the specter of a "nice Little Lord Fauntleroy" emerges, and you say, "Well, is that the image I would choose for myself?" In my community, however, if you played popular music or jazz, it was considered really cool. So while I wasn't interested in jazz and popular music solely because of the cool image, it certainly was a factor. When I was fourteen and a freshman in high school I wanted to be cool. I also became interested in listening to popular music and discovered, "Hey, I can figure out what they are doing on the record." I started trying to do it at home on the piano, and eventually I started playing in local popular bands.

Another important part of my musical background was my early childhood experience playing at church. As I said, all of the Wilson children had to study piano long enough to be able to accompany my father on Sunday afternoons, so when he went to sing "O Promise Me," or "Trees," or whatever the light classics of the day were, we could accompany him. Once you reached that point it was fine. As I said also, my father was also active in church music, and he got my older sister involved first, then my second sister, and then me. My second sister dropped piano, and my parents didn't force her to continue, but I followed my older sister, playing first the piano for the Sunday school and subsequently, as she had done, I became the pianist for the church. It was a very large church, we had a pianist and an organist. My sister and I also took turns accompanying the children's choir. Music was very, very important to us in the family. All of us sang in church choirs, except for my mother. My father sang tenor, eventually I sang bass, my sister sang alto, and my other sister sang soprano. We were always harmonizing spontaneously. Sunday church services and Saturday choir rehearsals were very important.

There were two kinds of music in church. The major ensemble was the senior choir. The music performed in the church at that time was primarily anthems and hymns. We learned how to play this repertoire early, which was very good training for a young pianist, because you learned how to sight-read rapidly. Occasionally, we had to accompany a soloist, so we learned how to sight-read other music as well. We also had a gospel choir, which wasn't as good as our senior choir in terms of the number of the people who participated and the quality of their singing, although there were a couple of people in that choir who were outstanding soloists.

Another important dimension of the gospel choir was that a lot of the singers didn't read music, so everything had to be done by ear. That presented a challenge for the church pianist, because usually the gospel choir had its own accompanist, who was somebody who often didn't read either but had a good ear and knew the songs. A person like myself who had learned to read first was challenged whenever the gospel pianist didn't show up, because you would have to accompany the gospel choir. I learned how to fake it well enough so that I could manage, but that experience was actually another good form of ear training. That was happening about the same time I became interested in popular music. I advanced from what would have been the latest top forty at the time, the rhythm and blues, which used the typical formulaic structures that I figured out pretty quickly, to jazz, which was much more of a challenge.

St. Louis, of course, was always an outstanding mecca for jazz. Miles Davis was from East St. Louis and had started there with early bands. There was also a black musician's union; I became involved in that, ironically, by playing the clarinet. The union had a concert band, and kids who progressed and played in the school bands were invited to play in this band. I was attending Sumner High School by then, and that school had an outstanding band and choir led by two outstanding people. One of those people was Clarence Hayden Wilson, who had been at one point the president of the National Association of Negro Musicians and who was an incredible musician. Wilson could play a wide range of instruments very well, including piano. The other person was Kenneth Billups, the choir director, who had also been the former president of NANM. The music at Sumner was excellent.

I remember going to Sumner in my freshman year, hearing the band play, and being really floored by the music. I was determined to get in that band as soon as possible, so I auditioned. Most freshmen students were just starting instruments by then, so I was able, before the first semester was over, to earn a spot in the clarinet section. By my sophomore year I had already moved up to second stand, and by the end of my sophomore year I had moved up to the first chair.

I think that I approached music on my own terms later on. Certainly by the time I was a junior in high school, though, I knew I was going to do something in music. I started out playing piano, switched to clarinet, and was successful at it. I had also been successful in singing in local and church choirs. I had started my own little band as well, a little jazz band; we were playing small jobs. I had actually started playing jazz piano gigs around fifteen and sixteen, playing around with some of the older professional musicians and trying to keep up with them. I also continued playing clarinet. We had music competitions, and I had advanced. By my junior year I became the first clarinet in the high school senior band, and at state contests I would win prizes playing clarinet solos. I was studying clarinet privately at that time. I was also still studying piano privately, and I knew that I wanted to do something in music. Additionally, Clarence Hayden Wilson was a strong mentor.

I had many mentors in the popular world of music. I had a group of friends; we called ourselves "The Knights of the Turntable," because we listened to Charlie Parker and became jazz aficionados at about seventeen or eighteen. I was also exposed to gospel musicians like Willie May Ford Smith, who is from St. Louis. My father knew her. Although I wasn't really active in the gospel music community, I was on the fringes of it. I knew about gospel music, I knew Willie May Ford Smith and A. B. Windom; I knew the O'Neil Twins, a gospel duo who were in grade school with me. Oliver Nelson, the phenomenal saxophonist, had gone to my high school. Grace Bumbrey was also in my high school.

As a matter of fact, in my junior year in high school, Washington University—which at that time was still a segregated institution and didn't become integrated until 1954, at the time of the Supreme Court *[Brown v. Board of Education]* decision—started a Saturday music theory class. They invited people who aspired to be professional musicians to come to that theory class. Our school was invited, so Grace Bumbrey and I used to ride the streetcar together to Washington University to learn music theory. At that point it was clear that I was on the music track. I was a kid who was identified as a talented musician. I knew that I wanted to go to college and be a musician. I didn't know exactly what I wanted to do, but I knew it would involve music. Also, during my junior year of high school I went to summer music camp at Lincoln University in Jefferson City and was introduced to the double bass. I started playing the double bass mainly because my name starts with a *W,* and all of the other instruments had been assigned by the time the end of the alphabet was reached. I really wanted to play the cello. At any rate, that was all part of my background.

You have to put all of this in its social context. The Supreme Court decision was in 1954. I graduated from high school in 1955, the year of the Birmingham bus boycott. Things were changing rapidly in the social context of the nation. When we moved into our neighborhood, we were probably the second black family who lived within a four-block radius of what was actually a Jewish community, but we had to go to the closest black school. I went to four different grammar schools, because each year the neighborhoods would change, and a school closer to us would be designated for black children. By the time I graduated from grammar school, however, I was living in a predominately black neighborhood, or at least a neighborhood that was 60 percent black. By the time I graduated from high school it was 95 percent black. By the time I graduated from college, it was very much all black. The social context at that time was that of a dramatically changing area.

I went to Sumner High School, one of two large St. Louis high schools. There were about three thousand students there. Sumner had an excellent music department. I mentioned some of the people who were there—Oliver Nelson, Grace Bumrey, three members of the Fifth Dimension, and countless other people who were extraordinary musicians. Some of them became famous, and some of whom didn't, but most of them were really very talented. We had outstanding role models and wonderful teachers both in the school and in the community. I also worked very hard academically.

In my freshman year, Sumner created a school within a school—a prep school, so to speak—and identified the kids who would participate in it on the basis of test scores as well as academic performance, though much more attention was paid to performances than to test scores. Those of us who were identified were placed in a special advisory group and given special counseling and training. The result was when we graduated, out of the thirty-five students in this special advisory group, which stayed together all four years, about thirty-three of us went to college. We had excellent counseling. By the time I graduated I had two or three scholarship offers. One was from Washington University in St. Louis. As I said, Washington University integrated in 1954, and there were two blacks registered. In 1955, when I went as a freshman, there were seventeen, most of whom came from the St. Louis area. This was out of approximately seven thousand students.

I went to Washington University to study music. I had already been introduced to the music department because of the Saturday music theory classes I took. The school focused on the liberal arts pretty broadly and had a small music department within its liberal arts school. We got a lot of direct involvement with instructors, because classes were small. Several important things happened during my sophomore year. I did very well in my theory classes, partially because the beginning theory was pretty easy, because of my experience in the high school Saturday classes, and also because of the quality of instruction we had had in high school. (I took a music theory class in high school, which Mr. Billups taught.) All of that helped prepare us for music theory at Washington University. In the sophomore music theory class, as is customary, we were doing twentieth-century techniques. My teacher, Robert Wykes, was a composer who had recently completed his Ph.D. at the University of Illinois.

He asked us to write music in different styles. I apparently did well on these assignments, because he said, "I think you have got something there. Have you ever thought about being a composer?" I thought, "Hmm." I had thought of it in a way, but in a way I hadn't. Then I began to reflect back on my experience, and I realized that since I started my first school band, I had been writing down things that I heard. I had been making little arrangements for my group. I had written head tunes and various things like that in a pop sense for the various groups that I did. Because of my father's interest, we had been exposed to a wide range of music and occasionally we would go to the symphony, but I really didn't have a solid grasp of Western European music. I didn't think of myself as writing extended pieces until I got to college, where I was exposed to an even wider range of music. I knew what a symphony was, but not in any great depth until I got into college, and then I began to really focus on it.

I think there are two kinds of music. First, as I said, I was already enamored with Charlie Parker and with music in the so-called jazz realm. In terms of the formal European tradition, the composers who I was really excited about were contemporary composers, like Stravinsky and Bartók. I think Bartók and Stravinsky were striking to me at that time because their music was different—it was exciting, it was challenging, it was dramatic. I had a lot of different ideas at that time. I felt my experience had been very rich. Within that two-year period, my freshman and sophomore years, I discovered in a lot more depth the music of Beethoven, Bach, and Mozart, as well as Tchaikovski and Brahms, and a whole range of other composers who I had heard of but I really didn't know. I remember saying, "Okay, I am going to listen to and know every one of Beethoven's symphonies. I am going to listen to and know Mozart's symphonies." It was a period of great discovery for me. Additionally, the way education was set up at Washington (and this is probably true of most places), in our music history classes we had to write a paper every week. We had to listen to a work and write a paper about that work, which meant you had to really study it in great depth. It was the first time I was exposed to looking at, following, and reading scores. Then I heard this really exciting music by Stravinsky and Bartók, and to a lesser degree by people like Hindemith. In the context of the fifties, in terms of contemporary music, the dominant composer, at least the dominant composer living in the United States, in addition to Stravinsky, was certainly Hindemith. There was a lot of Hindemith and Hindemith-like music being performed.

My sophomore year in college was when I decided, "This is really what I want to do." I had thought when I first went to college that I was going to be a band director, because my mentor had been a band director. By the time I was in college, a couple of years, I had discovered composition, and I said, "I really want to be a composer. I really want to write music." Then, in my junior and senior years, I was exposed to the Midwestern Composer Symposium. The symposium consisted of composition students from the Universities of Michigan, Illinois, Iowa, and Northwestern. Those were the four schools involved at that time, though Northwestern had always had fewer students participating. One year, 1959, which was my senior year in college, Northwestern couldn't come at all. Robert Wykes had a group of young students studying composition with him; the people from the symposium asked Wykes if he could put together a program of students from Washington University. He said yes, and I was one of those students. There were several other people who were interested in composition at that point, and we were all active in writing music; because it was a great honor for us to participate, we got the very best students from the school to perform. Wykes himself had been a flute player and was very aggressively arranging performances of student compositions. The guest composer that year, at the University of Iowa, was Wallingford Riegger. As was customary at that time, each school presented a program of works of its students. We were all undergraduates, but most of us were juniors and seniors. We presented our program; then a panel of composers, faculty members, one from each school, plus the guest composer, Wallingford Riegger, chose a piece to be played on the final program. My piece was chosen.

I had written for that program what was probably my second complete piece. (The first piece that I had written was called "Prelude and Line Study," for a woodwind quintet.) I was just studying a serial technique, so I was trying to use a modified serialism. My second piece was a trio for flute, cello, and piano. I was very pleased with that piece, and it was played very well by the trio.

The symposium started on Thursday, continued through Saturday, and then there was the final program of the pieces selected by the panel, on Sunday. My flute player, a very good flautist, had a commitment back in St. Louis, so she had to leave Iowa. I was struggling to get a flute player. It turned out there was a student there who was an excellent flautist. Richard Hervig who was then teaching at Iowa, said, "We have an excellent flute player who is an undergraduate here. It is also his senior year. He reads very fast and he is excellent. Maybe he will play it." He asked the student, who turned out to be Harvey Solberger. I showed Harvey the piece, and he agreed to play. It was very successful. I was also able to connect with a lot of other young students—composers who had been fairly successful in one way or another who were participating in the symposium. That was important for me. The piece was very successful, and a lot of the composers in the Midwest, faculty members, heard it.

After I graduated from Washington University, I applied to the graduate school at the University of Illinois and was accepted. I went there instead of going to teach in high school, which was normally the pattern for people who wanted a career in music; I went on to graduate school immediately. I graduated from Washington in 1959, got married, and went to graduate school in the fall of that year, when I was twenty-one. There I wrote several other pieces. I did a piece for piano and voice, a setting of an e. e. cummings work. The first commission that involved money happened a little bit later on, when I was in graduate school at Iowa. I completed my master's degree at the University of Illinois, and then I went to teach at Florida A&M. After that I went back to the University of Iowa to work on a Ph.D. It was there that a fellow graduate student asked me to write a piece for him for two bassoons and voice, and he actually paid me thirty-five dollars.

When I was teaching at Florida A&M, Wendell Logan was a student there. That was in 1960, and I was twenty-two years old. Wendell must have been about twenty, because he was a senior. I had got the job at Florida A&M in August of that year; it was the only job I could get, because things were still very segregated. Though I had done well in school and had a master's degree, the only place I could get a job was in a traditional black school in the South. It was a major step for me at the time to move farther south than St. Louis. This move was taken in the social context of Freedom Rides, when the civil rights movement was beginning to meet violent resistance. I stayed at Florida A&M for two years, and it was a great experience in terms of teaching. I was very young, and it was a lot of fun in some respects, but the teaching load was actually horrendous. I was teaching about six courses.

I could see that I would never be able to write much music if I stayed there, although I did write a piece for the dance ensemble. I had met Beverly Hilsman, who was the dance choreographer. She was an interesting artist, so I did some music for them. There were some very talented students there. One of the students who I met there was Wendell. Wendell was a senior at that point, and I didn't see him around the Music Department much, but that was because he was a starting football player; he played on the line. These were in the days when Florida A&M had a tremendous football team, when they would beat teams by scores like ninety-six to zero. The marching band was also fabulous. The Music Department was really based around the marching band. While I was at A&M, I was a very idealistic young kid and thought I knew everything. I thought I was just supposed to teach everything, and I didn't realize there was another dynamic going on. But I remember Wendell knocking on the door one day. There was this big guy standing at the door, and he said, "Are you Professor Wilson?" I said yes. He said, "Well, I'm Wendell Logan. I understand you are composer." I said, "Yes, I am." He said, "Look, I'm interested in studying composition." We became friends, and he became my first student. I hadn't even thought of having any students because I still considered *myself* a student.

Wendell and I worked, we got to know each other, and we have remained very close friends. I stayed at Florida for two years and then went to Iowa to work on the Ph.D. I was there from 1962 to 1964. I completed the Ph.D., and I still couldn't get a job outside of the deep South. I came back to Florida A&M, stayed there for a year, and then in 1965 I got a job at Oberlin. I stayed at Oberlin for five years, and then I went to Berkeley in 1970, I have been there ever since.

I think music simply is one's conscious organization of sound, a person's attempt to communicate something of his or her experience. I view music, therefore, as a transmitter of one's human qualities, one's intellectual and expressive qualities. I see music as a means of understanding something about existence and about one's own experience. I look at music from that very broad perspective, and I realize that music also does many other things. Music has symbolic meanings for people on a number of different levels, depending on what the music is. It can embody ethnic viewpoints, it can embody nationalistic viewpoints, it can embody a lot of meanings that people project onto it. I think all of that is multidimensional—multiple levels in this broader scheme of reflecting one's humanity.

I have written about peculiar qualities that I call "conceptual approaches to the process of music making," approaches that peoples of African heritage, because of their cultural background, tend to reflect. I don't mean to suggest that this is somehow in the genes. I believe it is culturally learned behavior. Just as Asian music has some general, defining, demonstrable qualities about it, the music of any particular group of people who have been isolated and have developed their own culture will reflect certain choices that have been made collectively and then refined over centuries. I think that is certainly true of any group of people living in a particular way. That is, in the case of languages, one can speak of linguistic groups (one can talk, for example, about Romance languages, or one can talk about languages of various parts of the world that have certain definable characteristics that tie them together, although each language is different), and I think this is true about music also, and about art in general. The art of a particular culture reflects the way people of that culture interact with the world of sound and the world of space and time. There are definable cultural characteristics. I think we can define some of those characteristics, but when you look at a specific composer, it is much more complicated. Although a composer might have certain characteristics and have a real propensity to do certain things, there are also so many other things that impact on that composer that it makes it very difficult, and perhaps even futile, to try to predict his or her choices, certainly in the case of a late-twentieth-century composer, who has been exposed to all kinds of cultural influences.

I think there are many factors that help to define what is generally understood as African American music. To avoid quantifying this, I would rather characterize it, because if you quantify something, you have to measure this much as opposed to that much. If one talks about basic qualities, the definition seems more accurate. I talk about it in terms of propensities, in terms of predilections to produce certain things. Now, I am talking about vernacular traditions, because I think you can find basic qualities more clearly here. That is what makes it vernacular—the fact that it is shared by a common group of people and everybody knows it immediately, because it is culturally learned. For example, I talk about the principle of metrical contrast, which has been called a number of things. I call it the "principle of rhythmic contrast." This is a tendency toward rhythmic clash on some architectonic level in the music, either metrically or rhythmically.

For example, look at the whole notion of polyrhythm. Depending upon who is defining it and what they think it means, what is in common between polyrhythm and something as simple as syncopation? In something as simple as mixed meter, there is a tendency to have a rhythmic clash—that is, to have an interaction between things existing on two levels. So, you have a fixed rhythmic group and a variable rhythmic group, in very simple terms, and you have some clash that comes about with the interaction of these two. I am suggesting that that is a cultural bias. All across West Africa, South Africa, East Africa, and some important parts of North Africa, one will find that same propensity to produce structures that create this rhythmic clash.

This doesn't mean that peoples of African cultures are the only people who do this, because it also exists in many cultures, but it is a common quality, when taken in conjunction with something else, which I refer to as a "heterogeneous sound ideal." By this I mean a tendency to produce musical textures in which there are timbral clashes, or a tendency to produce musical textures that use timbres that are distinct from one another. The Asian stew, in which one can see each pea, each carrot, and each bean, represents a different ideal from that of a blended French sauce. Both are valid, they just reflect different things. The idea of creating very dense musical textures and musical phrases at the end of which are interjections, often isolated by both rhythmic contrast and timbral diversity, is common in African American music traditions. The notion that physical body motion is an integral part of music is also common. There are a wide range of these shared musical conceptions.

Each one of these concepts exists in a number of different cultures. This doesn't mean that black people are the only humans who do this, but collectively the present mass of these concepts constitute what we think of as African, or African American, music. Those specific manifestations change over time and within various cultures, but they are present. I talk about, for example, the continuum from speech to song. If one looks at rap and the rhetorical schemes that are used in black speech and black oratory, independent of whether by a political or religious speaker, or if one looks at the relationship of musical contours to speech patterns that are mimicked in jazz performance and vice versa, there is this whole notion of the continuum of speech to song. It is an integral part of shaping African American music. If one looks at African languages, where the tonal pattern is an integral part of the language structure, there is also a continuum from speech to song. In some cultures it developed so elaborately that there are repertoires of codified patterns associated with speech music. This speech-song continuum exists as an important part of the tradition. All of those concepts taken together, plus obvious practices like antiphony or call-and-response, all reflect those culturally learned biases that are associated with music. I think that is something we carry with us if we have grown up in an African American culture. That is part of us.

What makes it so complicated is that these same qualities have affected, created, and shaped American culture, so it is hard to distinguish the source. That is why people outside of the culture find it difficult to recognize this in some instances; they assume that this is "American," because people simply lack a good historical sense. The process of things being modified from the African American culture to the broader culture is a very broad one, and as a consequence, a second generation comes up and claims it. For example, if you ask some white kids out in the suburbs who is the greatest jazz or blues singer, they might answer Janis Joplin, because that is who they have heard or because before she died she lived a blues life. Or they might say Sting, or Bonnie Raitt, because they put these artists in the same category without understanding the source of jazz and the blues. They would even be offended if you said, "Well, wait a minute, what they do is fine, but they are building upon something else, they are learning from something else. They are performing within a tradition that was established by something else."

A sense of history is extremely important and should be highly valued. That is why once I determined that the academy was not only a haven but a benefactor and the agent of support for the artist, I also realized that the academy is a place that shapes public opinion and ideas of the time. I think it is very important for people who are scholars to write, to express their views, to give their interpretations of history, to try not simply to correct past wrongs but also to provide insight into the meaning of their musical experience. I think that is vital. I think there needs to be a history that requires many scholars looking at this vital tradition that we call "African American music," constantly shaping it, constantly interpreting it, constantly introducing thinking, sensitive people to this tradition so that they can understand it. I think that is really important. I think the tradition needs to be studied.

I don't see a lack of passion for music in contemporary culture. As a matter of fact, I think the passion for music is just as strong as it has ever been; it is just reflected in different ways. The strongest—at least in the communities in which I see it happening, and I am talking primarily about the African American community now—is gospel. When a hot soul/gospel group comes into town on a Sunday morning, people hang from the rafters. People can't get there fast enough. When I see the number of young kids who have spent a hell of a lot of money to go to hear the latest rap concert, latest hot gospel group, or slick soul singer, and see kids who will buy synthesizers and other expensive sound equipment in order to produce their own rap group, it is amazing to me. I think the passion is there.

What I don't see, and what I think we have lost, is a certain amount of discipline. In my youth we had rhythm and blues, we had gospel, we had spirituals, we had things that were very much rooted in the oral tradition. But we also had an understanding that for certain kinds of things—if you were going to play jazz, for example—you had to practice your instrument. If you wanted to get a gig you had to learn how to read music; and although some people didn't, most people realized they had to read music to play in a big band sometime along the way. We knew we were going to have to be able to read the charts. The Duke Ellington ideal was there. We had that. We don't have that now, I think, with the exception of the group of players who have been inspired by Wynton Marsalis. I give Wynton Marsalis a lot of credit for this, because I think he really has done a major job in terms of focusing on the discipline of making music again, at a time when a lot of young musicians aren't paying any attention to that tradition. Even though Marsalis is musically conservative in certain respects, his focus on discipline is important. He spawned a whole group of other young musicians who share his respect for discipline, who are willing to put in all of the work it takes to play their instruments at the highest level. I think that is extremely important.

Because of the demise of music education in the public schools, the talented children of today suffer immeasurably. They don't have the band director that I, for example, had. They rarely have the mentors that I had in any of the forms of music in which I was active. As a result, it is harder for them. They don't have the advantage of direct association with a historical legacy.

In my reaction to the whole notion of Black History Month in general and special programs having to do with African American art and culture—which is often only performed during that period—I guess one has to face the historical fact that African Americans have traditionally been marginalized in this society.

When it comes to music in the written tradition, for example, conventional wisdom is that this is the province of European culture and people who are descendants of European culture; people from other parts of the world simply are not involved in this tradition. Of course, we know that there is a long, interesting, and important history of African Americans being involved in the written history of music, as well as their own glorious vernacular tradition. One can only begin to address marginalization by coming to grips with the fact that it has been historical. That means that one has to look at different avenues of addressing that marginalization. One means of addressing it is institutionalizing events focusing on things that heretofore have been lost, borrowed, or stolen. This idea of Black History Month grows out of the historical fact that black history, black contributions to the culture, to science, and to the nation as a whole, were minimalized; therefore it was incumbent upon African Americans themselves to say, "Hey wait a minute, look over here, let's begin to look at this accurately." One way of doing it was focusing on a particular time frame. Because the society as a whole is still not aware of all of the contributions, I think there still is a need for that focus. If one didn't do that, there would be a lot of people who simply wouldn't know about it.

Unfortunately, such awareness is not where it should be, even though some things have changed. As I mentioned earlier, we have a different situation now at the beginning of the twenty-first century than we did thirty or forty years ago. People know more, but the level of awareness of the music still is not as high as it should and could be. We have only begun to address some of the hundreds of years of conscious omission of the contributions of peoples of African descent. It will take a long time and special efforts to address that, so I support the kind of focus that happens during Black History Month or during special programs. Now, having said that, I think it is also a mistake to present music of African American composers, or the music of any particular ethnic group, only in those venues. I think that music should become a part of the overall repertoire that is performed all the time. That is the ultimate goal, and if we existed in an equitable world, one would have ample opportunity to hear this music represented as part of the overall programming. But we don't live in an ideal world, and there is still a problem, so we still need those venues, we still need those special programs. At the same time we need not simply be part of the larger scheme of things, we also need to redefine what is meant by the larger scheme of things.

I think, however, any means, however well intended, to address this problem can become distorted. Let's take it out of the realm of African American composers for a moment and talk about contemporary music in general. Look at the history of orchestras attempting to address the problem of lack of programming of contemporary music in general. If one looks back at the 1960s, there were initiatives that occurred in which various orchestras started special programs, like special festivals in contemporary music, designed to address the fact that much of the music that was played was written a hundred years before. Many people felt that the symphony should also do music of the contemporary time, and they began to do it by setting up special festivals. Theoretically speaking, that was good.

The problem was that occasionally people would simply do that, have a festival of contemporary music, and put all the contemporary music in that one festival. It would be attended by a special audience, and that would be the end of it. They would say, "Okay, we have paid our dues to contemporary music; now let's go on." Then they would go back and play their eighteenth- and nineteenth-century repertoire as they always had done. That same pattern has often been used by some orchestras. For example, I think the Detroit Symphony was one of the first that established a competition, a concert of music by African American composers. As a matter of fact, when they did their first competition concert, I was asked to be a judge. Initially, I refused. I asked them what music they had performed of African American composers in that year and what they were planning to do the next year, and there was very little. There was maybe one piece that they had done in the last two years, if any at all. I said, "Well, look, it seems to me that what you are doing is focusing all of your energy in the wrong direction. I think it is commendable to have a special competition, but that shouldn't be the end of it. It shouldn't be used to fulfill a responsibility to performing a wide range of music." I think that is a disservice. On the other hand, it was a service for some young composers; still, it didn't particularly mean much to certain other composers, whose works were being done on a regular basis. For composers of my generation and composers who had been around for a while and had had some success in getting their works played over the last twenty years, it wasn't a big deal. For the Detroit Symphony to read a work of mine or of another composer who had been around and had many works performed, and some even recorded, was not a major thing. Yet there were some young composers and some not-so-young composers who hadn't had the opportunity to have any of their work read by a major orchestra, and therefore for them it was a major thing. I didn't oppose their plan in principle, I opposed it if it was being used as a vehicle to fulfill their responsibilities. I made that very clear when I declined their invitation to judge. The person who was organizing the project passed this on.

I am happy to say that the next season they did program several works of African American composers. There wasn't just one, there were at least two or three. I was asked to judge the following year, and I did participate. So I am not unalterably opposed to such events, but I think they shouldn't be used as an excuse, or as a ghetto, to fulfill what should be a large and continuing responsibility.

I met a large group of black composers in the 1960s. I never met Florence Price—I think she had passed on by the time I became aware of her—but I did meet Howard Swanson. I was back in New York for a performance or something, I can't remember what the occasion was, but I think this may have been something that Eileen Southern had put together, because I know a group of composers got together at her house late in the '60s, at about the same time the Society of Black Composers was established. Dorothy Rudd Moore was probably part of that society, but I think the people who originally founded it were Talib Rasul Hakim and Carman Moore. Dorothy Rudd Moore and Kermit, her husband, were there, too, as well as Noel DaCosta, who, I believe also helped found it. Several composers who lived in the New York area were involved. Howard Swanson lived in the area. Hale Smith may or may not have been involved in it. But several composers got together.

I do remember meeting Howard Swanson, whose *Short Symphony* I had heard. I was very impressed by his work, and I found him to be a very gracious and dedicated person. Although I didn't know him that well, I only met him once or twice, he was an impressive individual in terms of his general sense of humanity, and he was also an excellent musician and composer. He was a role model, a person who had been writing music and had achieved some success in this field, to whom I could relate very well. I found that a very positive experience.

I met Ulysses Kay for the first time when I was a graduate student at the University of Illinois. This must have been around 1960. He was a guest composer at the university, and he talked about and played his music. Some of the ensembles on campus also performed his music. I found it very inspiring and very impressive, because here was an African American composer who at that point was clearly established. I think at that time he may have been an editor for one of the major publishing houses in New York, but he was making a career as a musician and a composer. He was a very solid composer and was well respected as he managed to carve out a career. That was inspiring to me.

I found his music convincing as well. Subsequently I met him several times. I would see him periodically at concerts and occasionally over the years when I was in New York at events with other composers. For example, Hale Smith was always very good about getting composers together. In addition, there were several festivals of African American music. Among the advantages of those festivals, like the one out at Indiana in 1969 and the one at Michigan in 1985, were the kinds of interaction that they fostered between people, between composers and performers. They provided an opportunity for composers to meet each other, to share ideas, and to encourage one another throughout the sixties and the seventies. That was one of the reasons why I was able to share ideas with Ulysses Kay. I also talked to him on a couple of occasions over the years.

When I heard he was ill I intended to talk with him, but he passed away before I had a chance. I really felt badly about that. Ulysses Kay was a member of the American Academy of Arts and Letters, and when I was elected to it he sent me a very nice congratulatory note.

I met William Grant Still for the first time at Indiana University, at the first conference that dealt with African American music and African American composers, which was, I believe, in 1969. Still was there, quite elderly, and I found he was a very gracious person, from a personal perspective. Politically, as I think I have said on other occasions, we were very, very different. He was not very empathetic with the emerging black arts movement at that time, not as it was being projected at that particular historical moment. He viewed the movement politically as being separatist and designed to look within and appreciate black culture. At the same time, as a Harlem Renaissance composer, he had, of course, dealt with earlier concepts of African American cultural appreciation, so he was a rather complicated individual in political and philosophical terms. As a composer, I thought he had a lot to offer.

As part of the tenor of the times in the late 1960s, there were some ideologues who weren't necessarily dealing with music but with the broader political ideology of art and culture who would say from time to time, "You should be doing this or you shouldn't be doing that." Occasionally such an individual who would say, "European music is dead." You would hear people who saw things solely in black-and-white terms saying that anything from Europe was dead, anything that did not grow out of clearly definable African American tradition had evolved from other people and was jaded, and therefore irrelevant. I was responding to that position in an article I wrote around the late 1960s or early '70s. There was a point of view, mainly in the literary circles of that period (journals like *Black World,* for example), that would caricature anything that wasn't identified as unalterably and absolutely, demonstrably African American or African. What I was saying in my article was, "Hey, a lot of this stuff that you think is not yours is certainly influenced by your culture; but moreover, your experience is so broad that it is also influenced by things outside of your culture as well. The critical thing is that you make the decisions, you filter things through your own experience. It is ridiculous to try to shun things that come out of other cultures." That is one of the fascinating things about being human—you can adjust to a lot of different things, you can interpret and reinterpret different things. Part of that discourse was a kind of anti-intellectual movement, and it also toyed with some notions that have been further clarified as a high-art/low-art axis. People who buy into that say, "This is high, this is low. Well, African American traditionally is considered low, but we are going to turn it upside down so that this is going to be high and that is going to be low." It takes a dialectical approach to the world.

My personal creative process entails a combination of things. A lot depends on the piece, and it is hard to really pinpoint, but the process is a series of things, borrowing and utilizing, from one degree or another, many things. For example, if I am working on a new piece I try first to determine in general what the piece is about, what it is going to be, what its instrumentation will be, and I try to determine the overall concept of the piece.

The macro level—that is, that large idea—is significantly impacted by the specific details. Those details are arrived at in the process of getting started on a work, or trying to compose a piece. Sometimes it is a combination of ideas, sometimes it is a result of improvising. I might start out by improvising something.

If a specific musical idea becomes clear to me, I might go and review my notebooks of little ideas that have come to me over the last few months. Sometimes, those will be written ideas. Other times, they will be ideas that I have put on tape, either by singing or by playing, and sometimes these ideas come full-blown. Other times they are fragments, little fragments, or a combination of little fragments. Then the issue becomes how to synthesize these ideas so that they become a larger, generative idea. What I am saying is that the process is one of always moving back and forth between the larger idea to the specific ideas.

How do I get to the specific ideas? When I sit at my desk in the morning, I am constantly thinking. It depends on where I am in the process, whether it is in the early part of the process, whether I am exploring a number of different alternatives. I will try idea A, idea B, and idea C. Sometimes I force myself to create something. If I am sitting there for two, three, or four hours, I want to come away with something, so I write something down. I might not be convinced by my idea, but I decide I am going to pursue it. Then I will come back the next day and review the idea again and decide if any of it makes sense.

Occasionally I imagine parts of a new piece with great clarity—with what I think Copland has referred to as a "sonorous image." You have this sonorous image, and sometimes it is very clear. At other times it is not as clear, and you work to clarify it constantly by stimulating yourself musically.

There are certain fundamental biases I have about music. I want music to make some kind of meaningful statement, to have some continuity from moment to moment. The notion of music as a narrative is one that is important to me, but there are different kinds of narratives that one can create. I believe that music is expressive, but music also has to have a structure undergirding it, that ties it together. I am concerned that by the end of the piece listeners have the sense that they have done something, that they have gone somewhere, that they have experienced something on a number of different levels. The whole notion of development is at the bottom of a lot of it, but different kinds of development. The development is not necessarily always creating something that is transformed from the beginning to the end, so that the end becomes a more complex statement of the first event. It might be the kind of structure in which a lot of fragments come together and shape something in the middle, so there is a sense of development, but it is not necessarily development in a Beethovenian sense.

There are other times, however, when I consciously won't use that kind of development, where I will simply make the piece kaleidoscopic. One can see something here, one focus on a little angle of it, and then one can see another angle of it over there. A lot depends upon the nature of the material. I guess I am curious about looking at a number of different approaches, and I try to make the developmental or the compositional choices relevant to the material that it is attempting to expand.

What I would like to accomplish as an artist is to create a body of work that is meaningful to the people who hear it. I would like to create music that speaks to listeners about what it means to share the human condition, that speaks about sensitivities and sensibilities, that helps to clarify what it means to be alive in the present century.

Dwight Andrews

Dwight Andrews, a native Detroiter, is known as a scholar/musician who works simultaneously as a composer, pastor (of the First Congregational United Church of Christ, in Atlanta), musical director, author, and academician. Dr. Andrews holds a Ph.D. in music theory and a master's in divinity from Yale University, with an undergraduate degree in music from the University of Michigan. He serves as professor of music at Emory University, teaching courses in music theory and jazz history, as well as courses examining the relationship between theology, society, and the arts. Known by many as the principal musical collaborator with the award-winning playwright August Wilson, he has also created the music for *Ma Rainey's Black Bottom, The Piano Lesson,* and his own *Seven Guitars.* Dr. Andrews served as the director of the National Black Arts Festival in 1998, held in Atlanta. He was awarded the first Quincy Jones Chair in Music at Harvard University (1996–97). He lives and works in Atlanta, Georgia.

My humble opinion about the issue of arts education is that it needs to be subsumed under a more sound philosophy of education in general. I think we have lost our moral and intellectual compass. We are not as connected to the idea that you educate people not simply to get a job but so that they have an understanding and perspective and relationship to their history and to their culture, of the shared American culture and all of the specific subcultures that make it up. Because of that, art is an absolutely vital way of understanding who we are today, where people have been at different points in our history, and why their arts reflect their perspective.

The real roots of my musical experience come from growing up in Detroit and being part of the public music education program there. When I was growing up there was a fantastic wellspring of excellent music teachers who were well-trained and broadly experienced musicians. Probably the most influential person in the first part of my life was Anderson White, who directed the band and the orchestra at Durfee Junior High School and Longfellow Elementary School. He was a tenacious music teacher; he was like a bulldog. When he thought he saw people with potential, he really drove them, not only in rehearsals at school but at private lessons, which he provided for half the musicians I knew, and he directed a community orchestra in a church basement. He himself was a jazz bassist, so my first experiences were with a music teacher who was really committed to teaching and who himself was pretty broadly based in terms of his own music experiences. He had been out and played with a lot of cats, so my introduction to early jazz musicians as well as to the Western European masters was through this music teacher. I got introduced to Yusef Lateef [jazz

instrumentalist-composer], Ramsey Lewis [jazz pianist], and the Jazz Crusaders [a modern jazz group], because these were all his contemporaries. We would go to these clubs and play on Sunday afternoons with a little junior high school jazz band. At the same time, we would be playing in woodwind quintets. Between Andy White and my experience at Cass Tech [high school in Detroit], where things just got deeper and more intense, I think, I owe my whole musical interest and passion to these great teachers that I had, and all these great ensembles and experiences. They really pushed you.

It was very late when I decided to compose. Like many musicians my age, I had a rock and roll band in the late 1960s and I wrote some tunes, but we were primarily doing covers. Doing covers provided me experience and training for my ears. In a sense, learning to take the tunes off records sharpened my skills more than anything else, but I really didn't consider myself a writer or a composer—that really wasn't my interest. My interest was in trying to learn how to play, and that remained my focus until after I graduated from Michigan and went east to go to seminary in the 1970s. When I went to Yale Divinity School, I found myself trying to make a living as a musician to pay for seminary. I started to get these little theater gigs, where I had to do a lot more arranging for different kinds of ensembles. I had had the training at Michigan, but I really didn't have the experience while I was in school. It was then, really, that I started both in the theater and also working with some choreographers, providing music for rehearsals. I started writing more and more and got interested in the whole idea of writing. I was fully grown, but I still did not regard myself as a composer. I was really just trying to learn about writing. I credit the theater and dance experience for my interest in composition. I was always working for some other medium, not for the concert stage.

Q: What relationship do you see between music and spirituality?

A: When I left Michigan as a musician to go to seminary to try to learn about the ministry and also about religion, I saw them both as two distinct disciplines. I thought ultimately I would have to give up the music to do the ministry. I did not see them as connected at all. When you are at Michigan, you are really training to be a player, period. I don't think at that time in my development I really saw the additional connections. For me, ironically, these connections came very late. In the last twenty years I have started to think of the interrelatedness of one's spiritual essence and music, to think of music as a way of both expressing and reflecting spirituality. I am still coming to grips with both spirituality and trying to use that understanding in my music.

People tell me that it comes through in my music. The spiritual experiences that I have had really come not so much from the act of composing as from the act of experiencing music. For example, I sometimes have a spiritual experience when I myself am playing, or when I am listening to someone else, either live or recorded. The music can transport me, take me to another plane. It's funny, I don't connect the actual act of composing, at least I don't yet; I don't have what I call a spiritual experience when I am trying to write music. I am trying to figure out what I am hearing and then how to get it on paper or on tape. I still think of it as a craft-oriented activity rather than a spiritual one. I know many other composers see it on a much higher plane, but I just haven't gotten there yet.

There have been several composers who have influenced me, and most of them have been people whose music I have known so intimately that it really just helped not so much to shape what I write as to shape the idea of me as a writer. Leo Smith's music, Oliver Lake's music, and Anthony Davis's [black American contemporary composers] music, those three composers really helped to shape me when I was beginning to think of myself as a composer. Also, because I was playing their music all the time, I not only knew what it looked like, but I had a sense of the sensibility of their music. Leo's conceptualization of time and music was probably the most radically influential, because he has elaborate systems of sound and silence, where silence equals sound. He radically reorganized my thinking about music and time. Davis, I think, opened me up in terms of sound complexes. Lake just reminded me of how important soul is to all music. He sets up a soulful sound no matter what he writes or plays. Those three stand out for me the most. On the other hand, there are European musicians who I studied intimately, and I was also influenced by them. The two who come to mind the most are Stravinsky and Beethoven, both of whom I highly regard for much the same reason. I think they really knew how to extend a musical idea to its rightful conclusion. I am drawn still to the music of both of those composers. I can listen to Beethoven's piano music forever and not get tired of it. The same goes for some of Stravinsky's music.

When I am writing music for the theater, I usually have very specific goals in mind. For example, when I did *Ma Rainey's Black Bottom,* set in the 1920s, I really did use many of the classic blues singers and early Louis Armstrong music as models for my compositions. I was really trying to copy directly from that language and that period. When I did *The Piano Lesson,* which was set in the 1930s, I used for my models the great pianists of the day, like James P. Johnson, Willie the Lion Smith, and those players. What has always guided me, what has always been my forte, is a certain aural connectedness from copying those tunes when I was in high school. I think I hear pretty well, and I think I have an affinity for being able to find the essence of a 1930s "stride" piano song, what makes it tick, just like I think I have some sense of what makes a late 1948 R&B song kick. I think I have a sense and an ear for the essence of these musics. In terms of pop traditions, the traditions that I grew up with are the ones that still guide me to a certain extent—not so much soul music, because I was really influenced by the Beatles. Their songwriting had a tremendous impact. Probably the most important song writer for me was Milton Nacsimento [Brazilian popular and jazz composer], because Milton's music has so much drama, theatricality, and simplicity. It always fascinates me how music can be simple and complex at the same time. Milton is perhaps the single most influential model. Milton, the Beatles, all the pop cats, I've listened to them all. But if I'm looking for inspiration, I would have to say I go back to *Sgt. Pepper's* or some of Milton's early music.

Q: How would you define "black music"?

A: Black music is itself such a broad playing field. My take on it is that black music is derived, first and foremost, out of the African American experience. I have a rather deliberately broad definition, because I think black music is more than the sum of its parts. It is not just R&B, jazz, soul, rap, hip-hop, and be-bop. It is not any of those—it is all of those, and much more. What makes it much more is the fact that the music is always a musical response, not just to music but to life. It is a particular way of looking at and responding to life through sound. If you are black and living in this world, that gives you a particular perspective. In a sense, I try to not think of black music as literally highly rhythmic or percussive, or as the use of call and response. Those things trivialize the experience that I have with black music. What I think is important about black music is that it is an individual expression. The individual voice is always a part of African American and black music traditions.

The black experience is so broad; for one thing, it depends upon what time you are talking about. If you are talking about today, there are many black Americans who do not share a common experience in terms of education, religion, culture, language, or mode of dress. Yet if they allow themselves to participate in an understanding of the historical traditions and want to acknowledge that in their traditions, that for me is black music. But black music has nothing to do with race. I think it has everything to do with an understanding of what it means to be black and wanting to identify, or not identify, with what it means to be the "other" in this society. If you identify with the other and want to acknowledge and lift up traditions that go beyond the concert music traditions, then, to my way of thinking, that is part of the black music expression.

Unfortunately, education in America today is so goal oriented, and with the most superficial goals in mind. The idea is that if somebody can pass a test or get a job and do it halfway competently, that is good. You don't have the old-fashioned idea that education itself has any value, that arts education has its own intrinsic value. To my way of thinking, we will reclaim a proper perspective on arts education only when we reclaim a proper idea about education, which is, I think, to prepare the citizenry for a democratic community in which people participate fully.

In terms of black music and black youth, the issue gets a little more complicated, because the boundaries around what could have been called black music are becoming so fractured by the way in which our communities are, in a sense, no longer segregated. In a sense, black music is as much a part of not just the black community but the white communities, and vice versa. It is very hard for me to get a handle on how black music functions in black culture, and in black communities today, except to say that I think music still operates in many black communities as a central expression to all of the experience. That is becoming less and less true, though, as African American communities become more and more stratified economically, politically, and socially. Sometimes one can encounter a black community in terms of racial identification, but these people don't identify with any of the racial attributes that we used to think of as being black. Increasingly, these racial labels are becoming dysfunctional on certain levels, if only because the African American experience itself is becoming so much more stratified. Leroi Jones predicted and described this phenomenon in *Blues People*. He said "If you study the music, you will understand the people. The music will change as the people change." I think what we see today is a part of that ever-unfolding process.

Q: How do you view Black History Month celebrations?

A: Black History Month programs serve a purpose, in that the majority culture still will not, unfortunately, allow African Americans to participate fully in the life of culture in America. From a very pragmatic standpoint, having a focus on the contributions of African Americans in one month is better than having no month. But at the same time, I am beginning to sense that the blacklash of Black History Month is that it seems to make it more likely that white people will not want to acknowledge black at any other time. Folks can feel like they have done their duty as long as they did something in Black History Month. It is a rather feeble attempt to counter a basically racist white environment in which we cannot fully participate and have not been fully welcomed. That is what it represents, a reminder of just how really racist this place is.

Q: What commonalities do you see between traditional or common practice and black music traditions?

A: I see some musical commonalities in Bach, Parker, Ravel, Ellington. What is most persuasive and powerful about them is their own senses of how musical time can unfold, how music can have an "arch." If you listen to Bach, or if you listen to Ellington, it seems like what needs to happen, happens at precisely the right moment, and couldn't have happened two bars sooner. If you look at Ellington, Bach, and Bird [Charlie "Yardbird" Parker], there are wonderful irregularities in their music. In other words, it is their genius and their understanding of the music that allow them to know that some particular thing needs *not* to happen where it is supposed to happen in terms of some external formal rule. Their musical understanding was so complete. Duke and Bach will take you on similar chromatic detours, ultimately not changing where things must go but understanding exactly how to use the language to create a sense of drama and tension. That is the one commonality. I really don't hear, when I listen to Ellington, aside from the fact that all of those composers are all tonal composers, the things that make me think of Bach, except for a wonderful sense of temporality.

Now there are better comparisons to be made, I think, between Bird and Bach, of course, because they are dealing in many ways with similar contrapuntal issues. In that sense, you can look at some of Bird's lines and see some of Bach's keyboard lines, a kind of two-to-one or four-to-one counterpoint kind of thinking, but obviously with a much more expanded or extended language. What is attractive about them is not that there is an analogy between Bird and Bach, but rather that these thinkers knew how to move through musical time— which is what I, as a composer, am always trying to work with. What is the sense of proportion, how long does this moment need to be before it needs to be something else? This is a deeper musical issue for me.

Q: What is your compositional process?

A: In my own work, I start by listening. I start listening to my head to see what comes out. I will rarely go to any instruments; for me the human voice is still my model, even though I am not a singer. But it is my starting point. If I can sing it, that gives me a way of starting. No matter what the piece is, I always start by singing. I need to hear something; once I hear it, and before I try to play it, I try to sing it. After I have gone through the process of listening to myself, to my inner ear, then step two of that process is trying to articulate it, which I never try to do at the piano, because I am not a pianist. But because I don't want my technique to be in any way guiding what my compositions are, I literally have to hear a piece in my head. Then I move from the head to the voice, and then ultimately to some external instrument to notate or to begin to play with the ideas.

I am very eclectic. I usually work in a very linear fashion. What I try to do, and I am not always successful, is take small musical ideas, a series of maybe three, four, or five notes, and try to understand its essence. I try to understand what this five-note series is about, and once I do, I can begin to say, "What are my possibilities?" In other words, I always try to totally exhaust an idea before I go to the next idea. I try to see what my possibilities are, what is implied in this idea that can spin out the next one. What happens if I juxtapose this five-note idea with maybe a rhythmic series of equal dimensions? I begin a playful improvisatory process that has much more to do with line rather than the vertical.

My work with August Wilson is really rather specific and rather particular, because he doesn't write musicals; he is only interested in straight plays. But because he feels and understands that music is central to the characters that he creates, virtually all of his plays have had very wonderful, powerful moments in which music happens—moments that are rare but precisely exquisite. My challenge in working with him has been to realize his musical dreams for his dramas. These plays are always guided by time, place, and people rather than specific circumstances. What I try to do is re-create a reality, but not as a composer; I have to suppress my composer's ego, to re-create an expression that really comes out of traditional African American culture. That is my role. In a sense, I am a re-creator in his works. I am really fortunate that he has elected to use me again and again.

Q: What would you say is your musical philosophy?

A: My own political stance as a musician is one of activism. I grew up in a generation of activists, I grew up in a time of hyped awareness of everyone's social responsibility. It is hard for me to separate that out from my role as a musician or a composer. Yet when I am composing, I am really thinking about art, not about protest. But at the same time, I am still a citizen. If my piece doesn't directly speak to a specific kind of social activism, I as a citizen, I feel it must. I use the privileged place of artist to be an activist. I think that is completely appropriate, useful, and vital. I don't think that artists can afford to lock themselves up with their art. In my experience, that just doesn't resonate. That is a rather privileged, classist notion of the role of the artist. I reject that role. I think of myself, along with all of my other comrades who work on the assembly lines or shine shoes for a living, as being both citizens and craftspeople. We all have a role to play, participating in the betterment of our communities. Sometimes that will involve our specific craft, or sometimes it will involve doing something different, being out in the street, being in a march, or building a house with Habitat for Humanity. I can't put myself in a vacuum. I don't think it is appropriate for artists to insulate themselves away from everything that is going on around them. I don't think it's appropriate, and I don't think it's useful.

Q: Where do you see American music headed in terms of artistry?

A: I see a state of confusion in contemporary American music in the concert world, the popular world, and the jazz world. All three are affected by the same things. They are affected as much by economics as anything else. In some ways, they are more and more driven by the lack of intellectual and moral compass that I talked about earlier. Economics is starting to dictate virtually everything—economics and politics. For example, in the areas of jazz, I am frustrated because I don't feel a sense of forward movement in terms of experimentation; the jazz tradition has always been moving forward. I see a certain amount of retrenchment, not just on the part of musicians but in the music industry. What you hear now are wonderfully proficient players playing like Donald Byrd [jazz trumpeter] and Freddie Hubbard [jazz trumpeter] played in the 1960s. It is great that people can re-create that music on that level, but I am not nearly as challenged by that as I am by people who are stretching the tradition to see the next step.

Unfortunately, in jazz, and to a certain extent in popular music, I sense a certain lack of the individual, forward-looking voices that I would want to hear. I suspect that they are out there, but I also suspect that the industry has a conservative bent and is just not putting those people out there. I am not hearing them on the radio or on the concert stages. I think, unfortunately, that we are in a kind of holding pattern, waiting to hear what the next step will be. In concert music, I think there is much of the same thing.

We are living in an age when composers are influenced by a variety of musics and traditions, but because race continues to fracture how we view the artist, if not the art, some people are more equal than others when they want to use other people's music. In a sense, Steve Reich and Philip Glass [contemporary composers] are eclectic in their use of traditional musics from around the world, but there is a certain expectation upon African American composers that I find very limiting. If you are a black composer, people want to hear what is "black" about it. I find that frustrating and silly, especially these days when composers like me or any number of other people have a variety of backgrounds and disciplines and are steeped in many traditions, not just one. I don't find orchestras or critics nearly as comfortable dealing with our eclecticism as they are with that of their white counterparts. To a certain extent I think this is due to the racial reality that white people have been ripping off other people's stuff forever and it has always been seen as a new interesting thing—George Gershwin, Paul Whiteman, Aaron Copland, and Leonard Bernstein. Interestingly enough, they are labeled as "great American voices." I just wonder at what point, since half of that music is based on our music, *we* become American voices, instead of always being seen as a kind of outsider, as the other, or a special something.

I feel like I am heir to so many different musical traditions, all of which I think I completely embrace and understand. Aesthetically, I just see myself more as a sponge rather than as a point on a line in a continuum. I feel like I am trying to soak up as much music from wherever I can hear it as possible. That is what my musical personality is. I am not sure, but I think if in another two or three generations, if people look back at my music, they might say, "Well, if you listen to Dwight Andrew's music, you get some sense of a person who was attempting to stretch." I think I would ultimately like to leave here with the idea of, "Here was a tireless soldier who tried to fight to make life more livable in all of its many manifestations—art, understanding." I am just trying to make the place better, and that is what guides all of this. I am trying to come in, look at the terrain, and see how I can make it a little bit better. That is the rather modest goal that has fueled all of these various manifestations. I do that through my art and through my teaching. That is what links all of my efforts together, the idea that I am trying to make it better for the next generation.

What I teach is that you don't take the easy answer to everything, you don't just listen to the surface of the music; you understand what it is connected to and understand to whom it is connected. For example, since I teach at primarily white universities, I try to get my students not to connect so much with the music but with the world out of which the music comes. In that sense I try to get my students to a new level of understanding and appreciation of the art and, ultimately, of the artist. Essentially, my experience in teaching is that people want to separate the art from the artist, when it comes to black people. They would much rather deal with jazz than with the history and the legacy of racism that helped to create jazz. What I am trying to do is to get people to understand the complexities of life that create the possibilities for the blues. People would much prefer just to deal with the blues and talk about how much they enjoy it rather than talk about why we have the blues. I am trying to get people to see that you can appreciate the blues but still understand where it comes from and why it comes from where it does. That is the hope, at least.

Ysaye Maria Barnwell

Dr. Ysaye M. Barnwell, a native New Yorker, born in 1946, is known for her voice, the solid foundation of the internationally renowned group Sweet Honey in the Rock. Dr. Barnwell spends as much time off-stage as an instructor and clinician in cultural performance theory and voice production. She has given her workshop "Singing in the African American Tradition" all over the United States, Great Britain, and Australia, making her work in the field a source of inspiration for her performances on stage. She has both a B.S. and M.S. in speech pathology (State University of New York at Geneseo), a Ph.D. in cranio-facial studies (University of Pittsburgh), and an M.S. in Public Health (Howard. University, Washington, D.C.). She has been a professor at the College of Dentistry at Howard University, and in addition to conducting community-based projects in computer technology and in the arts, she has implemented and administered health programs at Children's Hospital National Medical Center and at Gallaudet University in Washington, D.C. Since joining Sweet Honey in 1979, she has composed and arranged for ten recordings on Flying Fish, EarthBeat/Warner, and Music for Little People labels, as well as film and video projects. She has worked as a commissioned composer on numerous and varied projects including *Sesame Street,* Dance Alloy of Pittsburgh, David Rousseve's Reality Dance Company, the Liz Lerman Dance Exchange, the Women's Philharmonic of San Francisco, and Redwood Cultural Work, all outgrowths of her understanding of how creative artists are inextricably bound to society. Dr. Barnwell resides in Washington, D.C.

I am from New York City, and my father was a violinist. He named me after the violinist Eugene Ysaye, a Belgian violinist and composer. My father was also a teacher, and he taught me for fifteen years. I started playing the violin when I was two and a half. I was in all-city orchestra and concertmaster of my high school orchestra. I went through a special program in Juilliard while I was in high school, and that was a serious foundation for me. Everything I know now, I learned then. My father was so set on my being a violinist that he and my mother had a major disagreement when I was four. A spiritual reader had told my mother that I was going to be a singer. They used to go back and forth, and of course, for a really long time it looked like my father was going to win. I started singing in college. I dropped the violin when I went to New York State University at Geneseo, because I wanted to major in speech pathology.

I didn't do the church music thing, and I'm not sure why that was; we went to a Baptist Church, and I heard serious gospel music all through the fifties.

When I was growing up, going to school, I listened to gospel music on the radio and heard gospel music in church, but I didn't join the choirs. I think it was because people had a different expectation for me, because my father had a different expectation for me. I was the one who did the violin recitals and shared the program sometimes with classical voice students. People just never expected I would do gospel.

In junior high school I sang in a community choir that did spirituals; most of the arrangements for spirituals that I know in my head I learned then. I went on to college and stopped playing the violin, because the orchestra was not very good, it wasn't much of a challenge. I joined a group called the Geneseo Chamber Singers. We sang madrigals, motets, and sometimes would sing spirituals and folksongs. It was a touring group, so I did get to perform in that sense. My first vocal recording was done with that choir. The director of that choir also taught a folk music class where I picked up the guitar. This was 1963; I was in college from 1963 to 1967, and I got a master's degree in 1968.

The whole civil rights thing was breaking out. The school that I was enrolled in was all-white; there were seven black folks when I got there. That is significant, because those white folks ran me back to my black history. I was really fortunate. There were a couple of other influences that I should mention to you. My mother had a friend who never pressed her hair and was totally into blackness and the culture. She had Saturday morning sessions for those of us who were from ten to thirteen years old, where she would talk to us about Negro history. As a part of that, she introduced us to Nana Denizulu. Nana Dinizulu, who died about four years ago, was a major influence in bringing African culture and dance to this country. He brought the Akan religion to the United States. He taught the traditional dances, the traditional drumming rhythms, the costumes, all of that started with Dinizulu in New York, as far as I can tell. It was Dinizulu's African Drummers and Dancers, and I studied "for a minute" with them and got to dance with them in Central Park. That was a real strong influence in terms of Africa and African rhythm.

So in college, in 1963 with the civil rights struggle breaking out, I am learning how to play the guitar, I am listening to Odetta [a folksinger], who is now a dear friend, and I'm listening to Nina Simone, I am listening to Miriam Makeba, Buffy St. Marie [Native American singer and composer], and Richie Havens [folksinger]. I am also hearing the SNCC [Student Nonviolent Coordinating Committee] Freedom Singers who are singing the kind of things that the older people used to sing in the church I grew up in, but they are changing the words. I loved it. My three main influences were the women: Odetta, Nina, and Miriam. I feel like I learned how to play the guitar from Odetta and Richie Havens. I feel like I heard women's voices that had depth and range when I listened to Odetta, when I listened to Bernice and Rutha Harris, in the Freedom Singers, and I heard "serious attitude" from Nina. I had a god brother who my father had taught violin. He played bass with Nina for five years—that's Lyle Atkinson [bassist]. I got to hear a lot of Nina Simone. When I was home I would go to see live performances and sit and listen for hours. Those experiences were important in terms of learning how black women were using their voices, which was really different from white folk singers. Different voice color, different range, different purpose—it had intent. That was my lesson, that music was functional. That was different from the madrigal stuff I was singing.

I can tell you exactly when I went into the creation side of music. I had written a few songs, but everybody was writing songs. In 1976, I went to the Unitarian Church here in Washington, D.C., and before I joined the church I joined the choir. The interesting thing about that choir was that you had to be able to read music. They rehearsed at 9:30 in the morning what they were going to sing at eleven. They were singing in all kinds of languages. That meant that the black folks sat and listened, and the white folks sang, with few exceptions. That seemed ridiculous to me, and I talked to the minister about it. He told me I could do whatever I wanted to do. So I joined the church because there was that attitude, and I started a choir for folks who didn't have to read music, and that was mostly black folk. That's when all the spirituals I had learned in junior high school, all the stuff that I had ever seen conductors and directors do, I started teaching. The choir is still going; it's been over twenty years. A lot of the early influences started to come back at that point. The minister used to read Kahlil Gibran's *On Children* when he baptized children, except they don't really call it "baptism" in a Unitarian Church. He read this and month after month on the first Sunday, I would hear him reading, "Your children are not your children, they are the sons and daughters . . . ," and the thing just started to sing. I start there. I wrote music for those words, and the choir sang it.

When I set things to music, I only set them because they sing themselves. The text sings itself. I feel that other people should hear how the text is singing itself. That's the most that I can say about that process. I haven't done it a lot, but in every case where that has happened, that's what happened. I hear the tunes in my head. I don't write anything down, I sing all the parts into a tape recorder. Before there were four-tracks, I used to do two-track tapes, where by the time you get to the fourth or fifth part, you can't hear the melody. But I have always done it that way, and I think it is because I was always working out arrangements and things for a choir. I felt like I needed to be able to sing the parts. I had the range, I could sing the low parts as well as the high parts. I would just sing the next line, and the next line, and then it would all be there. I still follow that process.

Then, right about that point, in 1979, I joined Sweet Honey in the Rock, in D.C. Another piece came, which was called "Breaths," which was based on the poem by Birago Diop, who was a Senegalese poet. That too sang itself, but the interesting thing about that was that I had a different kind of consciousness about the piece. It was clearly an African worldview of death—that the dead are not dead, they are not under the ground, they are ever present with us. In all of the sounds of nature we can hear their voices reflected back to us. It is not specifically stated in the poem, but is clear to me that as long as we call their names and remember their works, they are still alive. That sang to me very loudly, but I also understood why I was putting certain rhythms under the melodies. Every single rhythm—there are three basic rhythms that go with the piece—meant something different to me. That was the first time I was conscious of that. I guess in a sense that links back to the Denizulu thing. I gave that song to Sweet Honey. I also gave "On Children" to Sweet Honey, and Sweet Honey recorded both of them. The choir, I think, still has both of them in their repertoire.

That was the beginning of writing. There is another poem called *No Images,* by Warren Cuney. I started setting it while I was in college. I used to sing it with guitar, and when I got into Sweet Honey, I arranged it for the group, so it is totally a cappella. A song called "More than a Paycheck" was the first thing in this period that I wrote the lyrics for. It is kind of a reggae thing.

I have a post-doctorate in public health. It was a nine-month program. I asked early in the program if I could take one month and go to Japan with Sweet Honey, and they thought that I was crazy. But I knew that I could fit what was going on into my program of studies. Somehow or other, they agreed to let me go. I was actually looking for a thesis, and I couldn't figure out what to do. I got over there, went to a city called Minamata, which I had just been studying because its ecology had been destroyed by mercury poisoning. While I was there I asked whether anyone had ever written any songs about what had happened, and people did not know of any. That started a whole train of thought for me, about the fact that (from the time I was a child I had heard Tennessee Ernie Ford singing, "Sixteen tons and what do you get? Another day older and deeper in debt") there are songs about environmental things, songs about work, etc. It was amazing to me that these people didn't know of any songs about this major incident.

I came back and decided that my thesis would look at the songs written by coal miners and textile workers to see how much folks knew about their own working conditions and illnesses. At the conclusion of that study, when I did the oral defense, I actually handed out to the faculty five coal-mining songs, five textile-worker songs, whited out the names of the diseases, and asked the faculty to guess whether they were about coal-mining or textile-work diseases. They saw the symptoms and the working conditions described in the songs and in every case they were able to name them. I decided that I wanted to add a song to the body of work/occupational songs, but my song was going to say, "It doesn't matter what kind of job you have, you are bringing home more than your paycheck." If you don't get sick, you are likely to get injured. If you don't get injured, you are likely to be stressed out. That is how that song evolved. I taught it to the faculty during the oral defense. All of these medical people were singing, "More than a paycheck, More than a paycheck." It was pretty wild.

It is clear to me from looking from an African worldview that music exists because it does something. It never is the art-for-art's-sake kind of phenomenon. If it doesn't make it rain, if it doesn't infuse herbs with a healing spirit, if it doesn't send a fighting energy into weapons that are being forged, then what good is a song? Quincy Jones asks, "What good is a song if it doesn't inspire, if it has no message to bring? If a song doesn't take you higher, higher, higher, what good is it to sing?" Because music is so integrated into every aspect of life activity for African people, I started asking how that applies for black people. It applies totally. We can see how our music has evolved; at every point that our history has taken another turn, our music has taken another turn. That to me is evidence of music's functionality. Then when you start to look at what the music says and how it was created and how it is used, it is totally clear that we have never dropped that aspect of who we are as African people. For example, when I look at spirituals, I see the whole history of slavery. Now, I have a slightly broader definition of what spirituals are, because I think that they are the whole body of songs written during slavery. I say that because African people didn't make a distinction between sacred and secular. In that sense, the music was very functional. It talked about every single aspect of life activity.

Coming into Sweet Honey, I find that whole tradition of music is functional. It serves people, it passes the values from generation to generation, it is the newspaper when newspapers aren't printing your story. It is the thing that gets played in the birthing rooms, gets sung at the funerals, that whole thing. That is what Sweet Honey does in people's lives, so I am told. It certainly is very much a part of how we see the world.

My experience is that Sweet Honey's music is primarily black, but black music, by and large, seems really to be more universal than almost any other music. My sense is that black music is very specific to our situation. Because it is so specific, it addresses what it knows best, and in that it becomes totally universal. This is why I think, for example, that people sing spirituals all over the world. When you say, "Nobody knows the trouble I've seen," people can identify with that even though—I am speaking particularly about myself—it wouldn't even occur to me that it would include someone who is Indian, or Japanese, or whatever, but they understand that. For example, I wrote a song that says, "There are no mirrors in my Nana's house." One of the lines says, "I never knew my skin was too black, I never knew my nose was too flat, I never knew my clothes didn't fit, I never knew there were things that I'd missed." I am amazed that when we sing that song I can see white people crying. I had a letter from a white male gay *a cappella* group requesting to sing that song, and I was stunned. I called them and told them I was stunned. They said in the letter that the song talked about such unconditional acceptance and love that they found themselves in the song. I said, "You can sing it because you really understand it, but you cannot change a single word. You have to sing, 'I never knew my skin was too black and my nose was too flat.' You cannot change that in any way." They agreed to that. My sense is that the more specific you can be about who you are, the more people understand that universally. I think that is what black music does. It is so personal that it cannot be ignored. It just really touches. In that sense I think our music is vulnerable, it is accessible. I don't know how else to describe it.

Black History Month, on one hand, is an opportunity that we ourselves can take advantage of. We can actually seek out opportunities to get an airing more easily during that period of time than almost any other time of the year. However, I always want to say to people, "If I come during February, will you invite me during another month?" I think it is ridiculous to focus everything and blow your whole budget in that month. We don't have that experience, by the way. What happens is we construct a Black History Month tour so that we actually are going South and do places where it is less expensive to tour than it is to fly the group in for one night and fly back. In a sense we ignore the Black History Month. We go to black schools during Black History Month. We go South, and we go everywhere else.

There are a few tunes that we collaborate on. Everybody in the group composes. We all have totally different styles and different methods of working, but we set deadlines for when we want to do a new album and we say, "You've got to bring in new material by this date so we can see whether or not it can make it to the album." Each of us teaches music differently. Everything is oral. I bring in my piece, and I know all the parts. Usually I bring in a rehearsal tape so that they can all hear it. Never is there an expectation, though, that they will sing it like I'm singing it. I hear who is going to sing what line, and I have a concept of where they are going to take it. On the same hand, I think people really see me as structured, so they are not as expansive in my work as they are in other people's work. Other people come in with only the melody and ask the group to arrange everything else. That gives us carte blanche. I know exactly, with my work, what I want people to do. But my work has been created under different circumstances. My work has been created primarily through commissions for music for dance. I've had three commissions for dance music performed by choir and one commission for a suite of songs for choir. "We Are" came out of that. A lot of the stuff that has been recorded has come out of those commissions. I have had to be much more structured.

The person who brings in the song teaches the song as best she can. Some are more successful than others, but some tunes are more complicated than others. Some tunes are traditional, and so you have to do them in a certain way. Others are contemporary and have a little bit more flexibility. We listen. We listen. We go around and around. In my case, people learn their parts, and once they do that, they are free "to go." I guess it is how I think spirituals are created. We try to figure out what it is the person who wrote it wants—"What kinds of sounds do you want heard? What do you want?" For example, one of the pieces on the album recording *Live at Carnegie Hall* is a piece by Evelyn Harris [an original member of Sweet Honey in the Rock] called "State of Emergency." It is about South Africa. When she brought that in she was talking about how things were going crazy in South Africa, who was right and who was wrong. At some point she said "It's [her song] gotta have this energy because I can hear the ambulances and the guns." I said, "Okay, let's put some sirens in." So, at the beginning of the piece there are two spiraling sirens, and they reoccur throughout the piece. It is a matter of throwing in pieces and trying to figure out what the person wants. Evelyn wrote another song called "My Lament." Each person in it is doing their thing; what I am doing is playing a clear cello line that comes right out of my classical violin training. It fits perfectly, I think, with what the song is.

People play with textures. We don't ever talk about rhythm, but the group is so rhythmic, that stuff just flies. I think that I have been with Sweet Honey for so long now that it is hard even to break down what we do. Earlier on, I think I could have done it. In my chapter in the book *We Who Believe in Freedom* [Doubleday/Anchon, 1993], I talk about singing songs on stage that we have never sung before. That happens in two instances. In one instance, Bernice might start a song and nobody knows it, but we will sing it. It is clear that we know the form, it is clear that we can figure out the harmonic structures— whoever gets on a line first stays there, and you just sing all around her. The other instance is when we do total "improvs" on stage. Somebody starts something, and we just sing with that. Each person is just weaving their lines, in and out, coming in, doing whatever. There are two recorded examples of this. One is called "Listen to the Rhythm" [on *We All Everyone of Us* (FF)]. In *Live at Carnegie Hall* there is an improv called "Our Side Won," around the Bork hearings [Robert H. Bork was nominated by President Ronald Reagan to the Supreme Court in 1987 but was rejected by the Senate]. I can tell you exactly how that started. We were in the dressing room and people on the news had been saying, "The bitter battle over Bork is raging." That just was such a great line that in the dressing room, I was walking around saying, "The bitter battle over Bork, the bitter battle over Bork." We get onstage and we know that in some point in the concert there is going to be an improv. It was my turn, I started something. The thing is going, it is almost over. Then I hear Bernice say, "Bitter battle." I looked at her and I said, "Yeah, bitter battle over Bork. Bitter battle, bitter battle over Bork." It turned into a little rap thing, "Bitter battle over Bork." I don't even remember the words. It went from this other improv of a whole different color into this rap at the end. That was the inspiration, that's where it started, and it showed up on stage. Other things show up on stage like that too. I don't think it is any different from a jazz ensemble. We don't work with a pitch pipe, and nobody has perfect pitch. Whatever key the song gets started in is going to influence the texture. The tempo is going to be influenced by whomever starts it and their mood. Things do change, and there is never the expectation that things are going to be the same.

I think artists are the storytellers, I think we are the people who pass values from those who have gone before to those who are coming afterward. I think we articulate things that other people are not able to articulate for themselves. I see this particularly with Sweet Honey. People are constantly saying to us, "I am so glad to hear somebody say this from the stage. This is what I have been feeling and thinking for so long." I think artists keep energy flowing in the universe, I really do. It scares me that budgets for the arts are being cut, because kids are not being exposed to that energy in a really healthy and constructive way. I'm scared. I certainly feel that what the young rappers are doing is on a continuum and is not new. I really hope that they know that it is not new. When I do talk to young rap artists and we get into this, I tell them, all the time, and I start tracing for them, from the griot [West African musician/entertainer] on, through the church minister, all of it. It is a continuum. What they are doing with their music is on a continuum. I don't fault what they are doing, I am nervous and frightened because of the "read" itself, which says we are in trouble. Our young people are saying these things because we are in trouble. If we had a different view of the world, they would be seeing things differently and using their creative talents in a more positive way. I don't like blaming, that is not constructive for me. I try to figure out where this is coming from. What was going on in society that caused the blues to evolve? What was going on that caused gospel music to evolve? What is going on in society that causes rap to evolve? What is the inspiration, what is propelling our young people into lyrics that are violent, lyrics that are abusive? That is where I try to have conversations with people. I get the question about rap music all the time in interviews.

I think our entire society is violent, and I think that is reflected in the music. I think therefore that young artists are not only to blame. They are maybe the least to blame because in some ways—I get nervous treading on this territory—I feel like they are courageous in putting it out there. On the other side of the coin, this music has become popular because someone has positioned it in the top-forty market; those people do not position jazz artists, or Sweet Honey in the Rock. It is what is inside and churning over. Putting it out there is probably more constructive than being violent. It is the same thing that happened in blues. I don't blame the blues composer because they talk about shooting women, when they talk about shooting their lovers. They talk about a lot of violent things in blues. What I say is, "What was going on in the society?" For me, when I look at homelessness, when I look at teenagers without jobs and without hope, when I look at people who are being laid off from work—at Howard University they gave them four hours to empty out their desks and get off the campus; they had a police escort, because they knew that if they didn't, somebody was going to go crazy. Well, what happens to young people in the midst of all that? What happens to young people who grow up in a society where everything you hear has to do with war, and very little has to do with the making of peace? What do they have to look forward to when monies are being stripped from education? They don't have a computer in their whole school, and yet the whole society is moving on the Internet, an information superhighway. What do they have to look forward to, and how does that get acted out? It gets acted out in really abusive and violent songs.

In my own work, I guess I do want people to be touched by something I have done. I think about writing a really beautiful melody, I really think about that, and I ask, "Will I ever write a melody that is just glorious?" I find that people talk to me, however, about my lyrics and what the words say to them. I want to continue to write music that feeds people, but I think my mission is getting people to sing, and also getting people to understand that music is functional, that songs are for them. It is not just my culture that has music to offer that touches people, all cultures do. I use mine because that is what I know the best, and that is what I teach to people, songs out of our tradition. I teach spirituals, I teach gospel songs, I teach music from the civil rights movement. I teach African rhythms to people because I think that it is in how that music is put together and performed that people learn lessons about who they are in the world and how they can be. In the way African American music is constructed, we learn lessons about cooperation versus competition. We learn leadership and how leadership evolves, how people step out and then recede back into the support system. We learn risk taking. We learn what it is like for us to experience diversity.

If I can, I get a group of people walking around doing a traditional African rhythm that has six or eight parts, I talk to them afterward and ask two simple questions: one, "What did it feel like when you met somebody who was singing your part?" and two, "What did it feel like when you met somebody who was doing something different?" In those two questions lies their whole view of the world in terms of the people they want to spend time with. Can they get excited about diversity? Some say, "Absolutely not, I want to stay with my own kind." People say that before they realize what has flown out of their mouths. My sense is that I really want to share the value system that comes embedded in African and African American music with people around the world. That is what I am doing. People think they are coming to sing, but they get much more.

Billy Childs

Billy Childs, born in 1957, is one of the most brilliant "stars" of his generation among modern jazz pianists and has emerged as an equally powerful voice in composition. He works as a composer, a producer, and a performing and recording artist. A native Californian, Childs graduated from Hamilton High in Los Angeles. He studied piano at the University of Southern California and later completed studies in composition under Robert Linn, graduating top in his class. Childs toured with J. J. Johnson, then played for six years with Freddie Hubbard. He went on to play with such greats as Bobby Hutcherson, Branford Marsalis, Dave Holland, Grover Washington, and Art Farmer. His solo recording career began in 1988, with Windham Hill, a jazz label, which produced his first four, critically acclaimed, recordings. His friendship with Chick Corea took him to Stretch Records in 1995. As a composer, Childs is known for his ability to unify the diverse elements of jazz, popular, and classical music. He has been commissioned by the Los Angeles Philharmonic and the Akron symphonies and twice by the Monterey Jazz Festival. "The Starry Night" (from *I've Known Rivers*) was nominated for a Grammy, Best Instrumental Composition, in 1995. Another album, *The Child Within* (released on the Shanachie label in 1996), was nominated for two Grammy awards. He has written in numerous combinations, including woodwind quintet and piano, chorus and orchestra, concert band and solo percussion, and fusion ensemble and winds. Still a performer in much demand, Childs resides in Altadena, California.

There are different starts in my life. I technically started in music when I was six, but it didn't sink in, and after a couple months, my parents gave up on me trying to take piano lessons. I did learn and remember the basics of what the teacher taught me, like what everything looked like on the piano. They tried again when I was ten or eleven. Again, I didn't really gravitate toward the teacher, so I gave it up for the second time. In the meantime, I did normal kid stuff. I played basketball, did my homework, had a paper route. But there was always music in my house. My parents were music lovers. They liked classical music and Duke Ellington. They played Duke a lot, and they played other music. They had Barbara Streisand, they had Tony Bennett, and they had Nat King Cole. My two older sisters were also influential. They all helped shaped my concept musically.

When I was fourteen my parents, being schoolteachers in the L.A. school system, wanted me to get a better education than they felt I was going to get in Los Angeles. They sent me to this boarding school for boys called Midland. There was no basketball, there were no girls, nothing, but there was this piano there. I played soccer, and while I was walking to soccer practice one day and I

heard a Hammond B3 organ being played in a way I never heard before. It turned out to be Emerson, Lake, and Palmer. I would go to the piano, because it was away from where our rooms were, and I would try to retain what I heard and then figure it out on the piano. That is how I got into playing the piano. I want to make one thing clear, though—Keith Emerson [a fusion/rock organist and band leader] was the catalyst that got me into playing the piano, and I got some ideas from him musically, but he is not, as some journalists like to say, the main influence in my work. They see that he is this rock player, and they think it is a really interesting story because I am a jazz person, so I just want to make that clear.

When my parents knew I was serious about piano and that I wasn't going to be moving from that direction, they took me out of that school, because there was no musical instruction. I was on my own. When I came back to L.A. I was about sixteen. USC had this preparatory school, this preliminary school called the Community Schools. I studied piano with a guy named John Weisenfluh, and I studied theory with one of the best teachers I've ever had, Marianne Uszler; she taught me a lot of what I use today about theory. I just continued taking those classes, plus I was taking jazz piano lessons with Herb Mickman; he showed me the fundamentals of stylistic things on the piano.

I had a couple of high school bands where we played little casual gigs, but my first legitimately serious gig was with J. J. Johnson. I was nineteen when I got called to do it. That was the first thing I did, and I was nervous as hell. This was J. J. Johnson, and we were going to Japan and playing in huge halls. We were out there with just a quintet, and I was really nervous, but that was great training to get over that kind of thing.

I have always been really fascinated by putting things together and seeing how it ends up. I liked building things, I liked drawing things, I liked creating things. I always really dug how things were created, the pulling together aspect of it. I was interested in who the director of a movie was, and things like that. What really happened was that I told my teacher, John Weisenfluh, that I wanted to go into USC as a piano major, and he told me I would never make it. He told me that I should go in as a composition major but forget about piano.

That was a rotten way for him to put it, I think, but actually I started thinking, "Maybe I should go into composition." I knew that I knew a lot about theory, so I went into the composition department, partly because of what this guy said, and partly because I dug composing. It is kind of a strange way for me to have ended up composing. But once I got in the department, I was really thankful that it turned out that way, because what I had intended to learn from school was not so much a bunch of repertoire but how European music was devised and how it was thought up, and to really understand it. That is how I got into composing.

Music is one of the main things that I really care about in life. I think that music is absolutely essential to human existence—the organization of sounds, to make something pleasing. I think it has a healing effect. I think it has the ability to stimulate people to think. I think it has the ability to make people feel things, to escape. I try not to attach too much importance to what I am doing, but I do think it is an important thing. What it has made me do is work as hard as I can possibly work to develop my craft and to grow as a person, to try to be a good person. I feel that what I am doing is really important. The contribution that I want to make to the world is something that is not to be taken for granted.

I know that gangsta rappers fall back on certain excuses a lot. They say that they are just like CNN for the neighborhoods, but news reporting doesn't necessarily make good art. To have that much power and influence over young minds, I think they need to be responsible. But how can they be when they are a product of a failed society? Take Snoop Doggy Dog, for instance. The guy was involved in a drive-by shooting where somebody gets killed! This is who is influencing young kids! His message on his early album, with the cartoon drawings, is just disgusting. They need to take responsibility, but I think in a system that systematically squashes every program in those neighborhoods, mind-expanding programs, outreach programs, music programs where they could be learning, they have no other choice, really. Their musical expression is taking their dads' records, sampling them into samplers and organizing those sounds, putting those pieces together the best way they know how. I think it is sad. Some people, like Public Enemy, have managed to make high art out of that process. I think what they write is poetry, it is historically sound, it is full of messages that are positive, and the production is concrete. It is a conceptually sophisticated way of dealing with sampling and sound design. There are some groups, then, that have made art out of this process.

When I am making music, what I do is fantasize about it, dream about it, and think about it. I have a process where, if I am writing a long work, I like to just think about it, start listening to a bunch of works to get into that total frame of mind. Then I always try to start with a melody. I think the way to communicate to an audience most directly is through melody. I always try to come up with a good melody and then expand on that, treat it contrapuntally, thematically, develop it, and come up with another melody. I write on a reduced score page; I have been doing that lately to write faster. I used to write straight to the score, but I was erasing too much. Now I just write on a short score and then orchestrate it. I don't think I have ever written anything that was twelve-tone—I take that back, I've written something for an assignment in class. It all depends on what I am going for. We all have our own rules that we have devised, and we need to break out of them occasionally to keep expanding. I have a set of rules. Lately, I've been hearing a lot of things triadically and a lot of things quartally and quintally, too. I like bi-tonality, I like seconds [i.e., intervals], I like bass lines that play clusters against the chord that is above it. I like inverted chords. I will take a major seventh chord and put the seventh on the bottom.

Your "voice" is a combination of what you bring to music, all of the music literature that has been done in the past, and how you deal with it. It is also your take on what has been done in the past. It is also how you do it differently. That is why I think people like to hear musicians play standards; it gives them an easier way of identifying who you are. They can figure out your take on something that is recognizable to them. You can't escape what has been done in the past. There is too much great stuff that has been done in the past. Your voice is going to have to be based on that too. It is going to have to be based on the past, but it is going to have to be looking toward the future. I think my voice comes out in my orchestral work, just in the way I treat things harmonically, the way I have always been doing it in my small-group writing. Like I said, I've been dealing with triads, I like dealing with fourths, fifths, and things like that, and I do that in the orchestra. I don't follow too many rules; I orchestrate what I think is going to sound good.

Getting ready for a recording date is different from a commission. The pressure is different. With a recording date, there is more of an emphasis on the need for the performance to come off perfectly for the album, for posterity. But when you are writing a commission for someone to perform, you have rehearsals, and then you do the best you can on stage. It is just that one performance. People are more receptive to a live situation, so you can make mistakes more; people still get the overall impact of the live music. In recording, it is like a painting. You have to get every detail right, the mix and all of that, so it is a different kind of pressure.

I have advanced more in my recording thing than I have in my concert thing. I listen less to what is going on in the recording medium than I do in the concert medium, but the process is generally the same. I don't believe in transcribing whole entire solos, but what I will do is take the best part of a solo and put the turntable on 16 rpm and actually get the lick and see what it is and why it works. I listen to Herbie Hancock, or Keith Jarrett, or someone like that, see why it works and use it, just like they did.

Twilight is upon Us was my second album, recorded in 1989. My third album was called *His April Touch*. My fifth album was *I've Known Rivers*. *Portrait of a Player* is just a playing [instrumental] album. It's like a trio in a very traditional jazz setting. I do a lot of standards, I create a lot of room for myself to just play the piano. On the others ones, I am bound by what I wrote. Some of my compositions not only have intricate heads [melodies], but I also write intricate solo changes.

My symphonic work, *American Voices* [Telarc, Akron Symphony], was a thousand times better than what I thought it would be. I had my doubts at the beginning. They said, "Concert music and African, yeah, African music, no maybe Indian, no African." Okay, that's two totally different ways of thinking about music in one piece. Plus, most ethnomusicologists spend a lifetime studying different aspects of African music. Here I am with two months to come up with something. I was going to come up with something authentic; I wasn't going to have some guy playing bongos and have the orchestra on top of that. I wanted to do that piece organically. I felt like I had no choice but to go to poetry and through that find commonality between Africa, America, and Europe. I actually learned how similar we are, as human beings, and that we have the same problems. But I didn't realize how similar the human condition is everywhere. That is a good thing that came out of it. The unifying link is the poetry throughout. It gave me a chance to write music that linked these things together and make it mean something, make the words mean something through the African percussion, make it all tie together. It also gave me a chance to write dramatic music and paint the words. Basically, it turned out really well, I think, because everybody took the project seriously. It could have been a drag, but the conductor, Alan Balter, was great. He dealt with it very seriously. Carmen Lundy, the vocalist, did too; she learned to sing it like it was second nature. Nana Asiedu and Thomas Kelly, who did the African percussion, took it very seriously and worked out their rhythms and chants, and it all came together. Everyone was really great.

I think the more you know, the richer your music becomes. Having a really firm grasp of formal structure helps your improvisation, it makes you able to shape it better, to make it more effective and more dramatic. By the same token, the ability to improvise gives you a certain spontaneity in your compositions and it helps you come up with ideas. Having a jazz background certainly helps. I think the more you know, the more things you have, the better; everything helps everything.

I went to the Grammys this year. First of all, I didn't win. I was only a nominee, but to be nominated was a great honor. My section was just the pretelecast; during the regular Grammys, we left. I found that awards in music is a concept that—I mean, as much as I would like to win an award and get recognition from peers—is countermusical. Asking who is better than whom, who is the best—who can say that? When I found out what I needed to know about myself, I was not really interested in finding out who was the best at stuff that really didn't have to do with me. Besides, I didn't think that in the pop category it was about being the best anyway, and the pop categories are the ones that are shown during the telecast. Hootie and the Blowfish the best new band? Get out of here!

I don't think music is progressing as much any more. There has been a trend in jazz to go backward toward the past, a retro movement of playing like people did thirty years ago. I don't see much progress there. Where I saw a lot of progress was in the early 1970s; in fact, the music was called "progressive jazz." A lot of different elements in music came together and were synthesized into one organic type of music. I think they were on the right track with groups like early Return to Forever, early Weather Report, Miles Davis with Bitches Brew, Mahavishnu Orchestra, and Herbie and the Headhunters. There were African elements in Herbie Hancock's music, with the heavy percussion. There were funk elements, there were jazz elements; it was a synthesis. I saw music going in a good direction; it was really headed somewhere.

Then that music made a whole bunch of money—and money corrupts. Then they started getting into the marketing aspect of that type of music and the possibilities there. I think the only way to create something new and interesting is to synthesize musics, to put them together into one organic new thing by incorporating different musics from other cultures. That is where I am trying to head. There are a lot of considerations, though, like radio airplay and marketing considerations, that stand in the way of getting that type of music to people. I think if people were to hear something new and exciting and refreshing, they would gravitate toward it. But I guess in this financial crisis time, industries don't want to take a chance on something not selling.

I would like my music to—at the same time it is making people generally feel better about themselves and the world—make them look at something in a way they hadn't thought of looking at it before. Maybe it can make them look at something in an artistic way rather than a totally factual one, or make them see something that I think that I see when I am writing something, or maybe make something beautiful out of something that is ugly, an ugly truth—ugly beauty.

I have so many things that I am really proud of that it is hard to name one. Among them is *American Voices,* the recording with the Akron Symphony. Another thing is this piece that I wrote fourteen or fifteen years ago called "Lunacy." I paid out of my own pocket for a chamber-type of orchestra to play it, and I consider that one of the best things I have written. There is another piece for the L.A. Philharmonic. There are some things on my albums that I like—for example, "Twilight Is upon Us," "Starry Night"—so it is hard for me to say which is the best.

I have been influenced more by the writing and conception of Herbie Hancock, of Paul Hindemith, of a lot of the fusion groups of the early 1970s, Miles's groups of the 1960s. Some of those things that Miles Davis did, like *Filles de Kilimanjaro,* for instance, and Herbie Hancock's *Mwandishi,* are really big albums in my life. Stylistically, I would describe my music as having elements of twentieth-century composers. It has elements of jazz. I try to avoid a particular, singular style, and I try to put different elements in my music. Thus far, my music that has been available to the public, through the Windham Hill albums or through the GRP albums, has incorporated an element of progressive jazz, of straight-ahead jazz, and some classical elements. Then in my orchestral things, the lineage would be from maybe William Walton or Paul Hindemith, Arthur Honneggar, and those people.

I am one of those people who just writes. I have a good idea, and then I write it down. I don't think about it in terms of the scheme of things. I don't mean to provide a means of escape with my music so much, but maybe people can take something from my music and relate it to their lives in a positive and healing way. Ultimately, I would like to bring a whole lot of musics together in one synthetic thing, to create a new form of music that works and that is positive. That is what I would like to do with my music.

George Duke

George Duke, born in 1946, remains one of the most visible composers, performers, and producers in contemporary popular culture. His *Muir Woods Suite for Orchestra* illustrates his interest in concert music, and his compositions remain some of the most revered and long-standing hits and classics in the industry. Mr. Duke attended the San Francisco Conservatory of Music, receiving the bachelor of music degree, majoring in trombone and composition. A veteran performer, George Duke has worked with and composed music for the best talent in the business, including Al Jarreau, Jean-Luc Ponty, Frank Zappa, Raoul de Souza, Dee Dee Bridgewater, Jeffrey Osborne, Melissa Manchester, Barry Manilow, Rachel Farrell, Najee, Dianne Reeves, Smokey Robinson, Gladys Knight, Johnny Gill, the Pointer Sisters, Anita Baker, and Miles Davis. His discography over the span of 30 years includes hundreds of performances, compositions, and productions. His work in the TV industry can be seen in the eight years he worked with the Soul Train Music Awards show, NBC's *Sunday Night Show,* and Disney Productions. In addition to winning several Grammys for his creative collaborations with bassist/composer Stanley Clarke, Al Jarreau, and Miles Davis's TUTU, he was named R&B keyboardist for two consecutive years by *Keyboard* magazine. His film scoring credits include the *Five Heartbeats, Karate Kid II, Leap of Faith,* and *Meteor Man.* Mr. Duke lives and works in Los Angeles.

Q: Describe the evolution of the *Muir Woods Suite.*

A: Essentially I wanted to do something a little bit different musically than what I am known for. I feel that as an artist you have to challenge yourself. I basically don't write orchestral music very often, though I realize I have the ability to do so. Unfortunately, I don't have many opportunities. The way it came about was that I had written a couple of things, the first movement or pieces of it, about six or seven years ago. When I had a spare moment I would sit down at my synthesizer and play it back so I could hear it. I wrote another movement, which wound up being the second movement. Finally, in the computer, I started writing the third movement. I didn't quite complete it, but I had the initial gist of it. Now, I had the first movement (or "phase," as we call it), the second movement, and the last phase in the computer, and that was the end of it for many, many years. Later on, I had another spare moment and decided I would like to finish the movements I'd started. About three years ago I went in to update it a little bit. I made a demo copy and took it to Quincy Jones's house, where he was having a party for Claude Knobs, who is the promoter for the Montreux Music Festival. I gave it to him and told him that I wanted him to listen to it, but I didn't think he was going to play it right there at the party. I

said, "Oh my God, it's only a demo! You were supposed to listen to it tomorrow in the office." He put it on and said, "Wow, man, this is great." People got quiet, and I was like, "Uh-oh." He said, "Man, I love this. We have got to do this next year at the festival. I want to do this." That started a whole chain of events, where they decided to do several nights of jazz with orchestra.

The problem for me was that I had to finish the piece, because I only had three movements. I then made a decision to take off three months actually to do it, to finish all the other phases, and tie it all together in some kind of way. That was the point at which I made a decision to include some jazz elements, because the original piece was totally orchestral. I had lived up near Muir Woods, so I knew the feeling of the area pretty well. To tell you the truth, when I first started this piece I wasn't thinking so much in terms of what it was about; I was just making music.

Later on, when I went back to Muir Woods, I decided the music sounded like the woods to me. I began to concentrate on that idea as I began to orchestrate the piece. That happened after I had already orchestrated the first part of the first movement. I said, "Okay, I got a title for this, and now I am going to make this a concept." I added the jazz elements later on after I was already commissioned to finish it.

Q: How would you discuss the evolution of your professional career?

A: First of all, in the early part of my career I had worked with Al Jarreau and Jean-Luc Ponty. Jean-Luc was very important to me, because he sounded like the Miles Davis of violin, and Miles was a hero of mine. I love the way Miles approached music, because he never did the same thing over and over again. The music evolved and it kept evolving; I liked that way of looking at music. It kept things fresh, because you never knew what he was going to do. Jean-Luc basically gave me my first shot at the "big time" in terms of making records. By working with him I met Cannonball Adderley [jazz saxophonist] and Frank Zappa [composer and jazz performer] and got my first record deal here in the States. Up to that point I had had my own group in San Francisco. This was the first time I decided that I needed to become a sideman for a while. I wasn't sure I could make a living playing music until I got the call from Frank Zappa. That's when I decided to quit teaching school, which I was doing at the time, and actually make a living out of performing. That is the long and short of it.

Now, Cannonball was like my dad. He was just an amazing source of information. He knew everything about jazz. He was an educator, an incredible humanitarian, he was funny, and he could communicate an idea better than anybody I know. A lot of my heroes used to come see him. I met Nancy Wilson, Joe Williams [jazz singer], and Miles, all the people who I was "into" in terms of jazz, because they would come to see Cannonball's shows—even Sarah Vaughn and Carmen McCrae. It was amazing. Just to hear him tell stories about that era, all those musicians I had grown up listening to, was just incredible.

Frank Zappa opened me up as a musician. He got me involved in singing. He was the first to take me seriously in terms of that. He told me I ought to sing. It was really a necessity, because I was the only one who was stationary, other than the drummer in the band. He said, "Man, the mike is in front of you. I've got to have you sing this note because everybody else is doing something else." He got me involved in playing synthesizers. I resisted that, I really didn't want to do it. He eventually bought a synthesizer for me and put it on top of my Fender Rhodes. I eventually started playing it. Adding humor to music as a legitimate vehicle really was Frank's whole idea about music. We can really put these things together. In a weird kind of way, he was almost like Miles—on a different level, in a different way, trying different things. He was never satisfied just to say something was good enough. And he rehearsed us to death. He was the first guy I met that knew as much about the studio as a recording engineer. I mean, he was really technically into that. That interested me, and I said, "Man, I want to be like that."

My mom used to take me to concerts when I was very young, when I was three and four years old. She would take me to see Duke Ellington and Lionel Hampton. She liked music. She took me to plays, she took me to ballets, and she took me to classical music concerts. So I got to see a full range of music besides hearing James Brown on the radio, and Aretha Franklin, and whatever was going on in the fifties. I was introduced to a smorgasbord of stuff, and that is how I got into music. By the time I was six years old, I knew what I wanted to do. By the time I was seven years old, I told my mom to get me a piano, because I was going to be a piano player. She scraped up enough money to get me a piano. She paid fifteen dollars for it. It was a little upright, and we put it in the house. I started taking lessons, and I knew from then on that that was what I wanted to do. I had no doubts. I wasn't sure I could make a living doing it, but I knew that was what I wanted to do.

At that time I was just trying to learn music. By the time I was a teenager I was trying to play some jazz and some Latin music. I actually started playing a Cal Tjader kind of West Coast Latin music with a jazz influence. I bought every Cal Tjader record you could find. I got into Les McCann; I combined that kind of churchy-funk that he was doing with the Latin thing, because that was the kind of stuff I was hearing in the church. I would go to church every Sunday, and I would see these people hollering and screaming and falling out. The music was kind of funky, and I could understand this. I could understand Les. As I began playing in the church, I found that if I played a certain lick the right way, it would effect somebody. It scared me the first time it happened, because I didn't know how much it was going to affect the audience. I began using that idea in the shows. I began trying these licks out in high school; when I played gigs, where I tried these ideas, somebody would go "Yeah!" And I would say to myself, "Oh, okay, that is what it is all about."

I guess if I had to put my finger on what unifies black music all over the world, other than the fact that somewhere along the line we probably have some kind of common heritage, I guess there is a certain feeling about what we do. There is an intangible. It is like trying to describe the taste of an apple. You may not know it, but you can feel it. I think we are the sum of our experiences. I have heard some black artists that I couldn't really tell were black. Generally I can, but I have heard a few that I wouldn't know were black from their music. It depends on how they grew up and what their experiences were. I happened to grow up in a black community; some African American musicians who grew up in Europe have a totally different bent. I just worked recently with some Parisian black folks. What unifies us is the fact that we are black folks trying to make a living. We have a definitely different bent on the music, but there is that something; there is a "kindred soul somewhere in there" that we can connect to. It is an intangible that is very difficult to describe.

Q: What are your views on the lack of musicianship among younger generation?

A: I am concerned about it. I know what I had to go through to get to my level of education in terms of music—a lot of hard work. I think there is a lot of raw talent out there in our community, but some of it is not being realized to its full potential, because they aren't putting in the work. They just don't know enough, they are not educated enough, in terms of music, to bring off what they would like to achieve. Because sampling has become so prevalent, many young musicians have no idea how to create music from scratch or extend careers for a long period of time. It does concern me, and I think it is a by-product of what is happening now in society in general, where everything is overnight, is very quickly done, a quick meal. There is no artist development in music because everything is done very quickly, in the short run, and then you throw it away. It is all a part of that same thing. I try, when I give seminars or clinics or talk with the artists with whom I am involved to let them know, "Look, man, you have got to look at the long run, not the short run." The whole idea is to be here twenty or thirty years from now. That is what the desire should be, but in a lot of cases it is not, because they don't have the education to make it last or be flexible musically. That is the problem.

Q: Do you see commonalities between the various music forms and styles you work within?

A: We all learn from each other. Jazz, for example, is a combination of European and African elements. That alone shows that there is some common element, some common ground. The difference is the rhythm and the intent. Generally African-based music has a different rhythmic intensity and intent. The European things tend to be more linear, more lush, and less rhythmic in terms of its syncopation. There are obviously exceptions to that rule. I love Stravinsky. I love his rhythmic concept. He even developed some ragtime stuff. Stravinsky was an incredible orchestrater. He was amazing to me. So if you get someone who understands both traditions, especially as black composers, it seems we should be able to combine all of that and come up with something that is incredibly different, fresh, and new. We have two different approaches. We can play the traditional classical concept of linearity and bring into it our rhythmic element and make it another thing.

I know from making the *Muir Woods Suite* that there is a little, I don't want to say animosity, but a little uneasiness there, because they couldn't do the rhythmic thing so well. But I was determined when I wrote *Muir Woods Suite* to make the musicians come into my world. I said, "I am coming to you bringing everything that I am as a musician, and a person with this piece. I am going to play what is part of your tradition, but I want you to play what is part of mine." It is tough for them to swing or improvise. There was some backlash not only from orchestras but certain radio stations. First of all, this is one of the first pieces I have written for an orchestra. I don't have a library of orchestral music. As you know, I produce records for a living in the R&B and jazz domains. This was something that was a test for me. So the way I started doing this was by playing the piano.

Q: Describe your creative process with the *Muir Woods Suite.* How does that process compare to the process of producing new artists?

A: I had an idea on the piano and began thinking orchestration pretty much right away. What made it different for me was that the majority of this piece was done in the computer. I wrote down the first phase, the second phase, the seventh phase. Basically, I had it all written before I put it into the computer, where I could hear it and make certain changes based on what I was hearing. It is a great thing to be able to hear the music right back. It meant a lot to me. After the first performance in Montreux several years ago, I came back and made some changes based on what I heard, so I am still making changes. But I am through with it now.

In reference to producing other artists, you have to gauge where each artist's weaknesses and strengths are, and that is a talent in itself. I would basically try to push them in certain areas. I steer the ship. If you are dealing with talent, people who have something to say, you have to nurture them and basically support them in following their dreams—not necessarily my dream, because I make my own records. But I try to have them get excited about this and bring something to the project. That is something else that is not happening a lot nowadays. Most of the stuff is done by producers. I prefer the time when, I think, the music was more creative and more diverse, when it was being produced and mainly performed by the artist. I think that is something that needs to change. The artists need to come to the fore, take control, and not let record companies have all the control.

If I am dealing with a new artist I try to find their strengths and weaknesses and build up their strengths and try to improve their weaknesses by saying certain things, guiding the ship, by making suggestions. Certain artists need more than others. Some need to be told, "You sing this line." If you are dealing with a Dianne Reeves [jazz singer] or Rachelle Ferrell [jazz singer and pianist] in that genre of music, you don't need to tell them that. You just guide the ship and say, "Why don't you try this? Did you think about this?" And they may say, "Okay, let me try that." That is the whole idea of production for me.

I certainly think artists have a particular role in our society. It's funny—I took a psychology course when I was in school, and the teacher said, "I can't teach you anything about psychology. The only thing I can do is to teach you to better understand yourself." I thought that was interesting. So he came to us, and he said, "Okay, this is what I want you guys to do. Answer the question, Why do we need music?" And everybody looked at each other. He said, "If somebody told you we are going to ban all music, you have got to be able to answer that as an artist because one day you may be called on to answer it." That was an interesting question. I thought about it, and the obvious answers are that music definitely plays a role as strong as building refrigerators. People need a release. They need to be able to dream, and that is something that you can do with music. Unfortunately, videos, I think, have taken the dream away to a point and cast the music in stone. People say, "That is what that song is about." On a certain level, I like music that doesn't lock dreaming down, because people can grab what they will out of a certain song, especially if it is instrumental, because then they can take the music anywhere in their mind's eye. I have had many comments about *Muir Woods Suite,* about where the music takes people spiritually, which is really interesting to me. It plays a role in terms of helping people. I believe music is a universal language, that it crosses all barriers, and I think it is a wonderful thing to have in society and very, very, very, necessary in terms of people's well-being, and my well-being too. For me, music is a release, but it also carries a message, various messages. That is why I think artists have a duty to be respectful of what their messages are, because the message is so strong and it can move people in so many different ways. You can get people to do things they might not normally do, based on a drumbeat. There is another thing I am concerned about now—some of the lyrics that I hear. I am amazed by what I hear on the radio nowadays, to tell you the truth.

We are role models, whether we want to be or not; young artists have to take that seriously and take that charge seriously. It is just like rearing a kid. You don't want your kid to see you come home drunk or beating on your wife, or doing this and that. You are setting an example for that child; even if it isn't your own child, someone is looking up to you. I have had more people at the end of a concert say, "I remember years ago being at a show of yours in such and such a place and you did such and such." And I say, "What?" I don't remember. Or somebody would give me a tape and I would tell them, "Just keep playing, just keep doing what you're doing, some type of constructive criticism." Sometimes at the end of my shows I have a spot where I bring up people from the audience and let them play. It is just a free-for-all, and we have a little jam and people get a chance to play, and they are thrilled. I'm telling you, man, years later they remember that as a highlight of their life.

It doesn't seem like anything new is coming up in contemporary music. Creativity is not totally supported, at least in this country. It is downplayed, and if you are a little different, a lot of times, that makes it tough. I think as artists we have to strive to move the music even though record companies say, "Hey, Anita Baker had a hit. I want four more of those." Or they say, "We can't get this played on this radio station because. . . ." You have to have a record that sounds like such and such, that fits in that slot. Well, you know, back in their day, Sly and the Family Stone and Miles Davis didn't think anything about what the radio was playing. I think we have got to get music back to that.

I have had a varied career. I have tried to do a lot of different things, and I consider myself a comprehensive artist. I do a lot of different things well, from jazz to different genres of music, including electronic music, and composing, writing, producing, and all of that. I try to do a variety of things, because it keeps me interested. Flexibility has made me stay current, listening to what is going on and adapting. How I fit in the tradition, I don't know. That is up to other people to decide. Some people don't like what I do, some people like what I do, so there it is.

Ultimately, I guess, I would like to be remembered for having made somebody smile along the way. I like to make people happy. I love art for art's sake, that is wonderful. But I think art, in order to be fully realized, has to communicate. If art doesn't communicate, it doesn't fulfill its destiny. That is the way I feel. I feel art must reach somebody. It has to touch somebody. Somebody has got to say "Yes." For me, if one person says "Yes," then I have realized my goal. Somebody understands, and then I am cool. There it is.

Jester Hairston

Jester Hairston was born in Homestead, Pennsylvania, in 1901. Mr. Hairston has become an internationally known and respected composer, and arranger. A "goodwill ambassador" under President John F. Kennedy, he traveled with his musical message to Europe, Africa, Mexico, South America, and the Soviet Union. His signature song, sung all over the world, is "Amen." A graduate of Tufts University, with additional studies at the Juilliard Institute of Music, Mr. Hairston became the assistant of master choral director Hall Johnson in 1929. Mr. Hairston conducted and prepared choirs for performances on Broadway, as well as the famous Hall Johnson choral soundtracks from *The Green Pastures, Lost Horizons,* and many other films. He served under the great film composer Dmitri Tiompkin for twenty years, honing his own skill as a conductor and arranger. Mr. Hairston remained until his death in 1997 the most sought-after and best-known living arranger and composer of African American choral spiritual traditions. He has also become a famous face and personality, appearing in such roles as "Deacon Rolly" on the TV show *Amen.* Mr. Hairston taught the Mormon Tabernacle Choir how to "sing black," a first. In his almost seventy-year career he has been awarded six honorary doctorates, the most recent in 1995 from the University of Southern California. Mr. Hairston lived in Los Angeles until his passing in 2000.

At the time of the interview, in Minneapolis, Jester Hairston was over ninety-four years old, and in town for a performance of some of his works. Our time was short, as he was very tired. He focused on the power of the spiritual as a form of artistic communication. His insight on that phenomenon, as far back as the performance practices of the 1920s, is extremely illuminating.

Q: How did it all begin for you?

A: I attended Tufts University in Boston. There I was a music major. But my folks were in a little steel mill town, called Homestead, Pennsylvania, near Pittsburgh. So I had gone way up north to be in a first-rate white school where they didn't call you "nigger" or anything like that. When I finished there, I came back to Pittsburgh.

Q: When did you start being involved in music professionally?

A: By staying around the places, I listened to people, like Paul Robeson, who were doing shows and performances and things, and so I too wanted to be in music. People thought I had the ability, like Will Marion Cook and all those folks. They said, "You go up there to school because we need blacks with

degrees." That's what gave me the idea to go to school. So, I left there and went up to Boston. I finished school at Tufts University, got my degree. Very few blacks went to Tufts back then.

Then, I went to New York. I worked for four years on a ship. I traveled back and forth from Boston to New York on this ship for rich white folks.

Q: How did you meet Hall Johnson?

A: By being around in New York. He probably would not have even spoken to me had I just gotten out of high school. But they liked the way I had gone through with my education. So, I was real glad the folks sent me up to Boston.

Q: Tell me about the things you used to do with Hall Johnson.

A: Nothing but Negro spirituals. He was very popular. He got popular right at the time I arrived there in Harlem. He was doing things with a regular choir. He was going with sacred and folk songs. They became so popular with the nice arrangements he had that he began to put these arrangements on Broadway, in minstrel shows, movies, and things like that. And that's where he got popular. I was just a little young kid who wanted to be in his choir. I had finished school in 1929. I was twenty-eight years old. In 1929, you were supposed to be on top by then, and here I was just getting out of college. But he really made me study and want to go into theater.

But they were impressed with me because I had gone to Tufts, one of the "big colleges," which were then very hard for a black to get into. I don't think I had to even take all the exams to get in. I had a lot of nerve. I guess they thought I was a wizard! [laughs]

Q: What happened after the Hall Johnson period? Did you just start out there on your own?

A: Oh, no! I stayed up with Hall Johnson right up 'til I got enough of a reputation to do my own things. I started arranging, before Hall Johnson, up there at Tufts. All I did was Negro spirituals. That was something new. You see, not very many blacks had gone to school, and here comes this little "darkie" from up north who knows how to arrange chords and so forth. Everybody thought I was a great musician. Hall Johnson took me in as his assistant. When everybody saw that I was Hall Johnson's assistant they all started coming to me. And so, I used what ability I had. I was really at first just a singer in his choir.

Q: Where did you get the inspiration for these spiritual arrangements?

A: My grandmother was a slave, born in Virginia on a plantation. She had been a slave all of her life. When she came up to be with my mother, she heard me arranging spirituals. I heard even more of them from her. I made my big hit out of "Amen." I went over to Germany and had a huge mass choir. It was "Amen" that made my reputation. That was one of the biggest songs of my whole life [he sings "Amen," accompanying himself on the piano].

It's the rhythm of it that sells the song. If you took this song to Tufts, where I went to school, and went to the harmony department and asked, "Can you pick out that chord?" they would say, "Can I pick out that chord!?"

Why, I kick students out of this class for doing more music than that! That's true, because there's no music in it. There are only three chords in the whole song. I have gone to Italy and had five thousand people singing "Amen" [sings and plays it again]. And you heard this chorus! When my grandmother was a slave, two generations before I was born, the people knew I was coming along out of her stomach. Then out of her stomach, here I come along singing this little song that everybody can sing. When white choirs sang this song, they sounded like they had some life in 'em, like the black choirs, and that's why the spiritual songs had the reputation they did—because they had life in them.

You could kill and lynch so many thousands of Negroes, and that song would sing itself, just like "Go Down Moses." That's a great song you see, and you can't kill it, and white folks know that. In the old days white folks would say, "Only they can sing that song." After a while, they tried to sing it, and they couldn't sing it. They heard blacks singing it in a Baptist church somewhere, who couldn't read any notes at all but could get their ears together and sing the song. It would sound like something that would rip through to the heart. The minute the song rips to your heart, color don't have nothing to do with it, with your heart, ya see. "Go Down Moses" sold for all those who wrote that kind of music. And then, after a while, they liked other kinds of spirituals too.

I've heard "Amen" sung in China. I've was invited to an international choral festival in Estonia, under Russian rule. I conducted a choir of, they say, 25,000 people. Now that's a lot of people. That's as many people as there are in towns that we have [laughs]. They were all in one church assembly, and here I was up on a platform. They wanted to see me conduct. There I was conducting "Amen." [He sings *a cappella*.]

The spiritual will meet things. I have taken spirituals into white sections in California that don't want Negroes to even walk on the sidewalk. But you go in there singing "Go Down Moses," and they'll get around and listen to you [sings and plays and sings it on piano]. Once you say, "Let My people go," you got all the white folks coming at you. And you sing, and you begin to save a few sinners, and then you got everybody with you. It's wonderful what you're saying about music and what it does for all these people.

Q: Is that a very important part of it for you?

A: Oh, yes, it touches them! And if you don't believe it, you go over there to Europe, to Germany. I've gone there with no blacks but me and two or three others that were with me, and you'll have thousands of Germans coming out to hear you sing. Because they, too, have music in their souls, once you hit a certain chord!

Q: What do you remember about what the musicians were doing in those days?

A: What the Negroes did that I admired them for was writing, and staying right in the "class" that they were in at the time, not knowing anything about European notes and dominant chords and so forth. They didn't know anything about that, but they could sing together. They put it together in such a way that it would reach the white folks' ears. whites would say, "We can't beat these Negroes to death. Listen to them, ya hear that chord? Listen to that boy, that's like my grandmother." Their grandmother came up with the same thing—with natural music, not music that you write for the choirs in school. And that's the way we got along.

Herbie Hancock

Herbie Hancock has established himself as one of the most important artistic voices of his generation. Beyond his work as a leading pianist/composer, his innovations in electronic synthesized music, his redefinition of jazz composition in popular radio and video mediums is unprecedented. A native of Chicago, he began his piano studies early, at age eleven performing the Mozart *Concerto in D-major* with the Chicago Symphony. Mr. Hancock entered Grinnell College as an engineering major, later switching to composition. He was awarded an honorary doctorate by the same school in 1972. After leaving Chicago, Hancock went to New York, working and recording with legends such as Coleman Hawkins and Donald Byrd at sessions at Bluenote Records. He received an invitation to perform and record with Miles Davis, and in the early sixties he recorded with the memorable "classic quintet" (1962–68). His cutting-edge work as a composer and pianist can be seen in works such as *Maiden Voyage, Dolphin Dance,* and the groundbreaking *Head Hunters,* one of the best-selling jazz albums in history. As an innovator in American music, Mr. Hancock has received numerous awards for his contributions, including Grammys, a BMI/TV/Film Award, and an Oscar (for the score for the critically acclaimed *Round Midnight*). In addition to his work on early films such as *Blow Up* and *Death Wish,* his credits as a film composer include *A Soldier's Story, Jo Jo Dancer, Action Jackson,* and *Harlem Nights.* Mr. Hancock recently reissued a series of works, including a project that critics called "jazz's new phase," *The New Standard* (1996). Mr. Hancock currently resides in Los Angeles.

Q: What is your impression of the contemporary direction in rap/hip-hop music?

A: From what I understand, there are people coming into rap who don't want to do that "reactive rap" kind of thing at all. Things are swinging toward something that is more creative and constructive rather than destructive. I read recently in a magazine that there is a new kind of rap that is more poetic—they call it "rap poetry." The article suggested that the people who are doing that depend less on the music, the music is truly in the background; the expression in the words carries the whole thing. Again, this is a positive, or constructive, kind of movement. I hope that is true. The thing is, I don't really keep track of what is happening on those different scenes, because I am too busy doing what I have to do. What I know is whatever somebody tells me or what I read, but I

haven't been able to sit down and observe it and come to a conclusion myself. You have to have time to do that.

Musicians may study something because they want to get close to it or find out more about it so that they can include it in what they are doing. I have done that in the past, but in this particular case, maybe because I am older and I have a lot more things going on, I try to trust my instincts about what people tell me. I try to keep my eyes open and observe. I think that the best of hip-hop culture is interesting, different, and special. Also, the clever use of imagery on the fly, improvised, by certain people is amazing. There is some garbage out there, too. There is some stuff that is not that "clever"—that is, as far as rap is concerned. As far as the music is concerned, I understand that it isn't necessarily in the foreground. It is in the background, comes to the foreground, and then goes back again. Personally, I guess, because I am an instrumentalist, I would like to see more of a marriage of the music and the text than what I have been exposed to so far.

The one positive thing I can say about it is that rap and hip-hop does call attention to certain issues. Often certain kinds of issues will be ignored if somebody doesn't wave a red flag. In this particular case, most of the issues that are raised are issues that people know about. We keep hearing the same things over and over again, until they have been run into the ground. I don't mean cop killing, we don't need that; I mean some of the other things. But that only takes you so far. It doesn't give you any solutions or any hope, it just makes you mad. We need some people with some answers, some hope, some solutions, something that is going to encourage people. I think that is starting to happen.

Q: What do you think about some of the younger "jazz lions"?

A: The good news about Wynton Marsalis is that almost single-handedly he made enough of a spark to set a fire that brought attention to jazz from the media, and brought attention to jazz from young musicians. That part of it was fantastic. That is good for everybody. The thing that I have the most problem with is when someone says that I shouldn't play this kind of music or that kind of music. They are taking my human rights away from me. That is the thing that bothers me. I should be able to play whatever music I want to play as long and as I want to do it. You can't complain about me selling out if I am doing it honestly—unless I purposely want to sell out, and that is my choice, too. But the choice is up to the individual, not up to people that pass themselves off as spokesmen for the whole idiom of jazz. I mean, nobody speaks for me but me. That kind of sums up my attitude.

The thing about the music of Kenny G, Najee, and that kind of jazz is that it does draw attention to the word "jazz." It causes a little confusion, though, because now we see a lot of jazz concerts that don't even feature a "Kenny G." The concert will include R&B, and they will call it a jazz concert. I think everybody realizes that jazz stretches out so far that maybe many of the promoters feel like they have license to do that, just to draw people in. I actually never asked any promoter about this, but I have a feeling that they may be trying to appeal to an older crowd—not the young twenty-year-olds but people in their thirties and forties. They might have the Isley Brothers, Stevie Wonder, or any number of people. To me, this causes a bit of confusion. It is mislabeling, and I don't think that's right. I guess the best thing about what Kenny G. does is that it's instrumental and on the charts, when almost everything is vocal. You never heard anything instrumental until Kenny G. came along. It is so rare, because everything is vocal. It does combine the blues side of jazz with a kind of soft rock, so I can't say that it's not jazz. In my opinion it is a form of jazz, a very soft form of jazz, and some people are better at it than others. I am talking about Kenny G. because he is the most popular guy playing that kind of music.

I see new developments in jazz with people like Gonzalo Rubalcaba. I can say Marcus Roberts, Mulgrew Miller, and there are others like Benny Green who are excellent, and there is Billy Childs. Of course there is Roy Hargrove and Christian McBride. There is Steve Coleman, Ravi Coltrane, and a bunch of young players out there. As long as they don't all try to cram into a single door, as long as there is enough variety happening out there and they are not afraid to spread the creativity, that's fine. There is a faction out there that is so concerned with the musicians' learning their history, and my feeling is that kind of thing is very stifling. That is the road to the destruction of jazz, once you start inhibiting the musicians; then they won't be able to play jazz. The very nature of jazz is that it is open. People who have different ideas shouldn't be discouraged.

Q: What are your current projects? How is your composition evolving?

A: I hope that within the next couple of years I will have pieces recorded with Deutsche Grammophon featuring works others have written and that I have written. I'm also interested in recording orchestral works, with myself and a symphony orchestra, with other settings that could be added to it. It could be hip-hop, it could be jazz, or it could be a combination of all three.

I remember the first piece that I wrote—actually, my brother, my sister, and I wrote it. We were all about three years apart, and I was probably about nine. It was called "Summer in the Country." It was a corny little song that we wrote. After having played piano a couple of years I was starting to write some things even then, but it didn't really come to fruition until I got involved with jazz. I can't think of any particular thing that inspired me, I just happened to like harmony. I happened to have a leaning toward the harmonic side of things, though I'm a rhythmic player. Maybe it's because I am a very curious kind of person, but I am always trying to see what makes things tick. I'm also kind of an analytical person. Maybe composition comes out of me hearing certain things and then hearing something else that sparks an idea, which leads to a setting for a composition.

What inspires me to write is having someone say, "Hey, I am going to pay you to write." Then I *have* to write. It depends upon what it is. If it is a jazz tune, one way that I used to write, and I often still do, is to start with a bass line then with a chord, rather than a melody. I am trying to work more toward starting with a melody or a combination of the two, because I think that is a better way to work. Then I build on top of that and put things together, like pieces of a puzzle. I don't see the whole thing at once, and I like it that way. I like the mystery of having just a clue as to what I am doing but not having all of the pieces together. I like the process of watching it develop, so at a certain point I can say, "Oh, this is what I was really going for," and I may not have realized it.

Q: Tell us about the Miles Davis years.

A: The first time I played with Tony Williams [drummer, composer] was about three or four months before we joined Miles. I think it was February of 1963, and we joined Miles in May. The first time I played with him, he just blew me away. I couldn't believe what I was hearing. This guy was so creative. He quickly became my favorite drummer. As soon as he hit the drums, he won. I just saw potential in this seventeen-year-old kid that was just amazing. I always loved playing with him, because he was very inspiring with the stuff he was playing. Even before we were with Miles, I would call him up and ask him questions about the things he listened to and the way he did things.

When we joined Miles's band, I had already played with Donald Byrd and Jackie McClean [saxophonist] and I think Kenny Durham, players who had played more traditional be-bop. I also played with Eric Dolphy, who was an avant-gardist. I played with him for about two months, but it was enough to plant a seed in me. Because I was fairly knowledgeable about harmony and so forth, the combination of the avant-garde influence and the traditional influence, I think what felt natural to me was a combination of the two of them. Miles at that time described it as a "controlled freedom." I think that is one way to kind of summarize what the band did. What that band did was so varied. A lot of the things that were the riskiest and most advanced were never recorded, but some tapes got floated around, some videotapes, that have some of this stuff on it. The band was evolving so fast that every three months we would be on to another thing. Tony brought what he had to the table, and I brought this combination of things to the table. Ron Carter brought his youth, stability, and invention to the table. George Coleman was a fiery player, and then Wayne came in and added a new kind of voice. Both of them had been influenced by John Coltrane, but they both expressed it in different ways. Everybody was bringing something to the table. Everybody knows what Miles was bringing to the table, his genius. He just knew how to put it all together and make it work on a superhigh level.

Q: Can you give me some reflections on [bassist, jazz composer] Jaco Pastorius?

A: I met Jaco Pastorius through a friend of mine who lived in Florida. He lived in New York for a while and studied with me, and then he returned to Florida. The first time I went down to Florida with the Headhunters band, I ran into this guy and he said, "Listen, you've got to hire this bass player that's playing with me. He's just amazing." I said, "Yeah, yeah, I got Paul Jackson." One day he gave me a tape, and I played it. It was unbelievable. Actually, Jaco played with us. One time Paul couldn't make it to Japan, and Jaco played with the Headhunters band. It was never released, but somebody who has the tapes wants us to actually put something out.

But when I met Jaco, he was very stable. He was a young family man with two kids, a boy and girl. He was living in Florida—a nice, simple guy, very bright, very funny, very serious about music. I didn't know at the time how much of a genius he was. Then, of course, he was hired by Wayne [saxophonist] and Joe [pianist composer] Zawinul, with Weather Report. At a certain point I saw Jaco's personality began to change. I am not exactly sure what caused it. It could have been a combination of things, chemical imbalance, stress related. From what I understand, their records were very expensive to make.

At one time Jaco expressed to me his disappointment and frustration. He was putting out all of this great stuff and he was not really getting paid for his effort. He had in his head that the better you play, the more financially secure you are going to be. It doesn't necessarily work that way, though sometimes it can. It's fallacious to assume that it does, though, and to live off of that idea is a problem. I think Jaco must have had some other kinds of mental problems, which may have been caused by a chemical imbalance in his brain, I don't know. His death [in 1987] was really unfortunate.

Q: What do you consider to be the role of the artist in society?

A: I just hope that we can make the planet worth living in. That is what I am working toward. If I'm working for that, that is enough for me. You could say, "Oh, you've got a bunch of awards, so you can afford to say that." Who knows, maybe if I didn't have any awards I would be saying something different. But in the long run, I just hope that humanity wins the war over itself. This can be done in a lot of ways. I pay more attention to things besides music these days. I watch CNN a lot, I read the newspaper. I don't read books as much as I really should, but I started a foundation called the Rhythm of Life Foundation. Its concept is that technology is for humanity. I was interested in science before I showed an interest in music.

Technology is going to play a greater and greater role in our everyday lives. Communication, entertainment, even shopping, education, all of those things, will be tied to technology. So technology is developing by leaps and bounds, but when I look in the newspaper and I see what is happening on the planet, I don't see technology really helping that much. Something is wrong with this picture. I think the technological community needs to look at the human being and the human condition, and ask itself how to use technology to address the issues of humanity. Not everyone has to do it, but that should be a major part of what technology does. I also think that will open up a whole new industry, too. I think it is something that is very, very necessary. Another thing is the situation with the haves and the have-nots. And this is not just about access. We have to rekindle the dream of the have-nots, particularly in our kids.

Rhythm of Life is a nonprofit organization. We will give awards to people and organizations that are working toward using technology for humanity and for the environment, with scholarships or whatever. We want to train some kids actually to use the technology, not just to express themselves but to develop programs that deal with their problems. Frankly, their problems are the same as ours, but worse. Their job is their schoolwork.

They have metal detectors in school. I don't have metal detectors at my job. All the other things I have to face, they have to face too. The issues of adults are the same issues that children face. The judicial system, the political system, peer pressure, the generation gap, gender issues, sexual issues, sexuality, all of those things children have to deal with. I have a strong feeling that the answers we will need will come from kids, maybe teenagers. We are really going to focus on our youth with this project.

Society is the responsibility of every human being on the planet, no matter what you do. It is our planet, and we are all here to do something. I have been chanting [Buddhist mantras] for twenty-four years, of the many things I learned, one of them is that being a musician is not what I am, it is what I do—and it is only one of the things that I do. I am also a father. When I am with my daughter, I am not a musician, I'm her dad. When I'm with my wife, I am her husband. I'm a neighbor to the people next door. I am a citizen. When I'm watching CNN, I am not thinking about music. When I read the newspaper and look at what is happening in the world, I am not thinking about music; I am a citizen of the planet. I am a son when I'm with my father and mother, not a musician. Those are all of the different things that I do, and there are more. What I am, always, is a human being. That is very different from how I used to think. I used to think, "I am a musician." Practicing Buddhism broke that down for me and let me see what was underneath that. I never realized all of that before. That changed my perspective on things. I am not limited to just doing music any more. I have to do things with my life. Music happens to be something that I am good at, but I would be foolish to ignore the other aspects of what I am and what I can become, any more than I should ignore the other aspects of what other people are and what they can become. It is not just me living on the planet. I live in a society, I live on this globe. Those are my concerns.

Stephen Newby

Stephen Newby, born in Detroit in 1961, received his undergraduate studies in music at Madonna College in Michigan, a master's in jazz studies from the University of Massachusetts at Amherst, and a doctorate in composition from the University of Michigan (1994). His principle teachers were Frederick Tillis, Leslie Bassett, Bill Bolcolm, and William Albright. Brought up as a P.K. (pastor's kid) in a singing and testifying Baptist church in Detroit, Newby, along with his mother (the church's director of music) and five brothers and sisters, provided all the music—which can still be heard in much of Newby's contemporary gospel and symphonic work. Dr. Newby spent several years during his doctoral studies in Dakar, the capital of Senegal, in West Africa, documenting the music of West African cultures, and conducting his music with the Martyrs of Uganda, a chorus with over a hundred voices. An eclectic Americanist, his works have been performed by several college and professional groups, including the Ann Arbor Symphony. His *Symphony No. 1*, performed by the Seattle Symphony, was honored as the best dissertation work by the University of Michigan in 1994. He has worked in theater, oratorio, and chamber forms and has produced contemporary gospel; he has released several compact disks of his works. He has worked extensively with the music division of Maranatha (a Christian publishing house), traveling throughout the United States. In addition he taught composition and electronic music at the University of Michigan before settling in the Seattle area. Dr. Newby currently serves as the pastor of music and resident composer of the Antioch Bible Church of Seattle.

The whole process of bringing secular and sacred music together was a struggle for me. I came from this missionary Baptist Church tradition in Detroit, where my dad was the pastor of the church and my mom was the minister of music. That was the musical environment in which I was surrounded. I started playing at the church when I was thirteen. I transcribed [gospel musicians] Walter Hawkins and André Crouch, and their kind of music became the music that was in me. While working on my master's at the University of Massachusetts in jazz composition and arranging—this was in 1985 to 1987—I began to fuse jazz and gospel styles, particularly. I finally came to the realization that the musical language in the secular and the sacred domains of African American tradition and performance practice were very similar. The only difference between the two musics was basically the thrust and the motivation, the drive and the consciousness of the music. I had already dealt with that kind of fusion and felt like I handled it pretty well, especially since I felt at that time that I really didn't

have the support of the church to introduce those genres and mix them together. It wasn't until later, until the mid-1990s, that I figured out theologically that God doesn't care about genre but cares about a willing heart.

After the University of Massachusetts scenario, when I got into the University of Michigan, my whole perspective on music took another fork in the road. I began to deal with twentieth-century issues of formal composition via the Western European tradition in a way that I had not experienced, never perceived, never anticipated before.

Once I did that I became engulfed in a particular style, and my personal voice was somewhat dormant while I explored these other arenas, these other scenarios. For example, during my first semester I was inundated with Stravinsky. I took a twentieth-century music course in conducting, a course in twentieth-century music history, theory, and a course in electronic music. It had a tremendous impact on me at that time. For lack of a better word, I was processing information, and it wasn't until I left Ann Arbor and went to Seattle that I began to realize the truth of my inner voice.

While at Michigan I began to develop technique from a Euro perspective, and that was fine, because it was the period I was in at that time. The fusion of what I see as gospel and orchestral music was a consequence of being raised in the church at thirteen; experiencing and working successfully with jazz and gospel idioms together at the University of Massachusetts under Horace Boyer [black American musicologist, gospel historian, musician], Frederick Tillis [black American composer], and Jeff Holmes [composer]; and then dealing with the paradox, the fork in the road, at the University of Michigan. I was always dealing with the dualism that African American men always face, yet I was suppressing the gospel and jazz to explore only the European. I also wanted to be accepted by my white counterparts, by my peers.

We are right at the beginning of the third millennium, and because of this I think twenty-first-century music has to move in a direction, once again, in which the composer is sincere and true to his or her inner voice. We are dealing with such a milieu, such a wonderful montage, in world music, in different world genres. I believe the music is accepted. Whether they choose to accept it or not doesn't bother me any more, because, in essence, I went through the initiation process of learning everything that all of the other people have learned. I feel I have a well-rounded musical background, because I speak three musical languages: the European, the African American jazz tradition, and the African American gospel tradition. I realize that my white counterparts are just beginning to deal with dualism in relationship to their pop culture in Western Europe and dealing with the music that is indigenous to their particular bloodline, their particular heritage and their consciousness.

I am convinced that for the American composers, the European tradition—the Bach, the Brahms, and the Beethoven—doesn't really deal with their consciousness. For some reason, European tradition has been the rule, the measure, and the increments by which we establish our particular biases and interests. We have been told that. I think all American composers actively writing today deal somewhat with that dualism.

I think that white composers are aware that in order to be true to your voice, to make a statement, you just have to be honest with your cultural background and incorporate that with the symphonic and orchestral—to know that it is all right. That concept probably didn't stick until after 1982, or something, with Steve Reich and minimalism. But we have always been ahead, because the Negro composer dealt with the dualism from the beginning. I use the word "Negro" because in William Grant Still's day they didn't call him "African American," they called him Negro.

In contrast, it wasn't until the late 1930s that white composers like Copland and Bernstein began to deal with the Western pioneering concept of America and the American sound, in, for example, Copland's symphonies and with his "Fanfare for the Common Man," and with some of Bernstein's work. But the William Grant Stills, the William Dawsons, they were dealing with the Negro's language from the beginning and making conscious efforts to attend to that truth. All of the white American composers never came to the realization until later that they needed to deal with the truth of American music.

Yes, we understand the importance of academia, we understand the Viennese tradition, but we are going to take all of that and work it. The black mentality has always been there. When we were in slavery, we had to deal with what was given to us, and then we incorporated our lifestyle and our perspective. We weren't given meat, so we had to slaughter the pig. We weren't given the food from the table of our masters, so we had to go in the field and take the leaves, the foliage, the roughage from there, and we worked it for our own use. The African American composer has always gone to academia, taken what was there, and then internalized it from his or her perspective. I really think our white counterparts are just beginning to deal with that kind of dualism.

The composer's role in society, as we move into the twenty-first century, is to re-create. The composer is a storyteller. The composer either reminds us of the past, explains what is going on in the present, or warns us of the future. I believe the role of art, if you look at its history, has always been to express where humankind has been. The canon is expanding. It is necessary for us to take on greater roles in order to realize fully our realities and our potentials as human beings.

As human beings, we have senses. What we take in is what we internalize and what we become. There is a little piece that I wrote, "Oh Children, Watch Where You Walk, Where You Stand, Where You Sit." We have to watch what we eat and get the right nutrients in order to take care of our bodies. We are also what we read and what we listen to, and we simply can't get away from that. The consequences of the decay of our society today—murder, rape, extortion, everything that is evil—seem to be at the forefront, because that is what popular music depicts. You have rap artists, for example, who present some of those issues. But what happens is the listener decides to take it and work it, just as the composer takes the Western European tradition and works it. We listen to that music, and it is going to come out in what we do. You listen to stuff that says, "Let me screw this lady, let me beat my wife up," and you are going to end up doing those things. You are either going to end up doing them or you are going to take a stand against doing them.

Once again, I think that pop music needs to address some of the social ills of our society. It needs to take responsibility for making this world a better place. Why do you want to live in the pits? Why do you want to live uncomfortably? Therefore, in our roles as human beings, as composers and as popular artists, we need to create an environment where we can live and be productive.

I don't want to be antiproductive. If something is presented to me that is contrary to life, if it presents death, I really don't want it. Although we have to die, nobody really wants to, and therefore the music and the art should re-create life. The art should move us to another plane, a higher level, another frequency.

Music and art should bring another challenge to us so that we can deal with the realities and the evils in this world and the ways in which we need to address them. I thought being in the motherland, in Africa, was an event that God gave to me. My mother hadn't gone. My grandmother hadn't gone. My great-grandmother hadn't gone, but my great-great grandmother was probably born there and came over here, and that scenario wasn't good. Going back as a free man and as an extension of my ancestors was a wonderful privilege. I felt that the trip was something that only God could have ordained. That is my religious belief, that is my theological perspective. I could take on, and be proud of, the reality of touching base with my ancestry. My experience in Africa had a tremendous impact on me, and I just sucked everything in, from the way people dressed to the way they smelled, the food they were eating to the colors of their eyes, to the culinary arts, I just soaked it all in. I was just on a high.

Musically, I worked with Pierre Lope [West African choir director] and the Martyrs of Uganda out there in Senegal, and I worked with the singers and drummers. I forwarded a choral piece to them, and they learned it. To be able to conduct them, I began to internalize their performance practices. For example, before my Africa trip the way I wrote percussion and perceived the drums was very different from my perspective after I returned. The difference is that I now realize that the drum is a voice. The drum is not like a metronome, it is not simply something to keep the beat, as we are taught from the Euro tradition. I now think of drums as the heartbeat, as a driving force in the music. When I was in Africa I began to hear melody in the drum, I began to hear counterpoint, I began to hear large forms in those performance practices. That has had a tremendous effect on my music. Even today, in my work entitled *Symphony,* for example, the fourth movement in the third or fourth section is a dedication to the great West African Diola [a Muslim ethnic group] tradition. The rhythms and the complexities of the percussion instruments are there. The rhythmic efforts that I try to re-create from the great West African tradition are not only in percussion; they can also be seen in the flutes, in the woodwinds, and in the strings. I treat the strings rhythmically, as if they are playing right on the edge of a conga drum. Ultimately, if you just look at the score and not listen to the pitches, but look at the rhythm, you would see the heart, the essence, of the Diola people.

In *We Must Be Reconciled,* my piece for choir and orchestra, I attempted to capture the African American piano performance practice of gospel music and intersperse those gestures, the voicings, throughout the orchestra. The lines of the strings, the way the first violins are divided in octaves, are fashioned in the way one would articulate a particular line on the piano. That is one example of how I explore the gospel tradition using a piano-performance style for the orchestra. Now, it is somewhat subtle, but if you were to take that orchestral score and attempt to play different parts on the piano, you would see the piano performance practice in the moving bass lines, in the parallel motion, in the upward-moving sixths, and in the diatonic chords moving in progression.

Of course, the vocal performance practice of breaking up lines and words is there in the piece as well. There is a line in the piece where in the Eurotradition you would say, "We must be reconciled." But in this work the singers sing, "We . . . must be . . . re-con-ciled." The phrases break up like that to make those words be said emphatically, unto God with all of your heart, your soul, your spirit. You want to be able to communicate emphatically to God and to the people, and you want to lead the people in that type of worship experience.

Today we call ourselves "African American composers," because people are interested in labels. People are interested in categorizing and are not interested in being unified, which deals with a whole other set of issues. Socioeconomic power, political power, theological power are all at play. Labels exist so that a particular unit is either higher or lower. Whether it is racism or not, it is biased, and it is prejudiced.

My heart would like to perceive everybody as who they are, but because the world is so evil, people want to label so they can create a standard of what they feel is important. Labeling is therefore a criterion. I hope and pray that two hundred years from now they will just label us all "American" and simply say, "This is American music." I write American music. Do we talk about Bernstein as being a Jewish American composer? No.

I think it is important, however, to talk about us as African American composers, for the mere fact that we have a whole bunch of brothers and sisters dying out there who think they can't do anything. They need role models.

To be labeled an African American composer is good on one hand, and on the other hand, no, it's not good—but I want to meet the needs of all people. If it is good for this individual, if it is going to make individual A's life better to not call me African American, then call me "American." I only want people to enjoy my music. I hope my music does something for people. If individual B needs to call me African American, then praise God, call me "African American." Let me try to meet the needs of all people so that I can serve them. Let my music serve people, let me serve people. I see myself as an American composer who is African American. More importantly, I am a composer who is Christian. I am doing what God is telling me to do—writing wonderful music as He gives it to me.

Michael Powell

Michael Powell, born in Chicago in 1956 but claiming musical roots and heritage in "Motown," has become one of the most sought-after and successful song composers and arranger/producers in the industry. Known as the composer/producer who put songstress Anita Baker "on the map," Mr. Powell has composed for and produced such greats as Aretha Franklin, Rachelle Ferrell, Regina Belle, Peabo Bryson, Randy Crawford, Nancy Wilson, Jennifer Holiday, Gladys Knight, Jodi Whatley, the Wynans, and many more. A multitalented industry visionary, during an era (the eighties) of robot-drum-programmed "Madonna-like madness," Mr. Powell re-revolutionized the industry slump by introducing masterful live musicians in productions that became the industry practice. One was the ground-breaking work *Rapture.* Nominated for numerous Grammy awards, including best record and best producer, the million-selling album that Anita Baker entitled, wonderfully, *Compositions* contains some of Mr. Powell's best work to date. He has three film soundtrack credits—*Lethal Weapon II, Leonard Part 6,* and *Dangerous Minds.* He has built a multimillion-dollar production studio in Detroit, the largest and busiest in the Midwest, drawing the country's best talent. Mr. Powell lives and works just outside of Detroit.

The first time I really was exposed to music was with my older brother, who aspired to be a singer. My mother worked nights. After she would leave for work, my brother would make us get up and sing. He used to beat us up if we wouldn't sing. He made us sing every night. I never really wanted to be a singer. It wasn't until 1968, when we moved to Detroit from Chicago, that I became interested in music. I was given a guitar as a present by a cousin of mine, who could only play boogie-woogie and the blues. He showed me how to play. That was the beginning of my life as a musician, but I wasn't playing seriously. I was just kind of picking it up here and there. In the early 1970s, when I was in high school, I joined a band. I set the guitar down and played the drums, because I had always wanted to play the drums. I got pretty good on the drums, but then a friend of ours who was in the band wanted to play drums, and since he owned

all the equipment, he could play whatever he wanted. He kicked me off the drums and told me to play guitar. That is what I did.

I started practicing and listening to people like George Benson [jazz guitarist]. One of my biggest influences was Jimmy Hendrix. Barnie Kessel and Joe Pass were also important. While I listened to a lot of jazz stuff, I didn't have the opportunity to play much of it. I got the opportunity to put another band together and go out on the road with the Detroit Emeralds. I played with them for years. We even went overseas. I also played with the Dells, Joe Simon [R&B, soul singer], and a lot of local groups. At some point I had joined Marcus Belgrave's big-band workshop and learned how to read charts. That was fun, reading music. I was basically self-taught. I never had lessons, I just listened to records, put the needle back and figured the music out in my head. After that, I was touring around the States and Europe with all of these different acts. The band I was with, Chapter Eight, decided to stay home. Chapter Eight did the local thing, playing in clubs, and we developed a following. We got a record deal on Areola Records and cut our first album in 1979.

I didn't know anything about producing, I just knew we wanted to cut a record. We were signed with this production company, and I cut some tunes. I was basically the musical arranger for the band. When it came time for us to produce a record, we looked for producers. Initially, we wanted to get Maurice White or Michael Henderson. Quincy Jones's name also came up. The production company, Fee Records, said they couldn't afford those people. Henderson was really hot and was doing a lot of stuff for the Dramatics, Maurice White was doing his thing, so we decided to try to find a local producer. The production company suggested a couple of people. I remember this one particular guy, whose name I can't recall, who had a record out on the radio. I remember hearing this record, and I knew the vocals and music were both way out of tune. We hated the record. When his name came up, we said, "No, no we can't use him. That was the worst record. . . ." They made us go over and meet with him anyway. So we were sitting there talking to this guy. Listening to him talk, a light went on for me. I went back to the production company and said, "Look, I know what I want this group to sound like." The guy told me to go ahead and produce the record myself. Derek Dirckson, who was the Chapter Eight drummer, and I went into the studio, cut a couple of tracks, and then came back to let the production company hear it. They said, "Wow, this isn't bad. It sounds pretty good." I know for a fact that our work sounded better than the guy they wanted us to get. We were feeling pretty good about it, even though we didn't know exactly what we were doing.

We depended upon the engineer to give us a lot of insight and direction. The engineer was very helpful. After we did the Chapter Eight record, I started doing productions for local artists. I worked with Jimmy Scott, a local artist, and I focused on sharpening my skills in the studio by writing songs and doing demos. After we cut the Chapter Eight album we went on tour, that was in 1981, and I was still doing some local production.

We were in a club on the east side of Detroit called the Cabaret Lounge. We gigged five nights a week there. Anita Baker was there in another band called Free Spirit, or something like that. Our bass player, Dave Washington, had gone down to the Cabaret Lounge on one of our off nights. Anita was singing background with this band, but she had one song that she would sing every night. Dave came back and told me, "Man, there is a girl at the Cabaret Lounge named Anita and she is ba-a-a-d." We went down the next week, and she sang her one song, and we were like, "Damn, she's ba-a-a-d." After her one set, we asked her if she would like to join Chapter Eight. At the time, Chapter Eight was a hot band around town—there was Chapter Eight, Brainstorm, and a few other groups. Anita couldn't believe we were asking her to join the band. She said, "Chapter Eight, you have got to be kidding!" So she quit the band she was in, joined with us, and we did the clubs around town until we went into the studio. That was her first experience in the studio, and I was probably the first person to ever cut a record on her. The record was just called *Chapter Eight.* The rest is history.

The thing was, if you listen to the Chapter Eight album, you hear a *band* playing, not a lot of synthesizers. We were real musicians, we had real bass, real keys [keyboards], and the whole thing. If I had been a keyboard player instead of a guitarist, maybe I would have leaned more toward a synthesized sound, but I was used to dealing with the Rhodes [electronic keyboard] and acoustic piano. That was how I was hearing music. We used live horns in the clubs we played, so we never really depended upon synthesizers to create the bulk of our sound.

In 1984, I started working on the Anita Baker album out in California, when I was doing a second Chapter Eight album. Anita had come over to my apartment and heard some of the tracks I was playing, and she said, "Wow, did you do that?" I said, "Yeah, that is Chapter Eight." Chapter Eight was a hard-hitting funk band. We could do ballads, we could do anything, musically. She heard those tracks, and the next day she came by and said that she wanted to do a record. She had signed a new deal and asked if I would help her out. She played some tunes for me, and from there we just did the arrangements and hired the musicians. I didn't really know anybody in California. I knew the names of the musicians, but I didn't know them personally. I depended upon Barney Perkins, the engineer, who was a legend in the music business. He suggested certain musicians, and we got them in there and started cutting.

Initially, I was only supposed to do two songs. The record company had all of these other producers lined up, people like Tom Bell, and I think they talked to Maurice White. The funny thing about it was that before I came into the picture, Maurice White was the person who they had considered to produce the record. He saw me out in California doing the Chapter Eight record and wondered if I would help him do his portion of the Anita Baker record. Whatever happened, it just didn't work out between him and the company. I did my two tunes, the record company loved them, and then asked me if I would do the rest of the album. I said, "Sure," and that is how we got into *Rapture.* Immediately after that, I did Regina Bell's first album. Then I did a couple of tunes for Grover Washington [jazz saxophonist]. From there it started snowballing. I worked with Peabo Bryson, James Ingram, Gladys Knight, Patti LaBelle, Rachelle Ferrell, Oleta Adams, Nancy Wilson, Jody Watley, the Wynans, Aretha Franklin, and Randy Crawford.

When I hear a new artist, I look for the raw talent. I look to see if there is true talent, no gimmick. It is in a sound, in technique, it is in the unique qualities of someone's voice. You want to hear something that is "today" but the key is to look for something that can grow and be huge ten years from now. I remember when I started producing I always used to say that whatever I did, I wanted it to sound good ten years from now, no matter what it was. I always looked at Stevie Wonder and Smokey Robinson—I don't care when you hear their songs on the radio, I don't care if it's twenty years old, their work is the jam! Strangely enough, *Rapture* is eleven or twelve years old now, and when I hear it on the radio, it is right there. It doesn't sound like old Anita Baker, it sounds like good music. I always look for longevity, because that is the hardest thing to hold on to in today's music. If you can get longevity in anything that you are doing in this business, then you are doing great. The music is changing so much every day that if you can come up with a sound or a concept that is going to stand the test of time, you have got it made. That concept still helps me today.

When people call me for certain projects, like a recent Nancy Wilson thing, for example, people say, "I've got this tune, and we need great production on it." They tell me my name is the first one they thought of, and that makes me feel really good. There is not a day that goes by when I don't hear some of my work on the radio, and it doesn't make any difference whether it is new or old. Everybody wants longevity. For one thing, if you use acoustic drums on a record, acoustic drums sound like acoustic drums, the sound doesn't change. If you use synthesized drums, you can say, "Oh yeah, there is that snare drum Cameo used on such and such a record back in 1978." But acoustic drums cannot be dated. You can't put a date on acoustic piano sounds, or guitar sounds either. Those sounds are always fresh. It is what you put into it that makes it work.

Technology makes me more effective in my work. Even when I am doing an acoustic session, I may use the drum machine for a "loop" [prerecorded, repeating musical pattern] to give it a certain feel. I can add to it, and it feels as if more musicians are playing. The thing about the synthesizers is that because of the digital realm, you can do so much with editing and time compression, sampling, and the whole thing. Technology is really a producer's tool. Technology is not necessarily a crutch; it can be a tool if it is used in that way.

Babyface [R&B songwriter, producer, singer] and I have a lot in common. We both worked in bands with real musicians. Babyface himself is a guitar player. I think he is a great songwriter, and I also think his productions are great. The same thing holds for Jimmy Jam and Terry Lewis [R&B producers]. They came out with their own sound, they were writing great songs, and they had great concepts for the music that they were doing. Teddy Riley [R&B producer, songwriter] came out with the new hip-hop jack-swing thing, and the young kids jumped on it because it was loose. It was not a precise, exact type of thing, it was more of a feel, like in the church. Riley's music felt good, and everybody locked into that hip-hop swing. Then people started copying that sound. That is the thing about the synthesizers and the drum machines. Anybody can cop the sound. Anybody can get it, copy it, and do it better than you. But if you are a musician, you are an individual.

I think the younger cats now are basically working off of feel. They will take a drum pattern and drop a couple of street loops in there. If you go to New York and you see these guys banging on cans or buckets, you might have five cats playing five different things. But if you listen to the pocket, the musical groove, it is right in there. That is what the cats are doing with these loops and samples, they are just putting together five different hip ideas, syncing it up, and it is working. They don't even have to know how to play a note of music. If it feels good in the clubs and you have a good hook, radio is going jump on it. I think that is another style, another form of music that allows some young cats who aren't really musicians to get involved and make some money in the music business.

I don't know how great that is, because it is so easy to pick up a drum machine. They even have keyboards now that will create a groove for you. We are now getting a whole generation of young cats who cannot play music. I think the tragedy there is that we are getting a whole generation of people who are in the music business who aren't musicians. If you asked them to play a song, they couldn't do it. Nobody is interested in learning how to play. They want to make the money, make a groove and get rich. But it is going back to real music now. As a singer gets older and that little hip-hop thing isn't working for them, or the sound is changing too fast and they want some good solid music, then they are going to have to come to cats like me and Babyface, Jimmy Jam, and Terry Lewis. There are some young producers coming up who are really musical—the guy who produced Brandy [Rodney Jenkins], for example. Those guys come out of the church.

I think what I do with the music I produce, even if I am working with a young artist, is make sure that there is some integrity in the music. I even have a rap group that I am working with, called Ordinary Black Folk. The music is original, and there is not a whole lot of sampling going on. People are hearing it and are saying, "That's phat." Ordinary Black Folk is always looking for something new yet, its music has a kind of old-school vibe to it, and the kids are digging it. I think it is important to keep the integrity of the music intact at all times. You can give it a street feel, but let it make sense musically. A lot of stuff I hear today doesn't make sense musically—some of these remixes, for example, where the drum is at one speed and the vocals are at another, with a different pitch than the bass. You have these guys at the record company who don't know anything about music who are just saying, "Oh, that's phat, press it up." Then you get records out there that don't make any sense musically or any other way, and that is really sad. The kids figure, "Okay, I can do that." It is not like it used to be when you would look at an artist like Gladys Knight. When she was singing, you didn't hear everybody saying, "I can sing just like Gladys," or "I can play just like George Benson." Nowadays they can hear something and say, "Oh, I can sing like her. That ain't nothing." Nobody really works on their craft or tries to develop it any more. It is more like, "What can I do to make some quick money?"

I also think that what is happening right now—everybody is looking for something new. We have sampled just about all of the music there is to sample. We are repeating ourselves. The music that we are listening to is second, third, fourth, or fifth generation down. It is not even original music. I think what people are looking for now is original music. That is what I hear when people talk to me about what they want. Even the rappers are starting to get hip now. They are asking for real bass players, real keyboard players, and live drums, so everybody is looking fresh. The only way you are going to get it is to create it from scratch. I think that is where it is all going now. I think people are concentrating on creating new music.

It is hard to measure my most significant achievement at this point. Some of the work that I thought was the best I have done was not the most popular. I think people will perceive the *Rapture* record as my greatest work. That album brought me a lot of recognition in the record business, and it also changed a lot of other producers' styles. When that record hit the radio in 1985, nothing else on radio sounded like it. When *Rapture* hit the streets and was played on black urban radio, nothing else sounded like it. That is why I think it blew up, because it was just so different. I think that was a great achievement for me, because I think it did do something in the music business to change a lot of other people's approaches to the music. Nobody thought that stuff would work, because everything else at the time consisted of up-tempo drum machines—and here comes this song with live musicians, and it is grooving. People were really into it. It worked. *Rapture* is one of the things I have done that I feel was really great.

I would want people to remember the integrity of my music. I always try to make sure things make sense, without being restricted. I want the music to be loose, but I want to make sure it feels good.

Billy Taylor

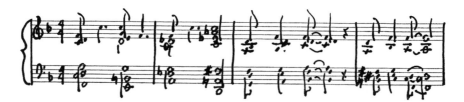

Dr. Billy Taylor, born in 1921, is an American ambassador for jazz and the arts, is probably one of the most recognized American public advocates of music in our time. Helping to legitimize the phrase "Jazz, America's classical music," he has spent more than forty years as a spokesperson for the arts. The winner of numerous awards, including a Peabody, an Emmy, seven honorary doctorates, and a presidential appointment to the National Council of the Arts, Dr. Taylor presently holds the Wilmer D. Barret Chair as artist in residence at the University of Massachusetts. He has been active giving clinics and lectures in every major university and college around the country—Duke, Princeton, Harvard, Boston University, the University of Michigan, Yale, Indiana, Vassar, and many more. He received both a master's and doctorate from the University of Massachusetts. His compositions have been performed by dozens of American orchestras, including the National Symphony and the Atlanta, Indianapolis, Portland, Denver, North Carolina, Savannah, Puerto Rican, and Minnesota Symphony Orchestras. He has served on the boards of the American Society of Composers, Artists and Publishers (ASCAP), the Rockefeller Foundation, as well as the National Association of Recording Arts and Sciences. He is well known as the creator and founder of Jazzmobile in New York. Billy Taylor has recorded over thirty albums and has performed and recorded with the likes of Ella Fitzgerald, Quincy Jones, Bing Crosby, Sammy Davis, Jr., Billy Holiday, and Charley Parker. He is also known for his radio and TV programs (such as *Taylor Made Piano*) and appearances (including as an arts correspondent for CBS-TV's *Sunday Morning*) highlighting the creative work of American artists. His work has also published *Jazz Piano: A Jazz History,* as well as several other books and major articles. Dr. Taylor lives in New York.

I grew up in Washington, D.C., and I come from a musical family. Everybody on my father's side especially was musical. Everybody on my mother's side was too, but they were primarily self-taught musicians and didn't have any real outlet for their musical talent. My paternal grandfather was a Baptist minister, so everybody on my dad's side of the family had an outlet for their talent. Most of them became trained musicians because of that. I was born in Greenville, North Carolina, but I was brought up in Washington, D.C., so the shaping of my consciousness for music happened there. Washington, D.C., in the days when I was growing up, had a wonderful black community. I lived about two blocks from Howard University, so many of the musical experiences in my early life were either at the university or in church, in my grandfather's church and in other churches where the great black artists appeared, since in those days they could not appear in the concert halls or with symphonies, at least not with the National Symphony. Most of the people I saw perform were African Americans,

and they were performing both traditional African American music and the European classical tradition. At Howard University there were many excellent performers, who were very exciting for me to listen to, because they performed on the same level as the people I heard on the radio.

When I was a kid a lot of activity centered around the church. That is where I first heard Paul Robeson. I went to Lucretia B. Mott Elementary School, Shawor Junior High School, and then I went to Dunbar High School. Each one of those schools had an assembly hall. In those assembly halls we had frequently (at least twice a month, sometimes three times a month) a visiting artist. I recall being in grade school and seeing acrobats and people who typed very well. There was one guy named Cortez Peters, who typed very fast to music. He would be typing rhythmically, and yet what he was typing made sense. He wasn't just hitting letters, he was expressing coherent thoughts. We had all kinds of stuff like that. My father was a dentist. His office was around the corner from the Howard Theater. Some of the show people who performed there were his patients. So I got to meet many of them off stage. I also had an uncle, my Uncle Bob, my father's middle brother, who knew everybody.

Uncle Bob was the hip member of the family. He knew all of the nightlife folks, the piano players, the singers, the show business people. He never went into show business himself; as a matter of fact, he went into politics. He was also a newspaper man and an army officer; he did a lot of things. Uncle Bob never went into music seriously as a professional, but he is the reason I play the piano. He played jazz, and he introduced me to Fats Waller by giving me Waller's record. Uncle Bob also gave me my first Art Tatum record, and he took me around and introduced me to some of the people who performed in the bars, restaurants, and night clubs on Hughes Street. I was too young to go in by myself. Uncle Bob knew all of the local musicians, so he introduced me to them. He was the first person who took me by the hand and introduced me to people who were already doing something that I aspired to do.

My biggest influence came from people who were in my generation. By the time I got to junior high school, I had taken some piano lessons, I had fooled around with the saxophone, and I had played the guitar. I wanted to get into show business in some way. There was a musician named Cooper Gibson who lived next door to my mother's sister, Alcinda. He was a very fine guitarist. I was so impressed by his playing that I bought a guitar. He showed me a few chords, and we began to play some duets together. We went on the amateur hour at the Howard Theatre, and because he was so good, we won. He was doing all the work. But for me that was a big deal; I thought showbiz was a very glamorous business. I would go to the theater. In those days it cost about fifteen cents to go to the matinee, so I would be there early to see the people I heard on the radio, people like Don Redmon, Duke Ellington, Cab Calloway, Jimmy Lunceford, and many other exciting performers. Every week there was a different band, so I got to hear and see all of the great black artists, musicians, dancers, actors, comics, and singers. I saw Lena Horne there, along with many others who at that point in their careers were not as famous as they ultimately became.

I was very interested in jazz, so I must confess that although I was tremendously impressed by Paul Robeson and by several female singers who sang opera, I was much more enamored with the jazz singers, like Ella Fitzgerald, Billy Eckstine, and other people who were singing the kind of music in which I was interested. The whole idea of finding some route to play this music well intrigued me, and I couldn't wait to study and practice in order to do that.

As soon as I began to play jazz with some facility, I began improvising and making up little melodies; soon some of them began to sound pretty good to my untutored ear. I would try to put something together that made musical sense, but I couldn't write it down; I was playing primarily by ear in those days. I would make tunes up, and then I would forget them. Many of them just went away. It wasn't until I attended high school and college that I began to write things down. By that time I had gone back to studying seriously and realized that you have to be literate as well as have a good ear. I was trying to write down some of the ideas that occurred to me for two reasons.

First of all, I had a very good friend, whose name was Frank Wess, and I wanted to play as well as he did. Today he is a wonderful flutist, but in those days he was playing tenor saxophone. Even in those days he was a tremendous musician and a warmhearted, funny guy. He would come over to my house, we would listen, and we would to play what we heard. We made up tunes that we liked to play. My first compositions really were just to show to the guys who were my colleagues—"Hey, do you like this? I just made this up." That was an exciting thing for me to do.

The second reason was one of the teachers at Dunbar High School, Mary Reese Europe [also a composer]. Everyone who came to Dunbar High School in the 1930s studied with her. I remember her as a wonderful, no-nonsense little lady who was very, very to the point. She wanted all her students to love music; she was the first person to tell me and others about Roland Hayes [concert singer]. We were trying to be jocks, playing football and other sports. We kind of sloughed off the kind of singing that she wanted us to do. I would go to the instrumental class, and I loved every minute, but about this singing and music history and music appreciation I would say to myself, "Okay, I'm not interested." One day she called several of us who were out in the hall making a lot of noise into her music room. She said, "I just have to talk to you young men. You seem to think that being manly is a matter of how many muscles you have—something physical." She told us about Roland Hayes's experience when he went to Germany and sang *Leider* for the Germans—how he walked out on the stage and they booed him and hooted and so forth, and how he stared them down. She said, "Now, can imagine yourself in a foreign country where you are the only Negro except for someone who might have come to see you? You are the only one. Can you tell me that you have got the nerve to stare down a concert hall full of people who don't look like you, don't think like you, don't speak your language, and don't want to hear you sing? It takes a man to stand up and face them and convince them that they should shut up and listen to him." She was so articulate. We didn't know at the time that Hayes was coming to our school. She had invited him. He was handsome and dignified, and he had a gorgeous voice. I had never heard a man sound like that. It was just beautiful. After we heard him sing she said, "Now you understand why those people listened to him in Germany." She was a real teacher.

It was experiences like that which gave me a broad range of desires. I wanted to express myself like that, but basically, because of my own means of expression, I was thinking, "How can I do something with jazz that does that for me?" I always had those ambitions for jazz. One of the reasons I guess I never desired to learn European classical music was because of a great pianist and composer who was also a student at Dunbar High. George Walker was already a very fine pianist. He would play at the assembly, and my jaw would drop. I would think, "Gee he plays well. My goodness, he must practice a lot." He was already playing Rachmaninoff, and I thought he was terrific. There were many other students who at that stage were dealing with the European classical repertoire in a very competent way. I just felt I had to make a choice. I could hear jazz possibilities that I wanted to do; I was actually studying piano with Henry Grant, a teacher there who was a good friend of Duke Ellington. He was also the band director. He played several instruments, among them piano. Through Mr. Grant I got interested in Claude Debussy and Maurice Ravel and the impressionistic composers. He said, "You are using all these chords that you think started with Duke Ellington when in fact you can find them in Scriabin, you can find them in Debussy and Ravel, and you can even find a few of them in Chopin. You ought to look at this other part of the tradition." With his help, I did just that.

I had all of these various points of information to draw upon—people like Henry Grant and Mary Reese Europe, the people who were teaching at Howard University in those days, the people who were in the choirs. There were some excellent choirs. In addition to the choir in my grandfather's church, Florida Avenue Baptist Church, there were several other choirs that were quite outstanding. We would go to hear them on Sunday afternoons. You would hear these wonderful singers doing things that were quite different from listening to opera and "classical music" on the radio. Radio was not commercial in those days, so I heard a lot of opera, a lot of light classical music, and a lot of jazz. All kinds of music was being played on the radio, so I had this tremendous variety of things available, whether I wanted them or not. I listened to the radio frequently, because there was always something of interest going on, either musically or informationally, but basically music. Because of this, radio was the most popular form of home entertainment for many people. Some people were singing gospel, some were singing popular music, some were singing and playing jazz. There was an abundance of high-caliber music available free every day and every night.

The people of the United States own the airways, but because we have not protected our own interests, we have allowed our representatives in Congress to give away a resource worth billions of dollars. In return for broadcast rights, we should at the very least receive in-depth news and information that would enable us to make well informed decisions on issues that are important to us, and we should have at least a fair and complete presentation of the diverse cultural gifts we have given the world. Jazz is America's classical music, so I believe it should head the list.

Back in the 1960s I realized that as far as jazz was concerned, we simply weren't getting the cultural message. I felt that jazz should be in the schools. I believe it should be available to as many people as possible, so in 1964, as members of the Harlem Cultural Council, Daphne Arnstein and I helped create the Jazzmobile, a unique outreach organization which brought great jazz artists into personal contact with young people of the inner city.

Q: That quotation, that jazz is America's classical music, isn't that yours?

Aren't you the originator of that great quotation? I always knew that, but I wanted to hear it from your mouth.

A: Actually, it came from the fact that while working for my doctorate, I began to talk about all of the things that went into jazz, such as jazz being a very hospitable music that takes information from other cultures and utilizes it in a way that is rooted in African traditions. Africans, because they had an oral tradition, accepted things that worked for them, often restructuring music to make it conform to their traditions. They reshaped those ideas to fit these cultural needs. Jazz followed that idea; it is an African American creation. When we were forbidden [as slaves] to use the drums, we began to do things rhythmically, melodically, and harmonically that had to do with the fact that we didn't have some of the support that we had had in Africa for various kinds of instruments. We didn't have the various stringed instruments, we didn't have some of the other melodic instruments that normally gave us support for vocal music that we used.

The more I looked into this, the more I felt, "Well, what is the difference between this and European classical music, which started off as folk music and went into the church and did all the things that seemed to me that jazz was doing?" The more I thought about it, the more obvious it became to me. I looked for the definition of classical music in the dictionary; the dictionary said that a classical music had to be in and of the culture from which it sprang. To be classical, music had to have longevity and to have spawned other types of music based on the parameters that it established, and so forth. The more I read what made a classical music, the more I realized that jazz fit all the criteria, that it had indeed spoken to and for the American people regardless of ethnic background or geography. Jazz speaks to and for us about Americana, in regards to many things that we say we hold very high. In this country, we say we really respect and honor the individual, and we think that because this is a democratic society the individual has the right to do and say many things that the same individual wouldn't have the right to do in a kingdom or in other kinds of societies. Since jazz celebrates that individuality, that personal expression, it seems to be the one indigenous music that qualifies as our classical music. Moreover, jazz conveys thoughts, impressions, and feelings that have been relevant to generations of Americans and non-Americans. This was, and is still, done through implicit, connotive musical symbols.

Q: Is jazz, then, the way to recapture the youth who have been lost?

A: Yes. I think that we can show them that there is much in this tremendously broad musical palette that we have developed in this country that is an important part of the African American experience, that has had such a profound influence on our culture. African Americans need to pull it together in the same way that the black community used to pull itself together when we all were forced by segregation to live together. The opera singers, the symphony players, the jazz singers, the jazz players, the people who sang in the barbershop, the people who sang on the street, they all knew the musical devices, which were common property, and they related to one another and influenced one another. It was a small community, and everyone took from other people things which were of value to himself and used those things effectively. That way, the music grew beyond the blues, it grew beyond dance music, it grew beyond concert music. It encompassed all the church and secular things that were a part of our existence.

If we can make this point to young people and show those young people that rap goes all the way back to Africa. You had griots, people who knew the history of the tribes, who traveled and were like the European troubadours. They had something else too, in that they took not only the information, they took the other cultural aspects—the manner in which you sing, the manner in which you use music, the manner in which you do many things that are a part of your collective memory. We can show a rapper that rap as we know it today originated right here in the Bronx, with a bunch of guys of West Indian background. What they did, unknowingly in some cases, was to take what the calypso musicians and singers had done before them, then did things that were slightly risqué in some cases and very risqué in other cases, and things that had a special meaning to their immediate group. If I were a calypso singer, that meaning would be a double entendre, because the person that I would be singing that to would get one message, while someone who was just overhearing it would not understand what we were saying, because it had another specific meaning to West Indians. The rappers picked that up, and since they were not musicians in many cases, they had to use scratching records and mechanical ways to get the rhythmic background and all the other things that they needed. They often used vocal sounds to create the background for what they had to say.

If they knew that the griots did that and that the calypso people did that and that, indeed, right in the generation that proceeded them, black disc jockeys used to do that, when they introduced records in the 1950s, perhaps their rhymes would be even better. All of the disc jockeys on stations that were programmed to African American audiences would do that rhyming thing to introduce the next record or to talk about whatever subject they wanted to share with the community. If they knew something was going on in the community they might do that in a rhyme. A guy named Jack the Rapper [disk jockey, impresario], who is still around and who has a convention of disc jockeys every year, was just one of many guys who did that. He has been Jack the Rapper since the 1950s, so rap didn't just come in with this current group.

Q: Let me ask you about your process when you sit down to write and a piece.

A: With a commission where they say, "Here's x amount of dollars, write us this piece for Lincoln Center."

Q: What do you do as Billy Taylor, composer?

A: It is interesting that you should ask, because I am wrestling with that very problem right now. I am trying to get the muse to strike. I do a lot of things. I play a lot, and basically I try not to listen to anything that I think will influence me in terms of writing, because I found that when I do I am not satisfied with the results. I hate to practice, so I'll set myself a very rigid practice schedule and decide to really work on this particular pianistic problem right now, and it will be just kicking my butt. I'll be working through it, and my mind starts to do other things. My mind says, "You don't really want to do this." Have you ever thought of so and so? I begin to get all of these other kinds of ideas that take me away from practicing. Ultimately I'll come up with something that I like. I'll say, "Let me try this." That sometimes gets me started. Then I have to work it out.

It is really funny, it is something that I am conscious of; I know why I am doing this. I try to force it, but that doesn't work. I really have to get into the practice thing and just say, "Let me really work on these things because I have a concert tomorrow, let me get it done." I'll start to work, and I'll work very seriously on some technical problems and that forces me to begin to get another kind of idea. I am now working on something that features piano, and I've got the germ, so the process is working. I've been up at the University of Massachusetts for the last couple of weeks, so I've been working hard to develop my ideas.

In addition to working with my students, every time I got a chance to go to the piano I would be running through something else. The piece is surely going to be overdue, but I've finally hit on something I want to start with.

The basic thing is to get something down. Once I get the germ of an idea rhythmically, melodically, or harmonically, then I begin to think of what direction I want it to go in and what I am trying to say with that particular piece. This piece is a jazz lullaby that I will be recording soon as a guest soloist on a new album by violinist Tracy Silverman.

Q: Do you think an artist has any particular role in society?

A: Of course. I think that an artist has not only a role but a responsibility. We have the attention of a lot of people, and it is up to us to say through our art, through any means we can, the things that, hopefully, we care about—that is, the welfare of the community, the welfare of people we care about, the direction the country is going in, any of the things that we as caring human beings would think about. If it is Bosnia, if it is famine in Africa, if it is the plight of women, if it is something like affirmative action, we should say, "Well, I don't think affirmative action should be discarded because I don't think it is finished working yet." That should surface somewhere in our music. Every artist I know addresses social issues in his or her own way. Ellington did way back before the term "black" was fashionable; he wrote "Black Beauty" back in the 1920s. He wrote "Black, Brown, and Beige" in the 1940s. Throughout his career he dealt with those kinds of issues.

Paul Robeson had his career ruined because he was a superintelligent person who cared deeply about the meaning of democracy and who spoke out in ways that were not acceptable from African Americans in those days. Powerful forces in this country tried to kill him, literally, by ruining his career. It didn't work, it frustrated him and made him less visible, but the man was so strong and such a wonderful inspiration to those of us who knew him that we all profited from his example of integrity. I didn't know him well. His son and his family lived in the housing project where I used to live with my family and so I used to see Mr. Robeson frequently as he came to visit his grandchildren. I had met him earlier when I had been the accompanist of Kenneth Spencer. Spencer was a wonderful baritone, and my understanding was that he was one of Roberson's protégés. I don't remember where I got that from; I suppose I assumed it from the manner in which they greeted one another and the tremendous deference that Kenneth, who was a wonderful artist in his own right, gave to the older artist. It was just wonderful to hear the two of them talk, just to be in the room with them. They were both very intellectual, very socially aware, and wonderfully artistic. It was just fascinating to be with them. I didn't even open my mouth; I just sat there and listened. They were talking about things that were beyond my experience, but they were speaking as activists, and they were wonderful, caring human beings.

Any artist of any generation, I believe, should use this kind of artist as an example. Just look at the wonderful things that came out of the Harlem Renaissance, when people did have a social conscious and expressed that in their painting and in visual terms—in sculpture, in acting, in film, in every aspect of aesthetic expression that was possible. So the short answer is that I believe every musician, in whatever way he or she feels is proper, should use his or her music to speak to whatever concerns that artist has.

Ethnicity is something that I have been very conscious of, and I have tried to use it in a way based on models that preceded me—people like Duke Ellington, Will Marion Cook, James Reese Europe, and many musicians who were legendary in terms of being able to say, "This is who I am. This is what I look like. This is where I live. This is what I care about. I am different from some other people, but that difference is something of which I am very proud." I was taught that very carefully by people at Dunbar High School, by my family, and by many other members of my extended family. They didn't just say this to me, they gave me concrete examples. For instance, when my father took me to see Duke Ellington at the Howard Theater, he pointed out how the Ellington Band looked. He said, "This is a man who is from this city, from Washington D.C. He has played for prominent heads of state in Europe, and he has done things that very few people who play jazz have done. You can see and hear the difference between the way he presents his music and the way some other people, who play very well, present theirs. I'm not knocking anybody's playing, but look at the difference between him and some of the bands we have seen recently here at the theater. If you are going to play this kind of music, this is one of the things you should bear in mind." My father never wanted me to become a professional musician—he wanted me to become dentist or something professional in another way—but he was saying that even if I was going to do this on an amateur level, I needed to bear in mind who I was and what I hoped to achieve. This is a level to which I should aspire. I would go to see Cab Calloway, and there he was, in tails and looking sharp. Jimmy Lunceford's band would come, and all these young guys were immaculate. The best musicians were the epitome of fashion of the day and everyone was well spoken. There were plenty of bands that played the Howard Theater. They used the vernacular and talked the hip talk of the day, but they did not impress me as much. I did that too, because I wanted to be a hip young guy, but by the same token, I also aspired to this other thing that in my view brought another level of listener to you and allowed you to reach a broader audience.

I remember seeing Nobel Sissle [composer, songwriter] present Lena Horne at the Howard Theater. I must say that though I really like Lena's singing, in those days I wasn't as interested in her singing as I was in Billie Holliday's. She also played the Howard, as did several other singers who had come there with various orchestras. But the way Lena was presented, I knew she was special. Not only did I enjoy her because she sang beautifully, but I thought she was really gorgeous, maybe she should be in the movies or something. I was also thinking of Ivy Anderson and some other people who sang the straight-ahead jazz of that day and used a personal approach to melody, harmony, and rhythm in ways similar to their instrumental peers. It has been interesting to me to notice how Lena, as she has grown older, has come even closer to the ideal of a jazz singer that I had; I'm sure that she had it in those days, too, but she needed to find her true self. Today, as a person who has achieved remarkable things, Lena epitomizes, to me, what a good jazz singer does. She does everything a fine jazz singer should do and more.

Jazz has become concert music. I think that I would like to see it broaden its base. The term "concert music" is loosely used now. What has happened is that the lines that used to be very formally drawn—a string quartet or a chamber group came into a concert hall dressed in tuxedos and long gowns and played very somber and very serious music. Now you find chamber ensembles playing, in some cases, much more accessible music and in some cases doing things that show the impact of jazz and popular music on the concert field. I am managed by the same person, Herbert Barrett, who manages Sheril Milnes. I am the only jazz musician he has managed for the last twenty years. I play basically in spaces that present European classical music. Just over the weekend we went out to Vail, Colorado, where we played in a classical series. I am the only jazz musician on its schedule this month. They may have one other, but basically we are their jazz presentation. We play with six or seven symphony orchestras a season. I play only jazz with them; I don't play Gershwin, I don't play other things, I play the kind of music that I write. The compositions I play with orchestra are the works that I write, because that is all I have available for them to play with me. It is not that I'm not interested in other kinds of music; it is just that, to make a point, if you want to hire me because I am a jazz musician, here is music, in my style, that I'm going to play with your orchestra. I think that rather than play what pop concert audiences seem to expect, I have to do what I do, because I have no interest in playing the music associated with most pop concerts.

I don't do the pop thing as well as some other people who wear funny hats and do other things that may intrigue that audience. I don't play my version of Beatles' songs and stuff like that. Jazz has worked very well for me. I played with the Philadelphia Orchestra recently. I have played with many different orchestras, but I think that as we proceed in the twenty-first century, jazz has got to be better treated by the African American community in order to develop its full potential.

I think much of the growth of jazz will come from that nucleus. Every significant change in the music has started with its roots, somewhere within that nucleus. Whether we are playing a kind of jazz that sounds like gospel music or playing the kind of jazz that sounds like Latin music, or the kind that sounds like an extension of the Count Basie or Dizzy Gillespie type of music, all of the music that was moving forward in the twentieth century came from the African American community. In addition to that, people who have come from a very European point of view, like Cecil Taylor [pianist, jazz composer] and a few others, are beginning to make headway in terms of making people hear what they are doing, simply because the palette has become so broad that what used to be thought of as sheer dissonance and unacceptable noise is now recognized as something else. After thirty years, audiences are listening to them with more respect for their artistry.

Q: In looking at all of things you have accomplished and what you are doing now, if you had to write down on a piece of paper "Billy Taylor's biggest contribution to American music culture," what is it, and what will you hope it to be?

A: I don't know, I guess someone else will have to write that, but I hope it would be that I wrote some music that would endure. I think that the strongest thing that I have done to date is to demystify jazz for a large number of people. I have done it on radio, and I have done it on television. I think that what I have been able to do is to show people that you don't have to have special knowledge, that you don't have to bring something special to the table to understand, appreciate, and love music on a very high level. I have been able to share this with a variety of audiences because of several things. First of all, based on my ethnicity, I am a black guy who has traveled all around the world because I was a jazz musician. Jazz has done that for me. Literally, I have been everywhere, to Australia, Africa, Europe, Asia, South America, the Middle East—I mean, you name a place and I have been there. I have been there because I am a jazz musician.

Jazz enabled me to have visibility, to give lectures on jazz in mainland China, to represent the U.S.A. behind the Iron Curtain in both Russian and Hungary, to be America's gift to the king of Morocco at one of his birthday celebrations. All this was because I am a jazz musician and because I am black. I would not be telling the truth if I said this would have happened to me anyway, because I am a great piano player or whatever. All of these things are related. I was one of three musicians on the national council, and I was visible. I was the second to be on the council, and David Baker [composer, educator] is the third. Duke Ellington was the first. There have been so many things. I got the Medal of Art, a national medal that comes from the president of the United States, as opposed to the Kennedy Center honors. I am the third jazz musician to get that. There certainly are many other musicians who are classically trained in the European tradition who deserved this and did not get it. I got it for a variety of reasons, including my visibility and whatever other reasons a president might have had to do this. It had to be based on some kind of artistic merit, because the president who gave it to me was someone I never voted for, George Bush. I am a registered Democrat. I never played the White House during the period when he was president. Nor did I play when Ronald Reagan was president. It had to come to him as something he did as the representative of all the people of the U.S.

So, I am very honored that I achieved these things and I am really very indebted to the Henry Grants and the Undine Moores, the Richard McClanahans, and others with whom I have studied, as well as the Tatums, Ellingtons, and others who in so many ways cleared paths for me. Will Marion Cook was the first of the American composers from the turn of the century who served as models for me. I can't recall whether he was a friend of Henry Grant, but it was Henry Grant who told me about him and who made me go listen to some of his music. He made me aware of some of the other people who were members of the Frogs, that wonderful association of talented musicians and other artists organized by James Reese Europe. That is a legacy to which I really feel that I am indebted. I feel a strong attachment to them. I hope that I can live up, in my generation, to the kind of standards that they set in theirs.

Tony Williams

Tony Williams, born in Chicago in 1945, established himself as one of leading drum artists in modern times. His composition work, first heard in his landmark fusion recordings with Lifetime, has continued to be one of the important elements in his creative output. This Grammy Award–winning artist is the only musician to have performed regularly with the three groundbreaking thinkers, Miles Davis, Jimi Hendrix, and John Coltrane. Mr. Williams began playing at the age of eight and developed "big ears" through the influences of his parents. After moving to New York at age sixteen in 1962, he performed with Jackie McLean. Soon after, in 1963, he was invited to join Davis's band, recording some thirteen albums with the "classic quartet," which included Herbie Hancock, Wayne Shorter, and Ron Carter. That group subsequently reunited and won the Grammy Award in 1995 for best jazz record. Mr. Williams was inducted into Modern Drummer's Hall of Fame in 1983 and has since conducted master classes in percussion, including teaching at the Mozart Conservatory in Salsburg, Austria. In 1990 he received a commission from the Wallace Alexander Geboude Foundation to compose *Rituals,* performed by the Kronos String Quartet. His first recording as a composer of orchestral music, *Wilderness,* was released in 1996. Mr. Williams passed away in 1997.

I started playing with Miles Davis when I was seventeen. When I got hired by Miles Davis in 1963, my feeling at the time was that I was the right person for the job. I felt I had prepared myself specifically for that job. I had worked really hard, I had studied all of my idols, like [jazz drummers] Max Roach, Art Blakey, Philly Joe Jones, Roy Hanes, Jimmy Cobb, and Louis Hayes. I knew what they played. I had listened to all of Miles's records, and I loved them. When we talk about influences, I tell people that if I had never met or played with Miles, he would still have been a major influence on my life, because of the way he played his horn; it touched me at an early age. I was prepared for that job more than anybody, because I knew all of the tunes, and I could sing all of his solos. I felt that when he called me for the job, he made the right decision.

What I wasn't prepared for was the emotional part of working with Miles Davis. As the years went on, I felt more and more alone, because I was the youngest. What is important to most people at that age is whether or not people like them. I wasn't prepared to be as isolated as I became. I was the only one around me who was my age, in the band or out of the band. I went to New York at the end of 1962, so I was still sixteen. People didn't realize that I was still an adolescent, and I didn't realize it either. I started having emotional problems. Looking back on it now, however, I am glad I did what I did. I wouldn't change

any of it, but that is what happened. The musical part, though, was a piece of cake, because I was so prepared for it. That was like going to the Olympics and winning a gold medal, knowing that you are going to win and just going ahead and winning it. After you win it, it is like, "So what?" Unlike the emotional aspect of the experience, the music was never, has never been, a problem for me.

The thing that people don't realize, and what I need to let people know, is that what I did was study all of those guys who were playing music, thoroughly. I made a mental graph in my head. I realized drummer A did a specific thing here, but he didn't do it there. Drummer B did this here, and he never did this. He knows how to do this, but he didn't do this too well. Drummer C can play this tempo really well, but when he gets to this tempo, the sound falls apart. That is what I did, and I made a mental graph of all of this. I didn't do this consciously, my mind just worked that way at that age. Elvin Jones [jazz drummer] was in that graph too. I would take exactly what these guys played and just add what one guy did with a certain style to what another guy did in a certain style and to what another guy did. I did the logical thing. It was simple logic, with the addition of my own emotional content. I wasn't really playing anything that any of them didn't play. I just played it all in a different place and added different things that seemed logical. I thought, "Well, gosh, if no one is playing this right at this spot, I might as well play it." If you see a big hole in a graph, you put your thing right in that hole.

What was recorded on the album *Nefertiti* was the first take of that track. We rehearsed it just once and saw that it was going to go that way. They turned on the tape machine, and what you hear is the first time it was recorded. That band was made up of the right guys at the right time. It wasn't about the piece, it was about the way that the guys started playing. When Miles wanted something, he had a way of saying, "Let's just see how it flows." When I make records now, people ask me if I can play like I played on some other recording with Wayne Shorter, Herbie, Ron, and Miles; I tell them to go get those people, and I will do that. I can duplicate it, but I don't like doing things in a vacuum just because someone wants to hear it. The reason why I play like I play is because of the people with whom I am playing. I am not going to play that way if I am playing with Hank Jones [jazz pianist] and Ray Brown jazz bassist]. I am going to play like they do. If I am playing with Cecil Taylor, I am going to play a totally different way. I just don't like people asking me to play a certain thing when there's nothing else going on around me that is helping me do that.

I don't get a chance to talk to the younger people in music—and I don't particularly want to, to tell you the truth. I am not really interested in that, because I am interested in going forward in what I am trying to do. I am trying to learn more about how to write music right now. I'm practicing the drums as if I were fifteen years old, because I'm trying to get better again.

When I was a kid, for example, the thing that excited me most was when I heard somebody and then said, "Damn, I wanna play that. Let me see how I can play that!" When I was a kid, my job was to go out and play with everybody. When I started playing in 1954, between 1954 and 1962, all I did, every night, was go out and play with somebody.

When I got a chance to travel to New York before I moved to there, I could go on any night of the week to Birdland and hear Art Blakey's band, Cannonball's band, and maybe Horace Silver's [jazz pianist, composer] band. There would be three bands at one club. Then you could go down to the Vanguard and listen to Bill Evans. Then you could go uptown to Minton's and listen to Johnnie Griffin and Lockjaw Davis's [saxophonists] band. Then you could go over to Count Basie's and listen to Jimmy Smith. Then you could go all the way back downtown to the Five Spot and listen to Monk. Then you could go over to the Half Note and hear Coltrane. You could do all of that in New York in one night. You cannot do that any more. That is what I had; I could feel these guys. When I was a kid Eric Dolphy came to Boston and played at Connolly's. I could just sit there and feel the force of Roy Haynes [drummer] coming off the stage, watch him sweat, watch his right hand and then watch his left hand. I could listen to Eric make mistakes and then try some other stuff. That is what a player has to do.

Wayne, Miles, and I didn't have discussions about music so much, we just played together. Wayne would bring in a tune, put it on the music stand, and they would just analyze it. Herbie would sit there, look at the tune, and figure out what it meant to him. Ron would do the same, and so would Miles. The only conversations that I have ever had were after the gigs. Herbie and I, sometimes Wayne and Ron, would be at a place having breakfast after a gig at four o'clock in the morning. We would say things like, "Wow, wasn't that great? Did you hear what we played on that second tune on the third set?" These were in the days when we played three, sometimes four, sets a night. This was in the 1960s. We worked hard. When I was kid, whenever I played with somebody, there was this magic that you played to reach. You played to reach a certain place.

You were always reaching. I don't see that, I don't hear it, I don't feel it from whatever is going on now in New York. Maybe it is because I don't live in New York. I am not one of those people who is looking for the old days, but the magic that happens is important to what makes music tick. Take that out, and the music is dry.

From time to time Miles would just tell me in different ways what he liked about my playing. He liked the way I played rolls. At times, though, I would get discouraged, and he would say, "Don't quit." There is a record that we made called *Four and More,* which I hate and everyone else seems to love. When that record came out, I was so depressed because I hated the way I sounded on it. I still hate it. At that particular time I was playing a certain way, and that record caused me to change the way I played. But Miles always encouraged me. I knew that he wanted me to play "all out," and he made no bones about that. He wanted me to play "all out," that is why he hired me. That was the great thing about Miles. That is the thing I have taken away from that experience. When you hire people, you hire them for what they do best. You don't hire them and say, "Don't do that." A lot of band leaders I have come across were like that.

One of the things that Miles is also noted for, that has added to his legend, is that he always had a great band. Why? Because he hired players who played a certain way, and he let them play that way. There are people who are big names who have never had great bands. When you mention their names, people don't conjure up the bands that they had at different periods. That is the thing that was great about Miles. He wasn't afraid; he would jump in feet first and then see what happened. He wanted people to shine. What I am saying is that some people want no one in their band to shine except for themselves. You can hear it time and time again in people's records. Miles wanted magic, so he hired people because of the way they sounded. People who reach are also going to make mistakes. You can hear Miles making mistakes, but that is because he is reaching. They say Henry Aaron and Babe Ruth hit so many home runs; well, they also had to strike out. They set strikeout records, because you can't hit so many home runs without striking out a lot too. You can't be afraid to make a mistake. The biggest thing I took away from Miles is how to deal with fear on any level, not just musically.

I was born in Chicago in 1945. My parents moved to Boston in 1948. Boston is a community filled with colleges, universities, institutions, all kinds of things. They have more colleges and institutes of learning in that area than any other place in America. The oldest high school in America, Latin High School, was established in Boston somewhere around 1838. When you are in Boston and you have all of this learning around you, you really understand what it is to be a student. Also, my father was a weekend saxophone player. He worked in the post office, and on weekends he would play saxophone with his friends. They would play dances, cabarets, and those kinds of things. My mom liked to listen to Chopin and Wagner, and my dad had Count Basie and Charlie Parker records, so I had a broad musical experience at home. As a kid, my kid friends and I were listening to the Coasters and the Flamingos. This was before Motown, in 1954 through 1956. I had these three musical things going on.

My dad would take me with him on his jobs, and I kept watching the drummer. At a gig I finally asked if I could play. My dad immediately said, "Yeah, but what instrument?" I told him I wanted to play drums, and he said, "Sure." That was really the turning point. Most parents would have choked and said, "Well, gee, I gotta ask the guys first," or they might say, "I've never heard you play." My dad didn't do that; he just said, "Sure, what instrument do you want to play?" It took me years to realize how strong that was. That is how I started. The first time I played a set of drums was in front of an audience. I was eight, and it was in the summer of 1954.

That is a major part of what makes me who I am, because I had to play right on the spot in front of an audience. It wasn't about, "Well, I'm going to get ready, practice, do this stuff and then come out." It wasn't that way.

I *had* to play, and I have had this ability all my life, to make the drums sound a certain way. I started playing with all of my dad's friends. Actually, Malcolm Jarvis, the trumpet player—who is actually Shorty, the one who went to jail with Malcolm X—was my father's best friend. Jarvis played trumpet, and he played like Roy Eldridge. My dad played alto and tenor; he liked Sonny Stitt and Gene Ammons [saxophonists], that kind of sound. I played with them for a long time. Then I graduated somehow when Allan Dawson [jazz drummer] heard me play. My dad invited Allan Dawson over to the house, and he heard me play. Dawson knew that he wanted to help me develop, so he became my teacher. In 1958 he invited me out to his club in Cambridge, called "The Club Mt. Auburn 47," which is one block over from Harvard Square. The first thing that I did away from my dad was sit in with Dawson and his trio at the club. A guy named LeRoy Falana heard me at the club and asked if I could play with him there on Sunday afternoon. Falana hired me, and he hired a bass player named Jimmy Tolls. He also hired Sam Rivers; that is how I met Sam. Sam and I started to get together, and he encouraged me to play more. But Allan Dawson was the first example I had of a serious, full-time musician. He did nothing but music. My dad and his friends were weekend warriors, but Allan was my first role model as to how you conduct yourself, how serious you have to be about an instrument, how serious you have to be about being on time, and how to be a world-class musician. Sam was more of an influence on my creativity, and by 1961 I was working a lot with him. By that time I had already started listening to Miles, 'Trane, and Ornette Coleman, and all of those things, which influenced me greatly.

I was working in Boston as the house drummer in a trio at Connolly's when I heard Eric Dolphy. Connolly's would bring saxophone players and trumpet players in from New York to play with the house band. One week Jackie McClean came in, and he heard me. He said I had to come to New York. I told him I was dying to go to New York. I had already been to New York a bunch of times on my own, and I had met Max Roach in 1959; one week I stayed with him. I met Art Blakey in 1958. They both let me sit in with their bands. New York was really great for me, and I was just dying to get there, because I was so bored in Boston. When Jackie said, "You've gotta move to New York," I said, "I would love to move to New York, but you are going to have to ask my mom." He came out to the house, and he told my mom that I would be staying with him, his wife, and their two kids; he told my mom he would look out for me. My mom knew my passion, and, to her credit, she let her only child leave at sixteen. I had dropped out of high school, because by the tenth grade I was so bored I wasn't doing the work. They asked me to repeat another year of the tenth grade, and I said, "Thanks, but no thanks." I dropped out.

My mom was a big influence on me. She and my dad had split up by this time, and for her to let me go was significant. By that time, however, everyone had told her that I was really good. My mom knew that my music was where my future was and where my talent was. She knew I was not just hanging out in the streets, so she let me go.

In New York I worked with Jackie and his band, and we also worked in an off-Broadway play written by Jack Gelber called *The Connection*. The play had gotten a lot of awards. Miles Davis brought Philly Joe Jones [drummer] with him when he came and heard me play with Jackie in a concert we gave one night. I didn't meet Miles then; he talked to Jackie. A couple of months later, Miles called and was looking for me. People were saying, "Hey, did you get the call from Miles?" I thought everybody was joking. They said, "Miles is trying to get in touch with you." A couple of nights went by, and he called me on the phone from California. That's how it happened—Miles Davis called me and asked me to join his band.

Q: How would you describe your evolution as a composer?

A: I listened to a lot of movie music when I was a kid, and my mom listened to Chopin and Wagner. Listening to the classical music that my mom played, and going to the movies and hearing that music, I wondered how they did it all. Music is the reason I play the drums. The drums gave me an instant access, I could instantly get into music, and I never had a problem. Listening to movie music as a kid, I was curious about how they wrote something, take it all the way through, and still make it cohesive. Later on, as I got older, and especially when I got with Sam and we worked with a group called the New England Improvisational Ensemble, I did things where you played to a clock. We played with numbers, or we played to a graph. This was a very experimental group, out of the New England Conservatory. This was around 1961. When I got to New York, I started listening to a lot of Bartók, Karlheinz Stockhausen, and Stravinsky. I had already written a couple of pieces while I was in Boston. When I was about fifteen, I started writing. Then I started taking harmony and theory in about 1964. I have taken private lessons ever since then. I was also into Indian music. When I got to New York, in those days, in the early 1960s—this is between the time of beatniks and hippies—we were listening to Indian music long before it was a fad, and that kind of music was very influential.

My musical interests all gave me something that I wanted to add to jazz. I took another look at the same material but from another room, so to speak. My musical experiences have made me want to combine elements that I didn't hear even in the kinds of experiments we did with "third stream" music in the sixties. For example, I have always loved the orchestra, and in this new piece that I wrote called "Wilderness Rising," we recorded the orchestra first, and then the players had to play with the orchestra. In most recordings, in a lot of jazz recordings, they record the band first and then the orchestra. What I'm saying is that there is a certain kind of sensibility that I don't hear that I would like to hear more of in a jazz setting. But it is also the kind of thing where I would like to get completely away from a jazz setting. I believe that African American music is not just jazz, R&B blues, soul, funk, or hip-hop.

I do think black music is distinct from other musics. I cannot define it in words, and I don't particularly want to, but I would like to be able to express what "black is" through music. I am also at a point where I believe you don't have to write cliché jazz things in music for it to be black. Actually, I find the biggest problem is not with the musicians or the music at all. The problem lies with the writers and the people who call themselves the "gatekeepers." These are the arbiters who don't play music, who don't create anything, and yet tell young musicians what to do. I find that the record companies, the managers, the agents, and writers who write articles in magazines influence these young people to maintain a certain sound that they think is jazz. There is a lot of music that hasn't been explored that is very valuable. I know after you hear something or if you eat something for so long—if you eat nothing but bananas, for example, you are going to get tired of bananas. If you put too much sugar in your coffee, you can't drink it. That is what has happened to me musically, so I am trying to find ways to do things. I am basically a drummer, so for me to write things, for me to have a voice, I have to write. I have to write things that I want to play, or I have to write things that I don't want to play. I have to write things in which I don't play the drums. There are no drums in "Wilderness Rising." There is no rhythm section. It is all orchestra, and that is what I am working toward.

I write as a composer. I don't write as a drummer writing songs. I think that my sensibility for melody and harmonic rhythm and structure comes out the same as it would if I played a drum solo. I don't think that it has anything to do with me being a drummer.

Every time I write a piece, the process is different. This last piece came about through certain events and a melody that came into my head. I started writing the piece, and then it changed. I decided that I was trying to express an extramusical idea about America. I am of mixed race; my mother is Portuguese, and my father is African American. On my mother's side, my great-great grand-mother is Chinese. That is what I am trying to express, and also how people in nineteenth-century America would have seen the wilderness and how they wanted to make something out of it. That is why the piece is called "Wilderness Rising."

The music grew through a lot of hard work. I work at the piano because I am very, very conscious of how things move. It is not just melody, I need to have a full palate. *The Story of Neptune* was something that I wanted to do for a long time. Those three pieces are a story that I wanted to tell. As a composer you have these notes, and you want to put them in a sequence that expresses your view of the universe and of life. That is all I am doing. I am doing what every composer does. I am trying to express something in a cohesive way so that people get a picture or feel something. I am not simply trying to show that I can write tunes, because anybody can write tunes. I am trying to show structure and direction. When I was a kid I realized that anybody could write a tune, but the real test is if you can write music that other people want to play. A lot of music is just vacuous and doesn't have something that touches people. When you can write something that touches other people, really touches them inside, that is what makes great music.

An artist does have a role in society, and that is to inspire other people. When I was a kid, I felt inspired by Max Roach, Art Blakey, Miles Davis, John Coltrane, Gene Ammons, and a lot of other people. I was inspired. I would just sit and listen. I would see their pictures in magazines and I would say, "I wanna be like that." This is before Martin Luther King and before Malcolm X. These musicians just made me know that there were black men who stood up for what they believed. Miles Davis and Max Roach were role models. I saw their pictures and thought, "Damn, these guys are some serious brothers. They are warriors." That is all I am trying to do, I am just trying to stand up and be counted.

That is what I think my role in society is, to first of all stand up for my instrument, the drums. I am not here to promote violins, promote saxophones, or to promote trumpets, I am here to promote drums. I have a list of drummers who are close to my heart, and I want those guys to be remembered. I play so that these guys, many of whom people have never heard of, will be remembered. The better I am as a composer, the more people will hear me and the more I will be able to tell them who Shadow Wilson was, for example. The better I am as a composer the more I will be able to tell them about Sonny Payne or Kenny Clark [drummer]. The more I write, the better I write, the more the drummer will be respected.

In ancient tribes the artist was like a doctor. They called him the "shaman." The musician, the artist, is very important to a culture. We're healers. I take my role very seriously, and I feel a big responsibility. That role is not something that was forced upon me, it was something I took on. It was something for which I decided to be responsible. No one said I had to do anything. I was proud to decide that I want to be responsible, to take up the challenge, to take up the gauntlet and fight the fight. I have always felt this way, because those people who inspired me need to be remembered. We can't let these people down.

Michael Woods

Michael Woods has emerged, in his own words, as the "Mingus reincarnate of his generation." Born in 1952, a native of Akron, Ohio, Dr. Woods's influences range from Miles Davis to Bartók, from Andre Crouch to George Clinton, to Beethoven. Composer/bassist and director of jazz studies at Hamilton college, he received his education at Indiana University, earning a B.A. and M.A. in composition, a doctorate in composition from the University of Oklahoma, and a second master's in jazz studies from Indiana University. In addition to being an avid performer, Woods has established one of the premiere concert stops in the upstate New York area at Hamilton College, drawing such performers as Clark Terry and Joe Williams, and leading numerous ensembles in his own works. In addition, Dr. Woods has had works performed by the Tulsa Philharmonic, Pro Musica Orchestra, and the Lafayette Symphony. Michael Woods lives and works in Clinton, New York.

I grew up in a Catholic church, and it had all the ritualistic things, and it was very sedate—very subdued in many ways, and I appreciated the ritual of that. I appreciated the beauty and the structure of it, but it was something that didn't give me the option for free expression. Then when I was, I think, a senior in high school, or maybe first year in college, I got baptized in a little Pentecostal school that was converted into a church. This experience hit home for me, it satisfied something inside of me spiritually, and my music comes from "that place." Before that time I had been searching for that place. I knew that place was there, but I didn't have a relationship to speak from, a point of personal conviction.

When I was eleven years old, my brother wanted us to be in a talent show, and he said, "Well, I can play a guitar, but we need a bass player." At that time, I didn't even know what a bass guitar was. So I said, "When is the talent show?" It was a month away. I had a paper route, and I saved money from my paper route and went out to Montgomery Ward. I got this bass guitar, and I've been playing one ever since. I've always been intoxicated with the sound.

Later on, I looked at music, and even before I got to the *Great History of Western Music,* I realized that the composer is the one who has the say-so at the macro level. Now, that rarely is understood, because the performer is so flashy. When you go to a performance and you see the violin concerto and the guys just burning the strings up, he has to be playing somebody's music. So I realized that the only way for me to achieve autonomy was to say it myself, or else I'd have to always be making somebody's statement, and people would not be hearing my voice or the voice of my people. All that came right on the heels of my beginning to play the bass guitar.

Of course, like every other kid on planet Earth, I would listen to the R&B and take the bass lines off the records. I knew all the James Brown bass lines, and all of the Memphis school, and Atlantic and Staxx records. I realized that was only one element of the tune, and I would have to know all the other tunes. So I began to hear guitar chords, piano chords, and melody lines. We had a little group together, like a Motown group. We had singing, and a dancing group, and a six-piece band, and we'd travel all over and play. This was in high school, and I was always the rehearsal agent. I can always tell people how many flats or sharps to use. This was the embryonic beginnings of my putting things together. Even though these were cover tunes, I still understood the compositional aspect of what I was doing.

I consider myself very privileged to have grown up during a time when there was probably the most fabulous black audio there ever was—great R&B music on the radio. I listened to that music and totally fell in love. I said, "I can do this! I can write songs like this!" I wanted to participate at the same level. I would get creative impulses, and my creative impulses just didn't quite fall into the slots that all these cover tunes did. So I said, "I wanna write my own." I began to explore; something about me has never been satisfied with the "black experience" as handed to me verbatim. I've always wanted to expand upon it. I think it was 1964, when the Beatles came (to the United States). I was twelve, when the Beatles came and I said I wanted to incorporate some of those sounds. I said, "What would it sound like with the crazy chord progressions that Paul McCartney does, with James Brown's bass lines? What would it sound like with Chick Corea's harmonies, and Tower of Power's horn section?" I always was asking what if, what if, what if, and nobody else was asking what if, so I said, "I'm going to have to do this myself."

I was drawn early on, to Mozart. Music gets into you subconsciously, without you thinking about it. When I was a kid, I mean still wetting my diapers, my mother would play classical music to put us to sleep, and I remember how pleasing the music sounded, particularly classical sounds of Mozart and Haydn. I remember how light and lyrical the music sounded, and particularly how pleasing the strings sounded. That music is very pleasing, and it's very melodic. Of course people realize now that the easiest way to put a kid to sleep is to play quiet, contented music, in major keys. But at the same time, Mozart, is very, very tasty, in the sense that he has different phrasings. I didn't know enough about the music at that time to understand the subject of it. But I did understand there was something about it that was drawing me in, that was capturing my imagination.

The beginnings of the Big Band era was the time when African American musicians particularly began to switch over from just their individual performance skills, Louis Armstrong, to compositional and orchestration skills, like Don Redman [jazz arranger] and Fletcher Henderson [arranger, composer, band leader]. I think there's a tremendous tradition that has been lost, with people not really looking at the really Big Band period as a compositional ferment. They look at it as flirt music, they look at it as dance music, or whatever, but I say, "No, no, no, this is very important."

For me, the big-band tradition reached its zenith in Ellington, because Ellington was the most creative orchestrater, the most creative of the composers, yet his music never lost its communal quality. That is the thing that makes him stand at the center of what I feel is essential to the African American experience. Now, you can branch off of that in any direction that you want to and recognize composers on either side, black or white. But Ellington, to me, hits it, because you can listen to his music, you can snap your fingers to it, you can move your body to it, and yet it can still mesmerize your mind. You didn't know what he was going to do, but you knew it was going to work, and that's what we're all trying to get to as composers. We don't want our music to become so predictable, or to become pedantic, or get to the place where it is just merely a technical display. Neither would we want to become so overgrown with emotion that it has no form, no function. What we're also trying to do as an African American people is try to somehow pull our own people into a broader contribution of the spirit.

Q: What is your philosophy of music? How does it function in your mind?

A: My particular philosophy is this—I have a certain degree of creativity, which the creator gave me, which I'm aware of, and which I take the opportunity to safeguard. Further, my philosophy is to embrace whatever will allow that gift to manifest, and whatever will keep her healthy, whatever will provide it opportunities. As an African American, I try to get my music to speak from the spirit first, before I concern myself with craft. The reason why I say that is this—music is sound, created by human beings, to help human beings to relate experience and meaning. It was that before it ever dreamed of being written in ink, and that's what it's going back to. All I'm trying to do is to get it to pass through the ink. And the only reason the ink is even there is to tell the players what to do, to cut down the rehearsal time. Music is not ink, music is spirit, that's my philosophy, and it's trying to go back to spirit. When you play it as a performer, you are trying to play it back to the spirit of an audience.

Q: What are your views on Black History Month?

A: Well thank God, at least we get recognized one month a year. If it wasn't for the February "slot," many black composers and performers wouldn't get played at all. I'm grateful that we do get some performances at that time, I'm grateful even if it's only a twelfth of the calendar year that somebody gets sensitized at least a little bit. You never know, you gotta do missionary work, and when you get that one month you may sensitize somebody for life. However, *Motor Trend* magazine does these road tests on all these cars. When the car first comes out they tell you how much power it has, how fast it will go from zero to sixty. Then they test the same car five years later and say how well it is holding up. What I'd like to do is hold society to their credo and give them little quizzes during the other eleven months, and say, "Are you still doing it? Are you still interested? Do you still care? Are you still compassionate? How about in July?" In other words, to only do it one month a year rings rather hollow. It's rather hypocritical—let's get our "diversity duty" out of the way.

Q: What is your composition process?

A: I'd liken it to the whole African American process in the United States of America. What are African Americans trying to do? We're trying to live the highest quality of life that we can live in a society that has maybe not all the necessary framework and designs for our success. Therefore, some of our search for upward mobility becomes a scramble, improvisation. We have to find out whatever will work, because there ain't no manual on how to be successful in a white, male-dominated world. So the same thing happens for me as a composer.

Any little scrap I can get is enough. If it comes by divine inspiration, hallelujah. If I just wake up in the morning and God has given me this awesome melody, wonderful. If He don't give it to me, then I'm gonna go to the piano and jump-start it. That's one way of doing it, divine inspiration. If not, then I'll just start with a concept.

Sometimes I only need to come up with a title. Then I say to myself, "What would move these people? What would satisfy these people?" Then I go back to the drawing board and try to do that.

The process of composition does not have to remain rigid throughout the composition. I do not follow formulas. In other words, even if I devise a twelve-tone row, I am not going to put pitch number ten next just to come after pitch number nine. If pitch number ten doesn't fit, if it doesn't fit the groove, if it doesn't fit the natural evolution of what I've begun, then I ball up the row and throw it away. I may stay with the general language that the row came up with, to put on "the floor," but I'd much rather work with a living thing than some pedantic form of execution. If I get a motif that I think is powerful and makes a cultural and emotional statement, I may indeed stay with that motif throughout the composition. But, I'm not doing it because it's a pedantic rule; I'm doing it because it has emotion that I know can continue to be conveyed, while at the same time it affords the listener "handles," an element that can unify the piece.

What if I was no good at jazz, what if I was a klutz, but I could write good classical chamber music? It shouldn't be presumed that because I'm black I can play jazz. I can, and it does give me an advantage, but we are also spawning black composers today that maybe didn't have roots so immediately in jazz. That has to be our prerogative. I would hope that our own people would not look down upon us by saying, "Oh, this guy really don't have his roots in the blues, or he really can't play no jazz"; we have to expand the definition of what black is, and "black" can be anything we say it is. I want to say that in defense of the guys who don't have "killer" jazz jobs.

I think that jazz gives you an advantage, because it allows you to think in a way that is spontaneous. It also helps you to analyze sound and its effect upon an audience at speed. The average composer sits in a room with a score pad in front of him and writes very, very slowly and looks at music up and down in a vertical fashion. A jazz musician works in real time. If you've got a burning rhythm section behind you and sixty-four bars to speak, you don't have two weeks to turn in the assignment.

Craft is almost a by-product of the force of the spirit that I want people to feel. For instance, when I have one of my tunes played, I want that tune to just roll out. I want my charts to sound like an eighteen-wheeler going down a steep hill with the brakes out—so much information, so much energy, so much force coming at you until little economy cars are pulling off in ditches trying to get out of the way of all that information, all that force, all that funk, and all that groove. That's my goal.

5

The Composer as Conductor and Composer

Leslie Dunner

Leslie Dunner, a native of New York City known primarily as a conductor, has conducted his own compositions around the world, including the premiere of his *Memoirs of a Shattering Glass Building* with the Transvaal Philharmonic in South Africa. Dr. Dunner holds degrees from Eastman and Queens College and a doctorate in conducting from the College Conservatory of Music, University of Cincinnati. He has held the post of resident conductor with the Detroit Symphony Orchestra, serving there from 1987. Dr. Dunner has led symphonies all over the United States, including those of Chicago, San Francisco, Dallas, Minnesota, New York, and Louisville, Kentucky. He has also held the post of musical director of the Dearborn Symphony Orchestra, as well as of principal conductor of the Symphony Nova Scotia and Annapolis Symphony Orchestra. He was the principal conductor of the Dance Theater of Harlem from 1986 to 1996. His awards include the Leonard Bernstein American Conductors Award, from the American Symphony League, and the Arturo Toscanini International Conductors' Competition. Leslie Dunner lives and works in Annapolis, Maryland.

I grew up in Harlem. I'm a New Yorker, originally. I went through the public school system. Because of the bussing that was done for integration purposes, I started out at a school in Harlem, and then I went to school in a Jewish neighborhood. That school had music, among the different things that it introduced to me. I found everything interesting, actually. They said, through testing for junior high school, that I had aptitude for music, art, and science. So I could take classes in those areas in addition to the regular curriculum. And I did. I think that really was how my musical training started. I started as a clarinetist in the public schools.

What is really interesting to me is that at that point I started to develop a classical music interest, but I was also very much involved in African dance and African music. The developmental path for me both musically and educationally was really split, in many ways. I found in high school that I had to grapple with these two different directions. I didn't think it was possible to make the two mesh. I felt I had to make a choice—one or the other—which was difficult, because I felt I was giving up the ethnic heritage that I had come to enjoy. I chose to pursue classical music.

My influence was not African American, it was African, from Nigeria. My family has its own church. In addition to that, I went to a Protestant church. The church was very, very conservative. To this point I have never been to a Baptist church. So I know nothing about what that is all about. Black church, as perceived from the southern influence, is not something that is a part of my background. My roots are not from the South. That's just not my heritage.

I knew in high school that music was going to be my focus, because they have special schools in New York. I decided to go to a high school of music and art as opposed to the Bronx High School of Science, which is the other school where I had been accepted. It is still considered the best public school in New York; it rivals all the top private schools in New York. It is very, very competitive. I went to the School of Music and Art [the Manhattan School of Music].

My family thought it was a mistake, because I started going to the music prep division, and they all felt, rightly so, that I was doing all of the musical coursework, the theory, the analysis, sight-singing, ear training, chorus, orchestra, at Manhattan School of Music. Why did I need it in high school? I was also doing extracurricular activities. I was playing in a college band, in the all-city orchestra and band as well. It was pretty intensive musical training at the high school level. I was doing the music school, the after-school conservatory, the weekend high-school orchestra band activities, and the college band activities.

After high school I went to college as an engineering student at the University of Rochester. Optical engineering was my major, and at that point in time, only two schools offered programs, the University of Rochester and the University of Arizona. The University of Rochester had the Eastman School, so I went there because I knew that while I couldn't take courses in music, because the program was so rigorous, I could at least be immersed in a cultural atmosphere. I didn't worry about the usual college fraternity sort of atmosphere. That was actually where I lived on the university campus; I lived in a fraternity for a year and then in the dorms. But I knew that the activities in the conservatory were going on.

At the end of my sophomore year, I decided it was not working for me. I remember exactly when I made the decision to discontinue the optics. I was in a course called "Geometrical Optics." I was taking geometrical optics and auto mechanics along with linear algebra, differential equations—it was a rough year. I went to my professor to plan courses for my junior year and said, "I just can't continue this way. I need to take a music class and I'd like to take a course in philosophy." I asked to discontinue one of the science sequences. To continue with optics, I needed to take physics; I had only taken quantum mechanics and chemistry, and I needed to continue numerical analysis. He said "No, you can't do that." I said "I really need to, it's a personal need. If it takes extra time, I'll take extra time and double major, but I really need to do this." He said no.

I left that class that day and went to see my adviser. I told him that I would like to change my major. At that point I didn't change to music, because I didn't have any prerequisites for the music major. Everything I had done in college was engineering and science. I had not taken the music theory exams, I didn't have applied music, I didn't have private lessons. I had to apply for all that, and in the meantime I wanted to drop out of school.

My parents advised me to take some time off during the summer, do something else, and figure out what I wanted to do. So I went to Europe. I applied for the International Summer Academy in eastern France for music. They did both music and visual art. I was accepted, I got a partial scholarship, I went to Europe and went to classes with great teachers. I became bored, and I met an artist who invited me to visit with her in Norway for a few weeks, so I went up to Norway, ran out of money, and did a hitchhiking race from Oslo to Paris with some friends, because I had no money. I had a great time. My parents didn't know whether I had made the flight, because the last they had heard, I was up in Scandinavia with no money; they wondered how I was going to get to France. I literally got off the plane and said "Hi Mom, hi Dad, things are fine, I'm changing my major to music." And that's when I made the change. I led the bohemian life, literally, and was transfixed. Even if I didn't have a successful life in terms of having a lucrative career, I was going to be happy in my endeavors. I had this urge to play as a clarinetist.

Composing and conducting came much, much later. It was not until my mid-twenties that I started developing a serious interest in conducting and composing. When I did get accepted into the music program, I decided not to do it as an Eastman student, because I was so far behind coursewise. I placed out of [validated] most of their required courses because of the background at Manhattan School of Music and in high school, so that gave me a good jump. The requirements as a university student for the music program left a lot of flexibility for electives—all of my sixty-eight credits in math and science counted toward my electives—so all of my other courses were in music. I went into overdrive and became involved in the theory program and started sitting in on the graduate theory courses. One of the courses had a guest lecturer, Leo Craft, who did a lecture on extended tonality and the influence of mathematics on the early twentieth-century composers, which, of course, was right up my alley. I was really fascinated by him.

Eastman and I did not get along. We had major problems. I actually dropped out of school before I graduated. I went back to New York and worked a lot of odd jobs, which was not good for me. So I decided to go back to school. I applied to Queen's College; they said they would not accept me as a matriculated student, because I did not have a degree. But if I could maintain a B average they would accept me, because I had enough course credits. I maintained a straight A average, so I was accepted as a matriculated student. Eastman then granted me my bachelor's degree. While there at Queens, I took courses with Leo Craft in particular, because he was the person who had influenced me. He decided not to continue one of the courses that I had become involved with at midterm, and I petitioned to teach that course. It was twentieth-century analysis and performance. I petitioned to teach it as a grad teaching assistant for undergraduates and got involved conducting a concert at the end of the year. I conducted the concert and decided at that point that I wanted to study conducting. I started looking at schools for conducting, and that is how I ended up in that field. It was not at all planned.

Composing actually started at Eastman/University of Rochester. My first taste of conducting was also while I was at the university. The university built, over the four-year period that I was there, a new student union on the river campus at the University of Rochester. It was an I. M. Pei design, but I think it was not particularly attractive. Most people felt it was very inconvenient—the mathematical thing, the shortest distance between two points is a straight line, that's the Engineering School. The favorite thing on campus was the shortest distance between two points, and that is what Wilson Commons, the new building, was. It was glass with a mud-colored brick structural support; the school solicited all sorts of artistic and creative output from students in the competition for the building's dedication ceremony. So I decided to write a short piece called "Images of a Shattering Glass Building." I had this dream sequence where you see the light reflecting through the building and it's very, very beautiful, but then, you realize that what supports this beautiful, refracting surface is really very putrid and ugly and so it is ultimately demolished. I submitted this piece. It was not received very well, but it did get performed in its original version for piano and oboe. That ultimately became a piece we did with the Detroit Symphony, *Memoirs of a Shattering Glass Building.*

As I have gone through my life, I have begun to think of the glass building as a three-dimensional representation of the glass ceiling that so many of us have experienced. That glass ceiling is all-pervasive. If you imagine a glass ceiling as a three-dimensional structure, no matter which way you go, things seem to be going fine for a certain time period. But sooner or later, as you are going through this dreamlike experience and your development is going along and your dreams are being fulfilled, ultimately, you come up against some barrier that you cannot see, feel, hear, smell, or taste. Yet, it is there, and no matter which way you turn, up, down, sideways, it is always there. *Memoirs of a Shattered Glass Building* came to represent the demolition of the barriers that are placed upon the individual from external sources. I said in the program notes, "It is my hope that people enjoy the music first of all, but also come to recognize that the meaning of the work is that when we are really comfortable and confident within ourselves, we can overcome any barrier, no matter where it comes from."

I can't say that being black hasn't been a help to my career. I am sure it has been a hindrance in specific instances, but more often than not I was not aware of racial barriers at the time that they were in place. I told a friend of mine that I had conducted the Dance Theater of Harlem and the sponsor had come up to me and said, "That was a great performance. It had never occurred to me that there could be a black conductor." I was taken aback and shocked by the statement, not so much because I was offended, but it had never occurred to me that you couldn't be a black conductor. In my educational experience, I hadn't known any black conductors. But, just because I didn't know any personally didn't mean that I felt limited from that field by not having that specific role model before me.

Both as a composer and conductor, I am sure that I have experienced the racial barriers, but I don't see them as racial barriers until I review and reflect. They are there. There is no denying that they are there. As a composer, especially with the activity of African dance and African music, I don't utilize specific quotes. But for me, music and dance are one, I don't see the two as being different, and that is probably why I am so successful as a ballet conductor.

I feel music physically. I literally *feel* the music. When I study a score, I look at the page and then I internalize the page in terms of my physical movement. My back, my arms, my legs, my head, my hands—I actually touch different sounds. In Africa, music and dance are not divided the way they are in Europe. They are one element. I think that is reflected in the music that I compose. I tend to be very percussive. Percussive does not mean heavy, necessarily; *Memoirs,* for example, is very gentle in its middle section and is only percussive for a while. In terms of my conducting, the reviews that I see, more often than not, are that the reviewer or the critic felt the pulse of the music. That doesn't mean just the speed, that means the actual intensity of the rhythmic continuity that is written into the music. That is, for me, the structure, like that glass building, and I don't want it to be ugly. It is very important for me to have that structure be beautiful so that everything that works around it, through it, and on it can be supported from something that is beautiful.

I think art education in this country has to be viewed as a critical component of the core curriculum. I think in certain cultures, the Japanese and the Jewish in particular, the cultural aspect, the artistic pursuits of those societies, and those philosophies embrace art and embrace creativity as a natural force for building mind, strength, and character. In this country, we tend not to see the development of mind in terms of character. We see the development of mind in terms of technical prowess. That leaves the individual short. I think the trends that we see with younger people not valuing their own lives or the aesthetic world around them is a reflection of our teaching to them. I know in Chicago, a few years ago, there was a study done in the inner city. Quite a number of kids were divided into two groups and were studied for the period of a year. They were all below-average students, without exception. Half the group was given courses in music, visual arts, song and dance, etc., the creative aspects of our culture. The other half were given the regular curriculum, with the emphasis in math and science. At the end of the year, it was found that in the group with the regular math and science curriculum there was some improvement, depending on the student's interest and development. In the other group, where there was a balance with the creative pursuits, there was an increase in all of their scholastic aptitudes, and all of them were above normal, 100 percent.

I view Black History Month as ghettoization of African American history. Ghettoization is always a two-sided blade. We have to view the positive side— and there is always a positive side. During the period of segregation, the positive side was that the black community was very self-sufficient and multitiered in terms of its interaction and development and its growth. There was more growth in terms of business for the community, and there were many more degrees of interaction between the different social stratifications. The same is true with Black History Month. It is great to have a focus on the development of all sorts of art forms. The Classical Roots Concerts that we did in Detroit tend to bring forth many different artists and many different styles of works, because they have it every season. The downside is, as with segregation, interaction between different kinds of people and exchange of different ideas from one group of people to another does not occur. That is what happens with the ghettoization of Black History Month from the rest of the cultural musical scene in America.

The people who are involved in those performances tend to stay involved in those performances, and the people who are not involved tend not to be involved the rest of the time, either. There seems to be very little interest on the part of organizations to have the two blend one into the other. I think the fix is to recognize the contributions of African Americans and celebrate them on a regular basis. Black History Month is fine because you can target some folks, but it has to happen on a regular basis and be a part of the regular consumer diet—the same way we see Easter as a celebration of Christ rising from the dead, if you follow Christianity, or Christmas and Thanksgiving as times for family. It is a celebration that is targeted for one specific time. But it is something that we do on a regular basis. You don't just give presents to friends and families on Christmas Day. You don't just go out to eat a nice meal on Thanksgiving. You don't just go to church on Easter.

During the period of the Harlem Renaissance, during the twenties and the thirties, there was so much development of an American style of music, with the jazz influences of black Americans. That went to Europe and became all-pervasive. So when you listen to Ravel, when you listen to Debussy, there are the influences of black Americans on their music. As you get into the forties and fifties, we have the same thing with Duke Ellington and Count Basie. The influence of their music went to Hollywood. Everything from Hollywood, then, is reflective of what was going on in the black community. We have to recognize that, we have to applaud it. The music that came along in the sixties, be-bop, and now hip-hop, is all-pervasive in our culture. That doesn't mean that it is good, that doesn't mean it is bad, that doesn't mean it is high art, that doesn't mean it is popular music, but it is there, and we should recognize that. I think that once we start to recognize that, we can start to appreciate the contributions of the different factions in our culture.

I think there are some basic differences of style. The music from people of color tends to be more rhythmic than melodic in conception, aside from church music, where the interest is not so much rhythmic as it is harmonic. Because the elements are different from the European point of departure, which is melodic, you have a very different base, but ultimately, all components are used in every kind of music, and so the influences one on the other are very, very positive. It is nice to have some things that are more one thing than the other and that are more one genre than the other. Jazz, for instance, is always jazz. Classical music, when it uses jazz influences, is still classical. It is more like stylized jazz, but it still can be recognized as being different. The two can work together and can influence each other for something that is enriching in many ways and reaches more people.

Q: Tell us about your compositional processes.

A: The first thing that happens is that an image flies through my mind. It's nonpitch, just contour, and that has already happened. The color has already happened, it's in my ears. At this point I know exactly what instruments I want to use and how I want to use them. It is going to be in three parts. Next, I will go the piano. I don't play piano at all. I can do either individual chords or I can do a melody. I can't play two hands at all. I can't type, I am very uncoordinated. That's a major difficulty. I will find my thematic fragments, I usually work with small harmonic sets; I already have pitch sets and tonal schemes, because I want this piece to be very tonal—bitonal, actually. Now, I will go through the process of trying to iron out the details. The difficulty for me as a composer, because I have no keyboard skills whatsoever—and I don't hear in concert pitch, which is another problem—is that it is hard to isolate what the specifics are, because the images don't occur in one pitch level but more as contours and colors. So, for me, the challenge is to isolate and write down the specifics before I lose them.

There are a number of different roles for a composer. The first is to be true to oneself as an individual, first and foremost. I have a friend, and we differ greatly in our opinions of the responsibility of the artist, because he feels that the responsibility of the artist is to be an instigator for social change, first and foremost. I think that is a necessary but unpleasant by-product. What we should do is kind of like the oyster that has a grain of sand inside. Its goal is not to set out to make something beautiful for the world. Its goal is to get rid of that irritation, and that is why it spins the pearl. The world benefits from the oyster's work and gets a beautiful pearl, but the oyster makes it in order to make itself comfortable. We as artists spin beautiful works of creation, whether visual, musical, physical, or conceptual, because we have a need to satisfy our inner longing and to find an even internal balance. Unfortunately, from my perspective, in order to do that we have to have a social climate that will enable us to "be." That usually means going against the times, because we tend to be more forward-thinking than the rest of society. So we are, I think, by our societal positioning, placed in the role of being an advocate for change, but I don't think that is our main responsibility.

As I get older, I believe more and more that ethnicity is important. I think it is important to be conscious of it and to have it as a strong influence in what we produce, so that when we make a work to present to the world, it really is a representation of ourselves. The training that we have in American conservatories tends to overlook that. In the first few years of the African American Composers Forum, one of our managing members [in the Detroit Symphony] made a comment to me that the works didn't seem to be very black. I said, "I don't understand what that means." He said, "Well, you know, the pieces are not jazzy, they are not into the blues or gospel." I said, "You are appealing to conservatory-trained composers. Conservatory-trained composers write works that reflect their training." Our training in the conservatories is European and Euro-centric. If our conservatory training reflected more of what we internalized as individuals growing up, and if that were recognized and valued, composers would be bringing it forth more. I think that is now the trend, because there is much more emphasis on developing and portraying ourselves.

In other words, either people were sending in overtures and symphonies that were in essence very traditionally structured, or they were sending in something that came straight out of church. There was nothing that shared both tendencies. You would get your twelve-tone tone poem or your serialized work, and a lot of the work was good, because those were the techniques that were utilized, your highly contrapuntal works. That is not what the average black person grows up with in the neighborhood. That's the conservatory influence. It is after that is mastered that the original influences start to permeate more and more. We start writing pieces that may have a more cultural base in terms of their name and their concept but utilize the Western European musical techniques. My songs are based on spirituals, but when I talk about how I worked on it, I talk about my tonality, I talk about the structure, I talk about the utilization of blues as intermediate, then the utilization of canon, or the utilization of *Sprechstimme* [declamation]. Ultimately, the Western influence and training that I had became the techniques that I utilized to give voice to what I experienced.

I think concert music is going to go in the direction of more audience appeal rather than what we had in the fifties and sixties, which was more esoteric. It is hard for me to talk about some of the things happening now in music, because that is not what I was trained with. But, as I tend to say, "School don't teach ya how to live." What that means is you get your training, you learn all the rules, and then you go out and learn that life has absolutely nothing whatsoever to do with those rules. You then incorporate the rules and life, and somehow make it work. If you are smart, you progress and change as life progresses and changes, and you change the rules. Ultimately, what that means as a composer and as a conductor, whether I like it or not, is that all of those things that are out there, because I am active in them constantly, start to influence me, and I start to change. I think it's good.

I think there are elements in contemporary hard-core rap and R&B that are really good. The elements that are really, really good tend, for me, not to be the lyrical, not the text, and they tend not to be the rhythmic, because I lose all sense of shape in what I hear now. The aspects that are good are those elements that I can recognize—if there is a shape, if there is a beat, so to speak, that is pulsating and not hammering; if there is a canon to the poetry that makes me feel uplifted; or if I feel there is a lilt, even if there is something that makes my back squirm; as long as there is a reference that I can identify that I feel is creative and good. I don't like gangster rap, because it promotes violence, and I don't believe in violence. The form of rap, though, I think is great. It is poetic, it is straight out of Shakespeare, as far as I am concerned. Listen to a couplet of Shakespeare, and put a whole lot of Shakespeare couplets together, and you have got rap. It's been around for centuries. The difference for us these days is that we don't have the melodic line, we just have the beat. Again, we are going back to the ethnic heritage of people of color, the beat and not the melody. Rap is pure beat and nothing else. But there is poetry there. It can create images that are not necessarily comfortable, images that come out of society. But to promote rap, and to promote violence, one against the other, I think is counterproductive, and I do not find it expressive.

Q: Do you think there is a perceivable ethnicity in scores by black composers?

A: When I review a score by a black composer, it does not speak to me differently than one by a European or Japanese composer. Clearly not. It depends upon the composer. I have to say first and foremost, no, no. I know that is probably not what you were expecting, and that is probably not what people want to hear. With "Ride on, King Jesus," or with something that somebody is submitting to me to review or peruse that has a specific cultural base, like gospel, like R&B, like jazz, something that is built on jazz licks from Dizzie Gillespie or from Duke Ellington or from Sara Vaughn, the score hits me very differently than something that says "Acquiescence on a Clear Night." Now "Acquiescence on a Clear Night" may have a jazz beat to it that I will discover, but I discover that from studying the music, not from looking at the title. "Acquiescence on a Clear Night" could be written by someone who is white or Chinese who likes the jazz beat. There really aren't commonalities; they are all different. Many scores are similar, because many scores tend to utilize jazz rhythms. But the ways those rhythms are used are so vastly different. Like minimalism, for instance—so many conservatory faculty members and trained students are writing minimalistic-style pieces that are based on riffs. I don't see the difference there.

I can give you my three strongest musical influences: first and foremost, Stravinsky; second Mozart; third Brahms. From Stravinsky I get coloristic and rhythmic intensity. From Mozart I get clarity. From Brahms I get depth of emotional line. My ultimate goal as an artist is to go down in history as being one of those great Americans who has done it all, in some way, shape, or form. What I want to do is opera, ballet, clarinet chamber music, and conduct every major symphony orchestra on the face of the planet. I want to compose works for many different forums. I want to do it all.

Bobby McFerrin

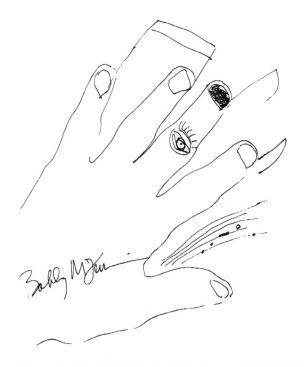

Bobby McFerrin, a ten-time Grammy winner, has been referred to by some as the "walking note," as synonymous with the idea of "creative force." An energetic performer and an industry innovator, making appearances all over the world, he became as well a famous household personality with the chart-topping 1988 song and video "Don't Worry, Be Happy." His work could soon be heard on TV commercials, including the popular *Cosby Show* theme. Mr. McFerrin also won a Grammy for his significant soundtrack performance on the film *Round Midnight.* In addition to an incredible recording and creating career (more than ten albums as solo artist) including collaborations with artists such as Bill Cosby, Herbie Hancock, Garrison Keillor, Jon Hendricks, Al Jarreau, Branford Marsalis, Manhattan Transfer, Yo-Yo Ma, and others, his creative forces in 1994 led him to the prestigious position of Creative Chair for the St. Paul Chamber Orchestra (1995–2001). This conducting appointment included educational concerts for children as well as two recordings on Sony Classical, and *The Mozart Sessions* (with pianist/composer Chick Corea). Born in New York City in 1950 to opera-singing parents, he began studying music at an early age. Mr. McFerrin continued his formal studies at the California State University at Sacramento and Cerritos College. In 1990, after becoming internationally known as a performing and recording artist, he began the formal study of conducting at the University of Michigan with Gustav Meir. He went on to conduct over forty of the nation's leading orchestras, including the New York Philharmonic, the Boston Pops, the Los Angeles Philharmonic, the National Symphony, and the orchestras of Atlanta, Dallas, Detroit, Seattle, and other cities. Bobby McFerrin presently lives in Philadelphia.

I don't know exactly what I am doing with orchestras except exploring classical music and learning how to do that. I don't have any long-range vision. If I am bringing anything to the orchestra it is simply myself, my spontaneous, in-the-moment self. I think all music should be performed like that. I think that the integrity of the moment is my goal. I am not someone who likes to rehearse a lot, because I like to leave stuff open to chance. For example, in the concert that we are doing here [St. Paul Chamber Orchestra], someone asked me a question about how we were going to work. They wanted to know if I wanted them to follow what was on the paper or me. I would say, "I want it like this"; they would get their pencils out, and they would mark it down. And then in rehearsals the following day I would do it differently. They would say, "Wait a minute, yesterday you did it like this. What do you want us to follow, the paper or you?" I said, "Follow me." The integrity of the moment is what is important. Sometimes you hear something a little bit differently. Now, today I am going to have to go out and explain to the first and second violins that in the Mozart piece we are doing I want to do something a little bit different. I have to tell them, because they mark it down on the paper. I have to tell them, "Okay, I'm not going to do this particular spot as an echo." We have been playing it like an echo, but today I don't want to do it that way.

I would love to be able to establish a relationship with any orchestra so that when they ask me that question again, I would be able to say, "Don't follow the paper." I don't really know their reaction to this type of thing. It is too early to tell. I know that the orchestras that I have worked with are not used to that. They are used to rehearsing and then doing the music that way. I am halfway like that, there are some things that I do like to hear certain ways every time we do the music, but then there are some really simple things that don't have to be done the same way all the time.

Q: How did you arrive at the structure of your opera with the San Francisco Opera in 1998?

A: I don't have a lot of the answers to what I want to do in the traditional opera setting yet; I will probably discover this on the way. I am sure that I will continue to work the way I always do. When I was working with *Voices,* many times I would hand them some music that was on paper and I would tell them to learn the notes. Then I would tell them, "Okay, now take the paper that is in your hand, ball it up, and throw it in the trash." That is what we would do. It was a symbolic way to let them know that now that they had the notes we had to put the *music* in the notes, forget the bar lines and just scratch it up. I probably do some of that in the creative process. I know that one of the things I want to do is workshop everything. After I have written, say, a month's worth of music, I get some singers together, go through it, find out what works and what doesn't, what sounds good, that kind of stuff. Then, I am sure, there will be moments where I will get the singers together, especially if I am stuck with something, and have them sing phrases and things like that. I am sure that there will be all kinds of notations, everything from traditional notation to things I won't want to write down, because I'll want it to come from the inside. I think there will be a mixture of traditional things and untraditional things.

I would like to see popular music go back a little bit and look again at what it was doing in the 1960s and 1970s. I think radio station formats have become too musically segregated. The top-forty format in the 1960s, when you look at it now, was so hip compared to what is happening now. The kids were exposed to so many different kinds of music. You could hear in an hour salsa music played by Herb Alpert, and then they would play a tune from a movie soundtrack, then they would play some James Brown, then they would play some Blind Faith or Eric Clapton, and then they would play somebody else, like Nancy Wilson or something. It was so spread out. There were so many different rhythms, beats, messages, textures, it was amazing. Nowadays, when you turn on the radio you hear one kind of beat, one kind of sound, one kind of message. I don't care for that.

I really like jazz that is "jazz"—Louis Armstrong, New Orleans jazz. I like what Duke Ellington was doing, I like what Herbie Hancock was doing, and Charlie Parker, and Miles. That to me is pure American jazz—the way the music felt, the inspiration in the black voice, the sound. Jazz has always been that way, if you look at its origin, its roots in spirituals and African slave songs, and then you look at African American church music, and then out of that you come up with the musicians who are playing stride piano and then be-bop. Jazz has always been a forward-looking music. I don't think "smooth jazz" is jazz. Whatever the radios call "smooth jazz" is not jazz. That is jazz that has gone in the Muzak direction, as far as I am concerned. The music that I buy is usually world music, particularly African music. That is my favorite music. It's funny how some music is repetitive and boring, and there is other music that is repetitive and just keeps getting so interesting. It manages to stay focused and interesting, and you wonder why. I think it's because there is a knowledge of the rhythms and tides of nature in it; it is not repetitive because the composer can't think of something else to do. The music is repetitive like a heartbeat, or like the tides in the ocean.

I didn't even decide to be a musician until I was eighteen. I had a jazz group my senior year in high school, and it was then I really started getting interested in music. The school counselor called me into his office my senior year and asked me what I wanted to do. I said, "Well, I know music best, so I guess that's what I will do." I wasn't struck by lightning. The "walking note" thing didn't happen until I was twenty-seven years old. Then it took three years, from age twenty-seven to thirty, I was trying to figure out what that was, what that looked like. I was doing solo voice and *a capella* singing in 1988. I was pretty much a solo-voice singer for eight to ten years.

The first thing was singing with Jon Hendricks [jazz singer] in 1980 in New York. We met in San Francisco around New Year's Eve. He was working at the same hotel where I was working, and I went and jammed with him one night. Then a few months later he called me. The group that he toured with at the time was made up of his wife Judith, his daughter Michele, and his son Eric. Eric eventually left the group, and I took his place. This was the week of my thirtieth birthday, in 1980. During a week I was working at Sweet Basil's in New York with Jon, Bill Cosby came to the club one night. I was doing one solo number at the time, a song called "Opportunity," which was written by Joan Armatrading.

Cosby then took me under his wing for a few things. He got me on the Playboy Jazz Festival, and I did a few things for him. In 1980 I hooked up with my current manager, Linda Goldstein. Then gigs started trickling in. I got on the bill of "The Art of Jazz Singing" in New York at the JVC Jazz Festival.

That was with Carmen McCrae and Joe Williams. A lot of people came out for that, and they saw me, and through that gig I got a record contract. I started recording my first albums; it was pretty much the record industry's attempt to get me out there in the pop/jazz kind of world, à la Al Jarreau. We did that, and it was moderately successful. Then Bruce Lundval [of Blue Note Records] asked me what my next album was going to be. I said, "I want to do a solo voice record." So my second album was called *The Voice*. It was just live performances in Germany in 1983, solo voice concerts. Then things started to take off.

I would not take a commission to write for an orchestra, but I would take one for a choral work, because I am a vocalist, and I am more interested in writing for voice than anything else. If they handed me a poem and asked me to write something for it, I would take the text, turn the tape recorder on, and sing the poem. I would just keep singing the lines, I would find the phrases, I would find what naturally comes out rhythmically. I would sing it and sing it until some idea struck me, some harmonic thing or whatever, or some melody, and that would basically be what I would do. I plan to write the opera the same way. Once I get the libretto, I will just sing it. I will turn on the tape recorder, open my mouth, and just go. If I get stuck I'll go to the piano and start pounding out some chords or something. That is basically how I write. I am not the kind of guy who would just lie on the couch and bang his head against the wall and wait for something to come up. I have to do it physically, I have to sing the parts and see what happens. That is what I do. Then, at that point I would start writing some stuff down. I would start writing what I recorded; it wouldn't even have to be complete, it could just be the first eight bars. I might take that much to some singers and start improvising on that and see where it goes. I have made some beautiful mistakes. I have made mistakes that have taken me to such a different place that I would never have discovered if I hadn't made the mistakes. You are playing the keyboard, and you hit the wrong chord, and you go, "Ahh, that's the chord I've been looking for."

Q: What kinds of initiatives do you think about in public music education in America?

A: I think that instead of taking giant steps, you take very small and simple steps. You just need to expose kids to music. That is it. Our teachers have our children for thirty hours a week, nine o'clock to three o'clock, five days a week. During those hours the teachers can play music for the kids. They can play music when they are entering the classroom, they can play music when they are studying, reading, when they come in from recess, when they are leaving at the end of the day. And every time they can play something different. They can play some classical music when they are studying, maybe some Bach or Mozart. They can play some kind of march or something when they come in from recess. They can play James Brown at the end of the day or the first thing in the morning, when kids are asleep and don't want to be there. Play some Coltrane. I think it is just a matter of opening up their ears. That is all they need to do. Maybe they should do this for a few years, do it every year, and when they get to a certain point, then you start taking the kids to concerts, take them to the movies and talk to them about the music in the movies. Take them to a band concert and ask them questions about certain pieces. Bring choreographers and painters and perhaps paint to music and talk about music in that way. Or they can discuss the rhythms in poetry. That kind of stuff. Show them the music that is in life, that is all around them without thinking about educating them theoretically, about composers who wrote this and that piece. Just open up the windows of their minds and let the light of music in, and then one kid will say, "That piece you played this morning, what was that?" And the teacher could tell them, "That was Barber's 'Adagio for Strings,'" and the kid could run out and find the music. Then the child would find more music, and that's what it would take.

Q: Should we be concerned about the role or image of popular musicians today?

A: Nothing, nothing, nothing is insignificant, nothing at all. Everything that happens bears witness to what is going on. I can certainly understand that rappers, for example, are reporting what is happening in their neighborhoods. That is true. But also, I have thought about teaching a course on what I would call "creative responsibility." It would simply be to get other creative people together to talk about the influences and the impact that our art has on society—because you can't tell me that it does not. Certainly, yes, we have the freedom to do what we want, but should we use that freedom all the time, when you think that your art is displayed in a public place, where kids may hear or see it? I would simply like to get these artists to just stop and think, two or three times down the line, about the piece that they are working on. I think the argument that they are just reporting what is happening in the neighborhood is valid, but they can also report on the other stuff that is happening in the neighborhood—the grandmothers that raised them, the papas who are working to feed their kids—they can report on those things too. They don't have to just report on the violence, the gangs, the drugs. That ain't the only thing that is going on.

I had no expectations for "Don't Worry, Be Happy." In fact, when I was working on my record that song wasn't even part of the plan. I was struggling with another tune, and I couldn't come up with anything. "Don't Worry, Be Happy" was this phrase I had seen on a poster. Lots of times when I am trying to memorize something, if I am trying to memorize a Bible verse, I sing it, make a song out of it. The tune "Discipline" came out that way [sings "Discipline"]. So I sat down, and I wrote the lyrics to "Don't Worry, Be Happy." It took me forty-five minutes to write the lyrics, and I think within an hour it was recorded. I had no expectations for the song whatsoever. I was just writing a song. I had no idea that the song was going to do that well. I think it was just the times.

I understand that we are a whole ball of mixed-up stuff. The song has two phrases—"be happy" and "don't worry." The "be happy" is always out there, but the "don't worry" part gets overlooked a lot. We worry about too many things. We think too much about the ills of the world and what have you. Jesus says in Matthew, "Don't worry about your life, don't worry about it." He is not saying don't be concerned about the ills of the world but that you should do what you can from day to day. You should keep yourself focused on simply helping your brother who is sitting next to you. You can change yourself and work with your family. You can work with the people who are with you. I don't know if I was really trying to say anything with that song, except don't live under a cloud.

Q: What would be your most gratifying accomplishment?

A: If I am remembered, I just want people to say, "He did what he could." I love music, all of it, and I love to explore it. I love good music making. I love classical music, but I can't say that I like all of it. I love jazz, but I don't like all of it. It depends upon the musicians, whether or not the music has integrity. Are they doing it because they love it, or are they doing it because they want to make a quick buck or something? I love music deeply. I think it's a spiritual art, the only art that can make a "community of people" instantaneously. You get people in a room together regardless of their age or creed or color, and make music better, you become one. It is amazing. At the end of some of my concerts I sing the Mickey Mouse theme. At one point I ask the audience to sing in harmony, and I can't tell you—some of the most incredibly beautiful sounds come out of two or three thousand people singing in harmony together. That just knocks me out. All of the sudden they become a community, a chorus of people who have made music together. I don't think there is any other art that can do that.

Coleridge-Taylor Perkinson

Coleridge-Taylor Perkinson was born in New York City, in 1932. He remains a major figure, inspirational and influential to many, especially in New York City. In addition to his concert work, he has become a much-sought-after television and film composer. Known mostly for his work on the films *A Warm December* (with Sidney Poitier), *Amazing Grace* (Moms Mabley), and *The Education of Sonny Carson,* Mr. Perkinson also has television credits that include the popular *Room 222.* He served as musical director and arranger for the *Barbara McNair Show* and for the Broadway productions of *Lena Horne: The Lady and Her Music.* Mr. Perkinson has also written ballet scores for the eminent Alvin Ailey Repertory Company and the Dance Theater of Harlem. He received an Emmy nomination for his 1985 work on *Bearden Plays Bearden.* As a composer he has done the musical arrangements and conducting for the album projects of such notable artists as Max Roach, Donald Byrd, Harry Belafonte, and Marvin Gaye. He received a commission from the Ford Foundation for a cantata for the renowned tenor George Shirley. He has composed in many varied combinations, from concertos to works for solo piano, from ballet to works for voices to theater scores, from string quartets to solo violin. Mr. Perkinson received his formal training at the Manhattan School of Music, receiving the B.M. in 1953 and then M.M. in composition, with continuing studies in conducting at the Berkshire Music Center, the Mozarteum, and the Netherlands Radio Hilversum. He has served as the composer in residence with the Negro Ensemble Company and has been a member of the teaching faculties of the Manhattan School of Music and Brooklyn College. He has held conducting engagements with the Dallas Symphony, the North Carolina Symphony, the Brooklyn Community Symphony Orchestra, and the Symphony of the New World, which he cofounded. Mr. Perkinson lives and works in Chicago, as composer and conductor in residence with the Center for Black Music at Columbia College.

Q: Tell us about the origins of your name.

A: My mother played Samuel Coleridge Taylor's [Afro-European composer] piano work. How she knew what was coming out of her womb I will never know, but she decided that would be my name when I came into this world. She slapped it on me, and it stuck. There wasn't much information regarding him given to me during my childhood, so I was not trying to ape his achievements at all. As a matter of fact, in the latter part of her life I had to do a symposium or something in Washington, and I was researching some material. My mother saved everything. In the midst of all of these old newspapers—I mean, newspapers that went back to the thirties and twenties—I found incredible things, I found some clippings of Coleridge Taylor. Here was this man who had

come here from England, conducting in a church uptown in Harlem. He had this huge black symphony orchestra and choir. I said, "My gosh, that is the same thing I was trying to do with the Symphony of the New World," not knowing that the likeness was even closer than I imagined in terms of what we were each trying to achieve. I had no knowledge of him doing things of that sort. I didn't even know that he had come to this country. I don't know if he made several trips or one, but he did it all. Here we were trying to reinvent the wheel; he had done it already. How successful they were I don't know.

Q: Tell us about the formation of the Symphony of the New World.

A: There were very few opportunities for minority musicians to perform in front-rank orchestral ensembles. They just didn't exist. This problem still exists today, but it is much better than it used to be. You go back to the 1960s; by that time you had probably the cream of the crop of minority musicians in this country in New York City. I am not saying that there weren't lots of them elsewhere, because I have found out lots of them were elsewhere, I have met them over the years. But at that time the largest kernel was right here. The opportunities to perform and play were not forthcoming, though, so a small group of us got together and started planning. It took two years of meeting at night, when people got off from their jobs, to put together the ensemble, the plans, and the arrangements. We had to become nonprofit. We had to address things in which we had no expertise. I think it was Harry Smiles [oboeist] and Harold Jones [flautist] in the group, and, of course, Benjamin Steinberg [conductor] was there with us.

I can't remember all of the names of those who were on the initial board that formed the Symphony of the New World, but it took two years of planning. We are talking about 1966 or so. There were a number of things happening at the same time—the Negro Ensemble Company, a couple of other things that didn't have to do with ethnic or minority organizations happened. That is how that organization began. Of course, the initial concert was uncanny. Benjamin Steinberg conducted the orchestra. I think there were thirty-three minority musicians; all of the first-chair people were minority musicians; there were women, Orientals, whites. It was an ethnically diverse orchestra, and it really did reflect the community. There was some of everyone there.

I remember one of the first-horn players at one of the later rehearsals had a schedule conflict and had to leave the rehearsal. Julius Watkins [French horn] took over the first chair. That was the first time many of us had heard him play. When Julius sat in the first-horn chair, and he played the horn solo; everybody fell out. You can be a very fine horn player and still not have the sound of a solo first horn. You can be a marvelous first-chair player and just not have that. None of the people who were in high places were aware of this man's ability. Things like that happened. I remember at that last rehearsal I was hoping Benny wouldn't let the orchestra play too much. It was a horse that is primed to run a race. They were about to burst out at the seams. I was saying, "Don't let them let it loose now. Hold it for tonight." There was that kind of energy in the orchestra. They played with a sense of metric time that was other than anything I had heard before. We played differently. We felt the time differently.

No matter who is on the podium, unless they know how to handle an orchestra, then it is going to take over. Any good orchestra with a guest conductor has a personality of its own. This was a new orchestra that had a personality that Benjamin couldn't have known, because no one experienced it before. If you weren't one of them, then you just couldn't know it. We knew it about ourselves, because that is how we felt about music and about how we played. That was one of the most magnificent-sounding orchestras that I had heard. If you are sensitive to it, you can hear it.

Everybody comes to New York. You can just sit here, not even interested, and you are bombarded with whatever is important, coming here in order to get a stamp of approval. You are exposed to everything, including to the people who are here. They come from far and wide to be judged, seen, and heard. It is wonderful to be here. Along with that, we have our own musical life here, which isn't wanting. At least it didn't used to be. I don't know exactly what it is now. I haven't been as active as I was in the past, and I am not aware of what is going on so much. I haven't been pushing at practicing my craft either as a conductor or a composer; I don't have a sense of what is going on in New York as much as I did at one time. There weren't as many performances and productions as there are now, so everyone paid attention to it, and you were aware of what was happening. Now there is so much of everything going on, from dance to music or theater, the energy is dispersed, so it doesn't have the effect that it once had.

I don't know that the quality of what is happening today is commensurate with what it was yesterday; those who were striving for exposure were the best of everything, from wherever. I think about the Negro Ensemble Company and look at the people who have had careers since then; of course, there were a lot of black actors who didn't come out of the company, but they all worked to-gether at one time—people like Moses Gunn, Rosalind Cash, Esther Rolle, Den-zel Washington, Adolph Caesar, I don't want to leave out anyone's name. There were too many actors for me to talk about who were there and who have careers now, but that type of thing doesn't exist anymore. We do have black theater companies.

I saw a production recently of a play by Lonnie Elder, a dear friend of mine who has passed away, *Splendid Mummer,* a monodrama about Ira Aldrich. It is a magnificent piece, a tour de force. To my knowledge it was never done on the big stage during his lifetime. I did the music for a production that Robert Hooks starred in and Adolph Caesar directed in St. Louis. I think there might have been a production in London at one time, then there was one at the Ameri-can Place Theater that Charles Dutton did. It was never done to the satisfaction of any of us, because it never got the care that a production heading for Broad-way gets, that nurtures it until it is ready. I have seen a lot of pieces that have not been produced that are magnificent pieces; all they needed was an opportunity to be seen—especially the work of Charlie Smalls, who did *The Wiz.* I know the work of Charlie Smalls. We were very close. He had other pieces that would have been very successful. This happens not only in theater but in film. There are some works of Lonnie Elder's that have never been seen, scripts that he was begged to write. They will give you all of the strokes, and then they get to the end and say, "No, we are not going to do this." They pay you off, take your work, and stick it in a drawer.

There is nothing that can absolve the media of the responsibility of dealing with creativity at large, whether it is black, yellow, or green. There is nothing that allows you to take the essence of someone's being and say that it is of no import. I am not saying that it doesn't happen, I am saying that it does not absolve the media. Oh yes, it happens. For instance, yesterday evening I heard something that was, for all intents and purposes, a rap score. It was just by accident, I haven't watched sitcoms, I am not involved with the television industry these days, but I happened to have the television on, and I flipped the channel. There were no words, but that whole feeling of what rap music sounds like was the theme of this show. This show was *Home Improvement.* Here it was, rap-sounding music that had the blackness taken out of it. All of a sudden they had put it through a wringer. They had taken out all of purities and watered it down, which is what has been going on for years. I can't even begin to talk about the music that has been dealt with that way.

When I was a kid one of the earliest songs I can remember was the Andrews Sisters singing "Drinking Rum and Coca-Cola." That was a version of calypso music palatable to the people who were not of minority background. When they do it that way, then all of the sudden they can embrace it. Then they can do the cha-cha, the meringue. Have you ever seen South Americans dance those dances? It is nothing like what we see. That is not what they are doing. The mainstream breaks it down and does it at the level of the lowest common denominator. That is like the problem we have in education. When you go for that low denominator, it waters things down to the point where they become ineffectual. They become ineffectual in terms of being able to make the statement that they could possibly make. All of the sudden they become commercially viable—that is what they are after. That is what happens.

Nothing has changed. Nothing has changed. We have the same battles to fight. Everything remains the same. It is disguised differently. It is like talking about the ensembles. There are now more opportunities to play, but there is still only one black player in the Philharmonic. I don't know if there are any in Philadelphia, I think there may be one or two in Boston, and I think—no, I know there are none in the Metropolitan Opera. That hasn't changed. One of the things I have resented for years is that the Philharmonic uses a slogan like "100 Years of Greatness," or something like that. A few people have suggested we ought to try to put together a group again. One of the problems we have is that there are many opportunities to play, we aren't as starved for venues in which to display our talents, but not on that high level. The problem is still there; from the moderate level on down the scale we can find venues in which to perform, but at the pinnacle we as people of color are not a part of it. At the same time, and I don't care what anyone says, they all accept public money. There is a law saying that organizations who accept those moneys are supposed to reflect the ethnic demography of the community. I can't speak for any other urban area, but I know we have one-third of the population here in New York and that is not reflected at that level. We have our person in there, but we don't have anything commensurate. Nor do I think that it should be legislated. I don't think that is the answer either; I think there should be an open-mindedness. If there were, we would be better represented. Commensurate representation simply isn't there.

Q: How did you approach working for TV and the film industry?

A: My standards for working in television, in film, in jazz, or in the concert world are all the same. I never approached any one of them differently than the other.

I have had good and bad experiences. One of the good ones was when I did the first picture that Sidney Poitier starred in, directed, and produced. It was a film called *A Warm December.* He was standing in the studio after the first session. He said, "Let me talk to you, Perk. I love what you are doing, because you are going to make my picture work. You know we have a red herring in the film, and there is something that needs fixing. Let me tell you what this scene is and how I feel it needs to go." He described the scene to me. I thought the music I had written for the scene was wonderful. What he said to me was, "If you think what you wrote does that, then that is it. It is my decision to make. But that is what the scene needs to do for me. Now, is that what that music does?" He left it up to me. Given that premise, I went back and wrote another cue. He didn't make me write it, it was really my decision. But I didn't often have that kind of person for whom to work. What he did was describe his problem. They were stuck with something that didn't work in the film. He didn't say that what I wrote wasn't good. He just said it didn't make him feel the way he wanted. It made me feel that way, but I represent one ticket sale, and I didn't have his experience of the industry.

The episodic things, like *Room 222,* were quite different, but they weren't any different for me. When I first got *Room 222* to do, the first thing I asked for was a copy of the theme. You had theme music that had nothing to do with the drama of the show. It wasn't interwoven or interspersed within the show, with so many different types of variations. If you have a half-hour show and two or three minutes of music, that is a lot. I forget what the norm was. Who was even trying to write variations on a theme in thirty-eight seconds? But I couldn't help it, that was my background. That was the way I worked. I had a good relationship with the people at Twentieth-Century Fox. Alfred Newmann was the head of music at Fox Studios. He was funny. I remember he said, "Coleridge, you are new here. I want you to watch a couple of people work. You have carte blanche, you can go anywhere. One of the people is great, the other one is an asshole." He wouldn't tell me which was which. I watched two people work. The one who wasn't an asshole was Jerry Goldsmith; he was doing *Patton* at the time. I also watched him work with his producer. They had little two-dollar bets on what was going to work or not in the way he had scored it against the film. There was a wonderful rapport. That was not always my experience working in Hollywood. A lot of it was uphill. I didn't win friends and influence people when I was out there, but I am proud of all of the work that I did.

I just happened to be in Hollywood. I was playing for Barbara McNair at the time. We were doing a nightclub act. She would get something to do in a film, or I would run into somebody who was working in the film industry. They would say, "Hey, do you have time to write my music?" I'd say, "Okay." Then I would run back to New York and get rid of some job, or it would end, and then I would be free to do something else. The truth of the matter is I worked in the industry for several years and never had a representative. I never had an agent or a manager. There was no one handling things for me. My telephone rang, and someone would offer me a job, and I did it. I didn't have a structured career. I didn't know to have one, because it wasn't by design. I permitted a number of things to happen to me rather than having someone structure them so that I could move my career forward in this, that, or the other direction. In a way that is good; that is why my career has been so varied.

Of course, if I had my druthers I would have had a concert career as a conductor and a composer, but then I think about how much music I would have missed learning about. One of the best things that happened to me was that I didn't have success early on. I had a modicum of success, but then the bottom dropped out. Because that success wasn't there early on, I had to find other venues in which function, and as a result of that, I learned so much. It is uncanny how much I found out I didn't know. I thought I had it together. No, no. I found out some of what I didn't know, because if one is really serious, one never gets it all.

My first film, which I happened to run into the other night on television, was *The MacMasters*. I remember when I got there, the woman who was hired as my music editor and I were coming out of the first screening. Having heard the conversations between the producers, actors, other people, and myself, she said, "Oh, we are going to get this score with great integrity. It is going to be so marvelous working with you." Her name was Irma Levin. She is marvelous. I had to sit her down. I said, "Let me tell you something. I know how to write music. I don't know anything about how to write music for film. I know you are my hireling. I know you are here to work for me. I tell you now, I don't know how to do this." She gave me a lesson every day, sitting right there on the movieola. That is how my film skills came together. If I had functioned in the manner that a lot of people do in that position of power, especially in that industry, I would have told *her* what to do. I didn't know what to tell her to do.

Q: What do you think of hip-hop music?

A: I didn't know what hip-hop was. Hip-hop to me is a finger pop. Hip-hop is some dynamite jazz. That is what hip-hop is to me. When I heard people say, "Oh, that is the hip-hop beat," I didn't know to call that a hip-hop beat. I said, "Hey, let me play on that feeling." But hip-hop to me is two-beat, as opposed to four to the bar; it is two to the bar. I don't know rap as a form, but the underpinning of it is a lot like James Brown. It is an ostinato on the bottom. The thing gets in a pocket and stays there. Rap is about pockets. Now there are several things one can do in a pocket. I think rap is a kind of pocket, and therefore it has been labeled. We know it when we hear it.

I was about to do some work with the guy who does *New York Undercover*. We talked about a project, and I said, "I can do this, and I can do that, but when we get to this certain point, I don't know how to do that." He said, "Oh, I've got that part." The quickest way to work things out, I discovered, is to know your strengths but be able to cop to your weaknesses so you can either learn how to do it or get some help. The part that I was saying I didn't know what to do with had to do with that rap underpinning. I may not like it when I hear it used without any diversity in a show or in a television drama. I may think, "Well, gee, they could have phoned that in." And sometimes that is exactly what they did. Maybe they are working to the limit of their ability, though, and maybe they need some guidance.

Q: Do contemporary artists have a role in our society?

A: It is tough to figure out the role of the artist. At one point I thought I knew the answer, but what I found out is that I don't know the answer. I thought that there was an obligation that one had as an artist. I didn't try to verbalize it. The first time the question was asked of me directly was by Dean Dixon. Dean said, "What is the role of a conductor in a community?" He wondered if we were interested in staying in touch with him. He wanted us to think about that and write a paper on it and mail it to him in Frankfurt. That was the first time I thought about what a conductor has to do. I began to see the responsibility, but I was still seeing it as an artist. I didn't see the artist as the social being I know he or she is now.

I didn't see the composer functioning in the same manner that I had seen ministers do. Like the artist whose job is to create this art form and disperse it, the minister's job is to walk into church every Sunday and lead his flock. He has a social responsibility to make them aware of certain things in their lives that they may be too naive to handle. The artist has that multiplicity of roles, and I can't enumerate them. Hopefully the artist has some kind of morality and conscience, and that he never gives that up just to be successful.

Q: What is your take on the impact of black artistry?

A: Tolstoy did not see the significance of the work of black culture. Of course, I think that is idiotic. I don't know what it seemed like before, but we know now that this is a global community. This is a very small community. We can call it the East, the West, the Third World, and whatnot, but the world is really tiny in the general scheme of things. Whatever we do has an impact. It is not difficult to show it, to prove it. Let's take Mardi Gras. Here we go, to Brazil. Those people prepare. They have samba school. It may or may not seem important. We are talking about a peasant population. But somehow, Dizzie Gillespie got down there and brought that music back. Now, had those people not been nurturing and furthering and saving that culture, which is a black culture from Africa mixed with whatever that culture is down there—I'm not going to try to describe what samba is or of what a lot of the music of the Caribbean or South America consists of, that music would not have gotten back here. It changed not only the popular music, it changed jazz; it has changed a lot of things.

Finally the West and the art world acknowledges the fact that Picasso and some of the other cubists pay homage to African art—not to African artists, who are artists of note, whom we can define, but rather to their art form. They may be wonderful artists, or they may be people who know how to carve this particular thing. Whatever it is, someone was exposed to it, and it went from there on. That is not to say that there isn't a higher level for the black artist to function on, but yes, there is an impact that we can have. I was talking about the New World orchestra earlier and its impact in the application (usually not consciously) of another sense of metric rhythmics. I heard it quite recently in Pratt's first recording. In it he plays some of the Brahms intermezzi.

All of a sudden I heard that same kind of energy in his playing that I was talking about in the Symphony of the New World. I have heard those intermezzi played by several pianists. All of sudden in my mind I said, "That is the way it goes." The way he was playing it was the way it goes. To pass this information on, to begin to show people there is another way, is extremely important. When I was conducting in Europe, I was doing Haydn. God knows they knew more about Haydn than I did. But all of a sudden I came in and gave them the rhythm for the notes. They said, "Wow, we never thought about it that way, Maestro." But that is coming out of the way I feel about things metrically or rhythmically, which is a black orientation. These are not the most magnificent examples to pass on, but it is very clear to me what that is.

We won't even begin to talk about it, but I have had the privilege to work with some wonderful dancers and choreographers, black and white, and I have seen them cross-reference information and materials, so that all of the sudden you don't know if it is this or that. Sometimes the pieces don't allow that. Yes, you can do an ethnic piece with Alvin Ailey, Donny McKayle, or Pearl Primus. Of course they can do ethnic pieces. Yet they can also do other things. I remember a woman with whom I used to play for dance classes, a woman named Drid Williams; she was Caucasian from Wisconsin. She could go in and teach Pearl Primus's ethnic class, because she understood the body. This woman could look at whatever Pearl had done, and she could break it down. She could make anybody look like a black dancer or vice versa. I have had those experiences.

I have seen people draw from each other's cultures and come up with a homogenous product that works. Or maybe you want to separate. Maybe you want to go from this to that and make the lines of demarcation even more distinct, but there is something to be gleaned from all of them, not the least of which is the black creative process and statement.

Q: Tell me about your own creative process.

A: I don't know where my own creative process starts. I know that I have to come up with an idea. I have just recently done a piece, another symphonetta for strings, my second, and I came up with an idea about folk melodies. The one that I chose was nice; it went, "Hush little baby, don't say a word, Daddy's gonna buy you a mockingbird." Then I realized that one of the reasons that I liked this melody was that it made me think of my relationship to my daughter. I didn't know my daughter when she was growing up. So, Daddy's gonna do this, Daddy's gonna do that. I am trying to make up for what Daddy didn't do. That becomes something for me to work on. At the same time, I don't know how it got into my mind. This is the most recent piece I have written.

I also know that there are some universal challenges that we like to tackle. The Paganini *Twenty-fourth Caprice,* the Brahms, the Rachmaninoff, that A-minor tune—yes, I want to tackle them. In this instance, I chose the Bach idea. That is what I hung the piece on. But I don't know where I start. You say, "I want you to write me a piece," whatever kind of piece. I get the commission, then it is up to me what I am going to write about, unless the commission is specific. Even when it is specific, and someone requests a piano concerto or something of that nature, I still go through that same process of finding a theme. I can do it on an abstract idea, but I think at this stage of my life the abstract idea has less significance. I am not going to call it programmatic, but there has to be a meaning other than just the science of the notes of the piece.

Q: How would you like to be remembered as an artist?

A: I would like to be remembered for contributing to what I think is a marvelous synthesis that can take place here, that has taken place up to this point, to whatever degree I have been a part of that. Describing that synthesis gets easy when we begin to break it down, but it also becomes difficult to narrow down. It is about the process of synthesis. I have had the ability and opportunity to show people of other persuasions that black creativity aspires to, and is capable of, the same level of achievement to which others aspire that's also a part of it. To have done something, even unknowingly, that is of black orientation, played for and experienced by black people, and to have them come away with a sense of their own beauty is important.

I don't know that we had any impact on what was going on in the world, but the piece that launched the Negro Ensemble Company was a song about the colonization of South Africa. We did this piece in a few places around the world. It had been done before, but our contribution was putting this piece together as a black company. I am going back to 1967; I didn't even know how old Nelson Mandela was then, or if there was even an awareness of him at that time. The piece itself talked about how this movement was going to happen, that this movement was a thing of the future. I had to find a way to say that and say it from the heart. If you lie in creative work, it shows up right away. So there was somehow an honest statement made about a movement that was going to overcome the problems in South Africa.

Now in a practical way, I don't believe we can beat people with cannons and machine guns using a bow and arrow or a spear. I want to believe it, but to have the strength of your convictions—that was what the piece talked about. The text of the piece was basically reportage and it would behoove me not to disbelieve it. At any rate, to be here today, to see South Africa turn around, to see Mandela come out of prison and take over—we said in the piece it would happen. I didn't think I would see it happen in my lifetime. I don't know if we were contributing to that or not, but we made an attempt at it. We helped put the conditions and the plight of Africans on the table so that the world could see it. That was a synthesis, and those who had an opportunity to view what we did, hopefully it made an impact on them. To make this global village come together in any form or fashion, I think that is a huge achievement. One of the things that I used to say when people asked me what I would like to accomplish in my life was, "To make Africa come together. To let them know that their similarities are greater than their differences." Families fight behind closed doors, but when we go out in the public we defend each other against whatever is out there. I would love for that continent to do that.

Here is another example of a synthesis. The Dallas Symphony played the ballet that I wrote for Alvin Ailey on Charlie Parker. They got to a certain part, and they played it, so "okey dokey." I got tickled. I realized, just like me learning and growing up, they had to learn how to play it. With any orchestra, what you do is you sing it to them. I sang it, and they played it right back at me, with all of the inflection and the understanding! They got right down! But, as I tell people, you can't write music down. We can put the notes down and say it goes something like this, but it is your training or your experience that tells you how to play that phrase. There I got a chance to explain something about how to play these jazz-oriented notes, and they knew. It is about, "Which way do we play this time?" Somebody has to say, "Do it this way or that way." Then they have that experience, and the next time they see that coming, they will know. That, to me, is the synthesis as best as I can describe it. There are so many syntheses. If I look for them, I will find them. Of course, I am learning all the time.

Patrice Rushen

Patrice Rushen, born in Los Angeles in 1954, has established herself as one of the most versatile performing artists, composers, producers, and arrangers in the industry. She has also established herself as one of the industry's leading women. She has served as the musical director of the Emmy Awards, the NAACP Image Awards, People's Choice Awards, BET (Black Entertainment Television) Awards, and the American Achievement Awards at the Kennedy Center, as well as Janet Jackson's world tour. In addition, her film score credits include *Indecent Proposal* and *Hollywood Shuffle,* as well as TV scores for HBO's *America's Dream* (with Wesley Snipes and Danny Glover), *The Women of Brewster Place,* and *Comic Relief.* Her work with such artists as Prince, Michael Jackson, Boys to Men, Aaron Neville, Carlos Santana, Herbie Hancock, and others, has established her as an artist and composer. Her work on the soundtrack of the film *Waiting to Exhale* paired her again with the leading commercial artists of the nineties. Ms. Rushen was enrolled at the age of three in a special music preparatory program at the University of Southern California, many years later graduating from USC as a music major. In 1972 she won the Monterey Jazz Competition as a pianist, which subsequently led to three critically acclaimed recordings as a band leader and composer on the Prestige label. Rushen released five albums on Electra Records, earning several Grammy nominations. Her most recent recording collaboration has been with the all-star band The Meeting (GRP, Hip Bop Records). She also serves as a performance consultant for the Yamaha Corporation, leading clinics throughout the United States and Japan. As an activist for the arts, Ms. Rushen devotes much of her time to teaching inner-city youth. In 2001 she served as composer in residence with the Detroit Symphony Orchestra. She lives in Altadena, California.

I was born in Los Angeles, and I started getting into music very, very early. Both of my parents worked. There is six years difference between my younger sister and I, so for six years I was an only child. My parents put me in a nursery school program. The teacher there was very musical. I was a small kid, and I was a little shy. During our activities, whenever we did anything that had to do with music—singing, dancing—any kind of activity like that, I would really

open up. So she recognized in me what she felt was an unusual musical aptitude—good rhythm, singing in tune, things that she felt were a little bit advanced for somebody who was about three years old. She knew of this program at the University of Southern California.

They had a preparatory music department designed for children. This particular study that they were doing at that time (they had a graduate course that they called "Eurhythmics") involved children and music students. They had small children in the course; the graduate students would study the kids and try to develop certain kinds of teaching theories about young, gifted children. You had to be screened to go through this program. Somehow I was in this program. I was going every Saturday to this lesson. They would use terminology that we could understand in order to help us identify what we were hearing. As opposed to major and minor chords, for example, we had "happy" and "sad" chords. For quarter and eighth notes we had "running notes" and "walking notes." This is the terminology we used to identify what we were hearing. We listened to the music and as we participated in this program, and they would make judgments and theories, do reports and things on their findings. At that time this program for small kids was new in this country. In other parts of the world they were just beginning to get into programs like this. This was before the Suzuki and programs like this that were geared to kids. This would have been in 1957 and 1958.

I started playing piano when I was five. I was classically trained as a pianist, beginning in 1959. I went through an entire piano program. I only had three teachers from age five to age twenty, so I had each teacher for a very long time. The teacher that I had through my preteens up and through college age was Dr. Dorothy Bishop. Among her other students were people like Michael Tilson Thomas. They had what they called a Comprehensive Musicianship Program, which I was in, which Billy Childs was also in. That's how I met Billy Childs. We met again years and years later, but he went through a program similar to that. It was about developing comprehensive musical skills so that no matter where you ended up, no matter what discipline you ultimately choose, your musical knowledge, your musical scope, your musical skills, your idea of communication through music, your ability to communicate through music all came first. The theoretical understanding and the technical aspects of it were organic to the reaction, to the passion that you had about the music as opposed to the other way—where you learn the notes, you learn the theory, you learn the harmony and all that stuff, and then you realize, "Oh, sounds great." We did it the other way. "It's red, it's blue, it makes me happy, it makes me sad, it speeds me up, it slows me down—why? Well, let's keep playing, we'll figure it out. It will come. It will come in your way. And by the way, play the correct fingering on this scale." So their ideas were things like that. That was my introduction through playing piano. By the time I got to junior high school, I had already been playing piano for seven or eight years. That is about the time, too, where you have a turning point. That is the time when you suddenly discover your peers.

At home, my parents used to have a collection of albums. My parents belonged to the Columbia Record Club, so every month we would receive these albums. My parents were big jazz lovers, they loved pop music, and they also loved classical music. Saturday morning was "clean up the house day." They used to put on a stack of records, and this stack would be so varied. It might have Perry Como, Miles Davis, Aretha Franklin, Oscar Peterson, and then Beethoven. I didn't realize that there were distinctions in terms of categories, or anything, at home. All I knew was that when I went to my lesson every week, I was going to be playing Mozart or Haydn or Beethoven or Brahms or something. I was not finding much Ellington in the stack of music we were going through to learn the piano, but I was hearing everything else. When I got older and began to listen to the radio and pay attention from the standpoint of the kind of music that my peers liked, the music of my day, the stack increased to include Sly and the Family Stone, James Brown, and Stevie Wonder. The jazz was always there, because my parents really liked jazz. They would give little card parties at the house, and that is what they were listening to. I would hear everything.

I didn't know if I was going to be a classical pianist or not. I didn't see a lot of black people doing that, and I think that still, somehow, this put some distance between what I was going to do with all the musical training that I had, until I started to play the flute. I started the flute in junior high, about the time that I was getting a little perturbed with the idea of practicing, because none of my friends had to do it. You know, in junior high you want to be exactly like everybody else, and I discovered that other people didn't have to practice every day. My parents were really smart, though. It was a social issue, really, not wanting to practice was a social issue. My parents said, "Why don't you choose an instrument that you can play at school with people?" A friend of my mom's was a flutist and gave me a flute and then suddenly I am plopped in the middle of the junior high school orchestra. You know, the flutes sit right in the middle. I thought, "Wow, listen to the sound!" You have rests, so you can pay attention to who comes in. Wow, the colors in the pieces! We were playing very badly, but still, it got through. In high school I played the flute, and I was in these honor bands where I played. I was still playing the piano at the time, and my concept of the piano broadened, because I was put into an orchestra environment, a symphonic band environment and suddenly it hooked up for me in a different way compositionally. It opened my eyes, and I wanted to know how to do certain things. "What do you mean your instrument is pitched in another key?" I wanted to know, and from that point on I started trying to write for some of those ensembles, just trial and error at first, writing for those ensembles, because I wanted to understand what they were talking about when they were saying stuff like "concerto." "Concerto, what's that?" I would ask. In high school I would write the arrangements for the marching band, because we needed arrangements.

I went to an all-black school, and we had about two hundred people in the marching band. I went to Alain Leroy Locke High. It was built right after the Watts riots in the late 1960s. We were determined to turn the image of the community around, and the band had incredible directors. One was a graduate of Southern University, the other was a graduate of USC. One was white, and one was black. There was this other young brother from Pepperdine College, it was his first year of teaching, and he was into jazz. We had a jazz band, we had a strong marching band program, and symphonic band program, we had a strong orchestral program. But we needed music for the marching band, and we didn't want to play any stock band arrangements, we wanted to play hip stuff. I started putting on the bulletin board, "What tune do you all want?" They said, "We want James Brown," or whatever was on the radio. That was one of the things I took on. I just said, "This is a way for me to learn what is happening." I started writing for the marching band. Then I got brave and tried to write something for the orchestra. All the time different people were turning me on to different books, but I didn't really study orchestration until I was in college.

I went to USC. I had gone through their comprehensive music program as a child, and then I ended up going to college there. I was a music education major. It was almost like a double major, with piano and performance. I didn't study composition there, and I didn't study orchestration there, but I did study composition and orchestration privately later on with a guy named Albert Harris. I was turned on to him by Quincy Jones. A friend of mine who used to work in his office was talking to him one day, and Dr. Harris's name came up. My friend and I looked him up. I was already making records, but jazz stuff.

In college I had a little band to help get some extra funds. I was playing locally, and then I played in a band that Melba Liston [trombonist, arranger] had. I also played with Gerald Wilson [composer, arranger, bandleader]. Liston and Wilson were instrumental too; they turned me on to stuff and exposed me from the inside. From being on the inside and from playing, the exposure was great. "How did you do that?" I would think. I wouldn't always ask, I would just listen. I was around these great players and excellent writers, and I would just check out what was going on and try to really pay attention, because of the sound. The sound was incredible to me, just the sound of everyone playing together. Melba's situation taught me more about shading and colors. I had always been attracted to harmonies, always. My favorite composers were Ravel, Chopin, Brahms, so harmony had always been a big part of my life. By the time I started gigging around I was really into jazz, and it was because of the harmonic thing, that is what attracted me to it.

Q: Did you see at that time any commonalities between Ravel, Debussy, what you learned in classical music, and what you were hearing on the scene in L.A.?

A: On the scene in L.A. I got more from what I would hear on the radio with records than from classical music. That is what attracted me to people like Bill Evans and Winton Kelly [jazz pianists]. There was a certain kind of connection to that harmonically and a certain kind of connection to that sort of sound, color, and this came out in their playing. I would think, "Oh, this hooks up sort of like that other thing, except that the other thing had with it a certain rhythm, a certain swing." I could identify more with it, because actually that was the sort of music that I had heard on the turntable when I was a kid. I couldn't identify at that point that there was going to be connections between Ellington and some things I would get to later on, or Miles, but it was there.

Q: What is your composition process? How do you put your music together?

A: It's funny, when I am writing just for myself it is one thing, but when I am writing on the basis of what other people need or want, it is something else. A lot of the music that I do for television or for film has a purpose, where the music is something that enhances something else. When I am putting music together that I intend to be played by an ensemble or for myself, or piano pieces, or quartets, or songs for albums, the music is the focal point. When it is for a situation where the music is the focal point, the process varies, but what is always the same is that I will just be quiet. This is the big connection for me, spiritually, to what we do as composers, what we do as players. There is something else that is going on, and it is not of me——that gets me started. It turns on the creative power and gets something on the paper or puts something in your hands, or some tune in your head, or whatever, and that aspect of it is the part that I can't pinpoint. As a young child, because I started composing early, I did some piano pieces before I could write the music down. I don't know what that part of the process is, in terms of being able to say, "It's like this," but that part has always been there for me. It never goes away. That is what has to happen first.

In the last ten years, I have been writing more and have been able to hear the instruments in the colors and the combinations of instruments, just from years of study. As soon as I either put my hands on that instrument or I stare at a blank piece of score paper, and it just happens. I write it down, and the form will grow from there according to what it is I want or that I am trying to do.

The first television show that I did as a musical director was the Robert Townsend HBO shows. Robert knew me because I had scored his film *Hollywood Shuffle,* and prior to that he had known me as an artist. He had been into my music, the commercial hits he had heard. When he went to look for a composer, he went to an agency, and I had just joined with this agency. My name was in pencil at the bottom of the list. But I was also the only name he recognized. That's how that happened. I did his specials, and when I finished those, there was another group of people who were aware of me in a different light. The next show after that was the NAACP Image Awards; again, it was because the producer had seen Robert's show. From the Image Awards, which I did for three or four years in a row, someone called me to do *Comic Relief.* The director of *Comic Relief* was the director of the Townsend show, so it was the second time that I was working with him. I didn't even know that he had been paying attention, because music is not the priority for those shows, although it adds a lot.

Then he directed and produced the Emmys the two years that I did them. He is a very demonstrative type of person, and he may have called me on a dare, I don't know, but when he called me, he said, "Hey, this is Walter Miller and I want you to do the Emmys." I was thinking I was going to be on a long list of people, that I was only going in for an interview, this will never happen, but what the heck? I went over there, and he said, "No, I want you to do it." I found out later that he had some major composer, and they had had a fight. He just said, "I am going to call Patrice." Once I did that show, I was definitely seen in another light, because it is a major prime-time industry show. I did the People's Choice Awards after that, and for a while there I was doing a lot of award shows, which was good. It was great training. You have to write very quickly—you have to compose themes for the shows, you have video clips that you have to score. Many times you have an artist whom you have to do arrangements for. For the Emmys you have to re-create all of the theme songs of the shows that are nominated. There are like seventy-five nominations, and only twelve shows are going to win, but you still have to have prerecorded every theme for every show.

Of course, the year I got the show was also the year they cut the music budget, so I didn't have the large orchestra. I was limited to about fifteen musicians. It wasn't a matter of just getting the scores and having them copied making some slight reductions; it was a major ordeal, because my band was small. To try to play everything from the theme to *Masterpiece Theater* to the theme to *Martin,* which are like A and Z in terms of style, was challenging. We had to play it live and make it sound good with this little band. We had two trumpets, two trombones, two French horns, three woodwinds, and then a rhythm section of two guitars, bass drums, keyboards, and percussion. That taught me a lot. Then I got a couple of small movie projects to do, and it just kind of grew from there.

Now what is beginning to happen is that in addition to the music that I do, songs for my audience as a contemporary urban/pop artist, I am still very involved in the jazz community, so there are compositions that I do there. My responsibilities with television have rekindled and opened up my desire to do more "serious" works. Now there is, as well, a "call" for a lot of those parts of my musical personality that you are not able to explore when you are talking about selling records or when you are accompanying other people. Because TV programs have mostly been small ensembles due to the budgetary restrictions that are always present, the last two years have really fired me up in terms of doing more extended work for symphony orchestra.

Q: The famous bass break in "Forget-Me-Nots"—where did it come from, why did you do it?

A: That whole composition was not unlike other things that we used to be able to do a lot more freely. You just play and write what you want to play, write without concerning yourself with whether or not it is going to get airplay or sales. For me, the greatest songs—again, this is part of that thing that came out of my childhood—are organic to something. You can place this here or put that over there, alter the bridge so that it is this and that, you can do all of that, but for me it is always better when it comes from your initial thought.

We were playing. Freddie Washington, the bassist, is from Oakland, California, and he wanted to get into the L.A. music scene. He came to L.A., and he lived with my family. He lived with my family for about six months, and we used to play together every day. We used to write a lot of stuff, but it would come out of just playing. That bass break just came out of playing. I think he started something, and that triggered something in me. I said, "What about this? What about that?" We just did it, and we said, "I'm sorry, I don't care what anybody says, that's funky. I'm sorry. That's funky." So we kept it.

Let me tell you a quick story about "Forget-Me-Nots." When we used to do records—I don't know if it was just because the record company just didn't know, or didn't care enough at that time—but I would do the recording and finish the albums and turn them in. You know, that doesn't happen now. No way! But that is what used to happen. I would turn them in, and we turned that one in, and the record company freaked. This is the same album that has "Remind Me" and "Number One" on it. They freaked and said, "You know, we don't know what we are going to do with this. We don't hear anything that will ever be on the radio or that we can play." We were devastated. It almost didn't come out, because they couldn't hear any of it. "Forget-Me-Nots"? They couldn't hear it. But that was back in the day when we were write-offs for record companies anyway, so they put the record out. And the bad boy caught on!

Some of them are still apologizing to me. They were taking me to lunch to tell me it was not happening. Then it caught on big.

We had learned a lot, too, about how you have to get into some self-promotion. You have to let people know, because you have to focus their attention so that they find it. If they find it, you can't make them buy it, or make them like it, but you can certainly let them know that it is out there. That is what we tried to do. We knew the company wouldn't support it, so we just tried to do what we could. I took some of my life savings and put it into independent promotion, into getting a publicist so that we could get the word out there. The idea was to just make people aware, but the record just blew up. To this day that is the single most important element that has gone into my continuous determination. It is almost like a creed—do your best and do something that feels right to you. The bottom line is, you have to like it. If you present it properly and it is well played and well executed, and if a person doesn't understand it or something, that's all right. But I don't think you can censor it or stop it when it is coming from a positive place. When it is not hurting anybody for you to do it, when it means something to you, and it feels right, there is going to be at least one more person out there who feels the same way. So go for it.

Q: What is your take on hard-core rap and even hard-core R&B? How does today's popular music compare?

A: When you talk about the music the young brothers and sisters are doing, there are a couple of things that come to mind. The first thing is the unfortunate limitation that some of the artists have from an educational standpoint. That energy of wanting to create is always there. It is ever-present and particularly fertile at that age. But in our public schools, which is where most of our kids are going to pick up their first instrument, or first hear, or see somebody who really plays and say, "I want to do that," that almost doesn't exist anymore. We are not going to private schools, and not everybody has parents who can take them over to USC every weekend or spend their life savings keeping the kid in music lessons. That doesn't happen. Like I said, the person who turned me on was out of a public nursery school situation, and we had a band and orchestra in school. We don't have that out here for the kids as much these days. So that creative energy, that desire to have your own voice, that desire that your peer group have an identifying sound, I think that's what made rap happen. They don't play, but they can relate to that rhythmic aspect of things, they can do these things. I think this is a large part of why the movement caught on, because it gave them a voice.

Now, by that same token, that is not the only aspect of education that is faltering. Language skills are faltering. I am not trying to say it is wrong to have a separate terminology, a slang, a separate language, that has always been a part of our lives, particularly in African American life. But not "in place of"—it should be "in addition to." That was our code. Whereas, now, I don't know that some of them know the difference. I don't know that they get the lineage and the history that the survival of our people has always been that we could do what the other people could do, but we could do our thing too; that being in our situation, our survival has been based on the ability to amalgamate, but to have our own too. In this situation, there doesn't seem to be the understanding about the discipline of that kind of survival. It allows for the language to be part of a separate language and code. It is in place of proper English. When I say "proper" I mean the ability to get in there so that you can really do your thing.

I find it unfortunate, too, that the glorification of a certain aspect of "gangsta" life, growing up that way, has become more than just speaking their minds about their situations. I do have some problems with the music industry financing it—conveniently and systematically, I feel—without balancing it with the other things that are happening. When you look at it, racism is alive; the kids are young, and they don't particularly understand it, and some of them maybe never will. This is a voice that they have, this is a way they do things, there are some of them who are making money. That's all they see.

I think using rap as a means of expressing their life conditions and wanting to put it out there in the form of the music they can relate to stopped a long time ago. It is an industry now, where it is about doing that a certain way in order to make money. I am not condemning that, but I am saying that there is no balance. There are other people out here doing something else too, and that was always a part of our music. There was always R&B, and there was jazz, and there was gospel and there was the support, and there were radio stations playing all of it, so that you got the idea that there was a palette of black music out there, as opposed to what we have now. I don't know about Indiana or Detroit, but out here in L.A., we don't really have an R&B station. They play oldies, or they play rap.

Q: What would it take, from your standpoint, to get us back to that, a larger palette of black music?

A: To be able to combine those worlds, the kinds of wonderful energies and progressive stuff that is happening in hip-hop, to mix it with the kinds of things we always had.

Q: Is it going to happen, or do you see it going completely downhill?

A: I hope it is going to happen. I think that it *will* happen, because I think that's what usually happens when people look back. Rappers are having to do that, because they are sampling all of the music that was done in the 1960s, '70s, '80s, even in the '90s; it is sending them back to find grooves. Their vocabulary was limited, and so it is sending them back to find grooves that may have been bit more unique. They are starting to include melodies again. I think what happens when you look backward is that you start to realize the importance of how that music was put together, that it requires a certain amount of skill and discipline. They are very creative in the way they use stuff. They are using my stuff; sometimes I hear it, and it's like, "What?" They are very creative, but they don't know how to put it together. They are going to find out how to put it together, because they are going to run out of things to sample. They are already up to me, they are already sampling music from the '80s. I have heard Michael Jackson's music sampled. Some of that is music of the '90s. It is about learning how to put it all together, and I think it is going to bring them closer to those of us who know and give us a chance to expose them to more of what is happening and how that music was put together. It is about learning music. I am looking for that to happen.

I asked a well-known rapper to participate on my new CD. I asked two of them, and one told me, "I don't do R&B." I told him, "You know that hit record you have out now, it's actually twenty years old, it is actually Sly Stone." I knew he couldn't hear me right then, but I told him, and I tried to be as loving as

I could, because I knew he didn't understand. I said, "If you adopt the industry separateness with your feeling and your attitudes toward music that you are using, you are setting yourself up to have a very short career. Because when they finish with you, you will have nowhere to go in terms of learning anything that gives you the assurance that you are going to be out here for a while. Your thing is built on someone else's thing. It is not about not doing that, it is about using that to be able to learn how to do it, and therefore to be that much more of a creative source longer, because you know what to do. If we separate ourselves from one another that way, I can't learn from you, and you can't learn from me, so what do we accomplish? You had a hit, and I had a hit. Now what?" He was really cool about it. He said, "Well, I'll take that into consideration, my sister." I said, "Okay, my brother, good luck." His career is history.

The thing that really is upsetting is that it is not out of anything other than the game that has been played and continues to be perpetuated. They don't get that there is a commitment and a discipline that is involved in playing music, just like the discipline and commitment that is involved in playing football, basketball, baseball, karate, dancing, broadcasting, writing. There is a passion that is there beyond just the doing, so that you can at some point contribute.

That is part of the responsibility too, because, like I said before, there is a spiritual connection to people who are touched creatively and have the ability to take what is on the inside and put it out there. That connection, to me, reeks of responsibility to give it your best, to learn as much as possible, and to listen, because I think that that creative stuff is a door that opens. If and when you walk through it, you have a responsibility of leaving something there for the next person who walks through the door. That can be in any kind of a way, from the sampling of your compositions or the body of work that you do. Maybe walking through that door turns you on to some aspect of your creativity that involves you being able to pass the word on—like teaching, or some combination of all of that—but you are supposed to make a difference. If it was such that everybody could do it, everybody *would* be doing it. The fact that you have been touched that way, I think there is something about that that says you are supposed to do something with it.

Q: Who was the inspiration for you to aspire toward these various facets of our industry?

A: For me, it was Oliver Nelson [jazz saxophonist, composer, arranger]. The behind-the-scenes, what is going on with television, and all that—I didn't make the connection that I could ever do anything close to that. We have got to see each other doing it. I am doing these television shows now, and people come up and say, "I saw you on TV leading the band"; for me, at the time I am doing it, it is a job. I enjoy it very, very much. It is demanding, and it calls on me to use a lot of my skills. But another person, another person of color, another black person, another woman, or whomever, will see me do it, and that may be the connection for them. It worked like that for me.

We take it for granted when we are in school that the person standing up there in front of the class is someone who we need to try to pay attention to. If the person happens to be of common ethnicity, that should be even more special to us, because the struggle to get to that place is the part we need to learn. That is the part you won't read in the books, and that is the part that you won't get even if you turn in every homework assignment.

Kevin Scott

Kevin Scott, a native New Yorker born in 1956, has been referred to as "a champion of works by underrated or underperformed American composers, with a specific concentration on the works of African American composers." Mr. Scott received his formal training at Lehman College, studying with John Corigliano and Ulysses Kay, later with Christine Berl and David Tcimpidis, and conducting with Yakov Kreisberg. Composer of a wide span of works ranging from string quartet to opera, his music has been performed by the Detroit, St. Louis, Houston, Atlanta, Shreveport, Minnesota, Brooklyn Philharmonic, and Minnesota Symphony Orchestras, as well as the Lyric Chamber Ensemble of Detroit and the Gramercy and Ciompi Quartets. His awards include the 1992 Unisys Composers Competition award from the Detroit Symphony, finalist in the National Black Arts Festival Composers Competition, and the Duke University/St. Augustine, William Grant Still Award for Emerging Composers. Mr. Scott's appointments as a composer are equally varied in repertoire and scope. He has appeared with the Brooklyn Philharmonic Orchestra, Opera Ebony, Opera Ammici, the Bronx Symphony, the African American Philharmonic, and the Chorale of Atlanta, and he has served as the music director of the Schubert Music Society Chorus. Mr. Scott lives and works in New York City.

Q: What would you say is the most convincing staple of your music?

A: What sound makes Kevin Scott, Kevin Scott? There is a harmonic base that's very dark and stoic. It's modeled upon the masters of the great Renaissance and the Baroque eras. And I work with two voices to start. I build the melody and the bass, and then I work in between all that. I want to hear not just the vertical sounds but a total horizontal element of sound as well. It has to be several voices—the past, the present, and the future—all in one. Kevin Scott's music can be interpreted as readily identifiable. I think most recently the more identifiable Kevin Scott has a dark streak, a dark side within him. People wonder why is there a darkness in my music. They asked Mahler the same question about his Sixth Symphony: "Why would you subject people to such bitterness when you are not a very bitter man?" He said, "Because I have been subjected to all that bitterness." And I have been subjected to a lot of bitterness—rejection by my peers, misunderstood by a society that is trained not to understand what an African American composer is.

When you mention "composer," it's interesting—everybody wants to think that a black composer exclusively writes top-forty hits, or blues numbers, or gospel numbers, or jazz numbers. But when you mention that you write

symphonies, concertos, operas, and the like, utilizing the forms of the great European tradition, you are viewed with suspicion. You are looked at as either an Uncle Tom or someone who is totally off the wall—or someone who just needs a shot of reality, as they say. The problem is: Who's in the real world, and who's not? My music, I feel, reflects a real world—a real dichotomy of values, a real sense of where we are, where we're going, and where we've been. The problem is we're moving forward without realizing where we've been. And my music takes a look at that.

A friend of mine asked me about that years ago. He asked me how would I classify myself. I classified myself as an "avant-garde romantic." And that's probably still the closest label that would fit. The reason I call myself an avant-garde romantic, as opposed to a neoromantic or anything, is that I have a problem with these so-called politically correct labels. I consider myself an avant-garde romantic partly because I feel I was born a little too late in the twentieth century. I feel I should have been born either earlier in the century, or in the latter part of the nineteenth century.

I am rooted, when I listen to music, especially orchestral music, in the great, grand, melodic gestures, the sweeping, dramatic gestures that you hear in the symphonies of [Gustav] Mahler and [Anton] Bruckner, the symphonic poems of Richard Strauss, even the music of [composers] Alban Berg or Carl Nielsen or [Ralph] Vaughan Williams. They have a sweep, they have a drive to their music, and that has always appealed to me.

When I realized that classical music was my forte, I saw that those composers had this magnetic drive, this grandiose, epic sweep. I'd even have to say movie music has had an influence on my music, from [soundtrack composers] Korngold and Tiomkin and Bernard Herrmann to John Williams and Jerry Goldsmith. They always had that feel for me. That's my music. But at the same time, I realized that I was living in the late twentieth century—not the late twentieth century but its twilight, the twilight of a millennium. And I now realize at this point, when you look at this new millennium, you have to say something new with what was already said. You can't just repeat it. You have to speak anew, yet reinforce the tradition with something fresh and spontaneous.

That's something that has escaped a lot of composers, and I think a lot of listeners too, which is sad. Listeners cannot deal with atonal music, or alleatoric music, or serial music, or dodecaphonic music, or whatever you want to say it is. We live in a society that's already dissonant. They want consonance in some part of their life. Composers have brought senseless dissonance into their scores to reflect the senseless dissonance in our society. Some composers, granted, have written dissonance for the sake of dissonance, or they've written dissonance because they want to show off their compositional technique, or because they're being curried by the elite intellectual establishment that sees only intellectual, bloodless, mathematical music as the music of the future. That's wrong.

You have to have emotion. You have to *say* emotion. This is why I consider myself an avant-garde romantic. I speak the language of the late twentieth century in my music. The harmony, the melody, or lack thereof, and definitely the orchestral colors, are of our times. But at the same time, I feel there's an emotional drama and sweep that we all have because we are human beings. I could sum it up. Since 1950 a lot of problems have come to a head. A lot of people will tell you concert music literally died in 1900. Others will maintain that it died with the death of Mahler in 1911, and others will tell you it died with [Giacomo] Puccini [Italian operatic composer], in 1924.

At a party I attended a couple of years ago, I was talking to a soprano about the glories of Puccini's last opera. I said, "Let me ask you, can you handle *Turandot*?" And she replied, "Yes, a beautiful great opera." I then countered, "Can you handle the first fifteen minutes of *Turandot*?" She responded, "Yes." "Well, let me ask you something," I continued, "Puccini's *Turandot* in the first fifteen minutes sounds like the Stravinsky's *Rite of Spring* almost gone berserk. Whereas if you listen to Berg's, it's firmly rooted in a key. The only thing that makes it very weird is the fact that Berg plays around with the orchestration. But yet you listen to Puccini and you hear *bahm-bahm-bahm bahm bahh!* [hums the opening bars of *Turandot*]. All of a sudden you've fallen into another sound world. That's not the Puccini of *[Madama] Butterfly,* not the Puccini of *Tosca,* which is very Wagnerian. That's Puccini realizing who Stravinsky and Schoenberg and Bartók were. And the listeners can't handle the truth. The same people who say, 'We cannot handle Berg, we cannot handle Stravinsky, we cannot handle *The Miraculous Mandarin*' say they can handle *Turandot?!* Come on!"

That's one problem we've had. People can't handle certain twentieth-century composers, but yet when you mention Puccini—who is a twentieth-century composer—they can handle it. The reason they can handle Puccini is simple—they hear the aria, and they can sing it in the shower. "Nessun Dorma" sung by Pavorotti or Domingo or Carreras. They can hear "Un bel di [vedremo]." They can hear "O mio bambino caro," from *Gianni Schicchi,* which is beautiful. But the rest of *Gianni Schicchi* sounds like Bartók, or an Italianate Richard Strauss. But they can't realize that. Nobody realizes this.

And the problem we have when we listen to music after 1950 is we're still continuing the tradition, but some composers broke from it—Sessions, Elliot Carter, Boulez, Stockhausen, Cage—they all broke from the tradition, but yet they still managed to, in some weird sense, reinforce that tradition. Me? I fit myself as a traditionalist when it comes to the form, when it comes to architecture. I believe in architecture as the foundation of music, the traditional form. But the problem is, everyone disbanded form as well as communicative idioms, and all of a sudden we got thrown into a new world.

People were not ready for a new world after 1950. They were not ready for the new forms, or lack thereof, or for the lack of melody, or the lack of harmony. [William Grant] Still even said that himself, that composers didn't know how to do harmony and melody to create emotionally communicative music. When he studied with Varèse, he had a sense of what Varèse was doing. It was in his earlier music. He put it in his music. It's still in his late music. Despite the fact that it sounds romantic, there's still a Varèsian element, subtly instilled.

I see myself reinforcing the tradition of form, in the form itself of sonata, variation, and rondo. But you have to say something new with the form, within the form. You can't just throw the form out and start anew. Oh, you can do that, sure. But you've got to realize what you've thrown out and why you re throwing it out.

I did that when I was young. I started off with form, or what I thought was form, and found out I wasn't writing a form at all. I went back to it and studied it hard. My fourth string quartet is the best example of where I stand right now.

And that's the way I can summarize it. The music is a return in my own past, to the music I grew up with—jazz, British rock, Motown, blues. But at the same time as I found myself writing this *Fourth Quartet,* I found myself also writing a Beethovenian quartet, literally: the first movement is a sonata allegro; a real scherzo and trio for the second movement; then a slow movement that's more rhapsodic than sonata. That's an A-B-A form. Well, it is A-B-A, but it has a sort of rhapsodic element to it, the way the slow movement of the Sibelius first and second symphonies are. And the fourth movement is a rondo of sorts. But yet I know where the rondo is. The language is basically now. It is still now. It is of our century, it is of our time. It is something that is also very identifiable and yet accessible, but yet looks forward without forsaking the past.

Q: Should music make a cultural reference?

A: I think it should be with the individual. I think individuals should be aware of where they came from. They should be aware of what they're saying, what idiom they use and how they say it. I identify myself as an African American composer or black composer. I also identify myself as a composer who happens to be black. But I definitely identify myself as an African American composer, because my heritage is there. My sorrows are there. My joys are there. My life is what my culture is. I would like people to become unbiased. I would love people who attend concerts, an audience of Americans who are Euro-centric in their behavior and their concept of what concert music is all about, to become unbiased; let them feel what they may hear. The problem is, they don't care what race, sex, gender, sexuality you are. To them, any music that has a date of 1900 and something—you fill in the zeroes—is deadly. They don't care about race anymore. All they care about is the century. That's the problem! Now, on the other hand, an African American audience should know that it's a work written by an African American composer, because they've been denied that part of their heritage.

There are personages that do influence me today. It's hard to say who at this moment. I would say filmmakers like Spike Lee do influence me in a political sense. I would say certain writings by poets like Maya Angelou or Nikki Giovanni influence me. Artist have to be aware of what they're dealing with and who they're dealing with, yet at the same time they have to be in some sort of solitude. The ones who tend to be in solitude, in their own sphere but yet aware of who is influencing them, are to me the true artists. Someone who notices their peers and just copies is just that, a copycat. They don't have an identity of their own. They don't have a mind of their own. They just go about and copy, because they feel it's the trendy thing to do. When that trendy thing is over, they'll find another icon to model themselves after, until they've used up that icon or they're bored with it. A true artist has to remain in solitude with themselves, and at the same time be aware of any contemporary thoughts. So, I don't know if anybody present really influences me. I'm influenced by everything around me, but at the same time I have to realize I am my own person.

Q: What's your take on rap music?

A: I mentioned at the Unisys African American composers forum in 1993, there is nothing wrong with rap music, technically speaking. Rap music is part of our heritage. Rap is a part of African heritage, period. Rap music, as we see it today, is an outgrowth and reactionary anger from the phony disco music and house music that blacks were hearing in the '70s. It was primarily promulgated by Italian-Americans and other ethnicities that weren't black, in that they were trying to sell a so-called black music to black audiences that really wasn't. Of course, there were some exceptions, like Barry White, and I think early Luther Vandross, Donna Summer, and such. They were into it, sure, but if you look at Donna Summer's material, I don't think there were any black men writing her material. It was Giorgio Moroder [Donna Summer's producer], which is interesting.

Rap music was an outcry, an outcry against disco. It was an outcry of anger of what was happening in the community. And so, by stripping it down to its barest essentials, just the voice and maybe a rhythm track, you have rap. That was rather early. The first rap was very interesting. We've always had gangsta rap, even the so-called gangsta bitch rappers, too. The reason you get these raps is because you get an even further anger. The anger in the rap music from the '70s was coming from an anger at disco music; the gangster raps we're getting today are from a combination of factors, especially the neglect of the African American in the '80s during the Reagan and Bush administrations, when we moved so far to the right politically, culturally, and every which way, and African Americans who were activists in the '60s and the '70s became the establishment, the "Buppies." If you say "Yo, brother," and they retort, "I am not your brother," they mean I am not your brother in terms of identity—that is, "I'm black, you're black." They can't even identify themselves as black because—I like to quote the line that Tommy Davidson said in *Strictly Business*—"You're whiter than the whitest white man!" And so naturally younger blacks are going to take offense at seeing their older counterparts who have sold out the community for the almighty dollar. They see them as the second Stepin Fechit, the second coming of Stepin Fechit.

So naturally gangsta rap is valid. What a lot of people don't appreciate, including myself, is you don't have to knock the black woman. You can say what is violent, but don't promote violence in such a way that you tell other kids to reinforce violence. You tell younger kids, you say, "Violence is all right. B—— is cool. Off the Man. Down with the Pig." No, you find other reasons to "off the pig"—not literally, please! You do it through other methods, through legal methods. You fight fire with fire. But no, what you get is some fanatics out there, and while they can say it's not fantasy, in reality it is fantasy. Kids are very impressionable. And that's what's sad.

If I write an opera, I probably wouldn't use rap the way we know it now, with a rhythm track and such. But it is inherent in the music. Speech patterns are inherent. The operas of Modest Mussorgsky and others who broke away from the conventions of the *bel canto* of Italian opera, from Wagner's Teutonic visions, adapted the vocal patterns that were heard in folk songs, in Russian, Czech, Lithuanian, or Polish. All of a sudden you had a new kind of opera. This was the precursor of what I would call "rap opera." Name me an aria in *Boris Godunov* that you can sing. You can't sing an aria in their operas, because there are none. They didn't want to write that so-called specialty opera, where the audience could go "Bravo!" The aria queens of the nineteenth, and even of the twentieth, centuries could get off and masturbate in the shower while singing "La donna e mobile" or a modern equivalent thereof. So, when a black composer can write an opera like that of Mussorgsky or Drago Tanacek and inherit the speech patterns of our culture, that's going to be a very positive experience, and that's going to be real rap.

Q: What kinds of things do you want to really do as a composer or as a contributor to American music society?

A: I would like to see my own works enter the staple of the repertoire. Maybe a lot of them won't, but I would like to see them respected by conductors and orchestras for their musical content, rather than me, rather than have them accepted because its politically correct and timely.

Right now, we're in the political element. All the political elements, sooner or later, are going to merge with the other elements and become a musical element. Twenty years ago the women's movement was established. There were no prominent women composers in the orchestras that were being played. Now we have Ellen Taafe Zwillich. You have Joan Tower. You have Augusta Read Thomas [composers]. They are being played and commissioned left and right by major American symphony orchestras, and that's because of the women's movement. There were women composers whom people like Sarah Caldwell and Judith Simognyi [conductors] promoted. Now, like I said, every concert you will find an Ellen Taafe Zwillich. You will find an Augusta Read Thomas. You will find a Joan Tower. You will find a Shulamit Ran on the programs, with no problems.

The same cannot be said for African American composers, especially black women composers. Name me one. You can't find them, but I could name several: Regina Harris Baiocchi, Lettie Beckon Alston. Those are two of the finest women composing right now. There are others, like Dorothy Rudd Moore. There's the late Julia Perry, who was a monstrous talent in her own right. There's Tania Leon, Margaret Harris. Who else can we name? Those are the most prominent right now. And, by the way, if you look at women's books on women composers, you won't find Tania's name or Julia's. You might find Julia's. You might find Florence Price mentioned. They will not mention Tania Leon—and Tania is already at the half-century mark and deserves to be mentioned in more than one book. But now we come to the point where African Americans need to be accepted by orchestras. I would like to be one of those at the forefront, to see that not just myself but my brethren and my sisters are accepted for their musical content, who write great music and they just happen to be African Americans. You don't see people saying of Ellen Taafe Zwillich, "Oh, she's a great woman composer!" No, you hear them say she's a great composer. I would like to see people say, "William Banfield is a great composer. Regina Baicchi is a great composer. Gary Powell Nash is a marvelous composer. Michael Abels is a fine craftsman. Kevin Scott is a master at his craft; he is a genius, he is a true maestro."

I would like to see our community and the white community say that about us, and not say, "Oh, just another black composer 'wannabe.'" I don't want to hear that. I don't want to hear them say blacks are incapable of writing music stemming from a European tradition. I refuse to hear that. I want to hear them say we are American composers just as much as anyone else is an American composer.

We need to challenge the canon, or what you're saying is the law, the law of tradition, the traditional law that has been handed down in an unofficial way by a society of elitists in this country. We're not talking about Europe. We're not talking about even Canada. We're talking about the United States of America. We have to challenge the canon, the concept of natural law, that is driving the programming of concerts, the programming of music, the teaching. It has to be challenged, for new roads have to be laid out. In education, you have to start by bringing in the composers, period. You have to expose inner-city children and the African American community to their own. Unfortunately, a lot of people are still with the notion that blacks are incapable of writing or being involved in classical music unless singing it. If you sing classical music, that's one thing. More power to you, because you're coming from the church tradition, and the church feels that classical music is not sinful, whereas, any secular music outside of the great European masters is sinful.

But when it comes to African American composers, you're charged by both black and white society. Blacks feel that you have betrayed our heritage. Whites feel you have no business in their heritage.

Well, guess what? Education is the beginning. You have to show that there are African Americans who want to express their feelings, everything that they grew up with, through this music. And they can bring the legacy of everything that we've written—blues, ragtime, jazz, R&B, gospel, folk, early rock—everything, into the concert world too. We can bring that in our own way, shape, and form. We may be rewriting the tradition, but we're still doing it. One way is through education, to expose the young to it. And the way to do that is to start educating the educators. Start educating black musicians, train them, get them interested in musicology, further their horizons and make them go out and spread the word. You can't just preach to the converted. You have to educate African Americans to educate African Americans about their heritage—especially one that has been kept from them.

Someone like Dr. Rae Linda Brown needs to go in and talk to other African American musicians, and see if they're good in history. Encourage them to become interested in musicology and then say, "You know, you need to go and try to educate other students." Black history studies, black history departments, black studies departments in colleges have omitted programs dealing with African American concert music. The colleges need to put that program back in, because kids aren't aware of it. You're a teenager, all you know about classical music is Bach, Beethoven, Brahms, and maybe Stravinsky, if you even know who Stravinsky is.

They need to know who William Grant Still is. They need to know who Hale Smith is. They need to know who Ulysses Kay is. They need to know who Bill Banfield is. They need to know who Kevin Scott is. They need to know the past, the present, and the future. They need to know who we are, because, again, you're omitting a part of our legacy. And we are the enemy. We have committed our own sin. And we have to continue to fight the other part of the canon, the administrators of our own symphony orchestras.

I could not encourage the way certain Dutch composers did in 1968, which was commit what they called the "Nutcracker Act." Black American composers don't have to be as drastic as staging events to disrupt concerts or protesting outside; but they do need to bombard and challenge the administrators with questions, to meet them, talk with them, and try to set up forums, to let them know who we are and where we are and why we are doing this. We need to make ourselves heard. If that doesn't work, then the second step has to be taken.

Julius Williams

Julius Williams, from the Bronx, in New York City, was born in 1954. He is one of a handful of composers/conductors who consistently wears both hats. He has conducted such groups as the Dallas, New Haven, Savannah, Hartford, Sacramento, Knoxville, Vermont, Brooklyn, and American Symphonies (the latter under Lukas Foss). Internationally, he has conducted the Volvodanska Symphony in Serbia and the Dubrovnik Symphony in Croatia; he has worked in Prague and Vienna with the Brno (Czechoslovakia) State Philharmonic. He served also as composer in residence of the Connecticut Nutmeg Ballet Company; he was the artistic director of the School of Choral Studies of the New York State Summer School of the Saratoga Performing Arts Center for eight years. As a concert record producer, he has again worn both hats, as conductor and composer, on a landmark recording on Albany, *Symphonic Brotherhood,* with the Martinu Philharmonic of the Czech Republic Symphony Orchestra. As a composer he has written operas and works for orchestra, chamber ensemble, musical theater, and film. His works have been performed by the New York Philharmonic, the Detroit Symphony, the Cleveland Orchestra, and the opera theater of the Aspen Music Festival. Educated at the City University of New York, Lehman College, the Hart School of Music, and the Aspen Music School, he has held positions at Shenandoah University, Wesleyan, the University of Hartford, and the University of Vermont. Mr. Williams serves as a professor of composition and conducting at the Berklee School of Music in Boston. He currently lives in Ellington, Connecticut.

My grandmother used to take me to church in the Bronx, where I was born and raised. To avoid sitting in the pew listening to the minister, I would opt for playing the piano or the organ, more often the piano, so I could be involved instead of being bored. I must have been nine, ten, or eleven. This gave me a chance to improvise and play, to get a sense of the way music could affect the Baptist minister. That influence, which occurred before I could read music formally, taught me volumes about music.

My main influences after that grew out of living in New York City and interacting with people like John Motley, a choral conductor in New York. John was the conductor of the All-City High School Chorus, he and another man named Richard Blankston. I wanted to be like John Motley, because he was an African American with a strong background and solid local connections, in particular with the NYC Board of Education. He was mainly a choral conductor. In addition to providing me with opportunities, he introduced me to Coleridge-Taylor Perkinson, who became my mentor as a composer/conductor.

The first time I saw Perkinson, my thought was, "Here is this black man

conducting the Symphony of the New World [a New York orchestra organized in 1966] wearing a leather suit! At that point I decided I wanted to be like this guy, I wanted to compose like this guy. Coleridge was a pianist, and at the time he was writing scores for television and film.

John Motley arranged for me to take piano lessons with Mike Longo, Dizzie Gillespie's pianist. At that age, I had so many influences. We worked with Dizzie Gillespie, Bill Cosby, anybody who came into New York. I had the ultimate music life as a teenager—sessions with Leonard Bernstein, Roberta Flack, being part of this group in New York City. I was lucky, and it helped in my later career.

The other person who influenced me early on was Fred Norman, whom I met through John Motley. He was the arranger for Diana Washington and another famous blues singer. I would go to Norman's house when I was a teenager, and he would give me lessons free of charge; he would look at my compositions and say, "Oh my God, take this back." Norman taught me how to orchestrate and arrange, and he never charged me a dime.

At first I wanted to be this pop star, I wanted to be this pop star piano player. I did a few gigs with James Brown and various other artists and finally decided; "I don't want to do this." There was a calling taking me into more depth with the music. There was the influence of Coleridge-Taylor Perkinson. And there was a desire to go into larger forms. That's when I made a conscious effort to become a composer.

At the time we had a teenage performing arts workshop that ran in the summer. We used to get paid to work in the Manhattan School of Music. I was about sixteen or seventeen, and we worked with John Corigliano [composer], Coleridge-Taylor Perkinson, and various other composers. At that age I definitely decided I wanted to compose and forget about playing pop or anything. The next thing that I realized, while conducting one of my own pieces, was that I started to want to be a conductor. That was the third step of the evolutionary scale.

By the time I started to study with Ulysses Kay, who was another big influence, I knew I wanted to be a composer. The conducting came a few years later, after I really decided I wanted to be a composer. Suddenly, all I wanted to do was write a new piece. I have hundreds of pieces in a box somewhere.

Is there a blackness to my music? A lot of people say you can't tell the difference, but there is almost definitely, rhythmically especially, a "blackness" in the music of black composers. In the last recording I did, *Symphonic Brotherhood,* performed by the Bohuslav Martinu Philharmonic Orchestra, in Czechoslovakia, there was a piece by Adolphus Hailstork. The orchestra read the piece, they played what was on the page, but they couldn't find that underlying pocket. I had to sing it. I thought it was right there, but it wasn't. There is definitely a color, a rhythmic factor, and melodic lines that reveal a person's influences. Maybe it is not just being black, maybe it's the environment where they grew up. It comes through. I guess if I had been raised in an environment where I'd never heard any church music or never heard spirituals, then maybe my music would be different. Most African Americans who are musicians are able to play jazz, pop music, and classical as well.

Music influences life, the same as art influences life. So often the public, especially when looking at the value of music programs in schools today, will think, "Well, if they are studying music, it must be a form of entertainment and is therefore not serious. It is not something we should really demand that they understand." With studies coming out about increased brain activity that occurs while listening to Mozart, or the fact that students having a musical background are able to score higher in many different aspects of education outside of music, it is becoming more evident that music is an important catalyst in opening up the creative mind. If education has to go to that "2001 dream," the mind must be opened, or technology will fall apart. At the Berklee School of Music we have all the newest, state-of-the-art, computerized equipment available. Computers are becoming more difficult to comprehend, but it's easier for musicians, because we understand how to think on many different levels. A few years ago, I couldn't hit a computer, now I am an expert; I think it is because of my musical mind.

I lectured recently at the New England Conservatory on William Grant Still, on music composition, education, and the use of African American music in the classroom. A lady jumped up and said, "They [African American students] know what music is. The students out there are way ahead of the teachers." That is probably true, because teachers are not listening to other types of music. To bring the young African American into a realm of music, we have to give them a broad range of knowledge. What so often happens is that like the football player or basketball player, they get the idea that they need to become entertainers, stars. That is not the goal. The goal is to make music, whatever form it is—to make music and to expand from that form into other things, to stay open-minded about other forms of music.

Is black awareness out there? The good point about Black History Month is that at least people are playing our music for a couple of days. Otherwise they wouldn't be playing it at all. But my opinion is that black composers' music should be played throughout the year. It's time to say, "This is good music, let's put it on the program." African American music captures the American tradition. So many musical forms are a takeoff of African American music. Any time you hear any "American music," it has roots in African American music. African American music is American music. What else is American music? Nothing.

There are universal commonalties between Beethoven, Ravel, and African American composers' music. Take Ravel's open harmonies. Jazz harmonic structures are very close to the period of Ravel. I know they were taking a lot of stuff. Ravel even said so himself, at one point when he was working with Gershwin. [Antonín] Dvorak came out and said, "You should use American music and African American and the Indian musics, they are the true models of what came out of America." They were taking this thematic material, lines from African American music; that was a big thing. All of a sudden everyone was writing jazz. Copland was writing *Jazz Suites* in the 1930s. Listen to Charlie Parker or Dizzie Gillespie, listen to the lines moving against each other; they truly understood improvisation. They knew how to move away from it. They were free. They understood fugue, they understood imitation, they were able to move from what was done two hundred years ago, what everybody abandoned because they wanted to structuralize everything, to a more natural form.

There is a lot of discouragement out there, and I would like for black composers, conductors, and artists to be more visible. I think my role is to educate and to show that we are here and should be taken seriously, and that this is part of our heritage. Too often black composers are grouped, or considered an adjunct or afterthought. "We are bringing you here so that you can keep the masses quiet for a while, and once you finish, go." Or else, "We need you here because we need to attract larger audiences." That is not the point. The point should be that we want to incorporate in order to make a better musical world. Sometimes, though, I ask, "Where am I going, what am I doing?" My role is, I hope, to educate and to create an easier path for younger musicians, so that the next young African American composer can hear his pieces performed, so that it's not such a stretch to have an African American composer get a Pulitzer.

Perceptions and stereotypes continue. When I was conducting in Dallas, I was dressed up in tails and about to do this concert at the Majestic Theater. I was coming down the elevator in my hotel, and there was a well-dressed woman in there with me. When the elevator stopped the woman looked at me, with my baton and my music in hand, and she said, "What do you do?" I said, "I am a musician." She continued, "Well, you must be the guy who's playing our jazz ball tonight." I just humored her. "I want you to play a certain tune if you can. I'll come over during the evening and talk to you," she said. Then she added, "I'm going to the symphony tonight. You should go to some concert like that." I was conducting a Beethoven piano concerto that evening for the Dallas Symphony, and I said, "Well, isn't there a composer named Beethoven? Isn't he deaf or blind or something?" She said, "No, no, no. He went deaf. You should go to a concert like this. Maybe it would increase your awareness of music and help you in other types of music." I said, "Sure, sure. You are right, I need to go because I don't know that type of music." I finally looked at her and said, "Well, at the end of the concert, can you go backstage and get the conductor's autograph and bring it back to me?" Needless to say, she did show up and apologize. But those are the types of stereotypes, that believe it or not, are hard to fight.

How do musicians respond to a black conductor? Most of the time, the orchestra is not a problem. Usually they figure that if you got this far, you must know something. They give you the benefit of the doubt. Usually I don't have any problem with the orchestra, maybe very rarely. It is usually getting through the first line, dealing with the administrators and their little biases, that can be difficult. They think, "Well, he had better handle this type of music. He can't deal with such and such." That's kind of funny, because we have studied the same stuff that they have studied, and just because you are working and doing African American music, they wonder, "I don't know if he can really do Beethoven, if he can really do Brahms." That is where the problems come in, with the administrators and some board members who are concerned with audience reception. You just shake your head. It is getting a little bit better now, but still, once in a while, that stereotype will come in there. Sometimes they say, "We will bring you in for our African American music concert, but we really can't bring you in for a regular program. Can you do some jazz pop?"

Concert music and the jazz idiom, I think, are becoming closer and closer. It is almost to the point that it will be common for both idioms to intersect. I am having a little problem right now with what is happening in the popular music industry, because of MTV. Are we entertaining or shocking audiences, or are we creating new art? At this point I am not quite sure where that is going. It is going to come to the point where either people are going to get so bored, they will say the music has gone somewhere else. Right now the popular music world seems stagnant. But as they say, as long as it sells they will keep putting it out.

Personally, I am not the greatest hip-hop fan, but I think the rhythmic structure and the idea of hip-hop is from our past. Hip-hop is not really new, it has been there. Today it is articulated in a more rhythmic and a more exciting way. I see that expanding. I see that crossing over into concert pieces somewhat; some concert pieces have hip-hop idioms in them. I would just like to see those composers expand their minds and their ears with hip-hop and move forward.

As a young composer it is sometimes difficult to create continuity within a piece. Personally, in my youth I had a tendency to write something, get bored with it, and quickly go on to something else. I go back to a lesson I learned from Ulysses Kay, as he was looking at a piece of my music. Ulysses Kay looked at me one day and said, "Julius, when you find an idea, run it, run it, and run it again. Keep on running it until you can't find anywhere else to go, and then change."

Ulysses was a mild-mannered person, one of the nicest persons in the world, who had a distinct way of teaching. His style was neoclassic; he was a student of Hindemith, so we were a little bit different in that aspect. He was a craftsman. When it came to using fugal matters or counterpoint, Ulysses Kay was a craftsman. I think I learned a lot about counterpoint in general from him.

Q: Tell us about your role and the experience of producing an African American recording with a Czech orchestra.

A: That was a good experience, but it takes a lot out of you. I had to assemble the financing myself, with the help of the other composers. Then we had to negotiate with a third-party engineer and production company in Europe and in Canada, and then deal with the orchestra. The orchestra was actually the easiest part. Constant phone calls, setting up schedules, figuring how much money you have, working with the recording company, hoping that they will make a commitment to putting out the recording—it is a very hard road to go. Then get the music over to a group of people who have no concept of African American music, that takes a lot of doing.

What I had to do was sing the music, jump up and down, walk on the podium giving rhythm, tap rhythm, or use an instrument to find the pulse. Usually the notes weren't the problem, it was always the rhythmic identity and the character of the music. I had to act out the music for it to come across. It wasn't a situation where you just start waving your hands and conducting—I had to become both an actor and a mime to communicate what I needed to get across, because I couldn't speak to them in a language. It was not just a language barrier but a cultural barrier; they really didn't have the cultural references.

There is a piece on the album called "Keep on Stepping, Brothers." When I told them what it was about, they asked "Whose brother, what brother are you stepping on?" Finally I looked at them and said, "Forget it, just follow me, mimic what I do." It worked out. They worked on it during the break, asking, "Is this it? Is this is the beat?" Finally we really got close to it.

The industry response to *The Music of African American Composers: Symphonic Brotherhood* was fine. We got great reviews, we got good write-ups, but the major industry wouldn't take it. They should have said, "Yeah, we'll give you more money." One recording company looked at the project and said they didn't want to deal with it because they weren't sure if it was going to sell. It will sell if somebody promotes the project, because suddenly now a lot of symphony orchestras are doing it. Now everybody else is coming out with something similar to that project.

Q: Do you want to be remembered as an African American composer?

A: I would like to be remembered for trying to make music and doing it with all my heart. I want people to say, "The music he made was something that came from his heart, that came from love; it was not just something that was thrown on a piece of paper." Anything I do musically is something that is part of me; I put my whole self into it. That is what I would want on my tombstone, that I made music from my heart.

Michael Abels

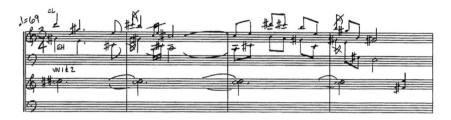

Born 1962 in Phoenix, Arizona, Michael Abels has gained widespread recognition for the work *Global Warming,* which was featured in the Detroit Symphony's 1992 African-American Symphony Composers Forum. The work has been performed by more than twenty orchestras throughout the country, including those of Chicago, Baltimore, Dallas, Cleveland, Houston, Atlanta, Detroit, and Indianapolis, as well as the National Symphony of South Africa, following the election of President Nelson Mandela. Doc Severinsen premiered *American Variations on "Swing Low, Sweet Chariot,"* and James Earl Jones and Garrison Keillor narrated *Frederick's Fables,* a four-piece work based on the book by Leo Lionni and commissioned by the Plymouth Music Series of Minnesota. Abels's arrangements for symphony and gospel choir have been performed by the Phoenix and Atlanta Symphony Orchestras. Abels began the study of the piano at an early age in South Dakota, where he was raised, later studying at the University of Southern California and then at the California Institute of the Arts, where he studied West African music with Alfred Ladzekpo. Mr. Abels lives and works in Los Angeles, California.

I remember *The Sound of Music.* I was probably three years old; I saw it in the theater. "Do Re Mi" and Richard Rogers. There is your composition—"One word for every note." What could be more simple? That was my favorite song for about three years. I sang it every day. I think that is how I grew to be a composer. It always seemed to me that it was really simple. You just had one word for every note, and then you "mix them up"—just like in the song—and there is the composition.

I lived with my grandparents when I was very small. I started on piano because I was trying to play "Do Re Mi." I knew that "Re" was higher than "Do," but I thought that "Re" was the note right next to it, i.e., D-flat. It didn't sound right, so I said to my grandmother, "What is going on here?" I had assumed that if I really wanted to play a tune I could just do that. I was now attempting to do that, but it wasn't coming out right. So she mounted this campaign to get me piano lessons with the only person around who taught piano. Somehow the teacher agreed to take me as a student, and so I began. I studied piano using your typical classical repertoire. I also studied a little guitar and sang in a boys choir. That was my access to vocal music—piano at four, boys choir from seven until fourteen. I studied piano until the end of high school. Until junior high, I hadn't really written anything that I finished. I had written a couple of little piano pieces, but when I really started to get serious about it was in junior high, when we would have concerto competitions on piano. I would do okay until I got to the finals, and then I would completely choke. This happened

two years in a row, and one of those little voices in my head said, "You do not have what it takes to cut it as a concert pianist." If you are bombing out in seventh grade in the finals, that is the sign.

Meanwhile, there was this Mozartian piano concerto that I had heard the first four notes of but had forgotten the rest. I played the first four notes, but I couldn't remember how it went after that. I played how I thought it went. I thought, "I know it doesn't go that way, but it ought to, so I should really write a piano concerto." This is how you think when you are twelve, you can just do whatever you want. So that is what I did—I wrote a one-movement Mozartian piano concerto. I already knew the techniques of notation for piano, but at that time I had never really bothered to study orchestration. I had a book that gave the ranges of the instruments, and I thought, "That's all I need!" So I wrote this piece, and then somehow, at a music camp in Arizona, I got it performed—and I got to play the solo part, thereby circumventing the whole concerto competition thing. I realized, "I just beat the system, and this could work for me." It was also then that I realized that the reason I could do this was because I was fascinated by writing music. Tunes would occur to me, but it wasn't like the music was spilling out of me; I found the tunes were a lot of work. But I was just fascinated with the challenge of realizing them. I thought, "What a really hard thing to do."

My biggest musical role model was Harvey Smith, the director of the boys choir, whose son, Mark, was a good friend of mine. Mark Russell Smith is now a conductor, the music director of the Springfield Symphony of Massachusetts and the Cheyenne Symphony. Mark was sitting next to me on the first day of music camp in Phoenix, and we basically grew up together. It is one of those remarkable friendships that is a gift from God.

Throughout our lives we have been linked musically, from little kids being in competition with each other on piano, to singing in the boys choir, to him performing in my cello sonata, to him conducting orchestral works of mine. It is amazing. His parents would sometimes have someone in their family who would not be able to go to a symphony they had tickets for. Mark would call me up, and he would always say, "How fast can you get ready?" Whenever I heard those words from him I knew we were going to the symphony. I would go to the symphony with his family, and it was then that it occurred to me how hard it must be to write orchestral music. I found it interesting.

My influences were all the American '60–'70s suburban pop cultural stuff, beginning with those Richard Rogers musicals through whatever music struck me at the moment growing up. I had a Billy Joel phase, a Bernstein's Mass phase, a Genesis phase—I think I'm clearly attracted to music that's highly developed but within the boundaries of a pristinely simple context. It's got to be rhythmic, melodic, and dramatic. It's probably no surprise that at age fifteen I nearly wept during the last scene and end credits of *Star Wars*. A pristinely simple context—good triumphs over evil, and instantly hummable, eight-bar themes—surrounded by seventy-five million perfectly orchestrated sixteenth notes.

The thing that fascinates me about orchestral music is first of all the complexity of the idea and the thought of all these highly gifted people being of a single mind to create something that is greater than any of them, that only exists in that moment that they have created. Composing is most like architecture, in that an architect does not make houses; an architect makes blueprints of the way a house ought to be. I think of myself as an architect, not actually a musician. I think, "If there were a group of musicians, this is what they ought to do to make some music." It is for that reason that I am attracted to orchestral music. Almost all of my ideas occur around the idea of an orchestra or large ensemble, or some sort of storytelling.

In college I had this total identity crisis, in learning about all of the things that I didn't know about music and all of the things that had been done. I was encouraged to go to a conservatory, but I didn't. The reason was because I wanted to experience people who were other than musicians. I was very unhappy being a musician, because I felt I was not a whole person. My only access to experience in life was through music. I thought I would leave and reinvent myself, and that only part of that self would be a musician. When people go to reinvent themselves, they go to California. I wanted to pick a good music school, and I was definitely going to California, so that is what I did. College was also the first time I encountered the black community. I had an identity crisis about that too, because I had been raised by the white side of my genetic family, and I didn't fully understand my background at the time. In Phoenix there was a small African American community, but not in the 1970s in the area I was raised in.

I was having a musical identity crisis too, because my formal music education, as far as I could see, was telling me I didn't have anything to say that hadn't already been said better by other people. I thought, "Well, I really love the sound of a huge orchestra. None of my teachers do. I really do so I guess I'll be a film composer, because they would allow me to work with huge orchestras." I thought that was what I was going to be doing. At that time I was meeting the black community and seeing what that meant for me. Gospel music was how I was really introduced to that.

I was introduced to Charles May, the man who is now the administrator of music at First AME [African Methodist Episcopal Church]. Charles May introduced me to Reverend James Cleveland. Reverend Cleveland had me arrange an album for a new group he was doing called "L.A. Gospel Messengers." This is while I was in college, during the time I was going to a black church. This was the first time I had ever been part of a black community. I felt very out of place, and it got me to thinking about my ethnicity, being mulatto and what that is. I felt like the one dorky guy who could read music but couldn't speak Ebonics. Everyone was very accepting of me, it was just my own self-identity issues that were being thrown up in my face in that environment.

I had this crisis that I was ugly. I was just ugly, and I didn't want to be a musician because I really had nothing to say. So I had problems! Somehow I discovered triathlon, so right out of college I was doing triathlon and doing commercials, underscoring and things like that, as a way to break into the film industry. I discovered that I loved all different kinds of music. That was the great thing about underscoring. One day I had to find a harmonica player who could read music, and the next day I was writing for dobro, "artistic whistler," steel drums, almost every instrument that exists.

I did complete the James Cleveland assignment. This was not my first professional work; I had already been doing commercials for a couple of years. I was getting Cs in composition, because I wasn't actually writing my assignments, but meanwhile I was doing charts for pizza commercials or whatever. It was really exciting to me, because this was music I had to write in one day—the next day it would be recorded. Whatever I would think of that day was what the music had to be.

This was in the days right before synthesizers were completely happening. Synths were used, but it was not like you had a sample of every instrument, so you still had to go out and call players. I got this tremendous orchestration education in the studios, and because that was what I was most interested in, my experience was valuable. In school, we would study Ravel and how everything he does is perfect, perfect orchestration. So I would go to my commercials and think, "Okay, I'll just have this oboe enter on G above high C." Then I would get to the session, and I would spend forty-five minutes punching it in on the synthesizer, slowing the tape down, and figuring out how to make the note actually work. I would say to myself, "Gee, this might have worked for Ravel, but I am never going to write this note for this instrument again, no matter what." I came up with my own rules of orchestration that I developed based on my experience.

I got to do all of these different kinds of music, and I loved that. Each time I got the chance to figure out how I could do this kind of music and what makes that style of music sound the way it does. I would sit at the piano and say, "Okay, now I am doing country. What is that?" I would sit down and play and say, "Oh, it goes like this." That was one education I was getting. I got to the point, though, that I hated everything else about the business. I hated the people I was meeting. I hated the business requirements. When my business partnership broke up, I was totally sick of it and decided I would rather have any other job than the one I had. Then I was able to start thinking about music as something that I loved again. My only access to enjoying my work was asking myself what I loved about music.

A couple of things happened after that. I went to see Steve Reich [American composer] lecture at UCLA, and I was really struck. He just told it like it was, for him. He totally dismissed everyone between Bach and himself as being irrelevant. Of course I disagreed with this, but I saw that he had an aesthetic of what he wanted to do. I had always thought there was something cheeky about his music, but I thought that he wasn't serious. I had heard his earliest pieces, and I thought his "music" was just a gimmick, that he was masquerading as a composer. Then when I saw that he had an aesthetic, that he really wasn't faking it; it was an incredible experience for me. I was very inspired. In his lecture he mentioned drumming at Cal Arts [California Institute of the Arts].

I went to Cal Arts and audited the class in African drumming. I had always loved rhythm; there I was creating it. As a pianist I hadn't done anything like this before, so that was cool. I got this job in an architectural firm, and then I just started writing music that I loved.

About that same time I went to the L.A. Philharmonic performance of John Adams's *Harmonielehre*. That was another moment when I was just floored. There was rhythm, and there was giant orchestral music. There was the emotion that I always have to have in music, despite years of being "trained" to know why music that doesn't move me is "good." I came to these realizations: (a) I don't care about music that is intellectually "good" if it doesn't move me;

(b) There is nothing I have to say that hasn't been said before—but I am kind of like a prism, like an interpreter. My spin on something is what I have to say. There is an emotional connection—it is visceral, and it is rhythmic. That is why I love music, as opposed to painting or anything else. I decided then that I was going to write the music I loved.

So I went home and wrote an orchestral piece that was huge, long, and very John Adams-like. I absolutely had to write that piece, to get it out of my system. It was so long and so difficult that at the premiere I antagonized every single person who was involved in it. From that experience I decided I would never set myself up that way again. I had a few other compositional goals, which are to do certain things with my music that would, in effect, hardwire successful performance into the piece. It was from there that I wrote *Global Warming*. *Global Warming* came from knowing what it was I wanted to say, plus these practical limitations that I was going to hardwire into my works so that they couldn't be performed badly.

It is very gratifying to me, the amount of play my music has gotten. If anyone had told me several years ago that this would happen, I would never have believed it. I think the practical part of this success is due to the fact that before I wrote something I sat down and decided this was a piece that was going to be performable on two rehearsals—and by a good orchestra, on only one.

I got over my identity crisis. As a kid I loved being mulatto. I thought it was cool, and I would tell people about it, just like you would tell them if you caught a cool frog or something. I would tell all my white friends, "I am half-black." I still think it is really cool. Each person experiences me differently. People don't look at me and say, "He's black." They don't say, "He's mulatto." About the only thing I haven't been mistaken for is Asian. They know I am not Japanese, but they are not sure that I am not Polynesian, Iranian, southern Italian, or Peruvian. That is a real gift, because no one likes to be pigeonholed.

I am honored to be a black composer, in that means I have colleagues, and it is fun to be a part of that. Every time you put your foot in the door as a black composer, you are going to walk through the door as a black composer. Composers of previous generations have talked about incredible discrimination they have suffered in their careers because of ethnicity. I am embarrassed to say it, but for me I think it has been an advantage. I look at that generationally and wonder at what point that pendulum is going to swing back. At what point am I going to have a career purely as a black composer? Those are the two things that I am most concerned about, rather than the way it is affecting my career now.

I decided that my music is about a perspective on something. I realized that no one is going to be able to analyze my music and say, "Wow, this is a new thing that has never been done." As I said, what I have to offer is my perspective, with music as the language I use to illustrate my point. When I write something, I choose a title that explains what the piece is about, what I am trying to say; I think about the piece to the point that I can choose a title that nails it. Or if it doesn't nail it for you, it makes you wonder what the piece is about, and I can then explain it to you. Once I have a title where I can nail my whole point of view in a single phrase, then I am ready to write from that perspective, because I have crystallized the idea. Then I allow my harmonic language to be whatever it needs to be to illustrate that point. What I would like to leave behind is music that gives people access to that point of view, that takes them to the place where I was, or where I want them to go with whatever piece of music it is. I really want to write music that invites people to listen to it, that someone could say they were happy to have experienced.

Lettie Beckon Alston

Lettie Beckon Alston was born in 1953, a native Michigander. She has received degrees from home soil institutions and a bachelor's and master's degree from Wayne State University. She became the first composer of color to receive the doctorate in composition from the University of Michigan, in 1983. Her teachers have included James Hartaway, Leslie Bassett, William Bolcolm, and George Wilson. A brilliant pianist and a composer of various instrumental combinations from solo piano and chorale to orchestra, her works have been performed by numerous ensembles, including the Detroit Symphony, the Pontiac-Oakland Symphony, and the Brazeal Dennard Chorale. She was a finalist in the 1994 Unisys Composers Competition. Her works have been recorded on Leonardo Records. A champion of new works, she produces numerous concerts yearly featuring a wide variety of composers. Dr. Alston is currently an associate professor of composition at Oakland University in Ypsilanti, Michigan.

I can't relate to a black woman's experience because I don't know what that would be in music. Women have not been in the forefront, because it has always been a male-dominated society. I would say it is probably easier for a woman to find her individual voice, because we have no role models. There are no Mozarts or Beethovens, as far as African American women go, or even white American women. I have to be perfectly frank—I don't feel anything different when I am composing as far as being a woman, a black woman, a young woman, an old woman. I write what I feel, and I think my environment plays an important part. I work very hard at just being me. I work well at trying to find myself, trying to find some free voice. I am an innovator. I want to be one who creates something new, a new sound, so that someone says, "Gee, that was certainly Lettie Alston," not because of my race or my gender but because of me. I truly am expressing what I feel. I am sure everything has something to do with something, of course, and I would think that perhaps my assertive behavior and attitude toward the career that I am involved in has provoked something in my music. I think that is more my personality, though, because I am energetic, I'm dynamic, and my music is that way as well.

Several people have interviewed me and probed to find out if there are any hidden things in my past. But I have blotted out many things that were negative in my growing up as a composer. Maybe something will surface at a later time, some animosity, or maybe something that being a woman compels me to write. Just recently, I became a little bit conscious of how people look into your music and see what you are. I wrote a piece called *Anxiety,* and I was criticized for writing it. Whenever I come across racism or a male chauvinistic attitude or

something of that nature, though, I always try to shut it out. I want to keep my focus. If I keep my focus I know I will be successful in what my goals are.

Yet it wasn't until I wrote *Anxiety* that I started feeling, "Wait a minute!" Men were telling me, "Well, you know, only women feel anxious. Men don't go through that." It was more a male-female thing rather than a black-white one. It made me very angry that they were looking into that. There is a piece called *Age of Anxiety.* Did anybody talk to Bernstein [its composer] about it? I said, "I should write another piece and call it *PMS.*" Then I started getting somewhat of a radical attitude. I wrote a piece just recently called *Biblical Quotes.* I decided to find positive women in the Bible, women prophets. I think it was because somebody planted a seed in my mind. I thought, "Well, people like controversial stuff now." I think I picked up on it because of that, not because I had any dark secrets or that I resented men.

I started piano at age fifteen at the Bailey Temple School of Music. It was a very informal type of thing, but I was interested in piano. Everyone in my family was taking piano lessons except for me. Mrs. McCullom, who was teaching, told my mother she wouldn't teach any of my brothers or sisters unless she brought me too, and I ended up being the one inspired. The Bailey Temple School of Music was a small community church group that promoted music for the members. I went through the old John Thompson books and played hymn variations. The music group also performed in some of the Grinnell [Music Stores] festivals around town and taking organ lessons from the Grinnell stores. All of a sudden I really got interested in the classics, and I just went forth. Before that I wasn't very interested in anything.

We have a lot of musicians in our family, a lot of jazz and blues musicians, but neither my mom nor my dad were musicians. My dad was a truck driver, and my mom was a seamstress who later taught economics in the public schools. There wasn't much musical influence in my immediate family. I would go to church with my parents on Sunday, but I rebelled, because I couldn't get into the gospel sound. That wasn't my inspiration. My inspiration was from Mrs. McCullom, who had come to the church and started me with piano lessons. I was just really turned on. That was just two years before I started college. When I started college I knew I wanted to be a piano major. I auditioned all these tunes, and they said, "That's not piano repertoire." I said, "What?"

I auditioned with a piano reduction of something like the Beethoven *Fifth Symphony* and all three movements of Beethoven's *Moonlight Sonata.* I was a very good reader, and I had good background, but my technique was weak. I ended up going into theory composition and keeping piano as my main focus. I went to Wayne State University as a composition and theory major from the beginning, but I did everything that a piano major would. I really wanted to keep up piano, and I was thinking of transferring to piano, but by the time they said I could be a piano major I was a composition major.

I really enjoyed composition, yet I think I was a bit radical when I decided to be a composer instead of a pianist, because I was a rejected pianist. I decided I would be a composer, so if there was any animosity built up in me at all, it was resentment that I was not a prepared pianist. But my parents and teacher were very encouraging and pushed me a lot. They would say, "Just take what you have and use it and go for it. Stop comparing and do the best you can. What difference does it make if you started five years before now? You just have to go five years farther." So I took that and decided this was what I was going to do. I decided to do composition because I felt that would be the closest thing to performance, and I was turned on by it. I was a little bit disappointed in having to study atonal music, though, so for a while I felt composition wasn't going to work. I thought I might have to go into public school music, but I was determined to stay in some area involving performance. Then I just started liking it. It started off, however, as a radical gesture. I decided to write some ugly music. Then all of a sudden I started listening to the twentieth-century sound. Stravinsky turned me on tremendously. Then I began to hear jazz, Duke Ellington and Oscar Peterson. I didn't really get into jazz, but a few of those flamboyant compositions that I heard turned me on and let me know that composing could be fun, too. I really loved the romantic period—Chopin and Rachmaninoff. I didn't care too much for Brahms. I loved the real wild pieces of the Romantic era, and so that's what I ended up performing.

Most of my early pieces had piano in them. I had piano and violin, or piano and cello, or piano, cello, and violin, or piano and marimbas, because I wanted piano to be part of my compositional experience.

Then I wrote something for chorus, something called "Help." I also wrote a piece for strings called "Head of Woe." My teachers always thought my pieces were so depressing. They wondered if that was because of their influence or if it was just me. I guess there was a dark side there, because I really longed to be a concert pianist. I was sad when I was composing in the earlier years. In the last three or four years people have been telling me that I should write and play more piano music. I guess I had become uninterested in performing anymore, because I always thought I was never going to be good enough for anybody. I decided I wasn't going to write piano music because pianists didn't want to perform it, and I would have to perform it. Then people told me that they enjoyed my piano literature, so I decided to start writing more. I just finished a piece I wasn't supposed to be writing; I was supposed to be working on something else, but this piano piece just came to mind. It is something that I really want to do now.

I feel as though I am reaching a more mature stage. My workload at the university is not as great as it was before. I am not as bound by all of those obligations and restrictions involved in trying to get tenure. I have other goals, and I think piano performance is definitely a part of them. I am thinking about an opera right now. I am thinking maybe my sabbatical next year might involve that and a little bit more. If I were to do something like a piano concerto, it may happen two or three years from now. I have been fooling around with a lot of electronic sound lately, getting into synthesizers and computers.

I was at Wayne State for the master's, and I think I went through such a hard program. I was very, very angry. It was such a hard degree to accomplish that I didn't have enough time to focus on composition the way I wanted to. Most of the pieces that I wrote for my master's were rushed, and I wasn't very interested in them. I just wrote them to get the grade. My instructors even told me that. Jim Hartway [American composer, educator] would say, "Okay, you wrote this wonderful piece, and that is all. You just want to write it and get it over with. But you don't want to do anything more with it." I said, "Nah, it's over." Everything went by really fast as far as composition was concerned, because my mind was focused in other areas.

The doctorate was a little bit more relaxing for me. I was seriously writing a lot of good music then. I have had more of my performances and a couple of publications out of the doctoral pieces that I have written. I think I was a bit more serious in my undergraduate and doctoral years. I don't even like to talk much about my master's years, because mentally and physically it was just not a good time for me.

I read something by John Ruskin [nineteenth-century British critic] once that art was the expression of one's soul. He was talking about composers of serious music and how composers try to communicate to their listening audiences. Sometimes they communicate their experiences, their personalities, their minds, and certainly their souls. I felt that description fit me. When I try to communicate with my audience it is out of personal experience, and it is more my personality and my soul. I know they always say soul music is the best thing you can deal with, and I think even in the avant-garde field, soul is a part of something that you can share with people. It is really difficult sometimes to express your inner feelings—it is hard to express a spiritual side, for example—but music can really convey those kinds of ideas.

I tried to continue some of those musical traditions of past composers, but I have never tried to focus on one composer or another. People always ask me who my role models and influences are, and I always hesitate to give an answer, because I don't view myself as a formalist but rather as an inspired being, if you will. My music is really not a solution to any problem, so I can't say that this is absolute music. I feel that programmatic music played an important part in my life in my learning to communicate, but I feel that music is more an expression of your feelings, and that works really well for me. I believe that most traditional systems can be a little bit harmful, for me at least, because you tend to sound like someone else instead of just using what you have experienced already. Every composer has had years and years of formal training, so we are all influenced by the past. I feel I am. I always try to organize my musical thoughts with some kind of organic germ. I think everybody does that, whether that germ is melodic or rhythmic or whatever.

I try to focus on some motifs for many of my works. Rhythmic moments often stimulate me more than melodic ones, depending upon my reason for writing. If someone has commissioned me to write something more accessible, I can focus more on the melody. If the piece is free form and I am just experimenting with sounds, rhythm and timbre play an important part. The type of instrumentation is important as well. I try to group ideas together, but I mainly focus on an independent style. In most of my writings I am trying to express myself—not the women's issue, not the color issue, but Lettie. I am trying to find what is Lettie: Lettie is energetic; Lettie is also very emotional, but not too emotional. I am sound, sober, organized, so my music reflects all of those aspects. But I am neither an avant-garde nor an experimentalist composer. I think I organize according to past forms. I tend to use formal designs as the shapes of my ideas and motifs—when I want them to recur, how I want them to expand, whether I want to build a wedge, whether this is my climax, or whether I want an arch there. I try to build my music, in that sense. More abstractly, I build first according to symbols and designs and then put the musical thoughts to it. When I compose I often don't know what my whole piece is about until much later. I am interrupted so often with my regular activities that I find myself composing in spurts. If I am given an opportunity to compose, however, I go straight through. You may not see me for a couple of days, especially if it is during the summer. I just go straight through and do it all. During the course of the school year, though, I write in sections. I may end up putting the design or the formal side of it together, or I may organize it a little more after I have conceived all of my motifs and ideas. It depends upon what I am doing. That is why I say I am influenced a lot by my environment.

I am not very impressed with a lot of orchestral music. I really seek to find new sounds. To contradict what I just said about not being an experimentalist, I would say that if there is any side of me that experiments, it is my orchestral side. I feel there is so much to learn with the orchestra. There is always something new that I experience. I could listen to two or three pieces before I write and say, "Okay, I m going to use that style and write something really traditional for this conductor."

Then I will end up going in a different direction because that sound is not what I really wanted. I find myself being a little bit freer with orchestral pieces. Since I haven't received any commissions for orchestral work, I always feel that I can do whatever I want, because I am doing it for free. It gives me a chance to explore and do what I want. I am like a kid with candy; conductors have actually described me in that way. I don't know if they really understand many of the things I am trying to express, because my goal with the orchestra is to find a new sound.

I would tell young composers to get all of the craft that they can, to get a good musical background and have a good foundation in theory, harmony, and counterpoint. I would tell them if they were not pianists they should learn to play, because composition is a performing art. Many people think composers are not performers, but you must be able to perform and realize what performance is about, so that when you compose you feel yourself performing. I would encourage them to able to play Bach inventions and Bach chorales, because that is the foundation. I would also encourage them to write rhythmic things, to do percussion pieces, and to write something for four or five percussion instruments, or maybe even venture off into six percussion instruments, nonpitched instruments. I think those are some of the things that stifle many composers. Young composers are afraid of rhythm, they are afraid of timbres, they are afraid of hearing more than two sounds. They should just forget about pitch completely, because they are liable just to emulate something to which they are accustomed. I would try to get them away from what they are used to and onto new ground. That is usually the first thing I try to get students to do, because that way they can explore and be really creative.

I also think that music preparation needs to start at a younger age. I think it needs to start in the home. We are so influenced by commercial music and by what we hear and see on television. Television is dictating what America should be, whether it is the African American community, the Chinese community, or the white community. I think the media has full control over what we are going to be, as far as it relates to the arts, specifically music. Music rules our society. It rules what people are going to be about. It takes over the soul, it takes over the mind.

Music can build the soul and mind, or it can destroy the soul and mind, depending upon what types of music or art forms to which our kids are exposed.

Allen Bloom [literary critic] has said that rock music is going to send all of our kids to hell. Actually, he is making a controversial statement so he can get feedback, but I don't know—it seems like an extreme in any area is detrimental. I just think we need more diversity. I don't think that rock music is destroying their souls. I like some rock music, I like to listen to dance music, I like to listen to Earl Klugh and Bob James. I like Michael Jackson. I am beginning to understand rap music a little bit more, because I have a child, and I am also trying to influence that child to be a diverse person. I am trying to expose him to enough music so that he will be able to make wise decisions. I think if our school systems were a little bit more liberal, our youth would be a little bit more liberal. Now it is like, "Rap is bad news, this is bad news. Acid rock is bad news." I think our youth is saying, "Well, I am going to reject you, because you reject me." Wasn't that the whole idea of minimalists? Minimalism was a radical movement. Everything was atonal; the minimalists decided they were going to take a part of the American world. The disco era, the rock-and-roll era, they took those ostinatos and the redundant, repetitious movements and put them to work in the minimalist movement. I think our youth do the exact same thing.

In the African American community, I would really like to work on reaching kids at a young age and also reach the churches, because I think the churches have a strong impact on our culture and our community. We could have a more diverse community, not only socially but also as far as the arts are concerned. Even in our dance forms, one form dominates another. We just need more diversity in our culture. I don't know if there is really an answer, something that would actually work. I have read several articles suggesting that kids who study the arts, who study something technical, like instruments, not just dance or visual arts, who actually have to read music, are more successful and tend to grow up to be the patrons that we all respect and need if the arts are going to survive. Like I said, it starts in the home, in the schools, and in the church.

I think Black History Month programs and concerts are great, because they give us an opportunity to showcase our stuff. A wise person once told me, "If you can't get it with your credentials, get it with your color." I thought that was such an amusing thing, because we have all of these credentials, we have such high expectations of one another as professors at universities, as holders of the esoteric. We reject the popular. But I really think we need to get out and show our stuff. I think people really look for our music in February, they look to have us in their programs, and it has been very exciting for me when I am invited. Then people who hear you in those programs invite you into other programs. I do not think it is like affirmative action, which can make us feel more inferior because they think we have gotten the job because they needed a black in the position. I feel if you are showcased in a New York Philharmonic performance during Black History Month, for example, it gives people a way to experience what you have to offer. If it is good, you will go far. Black History Month gives us the opportunity to show that we are good, and I think that is a very positive thing. I know some people say, "They only call us in February, and you never hear anymore from them throughout the year." That may be true, but we are such a small minority when it comes to the national and international scene, and it is going to take us a while.

I think there have been some attitude changes, not just because people see what is going on but because African American composers are becoming more diverse. It is not that we are always focusing in on Negro spirituals or African themes, but that we are showing that we are capable of working in different areas and are capable of doing all of it. It also gives us a chance to speak to what we really are. I find it delightful when someone asks me to write something with an African American or spiritual theme, because I was never exposed to that. For me it is exciting to get a chance to write something that I have never tried before. Most people think that is all we ever do, but we have been so diverse in our thinking, in our learning, and in our training that we have neglected our own race. So Black History Month does give us a chance to sneak in one or two of those wonderful pieces that we find really delightful and that we enjoy writing. I think that is very positive.

I also think I have inspired more white audiences with my works. I am teaching more of a white community. My music is not of the vernacular to them. I think what impressed them so is that I could be any composer. If they didn't know me, they wouldn't know who wrote the piece. I think that my African American counterparts have rejected my work because they feel that I have sold out. That makes me feel lonely, it makes me feel left out. It makes me sometimes feel that I don't know my own people anymore, and that it's not only black people whom I don't know, but my own family. I think that they expect me to write more on my own cultural background music. I do try to do a variety of things, but I think that it really drains the black composer to have to feed both worlds. Sometimes I think it stifles us to have to be so concerned with feeding our people and at the same time to have to feed the other people who are feeding us, if you will. I look at the concerts that we have, and I look at the audiences. I look at concerts I have in the black community, and who do I see? It is only when we have some national event or a Unisys thing [the Unisys Corporation sponsors the Detroit Symphony's black composer contests] that we begin to see all of the literate, esoteric colleagues we know. That is why we can relate to our own music—we are each other's support. It feels so good when I get to conventions and workshops, because I do feel that unless I write rap, or something else that is very laypersonish, if you will, it is not going to be accepted by the black community.

I personally have had an awful experience with the black church; my music is too "white" for them; I have been rejected by my church community. I feel that I have to be a part of the musical scene, because that is my inside, but I can't fit in with my own culture. It is really hard. I would love just to have a rap session with about ten composers on this one subject, because I think we all feel the hardship here. It is sad, and yet we have to be strong and say, "Well, look, this is something we have done, and we should not be ashamed." Why do we have to be penalized for being successful, or what we call successful? I am sure Michael Jackson is considered successful. Why is it that the educated musicians are not considered successful? We are considered rejects, and that is very painful for the black composer. I think it is even painful for the black performer. Go to a concert with Leontine Price or Jessye Norman [operatic and concert singers] and look at their audience—or go to a concert by Marsalis or Kathleen Battle. If you look at the audience, it is 98 percent white. And that is tonal music. They are doing jazz or the real traditional classics, like Bach; they aren't even performing late Romantic compositions. I think our form is more of a prestigious, elite art form, and that the blacks whom we do reach are those on higher financial levels. This is an expensive art form. But then, of course, when you compare Michael Jackson ticket prices with the Detroit Symphony, I would think Jackson's prices overwhelm the Detroit Symphony's. So we can't even really say it is financial.

I think it is the fear of losing their identity as black that keeps people away from our work. So many people just ignore this issue and are afraid of it, but we need to address this. We are afraid that we are going to lose our blackness if we give in to the norms of our society. To get a degree in music requires that you know European music; it looks like we are putting the white European person ahead of everything else. I think this works with any nonwhite community. I think you get the same feedback, but our musical form is rejected more in the black culture than perhaps in any other culture. I think black people are affected by how other people view their music, in both the popular and the esoteric realms. In the popular field our music is basically rejected by white America. Our black culture sees this, and we protect the standards of our music, and therefore anything that is nonblack in our music will be rejected by the majority of our race. Perhaps it is ignorance, or perhaps it is commitment to our culture—I can't say. Perhaps it is just that we are all afraid to do, and listen to, things close to European music or music of the early 1900s. Even Scott Joplin's music is foreign to many people. Furthermore, many people can't relate to jazz. If it doesn't have something you can dance to, it is not functional for them.

There are many different categories which we have to consider here, as far as people are concerned. There is the lower class, the middle class, and the upper class. We have the same classes in the black race that exist in the white race. We have to accept the fact that there are different classes of people and that their listening abilities are at different levels because of the things to which they have been exposed. Overall, however, I think that there is a fear of losing our culture, losing our black sound, or losing that blackness that we think we should all have.

I refuse to answer whether there is a historical line from me backward. I don't think that exists, and I don't think there is one forward, either, from me. That is not in my mind. I have never focused on one or two or eight composers. It's only that Lettie was *here,* and Lettie is *here.*

There are several things, however, that I would like to leave. I would like to say that as a university professor, I have worked to expose the black culture as something that says, "You can deal with this." I just want to perhaps be a role model and say that you can do things that are not common. As far as my music is concerned, I just want to share something different that other composers have perhaps tried to accomplish and have not. My goal is not to be famous or anything like that. I just want to be loved, I want to be adored, and I just want some of my music to live on. I hope that a few of my piano pieces show some unique techniques or levels of difficulty that will bring students to appreciate the late twentieth-century sound to a greater extent. The last thing would probably be to share guts and drive with the next generation. It is nice being a black female composer who has it all—the family, the husband, the career, the fame and fortune. Well, I don't know about the fame and fortune, but I'm blessed by God.

So many people seem to feel that married women, women with children, or composers with children cannot be successful and cannot function and be prolific in their writing. I would like to be a role model for all women in that sense, and for black Americans. I want my work to suggest that we can do things that aren't expected of us. My spiritual strengths have come through one Bible scripture verse: "I can do all things through Christ which strengthens me" (Phil. 4:15).

William C. Banfield (interviewed by Brian C. Brown)

William C. Banfield, born in 1961, occupies an endowed chair of humanities and
fine arts, and is an associate professor of music and director of American cultural
studies at the University of St. Thomas, in St. Paul, Minnesota. He served as assistant professor in the Department of Afro-American Studies at Indiana University
(Bloomington) and as composer in residence of the African American Arts Institute
at the Indiana University (1992–97). A native of Detroit, he received his bachelor
of music degree from the New England Conservatory of Music, a master's of theological studies from Boston University, and a doctor of musical arts degree from
the University of Michigan. His works have been commissioned and performed by
the National, Atlanta, Detroit, Akron, Minnesota, Sacramento, Dallas, Richmond,
San Diego, Savannah, Roanoke, and Indianapolis Symphonies, the Minneapolis
Symphonia, the Plymouth Music Series of Minnesota, and the symphony orchestras
of the Universities of Utah, Northern Illinois, St. Thomas, Massachusetts at Amherst, and Michigan, and Tufts and Butler Universities. Recordings of his works are
carried on Telarc, Atlantic, Innova, Centaur, and Collins Classics. He was a 1996
recipient of the Lila B. Wallace–*Readers Digest* Opera for a New America commission for the opera *Luyala,* premiered at Duke University in 1999. He served as a
W. E. B. Dubois Scholar at Harvard in 2001 and Princeton University visiting atelier
artist in 2002. He is the founder of the Undine Smith Moore Collection of Original
Scores and Manuscripts at the Archives of African American Music and Culture,
Indiana University. Dr. Banfield lives and works in St. Paul, Minnesota.

Q: What vision do you bring to your involvement as an artist/educator?

A: The endowed chair in arts and humanities, which I hold, was set up at my university to have scholars and artists within the academy encourage interdisciplinary studies. One of the principles of the endowed chair is that person would generate courses and initiatives that link the humanities in an interdisciplinary fashion.

That's one of the things that I've always been involved with, both as an undergraduate and in my master's program, as well as in the work that I began to do at the University of Michigan. In the past I have had to struggle with interdisciplinary studies, because they weren't a part of the psyche and the mechanism of the traditional college. I was discouraged. But it was quite prophetic and timely; such studies initiatives are now a part of the thinking of the academy, as we are trying to get people and students to think more about integrated knowledge and integrated experiences. Someone taking a course in political science needs to look at how art works or the media works within that discipline; that person becomes more informed and has a more balanced perspective.

This approach to the arts and education resonated with all the things I believe about education and educational initiatives connecting with artists and artists' roles in society. I mean, that was my master's thesis area. It was actually a master's in theology. I looked at Richard Wagner and the politics of Wagnerian opera and his understanding of philosophy from [Arthur] Schopenhauer and [Friedrich] Nietzsche, and his artistic attempts to struggle existentially with self and social meaning. And so as an interdisciplinary study, that master's helped me prepare.

I taught religion and Near Eastern studies at the University of Michigan. At Indiana University I taught in African-American studies and music, which are interdisciplinary programs. Here at my university we initiated an American cultural studies program. Together with twelve other faculty members, I proposed it as a minor in the study of American cultural experience as it relates to music, literature, and the arts. To accompany that we conducted a symposium on American cultural studies, which received enthusiastic support from the National Endowment for the Humanities. I invited cultural critic Henry Louis Gates and musicologist Susan McClary to come and help inaugurate the program. We proposed bringing together some thirty courses, courses that were already on the books and now are under the rubric of American cultural studies. This includes four courses that were developed: "The Theology of American Popular Music," "Black American Music: A Historical Survey," "Consuming Ideologies: Music and Rhetoric in Popular Culture," and "Introduction to American Cultural Studies." As director, I teach these courses, in addition to composition and a composition seminar.

Q: You often speak of the power of collaboration, and you certainly have had an impact on your students. But have your students influenced you in your own composing, in your own music?

A: Sure, most definitely. Working with students one to one in composition and creative construction really allows you to get beyond the books to a kind of real spiritual exchange, especially in composition. Music is the concrete understanding of someone's thinking, someone's reasoning, and someone's emotive makeup. I mean, this is what I believe music is. Some people believe music is a scale that you manipulate; well, I think most artists and most musicians believe that music is a creative force, a creative ideology. It moves and has its own way, but it also works within the psyches of artists. It's their world and their expression.

Those students influence me because they tell me what they are thinking. That teaches me and challenges me to rise up yet another level to get to what I need to say to encourage them to move toward what their dream is. Everybody is different. There are no two or three composers who have the same experience. Every time I have the chance to sit down with someone for fourteen or fifteen weeks, I can have an exchange with that person. Teaching like that is very taxing, in a good way. It takes a lot of energy. You can't just go in and prepare and then leave, because it continues to live with you each day. When they're writing, I'm kind of writing and responding to that. So that's very instructive to me.

Q: You mentioned teaching a course entitled "The Theology of American Popular Music." Mass media would have us believe that these are two contrasting ideas, that there can't be a religious or spiritual influence in popular music. How do you reconcile that notion for your students?

A: I do that in many ways. First, we go back to the foundations of music. There are certain principles within the Western notion, but I move from two angles, the Western European notion of history and philosophy, and the African notion of being and philosophy. When the students see that popular music is the marriage of both of those ideologies and look at the spiritual implications in them, they come away understanding very clearly that popular music is the result of both, a variation of what might be a spiritual quest for that blues singer, or that gospel singer, or even in some cases the rock 'n roll singer, and certainly the jazz performer.

When that's used for good purposes, it's very easy to see how one can have an understanding that creative agents have connections with things that are beyond the finite, toward the infinite. I think the West is where the philosophical understanding of it comes from.

When you look at cultures in the larger world beyond Europe, like Africa and India, they understand music to be primarily the connection between the individual speaking and the *Theos*. In African theology the whole notion is "We think, therefore we are," as opposed to "I think, therefore I am." Everything I do relates to my community; it has no reason, no meaning, unless that community is connected to the *Theos*. The connection between community and the individual is respected and understood within the community, and God gives blessings to that.

There is an African saying, "The spirit will descend with a good song." What that means is that God is connected to a song that is good, and that a song is good aesthetically when it relates to, and is a reflection of, the community in total. That's why in the black church when the spirit hits, there is ecstasy. That's part of the religious experience. Music helps to usher that in.

When we get to the Western European tradition, because of the way history has gone, that element gets left out. In order to hear the true voice of God, one would sit there in quiet contemplation. But if you go back to the Scriptures, it says, "Make a joyful noise before the Lord." You see, these two things always go hand in hand.

In short, the songs that became part of the popular mainstream grew out of camp revival meetings. These were revival-meeting spirituals and hymns from Europe. Africans had their own read on this, and they gave it a kind of stylistic spin; the commentators and Europeans were saying, "The Africans slaves are carrying on in ways that are beyond what these hymns are about."

The whole modification of popular music began with these black folks doing different things with this Western European music, and so we get the spirituals, we get the blues, ragtime and jazz, and all popular music. Whether it's country and western or rock and roll, it gets its aesthetic spin from that. Many artists have maintained that "spiritual" connection. They are saying, "What I do is a part of my spirituality." So if you look beneath a popular form, you will find these convictions that they have. The course tries to look at both of those things.

Q: You have mentioned in the past that the composer's duty is to reflect society. How do you do that personally in your music?

A: That has been an easier thing for me, because those things were always a part of my training. When I went to divinity school, that was what I set out to do. Then I went to West Africa and I saw that concern for one's society was always a part of the traditional African experience. So that, again, energized me. Then studies of people like Wagner gave me justification from the European notion. I think of myself as an artist using imagination, caring, and excitement about people and life to craft and construct works which connect and corroborate with, underline, or make commentary on things we all experience. There is a conscious effort to immerse myself, to be full of spirit and joy, anxious, excited, and awestruck—and black, American, born in 1961, and from Detroit. All of these things and a gazillion ideas, experiences, people, travels, and common lines from the texts of life compel me to write.

I believe music making is one of the great forms of a certain kind of literature that we have. I define literature in this sense—composers, creative music makers, are the authors of narratives, novels, the poetry that many recite in their inner worlds each day. We bring concrete sound to those unspoken narratives, and the music is a combination of all the literature we read, from poetry to film, to Alvin Ailey dance movement, to every rap, rhyme, song, blues set, or opera we take in. Music, from rough, vernacular blues to a symphony, is a text of marked significance that embodies the human condition.

My music is a synchronization of all those perspectives, and I try to create my own voice in that. I have opportunities to write music that I think comes from the heart and inspires people toward beauty or sometimes toward more critical societal reflection. But certainly I want somebody to walk away and feel like, "Wow, that music really said something, really moved me." If it moves people, then it's doing work of a spiritual nature; people are being moved beyond where they are.

I asked a theology professor, Gordon Kaufman, what theology should do. He said, "Theology's job is to illuminate the way and move people on." I always remembered that as something I need to be doing too, and so I always considered my music to be theologically based as long as it did that—illuminates people in some way and moves them on.

Q: In a recent interview you mentioned that the academy has done a lot of damage to the creative artist. Could you comment on that?

A: I tried to say that from an experiential perspective. Having gone through the New England Conservatory, then Boston University and the University of Michigan, then teaching at both Michigan and Indiana University, I am speaking from the perspective of an artist, having gone through these programs and seeing that in fact the academy (while it has done a tremendous job to codify conventions and histories) has done a lot of damage to creative artistic spirit. Because it is an institution, it is not designed to foster creativity. But it should be sympathetic and should inspire people to be creative.

We lose that when we get into our board meetings and become institutional in our ideologies and political and stylistic approaches. It does damage to the students. There needs to be a balance in courses, particularly in the arts, that deal with history and theory. But then theory and history should move toward conception, creativity, concept, and proper application, in order to allow students to step out, to be free and liberated from these theories. An artist may start with a theory then move on to self-expression. We don't deal with that, particularly in music. We stay with the theoretical and say that you have to understand this and do this in order to be musical. That's not correct. You're musical first, you're artistic first, you're creative first, you're human first, and then you learn things to help govern the rest.

I think there needs to be a balance. The institution should be set up with a balance of courses. What I hope to do within the curriculum of music and the humanities is to provide an understanding of what a creative artist, does in addition to theory to be memorized.

Q: Growing up in Detroit, what were your musical influences?

A: As is the case in a lot of African American households, it was a very eclectic kind of thing. Our house was full of Beethoven and Ellington, Pavarotti and Al Green. There was this wonderful mix of all these things. My parents would take me to the symphony. My church, which was a huge, progressive black church, would do the anthems and the Bach and Beethoven, but they also had a gospel choir. That's what African American ideology is all about. It is about this great amalgamation of these perspectives, both American Western and those things that are retained from African life and culture and that help shape African American identity. That's what I had around my house. We had Dinah Washington, and we had Beverly Sills singing some Broadway thing. This was what influenced me early on. I mean, Jimi Hendrix was a big influence.

But when I was in high school, I wanted to be just like both Ellington and Johannes Brahms, running around in Vienna trying to find himself. Then when I got into college and saw how hip these European avant-garde composers were; I was influenced by Stravinsky and what he was doing in mixing cultures. There were also guitarists, performing artists—Andrés Segovia as well as Jimi Hendrix and Wes Montgomery. Those things influenced me from all angles—definitely Ellington and definitely Stravinsky, but definitely Leonard Bernstein too. He was a big influence on me. I had a chance to meet him, and he encouraged me before he passed away to continue mixing the whole African American idiom within symphonic and American musical conventions. Bernstein encouraged me to create something that was absolutely unique in terms of my own voice, but absolutely American. That would be a contribution that I could make to this culture musically. I am continuing to try to do that.

Q. You are involved in so many different projects. What is the common draw for you? In other words, what pulls all of your interests together?

A: Creative activity, absolutely. I think I was just born to be creative. This has been a real problem. It's a joy now, because I'm older; I can walk away from some of the criticism and some of the challenges, because I have been blessed to have done a lot at a young age—I guess I'm still young. I have a little freedom and am not intimidated by some of the opposition. But certainly when you are involved in a lot of things you get more opposition. To whom much is given, much is required, as the saying goes. And so you take those things in stride. No matter what, the bottom line is creativity.

Q: In your article entitled "Creating Opera from Multiple Traditions," you refer to the end of the century. How will the new century influence your music?

A: The millennium mark was for me an attempt, at least in principle, to move out and ahead. Everything's not going to change anytime soon, but this realization that we are moving to a new period is very real in my creative thinking. People should be thinking that a hundred years is a pretty good period of time to test something out; if it isn't working after a hundred years, let's try something else. You know, I think that's a fair rule. So from that angle, I think everybody is thinking about doing some different things.

What kinds of approaches have we used? How has the public addressed these things? What have we done in education? What are we doing in our creative avenues and institutions? What things can we do that are new? What should we be implementing now? The millennium is a great opportunity for us to readdress all those things, and I'm addressing it musically and culturally. So many artificial barriers and categories have now been brought down, and our cultural, stylistic, and national sensibilities are converging. The barriers in art between what's classical and what's popular, and what's high and what's low, are breaking down.

That's one of the walls that we hope the contemporary artist is able to break down. If you come hear a symphony of mine, you're going to hear American influences of the blues and jazz, as well as popular music, things you wouldn't have heard in Beethoven. But Beethoven was doing the popular music of his day, which is something we don't talk about. That's not classical music. He took music from the peasants, in the traditional sense of how they meant it, from the common folk who were in the street. Their songs were then put in Beethoven's symphonies. That's what I think we need to be doing with a symphony orchestra and opera—using the "stuff" of our times to tell the stories.

Q: For you, what is the standard of creative excellence of the twentieth century?

A: Jazz, as a musical movement of culture, style, and as a language. Jazz is one of the most important creative movements in the history of mankind. That is not overstated. I can say that as someone who not only loves the music but has studied it. I can speak with authority in that regard. That of all human artistic movements—the spiritual, intellectual, cultural, political, and musical movements—it is one of the most important.

One thing that we haven't done in the traditional academy is study jazz music fully as a cultural movement. If you look at the lines of Charlie Parker, you find lines that are as intricate as Bach lines. Be-bop worked on this notion of outlining very intricate chords without even stating them. They were stated through the melody. So contrapuntally, it's the same kind of technique that Bach and so many of the Western European composers used to outline their tunes.

As a matter of fact, Charlie Parker never heard Bach's music until very late in his life. He once said to somebody at a party—and that person told a good friend and teacher of mine—"Why didn't you guys tell me about this guy Bach?" He started to study it. But he had already set down very intricate patterns in his compositions, based on this contrapuntal concept that defines and outlines very intricate sonorities. From that angle, jazz is a technical art form. But at the same time it's a very liberating art form, very much involved with human expression. It's the best of both worlds. It has taken on universal kinds of meanings. Jazz has made American music culture a staple around the world. It's unfortunate that it's not studied in the academy with the kind of critical tools that should be applied to it.

Regina Harris Baiocchi

Regina Harris Baiocchi, a composer, playwright, and poet born in 1956, is a Chicago native. One of the most pragmatic composers of her generation, Ms. Baiocchi believes in the notion of composer as "musical citizen in the community." An avid concertizer, with professional skills in public relations, business, and marketing, she is well known in Chicago for her composition work and concert organizing. A graduate of Roosevelt University (B.A. in composition), the Illinois Institute of Design, and New York University (graduate certificates in visual design), she received a master of music composition degree (M.M.) from De Paul University. Her works, ranging in form and style from gospel to solo trumpet and chamber opera, have been performed by local musicians as well as the Detroit Symphony. Ms. Baiocchi was nominated for the 1996 Cal Arts Award and was a finalist in the 1993 Unisys Composers Competition. She is a member of the American Women Composers Midwest and the International League of Women in Music. Her works have been recorded on Kaleidoscope and Leonardo Records. Ms. Baiocchi and her work can be seen heard and felt in Chicago, where she lives.

It is probably more important how the world views me than how I view the world. People are socialized to think that men are stronger and better when it comes to certain things, and that writing music is one of them. Because we are socialized to think more of men and their accomplishments, sometimes women composers are not looked upon with the same seriousness as their male counterparts. That is a reality that I face, but it is not something that I let hinder me. At low moments I might be depressed about it, but usually I am able to put it in perspective and move on. It is definitely an issue, though, even in the way women composers approach each other. Sometimes certain women composers like to be the only one in a group, because they feel they will be treated better, whereas in small groups of women within larger groups of male composers, we are more apt to have to be a man or to get out of the circle.

That does not change the way I write music. If am really bothered with something, I try not to write at that time, so that when I do write, I can do it with a clear head. There are times, however, when I am working with a really tight deadline and I don't have that luxury, so I just have to sit down and unload, meditate, or whatever, and try to get back on track and zero in on what I am doing. Usually when I sit down to write I have an agenda, not something that is consciously dictated by things within my musical psyche.

If a woman's sensibility does exist in music, I am not aurally astute enough to detect it. I can think of pieces written with great sensitivity by men.

In contrast, I have listened to pieces by women that are also written with great sensitivity. I don't think you have to stick your hand in the fire to know that it burns; by the same token, you don't have to experience things that generally happen to women in order to express them, either in words or in music. You don't have to experience things that generally happen to men in order to express those things in music. I have written some virile pieces, pieces that I think come across as very masculine. I have also written some pieces of music that, if I gave them feminine titles, you would certainly perceive as some of the most feminine pieces you have ever heard.

Music began in my home with my paternal grandmother, who played piano and organ for the Church of God in Christ in South Bend, Indiana. She also played in Chicago. It was my sister's and my job to walk grandmama to and from church. We hung around my grandmother a lot during choir rehearsal and services. We were also at her house when she was practicing. My father, who is from Kentucky, also played bluegrass fiddle and harmonica. When my mother was younger she was always a member of the choir. My parents are also both jazz buffs. I was exposed very early in life to a lot of jazz, a lot of gospel music, and I have been in choirs basically all my life, at least since I was four years old. Music was an integral part of my life, as well as the lives of my siblings. We pretty much had the same background, and then, as we got a little bit older, our interests started to develop. We took lessons on whatever instrument we were interested in, or whatever instrument was available. I began studying guitar when I was nine years old. I started writing songs using the guitar.

The notion that I wanted to write music came early in my life. By the time I was seven years old I knew that I wanted to be a poet, because I had found that I could express in words things I could not express clearly in conversation. I guess that is because I was such an introverted person and spent a lot of time alone just sitting, reading, writing. I also love penmanship. I love practicing the art of calligraphy. I knew from age seven that I wanted to write something. It wasn't until I got a little bit older, maybe nine or ten, that I thought that music was another branch of writing. Of course, by the time I got to high school I pretty much knew that writing music was the path that I wanted to follow.

High school was a very creative period for me musically. It was a very great learning period. I stumbled upon playing the trumpet; in many public schools they assign the instruments. In my case, there was a coronet left, and so they said, "Okay, you'll play coronet." I started playing coronet and trumpet in different bands and orchestras while I was in high school. I was very lucky, because I went to one of the best black schools in Chicago, Paul Laurence Dunbar Vocational High School. I was in marching band, concert band, choir, and jazz band. My teachers were very good about playing my arrangements; I could write something on Monday and hear it on Tuesday or Wednesday in band rehearsal, depending upon how quickly I could copy the parts. That was a very nurturing environment. It was definitely a turning point in my life musically.

I was about nine or ten, playing guitar, when I acquired the skill to notate my musical ideas. Once I was able to move around comfortably on the instrument, I started setting some of the poetry that I had already written. I started writing different songs, most of them for voice and guitar and a few for guitar and piano, but I really didn't have the piano skills or the knowledge to do anything lasting. I guess the one thing that helped was coming to grips with the fact that I was a mediocre trumpet player. While I enjoyed performing and I was a good performer, I was not a good trumpeter. I knew what it took to put on a good show, though, especially in a typical marching band like you see in some of the historically black schools—bands with a lot of dancing. I am a very good dancer. I have a great sense of rhythm, so I was good at performing on the instrument, but I knew that I just didn't have it as a trumpet player. I couldn't see myself playing trumpet for a living in an orchestra or in a jazz band. I realized that early on. I knew that I liked arranging music and writing music, so I decided to concentrate on that. I decided to be the best arranger and composer that I could be.

My high school teachers were my role models. Dr. Willie A. Naylor [trumpeter] had some local notoriety and did a lot of recording on some of the Chicago labels, with people like Tyrone Davis and Curtis Mayfield. Willie Naylor was one of my early influences. Another teacher, named William Gardner [trumpeter], was an influence, as was Nathaniel Green [pianist], who was my choral director and who also taught me counterpoint. There was Stanley Pollack, another great influence, who used to be one of the trumpet players with the group named Chicago, which is out of De Paul University. There was yet another trumpet player, named Lionel Borderlon, who had a double major in theory and trumpet, who was also very helpful. I was very interested in theory and in knowing the hows and whys about music. Composition seemed a very natural next step as a way for me to express myself.

College was a culture shock. I had been in this very nurturing environment, where in grammar school and high school I was taught black history—not only black history in America but pan-African history as well. Everyone knew my parents too. Even though I went to a high school with five thousand kids, it was still like being at home, because the music school was very isolated and everyone there knew everyone else. When I went to college, I was the only black person in the composition and theory department for a while, and I was also the only female in the department. It was very obvious that the school was not set up for me. I studied music with a man who did not respect the fact that I had an affinity for writing pop music as well as jazz and classical, blues, and gospel. That didn't work, and I was always being rudely reminded of the fact that they were teaching me how to write classical music. I tried to present the music that I was hearing, and a lot of times it was rejected as "pop shit." I was often told, "This is not the vein in which you should be writing." I found myself writing for a grade and keeping my real music at home.

I became aware of my ability to do left-brain and right-brain composing, one for school and one that comes from myself. I realized that I could probably do just about anything. Yet, I also realized, very early in the game, that I probably would not get very much support from the regular structures that some people were able to depend upon. I knew that if I was going to experience any degree of success at all as a composer, I was going to have to bring my music to the audience myself. That is basically what I did. I tried to participate in as many student recitals as I could. That was kind of hard, because I am an extremely introverted person. I am very shy, and performing is not something that I do naturally. A lot of people find it very hard to believe I am shy, but that is because I have learned over the years how to perform in public without falling apart.

A friend of my father's (Bishop Dominic Carmen, SVD, who performed my wedding ceremony) was pastor of St. Elizabeth Church—the oldest black Catholic church in Chicago. Carmen asked me to help him out until the church found a choir director. Well, four years later, he was still looking for someone. I ended up with this job without really having any skills to be a choir director. It was a *kairos* ("the time is at hand") moment in the history of the Catholic Church: masses in the vernacular replaced the Latin mass, and Catholic faithful were making the transition from singing traditionally white Catholic hymns to singing traditional music of each church's congregants. In my case, I was working in the oldest black Catholic church in Chicago, and they wanted music to reflect the culture of African Americans.

Unfortunately, many of the people in the choir that I worked with, especially the adult choir, where the average age was about seventy, did not readily welcome our own music. The young people welcomed African-inspired music with great enthusiasm. They wanted to do contemporary gospel, so I started doing that. The older people, while they liked music that was rooted in black culture, tended to do more laid-back, inspirational-type things, like spirituals and "traditional" gospel. I was commissioned by the pastor to write something that the adult choir would be able to get into and that the congregation would also have some affinity for; the church was actually divided between the young and the old, the "hip" and the "square." I started writing church music. I loved it. Then started doing round-robin concerts in black churches in Chicago. But I realized very early on that even though I enjoyed it, I didn't want to be a church musician. I think it takes a very special person to be a church musician. That is not what I am, that is not what I wanted to be. Besides, it is just too political for me.

I started working in public relations, just because there are no jobs in music. I discovered that I really like public relations, and I also discovered that it was a very natural place for a musician to be; it taught me how to promote myself and my music. I made acquaintances with people in print media, radio, TV, the whole broadcasting world. A whole different world opened up, and I realized that I was in a good position to promote my own music using the skills I learned while I was practicing public relations. Once I started getting into design, layout, and promotions on a high-level basis, I was able to attract the attention of people who hold a few coins in Chicago. Once one person sees that you are given a chance by someone, they think, "Oh, it's okay, this person does deserve the money and she knows what to do with it." Things took off from there.

Aside from the church pieces, the one thing that probably launched me into the situation that I am in now is being offered a job by an organization called Mostly Music, Incorporated. Mostly Music's founding director, Joyce Turner Hilkevitch, produces anywhere from 100 to 150 concerts a year. As the name implies, most of them are music, but some of them are dance recitals. Some of the concerts involve poetry or other arts. Mostly Music commissioned me to write a piece, then it offered me a job as its composer in residence. A lot of its audiences are schoolchildren; most of my children's music was written for Mostly Music. The rap that I wrote was commissioned by Mostly Music for a high school program that I was producing. Once Mostly Music came on the scene, other funders followed. In my last year in college, I joined an organiza-

tion called American Women Composers—which is now American Women
Composers Midwest, because the national chapter was absorbed by the International Association for Women. Now I am a member of both groups. American
Women Composers Midwest commissioned me to write music. They had been
courting me to join the group, which I really didn't want to do, because I tend
to be a loner. When I got the commission, I wrote two songs based on an essay
by Zora Neale Hurston. Every time the songs were performed people would ask,
"What opera is this from?" Of course, they were not from an opera at that time,
but that led me to write the opera *Gbeldahoven: No One's Child* (1996). A lot
of things in my life are interconnected like that. Nothing really explosive has
happened, but there is a whole sense of connectedness. I feel that my life is now
a series of connect-the-dots.

Winning the Detroit Symphony Orchestra competition reminds me of the
way my whole life in poetry has gone. Someone sees a competition and tells me
about it. I say, "Oh, I don't have time for that," or "I am doing something else."
Then, at the eleventh hour, someone convinces me to submit a piece. I was
shocked when I got a call from the Detroit Symphony; I figured that since it
was a national thing, they would get a lot of entries. I think the nicest thing for
me about the Detroit Symphony Orchestra experience was meeting other black
composers. Even though Chicago is a very large city, and even though I travel
to New York and the West Coast fairly regularly, I had not had any intimate
relationships with many black composers. I could count on one hand the black
composers that I knew before the Detroit experience.

The DSO-Unisys competition was a nice experience. I was surprised and
happy to be there. It inspired me to do other things. After the Detroit experience,
other orchestras became interested in my work. I have gotten calls from orchestras around the country asking me to participate in certain things. People have
also discovered that composers can relate to other people; I have gotten a couple
of lecturing jobs because someone heard a presentation that I made at Wayne
State University. That has been helpful.

I think of music as my passion. If I didn't have a passion, if I didn't have
something to be really excited about, something that really set me on fire, I
would rather not bother with life. That is the way I feel about it. Music is the
one thing that keeps me going. If I woke up tomorrow and there was no music,
I would want to fold up my tent. Music is that special to me. I rarely spend a
minute of the day not thinking about music, not hearing music, not wanting to
hear music, not wanting to write music, or not wanting to play. Music is my life.
I do a lot of things to try to keep that feeling fresh. I take jazz piano lessons.
That has opened a whole new world for me, in terms of rethinking harmony and
chordal structures. I am studying with one of the greatest jazz pianists in Chicago, Alan Swain, and I am also studying composition with Hale Smith, one of
the greatest twentieth-century composers.

If I had to describe black music, the one word that would come to mind is
"soulful." Also, there is a connectedness in black music that in European music
only the great masters are able to accomplish. I mean the connectedness that
links people across cultural, racial, and gender lines. This is the kind of connectedness that doesn't respect ageism or sexism or any of that kind of stuff. Usually
black music that speaks to me, jazz or some of the indigenous music of Africa,
is quite arresting. I stop dead in my tracks, even when I am engaged in a conver-

sation. A certain piece will come on, and I will just space out on the people with whom I am speaking. I can step into the composer's or the performer's zone; that doesn't always happen for me when I hear European music. There are some exceptions to the rule, and those are the people to whose work I like to listen.

My favorite female vocalists are Cassandra Wilson and Betty Carter. When I listen to Betty Carter and see how she stretches and pulls her whole harmonic structure, it recalls the fact that she is from a culture that cannot be confined to a twelve-tone series. There are a lot of microtonal things happening with Betty Carter, not only when she is improvising but within the structure of a standard tune. The same thing is true with Cassandra Wilson. On one of her latest CDs, I heard "Strange Fruit," a piece that was cowritten by Billie Holiday. Wilson's work is so different from what Billie Holiday did, though; Wilson's interpretation is so earthy, so worldly. It is a kind of music that makes it difficult for critics to pigeonhole her work. They say she is a jazz singer with a blues twist, but there are some classical things happening in her work as well. Wilson's music is so difficult for people to categorize, because it is truly world music. She also did the Stylistics' "Children of the Night." When I listen to the Stylistics' version of it, the song seems to be about the child being thrust into the night; when I listen to Cassandra Wilson's version, it is about the night coming out of the child. That is the kind of thing that black music does for me. It is like looking at a prism or a kaleidoscope. You can turn it and see different perspectives. I don't always get those three or more dimensions when I listen to European music.

I find African American Heritage Month and programs like that interesting. Because I have been in public relations and institutional advance work, I know that a lot of times organizations are forced by their funding sources to do certain things. In other words, someone like [the John D. and Catherine T.] MacArthur [Foundation] says, "Hey, if you don't include more people of color in these things, we are going to have to reassess our funding policies where your organization is concerned." So a lot of the major orchestras and a lot of the major opera houses are widening the circle, to hang onto the money they are getting. Many of them claim that they are doing it because they want to enrich what is going on. That may be true, but I think they are also doing it because they have to do. I don't think that is necessarily bad. I don't care why a door is opened; the important thing is that the door is opened. Once I get in, I feel that I can make a lasting impression. I don't think that is a bad thing, I think it's good, regardless of what happens. For example, sometimes you hear people singing Abraham Lincoln's praises for freeing the slaves, and that is not what he did at all. What Lincoln said was if freeing the slaves was going to save the Union, then slaves should be freed. Lincoln was not necessarily antislavery, he was pro-Union. I think the same thing happens to musical organizations. They are doing this for self-preservation, yet nothing but good can come from it.

Being identified as a black woman composer, an African American, definitely does not minimize me. To say that it minimizes me would be to say that "black" minimizes me, or "woman" minimizes me, or "composer" minimizes me. I don't think any of those three terms can minimize or maximize anyone, especially not myself. I am probably more political than I think I am, but these labels remind me of the word "minority," a word that I resist like the plague, because it insinuates that there is something "minor" about the accomplishments of people of color. If you look at it strictly from a numbers perspective, the term is inaccurate, because worldwide, people of color outnumber whites. To me there is a connectedness in one sense, but in another sense "minority" insults me. Call me a "black woman composer"; none of those three terms are derogatory. I am proud to be black, I am proud to be a woman, and I am proud to be a composer. If someone feels the need to label me, that doesn't bother me at all.

My composition process changes from project to project, from day to day, from mood to mood. I am a very moody person, and I think that is important for a creative person to assume these different roles and step into different psyches. I was working on a piece today that was from my opera, and I tried to get into the character. One of the things Hale Smith suggested that I "become very familiar with the biographies of my themes and the biographies of my characters." To that end, I sat down and wrote a profile for each of the characters in the opera. One particular character is a female servant, a young black woman. It was difficult to get a handle on who she was; because she doesn't have a name; she is just referred to as "the female servant," as opposed to "the male servant." I am usually pretty good about naming things, but in this particular case I really saw no reason for it. I think that not naming her is totally justifiable in the world of playwrights or librettists. Just realizing who the person was, though, wasn't enough to write her aria. I started thinking about some women who could possibly sing this role. The woman I had in mind at first was a jazz singer, but the person I ultimately chose is a classically trained church musician who sings jazz also. So I started writing for this particular person's voice. I find that easier than just writing the song, otherwise I end up writing for my own voice or things that I like to hear and not necessarily writing things that the performer can do. That is how that particular piece started. The woman who is going to be the female servant is named Barbara. I started thinking about Barbara and some of things that she can do with her voice. I know some of her weaknesses and some of her strengths; I tried to capitalize on the strengths and minimize the weaknesses. Then I just went inside the character and said to the audience, through song, what I wanted them to walk away with. So when the audience goes home, providing this female servant has touched them, they will be able to recall the music and know why it stuck with them.

I did a concert reading of the opera, basically piano and vocal renditions of the arias, which will ultimately be scored for chamber orchestra. I am aware of the role that the piano plays here; I want to make sure everything is done to accentuate the voices. I started out with the words, and then I just wrote the melody as I heard it. Then I went back and looked to see if the rhythm of the words matched the rhythm of the melody. I made adjustments—usually in the favor of the rhythm of the words, unless I was trying to prove a point. I made some other technical decisions, connecting certain notes with certain vowels, using certain notes to accentuate vowels, using certain notes to accentuate consonants, and so on.

I think an artist should be an integral part of society, because art reflects life. Sometimes, of course, life imitates art, and vice versa, but I don't think an artist can be successful without being attuned to society. Sometimes artists are in tune with the past, sometimes they are in tune with the present, and other times they are able to anticipate the future. Artists have to have some sort of link. One of the things that would help elevate our role in society would be to link the educational system, in the institutional sense, to the familiar realm. My whole philosophy about education is that it basically takes place in the home. School is a supplement to what the home environment gives. If the foundation is weak at home, chances are the pupil is not going to be successful at school. Conversely, the same thing happens with an artist. If we are not attuned to who we are in our homes, with our individual selves, if we are not attuned to who we are within the structure of our families, with who our families are in the structure of our neighborhood, etc., I don't think very much success can be achieved.

I think my work is stylistically all over the place. For example, I am happy that I was able to write a rap piece. Something happens for many kids who are in the audience where that rap is presented. Once they hear that piece they seem to forget about all the other pieces that I wrote. Purists, classical musicians, concert musicians, often look down their noses at that piece. I have also ended classical concerts with a gospel piece, one of those foot-stompers and hand-clappers. People seem to like it, but it is not what they expect from a person who has master's degrees in music. People expect only "highbrow" expression. At other times I feel like I am still a student in music, especially in jazz and when it comes to world music. Every day I realize that something I see is just the tip of an iceberg. I have a feeling that once I unlock this musical mystery, this phase of my life will end.

The list of my influences is long, but the first person I would start with is Hale Smith. He is a person whom I really respect, because he has feet planted firmly in many different worlds in music. He is a great concert composer, a great jazz composer, a great jazz pianist and arranger, and he cut his musical teeth on the street. He has worked with army bands, doing arrangements and serving as their conductor. He has done spirituals. That is a pretty wide range, not to mention his work in classical music—orchestral, chamber, etc.—and in blues, and some of the other things he does. To me Hale Smith's musical experience is an ideal situation for a black composer. That is not to say that all black composers have to write in these various idioms, though that is what I aspire to as a composer myself. A lot of people who write concert music exclusively do it very well. There are a lot of people who write jazz exclusively and do it very well. Sometimes people concentrate on one niche, and there is certainly a lot to be said for that, but I think if you can exist simultaneously in other worlds, that is the way to go.

Other influences would be Dorothy Rudd Moore and Julia Perry. There are also people like Lena McLynn [black American composer], who is here in Chicago. Betty Jackson King [black American composer], who passed away a few years ago, was another influence. She was New Jersey and Chicago based. Quite a few people I meet in Chicago are not known in the world of music. Many of them are church musicians, and they are very inventive and very creative. That is a rare thing nowadays, because when you turn on the radio or the TV, everyone basically sounds the same.

Vocal and piano music are the things that I enjoy doing the most right now, but if you asked me tomorrow I am sure I would have a different answer. I think one piece, my piano sonata *Liszten, My Husband Is Not a Hat*—created between 1994 and 1995, and obviously inspired by composer/pianist Franz

Liszt, whom I love—summed up my life as a composer in those years. I have other pieces that are milestones, for myself if for no one else. I think that if I could not write piano music, if I could not write vocal music, I wouldn't feel like a whole person. And yet I feel the same way about public relations. If I could not practice public relations in some form or another, I don't think my music would be as true. I think my music is good because I take breaks from it to practice public relations; my public relations is fresh because I take a break and write music. I have that balance. I can juggle that with family and friends. I think socializing is very important, because that is where I replenish myself, through interacting with other people, either in person or through books or movies. If I cannot do that, everything I write will lack the vital dimension that makes my music ring true.

Anthony Davis

Anthony Davis was born 1951 in Paterson, New Jersey. The range, scope, and impact of his work, and the artistic, critical, and commercial success he has earned have established him as the leading composer of his generation. His *X: The Life and Times of Malcolm X* played to sold out audiences at the New York City Opera in 1986 and was later recorded and distributed on Gramavision Records, earning a Grammy nomination. Davis graduated from Yale University despite having to commute to New York venues as a player. His group Episteme, which he describes below as "a very sophisticated group of musicians," brought him into contact with New York avant-garde players and forces, such as Anthony Braxton and Leo Smith. Anthony Davis has been commissioned and performed by such groups as the American Music Theater Festival and the Houston, San Francisco, and Kansas City Symphonies. In addition to three successful operas *(X, Under the Double Moon,* and *Tania),* he received a commission for his *Amistad* from the Lyric Opera of Chicago. Davis has taught at Yale, Cornell, and Harvard University. Presently, Mr. Davis teaches at the University of California at San Diego.

I started on piano. My parents lived in New York City, but I was born in Paterson, New Jersey, where my grandfather was a physician. My family lived in New York till I was about four, and then they moved to Princeton, New Jersey. At Princeton I really started playing classical piano. I started studying in the first or second grade. I had heard my father play piano, and I started playing things that he played, by ear. Because of my interest, my parents decided to give me piano lessons. I started lessons at this really nice school called the Francis Clarke School. I think I was beginning to think of being a composer when I was fifteen. I started composing some when I was little, because at the Clark School you are required to do a recital every month, and we had to do one piece that was our own.

I didn't compose again, until I was, I guess, going into tenth grade, and it was simultaneous with an interest in improvisation. I started to improvise and compose; it was just one and the same process to me. I was inspired by Thelonious Monk recordings that were given to my parents. When I was in tenth grade, my family went to Italy for a year, because my father received a Fulbright. When I was in Italy I really began to play, to play jazz and also to experiment with my own compositions. I may not have written down what I played, but they were still compositions, or more accurately "remembered improvisations" that had the structure and form of written compositions.

This happened to coincide with my self-discovery as a black person—you know, what it meant to be black—we are talking about the late 1960s. After Princeton, my father taught at Penn State University, and we lived in State College, Pennsylvania. I think my brother and I were the only blacks in the junior high. We felt quite isolated, but at the same time that was a motivating factor for me. I felt I was different, and I didn't feel at all inferior or in any way inadequate because I was different. I think it was more and more the reverse. But I also had to be armed with knowledge of my culture and of who I was.

I always had experiences with classical music. I loved classical music. I loved Chopin, Beethoven, and Mozart. I liked Stravinsky, and I was playing Prokofiev and a lot of other Russian composers, like Rachmaninoff. So that was part of my experience. At that point I was around mostly classical musicians, although I knew of Billy Taylor. Billy Taylor lived in our apartment building in New York. I think I learned more from playing with my peers and developing my own music with my peers. We were all going through the same process. Later, when I was in New Haven, Connecticut, at Yale University, I met Leo Smith [black American improvisational composer], who was very important to me.

At Yale, I was originally a philosophy major; I wasn't a music major until my last year. The reason I went to Yale is interesting. I went there because of the philosophy department and also because Mel Powell [a composer] recommended it. He had been at my parents' house when I was away at school, and he had suggested it. When they told him that I was interested in jazz and composing, he said I should come to Yale.

I was already performing with my own group. We were playing concerts at other colleges and regular concerts in New Haven. I played with quite a sophisticated group of musicians. When I was at Yale people like George Lewis [trombonist], Gerry Hemingway [drummer], and Mark Dresser [bassist] were in New Haven. Through Leo Smith I met a lot of people from the AACM [Association for the Advancement of Creative Musicians], like Anthony Braxton and Leroy Jenkins [black American improvisational composers]. Also, even before I graduated I was going to New York to play concerts and gigs. I was playing there with Rasheed Ali [drummer] and with other people.

Well, my undergraduate career was extended; I took six years to get through Yale. I left school for a while, when the draft ended, to work on music. I was consumed with working on my music, and I spent a lot of time playing in New York. I was even starting to make records with other artists and touring. Then I returned to get my degree. At this point, I really concentrated on music, because I had decided that I wanted to be a music major. After I graduated in 1975, I stayed in New Haven for two years teaching at a school called the Educational Center for the Arts. Again there was a great group of musicians, who were all teaching at the school and playing together, and we did a series of concerts. It was an ideal situation, because then I could go into New York whenever I wanted to do concerts. Through Leo Smith I was able to meet many prominent figures in the avant-garde scene.

I guess that my philosophy of music is that I don't believe in pandering. I'm not an entertainer; I don't create music for mere entertainment. I'm creating art, and therefore I'm willing to accept that not everyone is going to like my music. I understand that not everyone is going to embrace my aesthetic. On the other hand, I feel that there is something in "great music" that can appeal to a large group of people. There has to be something visceral, in a sense, about the music, something that interests you and makes you look further, makes you look underneath. That is something you learn from the great composers like Ellington or Wagner. I think that was a great lesson to be learned, especially as an opera composer. Opera has to exist on so many levels of cognition, levels of understanding—how people relate to the voice and the melody, how people relate to the dramatic structure, and deeper levels that relate to the harmonic medium or subliminal messages, etc. I love the idea of layers of complexity. They can be underlying, they may not be perceived by the listener right away, but they are perceptible to me and therefore eventually to others.

I don't think we should assume that young audiences are alienated from modern music. We shouldn't make assumptions about what young, fresh ears can comprehend. Young people who have never been exposed to my music before haven't learned that they aren't supposed to like it. The negative message—and I think of it as negative message—is that there is a canon of serious music, which is white and European. I think that black people don't feel they are supposed to participate. They don't feel that they're allowed to think that something else has as much validity; that's a form of self-denial and self-destruction. It's very important that we expose people to music at a young age before they have been made to feel prejudice, in the ways young classical musicians become prejudiced against improvisations, or against modern music, or to think, "That's too weird." Institutionalized learning attempts to make twentieth-century music the last subject taught. A student is required to digest the whole European musical tradition before they ever hear of Schoenberg, Stravinsky, or even Ellington. Students should be exposed, from the beginning, to twentieth-century music, so it is no longer alien.

Unfortunately, programming in Black History Month is always tokenism. The fact that there are opportunities for African American artists finally to have music played and have some exposure is always good, but the fact that these opportunities are isolated ghettoizes the music. I hope that the music will be taken seriously for what it is and what it means. We are composers and musicians, not civil servants. We're not here as tokens to relieve the political pressures on white cultural institutions; that's not our function. There is a lot of work to be done. I love working with children for example. I love that aspect of it. Every composer needs the love and commitment of our musical institutions, and that battle will take over time.

We as African Americans offer a new aesthetic of music; that is why our music is so threatening. We've challenged the primacy of the European musical tradition. It takes so long for those institutions or individuals within it to accept us as creative individuals. I think that's the main thing, an ultimate goal—to accept the difference, the new aesthetic of music. Being black provides me more opportunities, but it brings me more resistance. It's always a trade-off. There are opportunities, but if it's one month out of the year, what does that mean?

Q: What do you consider to be the role of the artist in society?

A: We have to be involved in making a difference. It's self preservation; if we don't, we'll be irrelevant. We have to be involved in transforming our society, working with children of all ages, exposing them to music, teaching them a political consciousness in order to protect the whole artistic world. We must have a political consciousness that looks at what's going on that affects all African Americans. There has to be an awareness, a realization, that we do necessarily have a leadership role in all this.

Q: Do you think popular culture is destructive?

A: No, I think that art reflects society. It is important that we see the picture, even though there is good reason not to like that picture, with its rage and frustration. I wish it didn't have certain manifestations, I wish it wasn't demeaning to women. But I sense the passion. It isn't edited, but it's necessary, and I think it may be necessary if we are to get to the next level. Eventually there will be someone who does something deeper. There were poets in the early sixties who did black rage poems, and some of those poems weren't very good. But emerging out of that you have poets like Amari Baraka, for example, who is very powerful and writes beautiful work. You can't assume that something's an artistic dead end. If something speaks to a generation, we must look at it. We can't just say, "Well, that's not good for them." We have to understand it first and also realize that it evolves.

I would say right away that the most important African American composers are Ellington and Monk. I still think that in historical terms, to divorce concert music traditions from jazz tradition and the jazz composer is to cut off the heart of the music. Willie Ruff, for example, had this concept of the "conservatory without walls." He brought in Ellington, Mingus, Willie "The Lion" Smith, Ray Brown, and even Dizzy Gillespie to become fellows of this school. But I think that this institution was not thought of as seriously challenging to the European canon. But my own feeling is that Ellington and Monk, in the first half of the twentieth century, were probably two of the most important American composers—period, without qualification.

Ellington's contribution was profound. His conception of the creative orchestra, the sense of working and developing extended forms, employing improvisation, the idea of expanding and synthesizing all the elements of jazz, merged in the twenties and thirties into a completely new idea. So I think Ellington is still our seminal composer. I sometimes think that all this categorization is ridiculous. I was aware of William Grant Still, but I never thought he was as important as Ellington or Monk or Mingus, or the whole jazz tradition. I always felt that—not to belittle William Grant Still—Ellington had much more to do with what constitutes our "original voice." I think that the basis of American classical music is Afro-American music, I really do. I think that it is what makes our music unique, what makes it different, what differentiates us from the European concepts. That has always been very important to me. There's been a lot of resistance because of this realization. We are in a cultural war to define an American aesthetic. The jazz revolution has affected every corner of America music. Every American composer, white or black, has to define his or her music in relation to the African American tradition.

Q: What is your view of the notion of white composers using traditional black materials and exploiting them?

A: Using and exploiting traditional black materials is a kind of colonialism—the idea of looking at us as "raw material," to be exploited for their "higher plane" of activity. [Here Mr. Davis is referring to the Leonard Bernstein race-absorption thesis. See chapter 1.]

Gershwin and Bernstein were not racists. They were involved and engaged, and they realized that this music has a tremendous power. Whether they could accept that power and all the implications of that power is another thing. They probably couldn't, because the black cultural materials spoke to their identity.

Q: What direction do you believe contemporary music will take in the twenty-first century?

A: I think Don Byron [jazz clarinetist, composer] is very exciting as a musician. I think there's a lot of interesting music being done. I've always felt James Newton was very gifted. George Lewis has done a lot of important experimentation with computers. He definitely is an innovator.

I hope to be part of that innovation. In my operas we'll see a transformation of the traditional orchestra over time. There will be more players who are improvisers incorporated into the orchestra. I suggested to the Detroit Symphony that if they are really serious about having a jazz orchestra for kids, they should hire real jazz musicians as integral parts of their orchestra.

That kind of experience is very important so that the musicians can really deal with the pieces that will soon be created. They may involve techniques and skills that are not normally taught in the classical world. But I think that more and more, on the conservatory level, jazz has to be part of the education process from the beginning. When music is taught, improvisation should be taught too. Improvisation can be used as a tool in education, particularly in the conservatory level. There should be no musicians who graduate from conservatory who can not play blues. In our country, there should not be a musician who graduates from a conservatory unaware of the American traditions. That would be like going to the Paris Conservatory and never listening to Debussy or Ravel. That wouldn't happen. Only in America would that happen.

My goal is to be the American composer who helps to define opera for the next century, to give opera its unique American voice, and leave a legacy of works that do that. I also hope to have an influence on other composers who want to work in that direction. I want to bring the aesthetic of the improviser into the orchestra, whether as the informing aesthetic of my musical composition or as musicians brought into the ensemble. I am looking forward to the day when aesthetic takes root within the orchestra, the way it took root in the creative orchestras in the '30s and the '20s.

Donal Fox

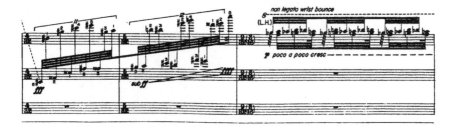

Donal Fox, born in 1952, stands out as one of the leading avant-gardists of his generation. A virtuoso pianist as well as a conductor, Donal's work primarily focuses on the power of improvisational properties, devices, and free association, and the dense complexities of strict contemporary composition systems. Comfortable in many idioms, from Western classical periods to blues and be-bop, he is considered a New Age eclectic composer, fusing several styles. He is a native of Boston, and his early teachers included T. J. Anderson and Gunther Schuller. Mr. Fox has several recordings to his credit (New World Records, Evidence, Music and Arts Wergo). Trained at both the New England Conservatory and Berklee School of Music, at seventeen Fox received a scholarship to study at the prestigious Tanglewood Music Center, later receiving a commission from the Fromm Foundation. Fox has worked with such artists as Oliver Lake, David Murray, Billy Pierce, and William Brown, and the poet Quincy Troupe. Fox was commissioned, as the first black composer in residence with the St. Louis Symphony, to do improvisations with the orchestra as soloist/composer, and to write a piano concerto for the orchestra. Fox went on to produce several works on his home soil of Boston, including the ballet *Gone City,* with the Boston Ballet. As a concert pianist, he premiered Anthony Kelley's *Piano Concerto* with the Richmond Symphony (1999). Other collaborations have been with Boston's Dinosaur Annex, Musica Viva, and the Boston Symphony's New Music Ensemble Collage. Mr. Fox, a 1997 Guggenheim recipient and 1998 Bogliasco Foundation fellow, lives and works in Boston.

I was born in Boston. My father's first degree was in music composition at Boston University before he went into physics, so at home there was always music paper around and certainly recordings. One of the recordings I used to like to play as a kid was [Stravinsky's] *Rite of Spring.* They said I used to steal the record and put it on my little record player to play. And there was Bartók's string quartets, and there was Charlie Parker, and Miles Davis's *Birth of Cool.* That's the music that was in the house, so early on I was getting these combinations of sounds.

Piano was my principal instrument early on. At six years of age, my father had a friend, and they set up an exchange program. My father taught his son recorder and flute, and in return, his friend taught me beginner piano. Then I immediately went on to more formalized lessons with Edna Nitkin, who I found out later had competed with Leonard Bernstein in a piano competition here, when Lenny was in high school. She won. Edna Nitkin. I saw her a few years ago. She's in the Bernstein autobiography. So I had her those early years up

until ten years of age, and then I studied with Jeanette Giguere, who was a teacher at the New England Conservatory of Music. I had her both in the Prep [Preparatory] Department and in private lessons and studied with her until I was fifteen. She was a French Romantic and really got me into the whole thing of touch and sound coordination. She gave me the fundamental basics, and then I was able to take it on my own, even though I periodically saw her for a few years up until I was twenty. I think hearing Miles and Parker, Stravinsky, and Bartók definitely imprinted upon me the need to create something—to make music.

My craft—or, the craft that is usually used in composition—is primarily from the European tradition. We have to remember that at this point it's a blending of all these cultures. You can't keep separating and creating these vacuums of thinking that jazz is over in this corner, and classical is in the other. For example, the saxophone is French; African Americans took that and did something with it that they didn't dream of over in Europe, and then brought it back. The Rolling Stones took the Motown sound and went back. So there's this blending. The Europeans have this strong history, but one school of American composition will say, "Well, we have John Knowles Paine and Charles Ives." But I am now into the cliché phrase that we hear all of the time, that is that America's classical music is jazz. I think that is true. Jazz is our real creative source, in the sense of giving something to the world that didn't exist elsewhere.

When we say the word "jazz," just like we say "classical composer," people have stereotyped images. You say "classical composer," and they think "Oh, he's got that serious, boring music," or however they want to think of it; "I'm going to have to go sit down in my chair and listen." You say "jazz," and they think—unfortunately a lot of people say—"Oh, the club with smoke, and there are some drugs in the background." But those are the extreme stereotypes. When I think of jazz or African American music, as in the spirituals or blues, I think of the spirit of it. If you live in America, you have embodied that experience, and it doesn't matter what your nationality may be. But if you are brought up as an African American, there are other things that come with it, the social elements that we experience that a white American doesn't. If you can follow and express that through musical means, I think you are on the track. In the study of European composition, I think, there's another spirituality. What I like to do is find the connections between the spirit of Beethoven and the spirit of Monk. What is that essence that I like about Monk, that I like about Bartók, that I like about Beethoven, that I like about Bach. that I like about Charlie Parker? There is something there that has to do with that creative element, that center. That is what I try to plug into.

What strongly influenced me as a composer in the sense of my craft and studying scores was initially European—I mean, Bach, Mozart, Beethoven, whom I still adore. Then we get into the twentieth century; Stravinsky, Bartók, and Penderecki had a great effect upon me. Penderecki was a Polish composer who did a lot of experimentation with Don Cherry [trumpeter] and Ornette Coleman in the 1960s; you had free composition and free jazz meeting each other. I am less fond of the Americana-type composers. I respect the things Aaron Copland has done, but most of it, to me, doesn't have the weight of the great Europeans. I mean, I want quality no matter where it comes from. Just because Roy Harris and David Diamond [composers] are American doesn't mean I have to jump up and down about them. I would definitely want to go to Mingus and Ellington in terms of originality.

Q: Who do you consider to be the quintessential American composers?

A: Maybe Charles Ives, because I need the structure. I don't think Duke Ellington; it's not necessarily his fault, per se. There are a whole bunch of reasons—social climate, the three-minute limitations of 78 rpm records, not having the venues, not being offered enough commission money, you know. Beethoven is about structure and emotion. Ives is working with structure. Duke has the spirit, but the structure is not substantial enough for me. Mingus has got more, but I don't think there has been an African American composer who is steeped in the tradition of African American music but combined that with European structures of larger forms. Yes, we are getting closer now; I think the new generation is starting to do that. But the older generation was still sort of split.

Q: How does music function in your mind?

A: There is an abstract place that works purely with the materials I have at hand. They have no intrinsic properties, and they have their own logical development. I don't particularly put any social order or hierarchy on it. Then there is the awareness of the world around me. I have been writing for ballet. There is a piece, *Gone City,* that became very sociopolitical, not in the collaboration with the choreographers but in the context of the piece, what was running it. A piece that includes improvisation that I'm performing in front of an audience creates a lot of impact. If you put me in a room and say, "Here are some notes, and here are some chords," I tend to get into what those notes or chords mean and try to find a link to my emotional being. That may conjure up a narrative of anger over Bosnia, or celebration of Russia, but it's not like I go to that source first, to the larger political arena, and go, "Aha, I hear a melody."

Q: How would you deal with cultural illiteracy in this country?

A: Lack of cultural literacy? You have literacy in the sense of language; that's waning. You have cultural illiteracy that includes the arts, and then there is musical illiteracy. The simple answer is education, reach the young generation early and showing how culture is important to overall intellectual development and emotional development. There is no question that in my early days, besides what I had at home, which was a very important element, I had access to music schools. They supported the relationship with my teachers who worked in the school system and the conservatory. I remember playing French horn in the little school band when I was in the sixth grade or something; I had a friend, and it so happened that his father played the violin and my friend played bassoon. So there is this relationship between your cultural connection and your social environment that makes it okay to do cultural activities. If you are in a world that is very narrow, where the focus is to make money or whatever the "now" thing is, you miss out in a lot of other areas.

I always equate it to food, in a very simplistic way. We all need to eat. It's true by eating white rice and black-eyed peas with some beverage you will make it for a long time, but if that is all you have, it is kind of limiting. If you never had gourmet Italian, some calamari dipped in a fresh pasta sauce with fresh basil right off the vine, you have no reference point. I guess it is how we create these reference points. People need to realize there are things other than the narrow little circles they are walking in. But that comes back to education.

Q: What's your view of Black History Month celebrations?

A: I have the same mixed feeling that women do. You go up to a woman composer or a woman saxophone player in jazz or something, and you say, "Oh you play sax, that's great. Have you heard of that all-woman jazz band in New York?" Do they jump up and down? They go, "Hey, man I can play, and I can play with anybody." They are a little defensive, because you immediately categorize. "Hey, you can play in that all-woman's jazz band, but you can't play in the vanguard with the guys, can you?" It's an assumption. It is the same thing with African American composers in Black History Month. "Hey, that's great, you're a composer, Mr. Banfield. So listen, we've got a program in February." It's the same thing. "Wait a minute, that's all I am to you?" Does this help? Maybe it did when there was no other opportunity at all, when there was no other visibility. I mean, you take what you can get, right? I think we are a little more sophisticated now. We shouldn't settle for that.

Q: What do you see as the commonalties within European and jazz music?

A: Theoretically, I think you can easily just take up the music and see the musical connections. I mean, you could take the angularity of the Beethoven line and take the angularity of Monk. Parker loved Bach. A lot of the lines that Parker started using came out of Stravinsky's *Firebird Suite*. People have been borrowing for years. Musicians don't live in a vacuum, you know; that is something the critics and groupies do, people who have territories to keep. "We're jazz, man, so we're cool. We don't dig your thing, man, we just live here in a vacuum." Those are the people who aren't making the art. The people who were making the music—Mingus or Duke or Parker or Monk—were looking at all of the sources they had at the time. Look at Henry Threadgill; you see Ravel on his piano. He doesn't cover it up and think that's not hip.

What are the sources? In relation to the creative spirit, we are not reinventing the wheel. There are twelve notes, and we can take any European music, we can take Ravel or Debussy, and I can show you harmonies that Stravinsky just lifted off the page and then passed through his rhythmical filter, changed them. Black music went over to Europe and affected the French. Ravel came here and influenced music later in his life, but earlier—we are talking about 1905—he was writing pieces with extensions on the seventh chord. He didn't use them in the way that African Americans use the extension, but we have extensions. There is the similarity. We look at Beethoven's rhythms and the punctuation and the angularity and the percussiveness; then look at Monk's angularity. Look at the wit of Stravinsky, and look at the wit in Monk. We are in the same parameter.

Q: Let's talk about your process of composition.

A: Well, it has changed. In earlier things like *Dialectics*—I say "earlier," because it comes from a different gestation period—it was probably more linear. It came from cells. I had these little motifs, and I would have a sketch of a motif there—a little building block there, building block C, D, and F—and I would see how they could link up in all the various parameters. Then I would start building them in a contrapuntal way—not in the sense of note against note, or point against point, in the Bachian sense, but entire textures, polyrhythmical concepts, and polyharmonic concepts. In that period of composition, I was not as interested in starting with clear harmonic cells; the sounds were created out of the textures. I liked a sound, and I would move it around. I might analyze what that sound was, to manipulate it further.

Now, I am shifting more and more into finding a harmonic rhythm, some common language that existed for all the composers before us and that gave tremendous foundations for developing the music. What I really enjoy doing right now is taking any score or any composer and seeing how pure composers manipulate the harmony, for example. There is Ravel's "Sonatine," where he uses the diminished triad. Take that same diminished triad, take it out of the composer's score. Take that diminished triad out of Brahms. Take the same diminished triad out of someone else's score. It is amazing what we find in the style of the composers, how they manipulate the harmonic language in the sense of voicing the harmony, the vertical placement of it, the color and texture of it. That's more where I'm at than the cells and chord building. I still have the contrapuntal techniques, but I'm really taking on a simple harmony.

Take a chord, let's say it was C-seven with a sharp eleventh on it—right, a sharp nine, a flat nine. We can hear that one chord and say, "Let's write one minute of music on that one chord." To me, that's what a composer is about, it is the power of imagination. Beethoven ended the entire last movement of the *Appassionata Sonata* on one harmony. Powerful. Can we just take the triad and have the same power that he had at the end of that sonata? Or the simple harmonic sequence at the end of the *Moonlight Sonata?* Or the simple A-minor triad using the slow movement of the *Seventh Symphony* of Beethoven? That's the power of the imagination. That's what I'm really trying to say. What imagination do I really have? How much power do I really have? I should be able to take the simplest elements and make profound statements.

One approach would be to take the simplest elements and not try to be "original," just feel that my voice is there. I would create melodies that are triads and other simple seventh chords and not worry about it. In the old days, I would say, "Oh, no, I can't use those simple elements. That's cheating." I would fret about it and say, "I can't do the commission." The other approach is, "Okay, I'm going to create an ensemble in which I participate as a performer, and I want to create in 'real time,' at the moment." I don't want to commit myself to the whole melodies. I want to have sketches of melodies; we are going to improvise around them so that the music can keep evolving. That is probably close to what I am doing right now.

Q: What did you attempt to do with the *Dialectics for Two Pianos* [works by Andersen, Baker, Fox, Wilson]? Did it achieve in recorded form what you wanted it to?

A: The recording could be better, you know how that goes. Each performance could be better. But the concept of the piece is what I wanted. What's interesting about *Dialectics* is that when people get wind of the fact that there's some improvisatory elements on the recording, they go, "Oh, that's the improvised piece, *Dialectics.*" But, of course, the piece is completely notated. So the sense of wildness and abandonment was actually completely controlled in the composition. That's one area.

The other was, which is why I love that way of writing, is its control—which in fact I think I went overboard with in a way—in getting every little detail. "Okay, you'll go 'ah,' in this way, and you will play this rhythm that way." There was so much information that the performer almost gets uptight trying to get it down. But I was trying to capture all these little twists and events that happen in vocalization when you get excited, you know, when you are jamming in the contemporary texture or fabric.

I have abandoned the esthetic of the academic, institutionalized European composer—Elliot Carter, one of the senior members, or Milton Babbitt [composers] for example. They tend to be isolated from the social musical fabric of America, particularly the African American experience. I found that I could sit down with very competent, totally trained musicians from both the classical and jazz worlds and improvise in an ensemble setting music as complex as, and at times more interesting than, all that music which is elaborately notated. So I began questioning this overly cerebral, left-hemispheric control over materials, which is almost a justification for this type of art. For me, music is sound, and if it is not happening as a sound source, I don't care if you have a fancy score or no score. It either moves people or it doesn't.

Q: Do you think an artist has any role in shaping society or commenting on society?

A: Definitely, rap artists come out of the fabric of our society. There is anger there, and there is anger in the urban black community. Rap represents elements that we may not be fond of, but they are there, and the rappers have commercial access. How they affect the next generation, how seriously young kids listen to the words of rap and what it does to the culture, I'm not as clear about; that is more of a sociological question. Musically, rap is evolving. You have this hip-hop or hip-bop, all these different layers keep changing. It is going overseas. US3, that group from England, comes back to the United States with musical lines taken from all those various Blue Note recordings; that raises the ante. It raises the sophistication of what you use when you borrow material and how you interact with the musical elements. So with jazz, you get Pharaoh Sanders [saxophonist], Donald Bird playing with some rap groups on this AIDS benefit video; I see something happening here that can be very important. Actually, there is something else as well. There's a producer, Hal Willner, who did something for Columbia. He took Mingus's music and all these various musicians from New York, and he had someone read from Mingus's autobiography, *Beneath the Underdog.* This is rap—Mingus was rapping. This stuff has all been there. It is all in the air, it's not like totally inventing something. It is how you put it together.

Q: Has ethnicity been a disadvantage to you as a black composer?

A: For me, it is about respect. Agents in Europe respect the black musician/creator. So I have no problem saying proudly, "I'm an African American who plays concert music and jazz and I can come over with a jazz band, I can come over and do my compositions." They say, "That's great." There's respect. If I am respected as a human being, and if included in that respect is the distinction that I am an African American, then, great. It is in America, which is full of racism, that they want to compartmentalize black artists. The euphemism is, "We don't necessarily think you are as good as your white counterparts." That is when I start rebelling. I mean, I am a human being, and my name is Donal Fox, and on the phone you probably can't tell my background. The reason you can't tell is because you have stereotypes about what you think black people should talk like. I'm not falling into your trap. If you have a problem when you see me, then I know the reality, and we start over again. But I'm not going to feed into that racism that way. So—do you respect me as a human being? Do you respect me as a composer, as a musician? If you pass those tests, I am willing to go along with you. If I smell that you are using me as a symbol to appease the racist elements in your canon, I say "no deal."

Q: Did you have models—that is, black composers—growing up?

A: Was I aware of black American composers per se? Not really—but then, I have always been somewhat "colorblind"; I am the product of a mixed marriage. I have a Panamanian mother and Jewish father. I listen to the music of the composers I like. I mentioned Stravinsky, a Russian; Bartók, a Polish Hungarian; Bach, a German. I didn't think white or black or red or brown, I was thinking the style of music and only a little about the nationality.

I loved Miles. I didn't immediately love Miles because he was black. I love Miles because I love the sound. I think a lot of those pressures of ethnicity and where you fall in those categories come from society. I got older and was forced to start to pick: "Are you a black man?" "Which side are you on, politically?" "Are you a composer, or are you a black composer?" Those are the outside sources. Inside I was thinking, "I'm a composer."

When I started studying with T. J. Anderson, I was proud of him, because here was a black man doing what I'm doing. There is pride in seeing somebody else who is successful. But I didn't immediately feel that there was this whole other category I had to join. Once I was accepted through my craft, I didn't feel that people judged me other than on my craft. Then there is the other layer, which is the audience. That is the class layer. That is where I became aware that black people, in general, don't attend art music performances. They are usually into pop music or jazz. But even with jazz, in some clubs you notice there are usually Asians or upper-class whites. There is not a large black audience there. Contemporary classical music, forget it. For example, I would say to my neighbors that I was having something done at Tanglewood [in western Massachusetts], that I was having something done over here at Jordan Hall [in Boston], and they would say, "Oh, that's nice." But they were not going to show up. I felt isolated from my own people. Then I said, "I'm playing at the Regatta Bar [in the Charles Hotel, Boston]. You can come down, have a drink. It's a jazz club." Half the neighborhood came.

How do I connect with my people through the music? It has a lot to do with class and an environment that makes people feel safe. Symphony Hall [Boston] has always said, "We don't want you." It's not that they don't want to hear my music. This is why I have become interested in combining my compositional process with performing. For example, I can go to a jazz club and invite people, and they feel safe to come; they can have a drink and not feel too much pressure, and the music is geared to them. So even though I do sophisticated things musically in that environment, I'm communicating. In a concert hall setting, it is a lot harder to get people to feel comfortable if they are wondering if they really should be there.

It gets complicated, because you are dealing with an institution that is modeled after the European institutions and that at the turn of the century embraced this high culture from Europe and said, "We want to be part of that." The elite of America, Brahmins, people who had some wealth. said, "Let's create an orchestra." The New York Philharmonic Society in New York, and so forth, said, "Let's bring this great music from Europe over for our elite listening audiences." That is why we still have this sense that the symphony and Lincoln Center is not really modeled for the average American. It is modeled for some elite group. There is some historical truth to that. In other words, if you come in just as a composer, no matter what your nationality, they're already suspicious, because it is new music, not part of the "great works" of art. You get that hassle, anyway.

When you come in as an African American composer or Hispanic, or whatever, there is this whole other race issue that says, "Well, you black people in this country, now, your history is about slavery." I'm exaggerating about how the mind works, but the connection is, "You do your sports, and you have your pop Motown stuff, but what do you have to do with our high art?" Then I have to deal with proving myself. Usually I try not to get too caught up in that, but I have found that I use the language that the orchestral musician is familiar with better than they do. Then I say, "I know your language, now you have to learn mine." I have found that this is the most powerful way. For me just to say, "I'm not going to care about your language," will reinforce their attitude—"You see, you don't know our thing, so you can't speak unless you have that black dialect." Then you come in and say, "I think the issue here is incontrovertible and we should work dialectically on certain areas" but "Yo, here is what I really want to talk about, motherfucker." You see? That to me is the power.

Q: Where do you see contemporary American music headed?

A: Generally, we definitely have more cross-pollination. That is clearly happening. We have Brian Eno and Phillip Glass hanging together, and we have Paul McCartney writing a piece to perform at a London Symphony. Clearly, jazz has influenced many American composers, Copland and others, and European composers. There are more and more jazz composers writing for big band and writing for orchestra, getting commissions and Meet the Composers grants. I see those two styles of music and the bridge between them; they are getting closer and closer together. Anthony Davis is an example, blending his background of free jazz with classical compositional techniques and his interest in opera. The more that happens, the more and more successful hybrids there are. Eventually, it is not even a hybrid, it's just going to be a musician who really has this knowledge that is unique in America.

The pop element is trickier, because that is so connected to a commercial element, to the bottom line. I don't know the long-range influences. Some things of value are discovered in the overlay of rhythms in pop music, but because it is driven so much by the market, the musicians who get involved tend to downplay their artistic side; they want to have a hit. In jazz and in concert music, even though jazz does exist in the marketplace, in a marginal way, it also has a very strong artistic base. Many jazz musicians who work and decide things—even Mingus, who struggled his whole life to survive—make decisions primarily artistically. When you make a pop record, you are talking about what is radio friendly before you even begin writing the music.

Q: Are you engaged in any new aesthetic movements? If you are not, do you foresee anything coming in terms of composition process? Twelve-tone rap?

A: I've abandoned all those systems, because if I have a legacy, something you leave for your family or the next generation, it is the quality of the music. To go back to studying harmony of various composers from the past, the compositional materials used by these creators and how they manipulate their materials, the point is the power of their imagination and the quality of their solutions, the emotional impact of those decisions and how it affects the sound and how it affects the listener. If you get to that level, I don't care what elements you are using.

The problem with twelve-tone—maybe there are some intrinsic limitations to twelve-tone, one could probably argue that—I think it has to do with the limitations of the composers who have used it so far. Why limit yourself to twelve-tone? Whatever element you want to take, any of those elements can be used separately or together. It is how we use them and what listeners are left with as an impression or imprint. Have we created an artistic world that is worth our listeners' time? I'm not going to judge that. I listen to Erik Satie [French composer and pianist] and I think "That's great, that little world he made." On the other hand, I can hear a complicated dissonant piece and realize that I can follow that because I am a trained musician. I know the average audience probably can't. But I don't say that is not valuable.

I am now experimenting with whether I can re-create that angularity or spirit that I feel in some of these more complicated dissonant relationships, but with simpler means, so that I can bring the audience on a journey. Now, in performance, I have been doing that with the jazz audiences; I'll play a pretty ballad like "My Funny Valentine," but without the melody, or I'll play it with unusual harmonic voicings. Because they are familiar with the song and they see the title, there is a certain comfort zone, and I can push it a bit. Then I'll play one of my pieces that really pushes the envelope. Now, if I sat down and started with that piece, they wouldn't have a reference point. They wouldn't trust me. I say in performance, "I know your language, and I have done something that you are familiar with. You are happy now; and that was a pretty piece, and you applaud and you smile. Now I'll give you something that you have to stretch and push a little bit for." The audience goes, "Well, he is a nice guy, and he played 'My Funny Valentine,' so we had better listen to his 'Demon,' because maybe there is something we should learn." That is what I am trying to do.

Q: What is the most shocking or stirring news event or media thing that has compelled you, or pulled you, to respond musically?

A: I work as an abstract composer, which means that my life is entwined. We have to have a life in order to be a creator, because we are filtering all these emotions, and somehow they come out musically. My weapon for defining who I am in the world is music. I don't know if it is a one-to-one thing; I don't look at the horrors going on in Bosnia and the United Nations and immediately go to the keyboard and go "Aha." But all those feelings and all that struggle and pain in a world that can't seem to find peace, and that nationalistic strife and manipulation of power through economic means, and the injustices that we can speak of—all that affects me and urges me to create beauty. I am now interested in creating beauty, whereas before I was expressing all that tension and anxiety.

Q: What do you think of Anthony Davis's work?

A: I respect him. I look forward to what he is going to create. He is a force. It's funny, you come in and you see Bach on my keyboard. Bach is unbelievable. That is contemporary to me; Bach is not something historical. It's alive. I play Scarlatti, and then I go to Mingus's "Porkpie Hat" and don't miss a beat. The audience doesn't miss a beat. Scarlatti is now.

But the question right now is, who would I go out and pay money to see? It is not so much the names of the people as it is the energy and creative force behind the music. I saw young Roy Hargrove [trumpeter] with his new quintet. He's got a new bass player who I know used to play at Wally's [a Boston club]. He's nineteen. He's got this drummer who is eighteen. The energy in that group! It wasn't that they created new music or anything like that. The total swing, the total energy of that thing had my hair standing up on my head. It was just an intensity and a focus. I saw Roy four years ago. He was rehashing be-bop, and I said "I don't want to deal with this." But now something is happening there.

In hip-hop, I haven't kept up with all the names, but occasionally I put the radio on to hear what is going on. I am curious to see how the hip-hop thing develops. I have done stuff with Quincy Troupe, the poet, and I am interested in creating a compositional fabric where hip-hop could be included. The thing with text and words, though, is that they can be narrowing. Since I work as an abstract composer, sometimes text really defines what the message is so concretely that it doesn't leave much room for me or the listener to interpret outside of the text. Musicians that have been proven over time—Gyorgy Ligeti and Krzysztof Penderecki—to me are still creative forces, even though I don't try to emulate them per se. Ligeti is a really strong, independent personality. Monk is inspirational to me too, the way Bach is.

I've transcribed most of Monk's stuff; I was just looking at "Rooty Tootie," the big-band version and the original version, from the *San Francisco Trio* recording. On that same recording I was studying "Think of One" and comparing it to the *Criss-Cross* recording and to all his other versions of "Think of One." I get a lot of inspiration from Monk's evolving interpretations. I am less influenced by Duke Ellington, for example. I know the classic pieces. He is prolific, and he is a force in America, but I don't put on a Duke Ellington record that often. Monk will turn me on, Mingus can turn me on, or Miles. Miles is creative, not in the sense of a composer, but of his sound texture and his spirit. *Kind of Blue* is a place, a place that sounds fresh. Just listen to the way he thinks in his trumpet.

To be honest, Bach, Beethoven, Scarlatti, Miles, Monk, Mingus, Charlie Parker, any of the new forces that deal with those spiritual worlds excite me. If you take classic pieces of this century, such as by Ravel or a Stravinsky, I am excited when I dissect them. There are very few contemporary classical composers that really excite me, other than the fact that my training and my craft allows me to go and listen attentively and be excited in the sense of understanding what is going on, in a purely technical way. The visceral experience that I have when I listen to Bach's *B-minor Mass* really comes to mind. At the end of my time, will I have written music that has an enduring legacy? Can I write music that has the power of the Mozart *Requiem,* that has that enduring spiritually? I don't know. I'm not sure that I can accomplish that, but I am striving for it.

If you are writing a lot of symphonies, you are connected to the symphonic world. That is a clear category. But you see what I mean about the categories? I think I am in a marginal category. I am documented both as a classically trained musician and an improviser. That already confuses people. I have European and African American interests. I have recordings out there where I'm playing with some of the key contemporary jazz artists, and then you flip over in the store's computer and you see me over there in contemporary classical stuff. I don't know where that fits in the continuum. I am not even worrying about it any more. I used to worry about it and say "I want to be in this or that category." If I write six string quartets, I thought, maybe the music historians will connect them with Bartók's six and then with Beethoven's late quartets. Now I've left that and decided to just create some music and keep my creative forces connected. That's what holds me and my music together. The categories are going to fall where they fall. I am not going to keep spending time trying to be clearly marked as to what those categories are.

The greatest achievement would be to leave music that has value to my generation and the generations after me. I want it to have some educational, emotional value other than to my immediate world. If that value is substantial enough, then of course, it would be embedded in history, because each generation wants to review the value of that work. I don't have this false immortality thing anymore; the important recognition is the respect of my peers. Now, there is material recognition too, that is part of the way the world is set up, but credibility and respect are key factors. If I can reach my contemporary audiences without compromise and hear that applause or hear that curiosity regarding what I am going to do next, I will have some satisfaction. I hope that in the twilight years of my life there will be a body of work that has real meaning outside of the university.

Jonathan Holland

Jonathan Holland, born in 1974, a native of Flint, Michigan, stands out as one of the youngest American composers to have received such unprecedented success in major symphony performances. A graduate of the Curtis Institute of Music and a student of Ned Rorem and Bernard Rands, he has had works performed and commissioned by the Atlanta, Baltimore, Detroit, Minnesota, National, Philadelphia, St. Louis, Chicago Civic, and Plymouth Music Series orchestras. His *Martha's Waltz* was chosen by the Detroit Symphony's director, Neeme Jarvi, to be performed on its European tour in 1994. He received a Ph.D. from Harvard University in music composition in 2001. He has received awards from Meet the Composers/*Readers Digest,* the American Academy of Arts and Letters, ASCAP, and the Presser Foundation. He has been a competition finalist with the National Black Arts Festival and the Unisys Composers Competition. Dr. Holland currently lives and works in Boston.

I think there is definitely a Curtis Institute sound, one that is conventional, traditional, and very much based in tonality. There have been people who came through Curtis who don't write in that style, but for the most part the music here is predominantly influenced by the Americana tradition. While a composer at Curtis, I felt that I was writing in that particular style, but I am not sure if I am still moving toward writing that way or not.

Studying with Ned Rorem was exciting, largely because he knows everyone. There were three students, myself included, who went to his house in New York for lessons, and our lessons usually began with lunch. One day Thomas Thomasini, the new music critic for the *New York Times,* stopped by during lunch because Rorem was proofreading his new book about Virgil Thompson, Rorem's most influential teacher. Another day, we had to leave early because Rorem was having lunch with Steven Sondheim.

The fact that Rorem studied with Virgil Thompson definitely contributes to the tradition of the Curtis sound. Rorem has a definitive style, but he is also good at looking at another person's music and telling him what he is doing and how he could do it better, without imposing his own aesthetic.

I am originally from Flint, Michigan. My dad's father was an opera buff and conducted a church choir. He passed on his piano to my dad, and we still have it at home. My mom plays it for enjoyment now. When I was very young, I used to sit at the piano and make up my own little songs or just listen and sing while my mom played. My parents attended many concerts, and there was al-

ways music in our house. They decided when I was about ten to let me have piano lessons. I took piano for a year, and then my teacher moved away. I wanted to continue with music, but not with piano. I eventually ended up taking trumpet lessons. In junior high, my band teacher taught us music theory and music history in band class, something that is not usually done in junior high. We would have tests where we had to play all twelve major scales in less than a minute in order to get an A, no matter what your instrument was. During those two years of junior high school, I really got into music and decided that it was something that I wanted to pursue.

For high school, I decided I wanted to go to a school with a strong music program. I attended the Interlochen Arts Academy, originally as a trumpeter. During my second year, I became frustrated with playing because I wanted to do more musically than I was ready to do physically. I had always had a desire to take composition lessons, although I am not really sure where that desire came from. I began taking lessons on the side, not really taking them seriously. When I started to win competitions, I thought, "maybe I should stick with this for a while." When it came time to apply to college, I hadn't seriously thought of studying composition. If I wanted to study music, it would most likely be part of a double degree. I applied to Curtis as a composition major, simply because of its reputation. I did not know anything about its composition program or even who taught there. When I found out that I was accepted, I jumped at the opportunity to go.

I have to have music. Not long ago, I wasn't around music. I had no radio, and I didn't hear any performances for a few days. After a while, I noticed that I was always humming something, usually just random things that popped into my head. Music is just something that I have to have. However, I think that I get tired of listening to the same thing all the time, which may explain why I am a composer. I used to go through phases of listening to one composer for a long time and then switching to another. Now there is no one composer that I listen to, and I often find myself listening to music to hear how the composer put his or her music together or how he or she used the material.

I am interested in writing music that is more "relevant" to now, something that is more challenging than what I have written in the past, yet something that is still accessible and not too academic. There are many techniques that have been created in the twentieth century that I would like to utilize.

I have to admit that most of the music I listen to is popular music. I imagine that it must come through in my music in some way. It is not, however, a conscious thing. I listen to everything—top forty, rap, techno, jazz, etc. When I write music I don't think in terms of trying to imitate or fit into a specific style. I definitely don't think in terms of trying to represent "black music" or writing the kind of music that black composers write, if there is such a thing. I just write, and if those things come through in my music, that is fine. It is just not an issue for me.

The piece I was commissioned to write for the Detroit Symphony presented a challenge for me. They asked for a five-minute piece, and I knew that it would most likely be used as a concert opener, which meant something "flashy." I had to compromise between giving them what I thought they were probably expecting, a crowd pleaser, while at the same time doing something artistic, which could mean something that people would not like. I decided to write a piece using the smallest amount of material possible, which in this case was a two-note ostinato. I then took the two notes and developed them into motifs. The entire piece ended up a continual development, from beginning to end.

I used to compose at the piano, but recently I have been trying to get away from it. Part of the reason is that I often fall into a trap of playing something, deciding that it sounds good, and then just throwing it into a piece without knowing whether or not I can claim the idea as my own, even though I just stumbled upon it accidentally. I suppose these ideas are valid either way, as long as no one knows, but I think that it helps me if I am not right in front of the piano all the time. Usually when I compose I begin by taking little motifs. I play around with them and try to develop a larger picture of what the piece will be and what I want to do at certain points. Then I take the material and try to manipulate it into what I want it to be while also trying to let it develop on its own.

I experiment, I challenge myself, and at the same time I keep in mind who is listening and who I want to be writing for—the normal concert goer. I see myself writing music that is going to challenge its listeners, but at the same time does not alienate them because of its inaccessibility. Many listeners today don't seem to want to have to listen actively when they go to a concert. They get scared off or offended when something they are not familiar with is introduced to them.

I have no idea where contemporary concert music is headed, because there are so many different styles in which composers write today. Many people seem to think that "hard-core" modernist composers will begin to soften up, because no one wants to hear the kind of music they are writing. Others tend to hope that audiences will tire of hearing the same pieces—Mozart, Beethoven, etc.—at every concert and will begin to desire newer pieces. I think it is just too hard to judge at this point.

I don't see why black people would not understand my music or see it in a different way then anyone else. I think that anyone that has an interest in "contemporary classical" music could find something to relate to in my music, regardless of their color.

To bring an audience back for new music, or maybe to help convince audiences that new music is not as scary or inaccessible as they think it would be, are two goals that I would like to achieve someday through my work. I want to make my contribution as a composer to the process of bringing people back to music, in the present tense.

Anthony Kelley

Born 1965, a native of Henderson, North Carolina, Anthony Kelley has emerged as one of the formidable voices of his generation. Even before finishing his doctoral studies at the University of California at Berkeley with Olly Wilson, broadcasts of his works could be heard on National Public Radio. Mr. Kelley was awarded the coveted Meet the Composers residency and was appointed composer in residence with the Richmond Symphony in 1996. Kelley earned his bachelor's and master's degrees from Duke University, studying with Robert Ward, Stephen Jaffe, and Thomas Oboe Lee. While a composer of several forms and styles, his symphonic pieces have received performances from orchestras such as the Baltimore, Detroit, Atlanta, North Carolina, Richmond, Oakland East Bay, and Marin Symphonies, and the American Composers Orchestra in New York. Kelley has received numerous awards and honors, from ASCAP and the American Academy of Arts and Letters (the Charles Ives Award), and others. Dr. Kelley currently serves as an assistant professor of composition at Duke University. He lives in Durham, North Carolina.

I was born in North Carolina, in Durham. That is also where I spent my graduate and undergraduate years. I was raised in Henderson, North Carolina, which is much smaller than Durham. The southeastern United States has its own set of cultures. There are suburbanite, accented cultures. There are deeply rural cultures. There were tobacco farmers' sons and daughters going to class with me when, for example, both of my parents were educators. My mother taught first grade, and my father taught sixth. My mom used to sing church songs in the house all the time. They were pretty much standard hymns that you would find in any church, white or black, but she just liked hymns. Every once in a while she would fall into a spiritual or something. But when we would go to her hometown, which is Candor, North Carolina, that was a really different type of culture. We are not talking suburbs and things; this is really deep South. There I would see my great aunt's and my grandmother's churches. I spent many entire summers with my grandmother, because I really liked it down there. All the fruit you can imagine is right there in the garden.

In the churches there I would hear the clapping and stomping kind of music, where it seemed like the human body was more of a musical factor than the instruments. Harmonies were made automatically and spontaneously by these gatherings of sixty- and seventy-year-olds. There were specific types of harmony that come from that type of music. I used to love hearing that. It surrounds you; the whole room is filled with wooden thumping. This was where I spent a great deal of my childhood and early adolescence.

My father died when I was in the ninth grade, in 1979, when I was about

to go into high school. I had to finish my ninth grade year with this loss. I remember I had begun to study piano when I was in sixth grade. I studied tuba when I was in junior high band in the seventh grade. I was doing both concurrently. My parents agreed that they would not buy me a piano until they thought I had learned enough to make it worthwhile. I would always have to walk up to the elementary school after school and practice until the janitor would kick me out. It took an effort for me to keep learning music, so I guess I valued it more. That was a big factor, that the burden was on me to prove to my parents that I was going to be musical.

My high school years I spent in a boarding school in Wallingford, Connecticut, twelve miles from New Haven. The school was called Choate Rosemary Hall. I won a scholarship that was sponsored by A Better Chance, Inc. (ABC). This is tenth through twelfth grades. We studied everything, but it was college preparatory, so the classes were intense. A bunch of rich kids is what it actually came down to; it was John F. Kennedy's school, it was prestigious. I won a scholarship, and I was curious about why people spent so much money to go to a school that I probably couldn't have gone to without the scholarship. I went to the school out of pure curiosity. There were things I liked about it. I liked the way the teachers treated me. I also liked the way I was finding things out about how to get around in the world, connections and things, like making sure you are productive in society at a certain pace. I had good role models.

There was one teacher, Ralph Valentine, who taught music theory there. I started that, oddly enough, my senior year, after spending the fall trimester in France. The teacher, who was a funny, hilarious guy said, "Why don't you take my course? Come and take my theory class." I did. This guy was so witty that I just wanted to be like him. I think he still teaches at Choate Rosemary Hall. He is an incredible organist. I heard him reharmonize Christmas carols on the spot during the Christmas festival we had. It just blew me away. "What is he doing?" I began to understand what harmony meant. That is the thing I search for in music, even to this day. It's the harmony, the content of the overtones and how they interact, that's what I really search for, combined with this rhythmic thing that I am into with the popular stuff. Valentine was a huge influence. He tutored me so I could catch up with all that I had missed all those years. I actually caught up with classes filled with advanced-theory students.

I had been studying piano all three years in high school. I would learn pieces like Dmitri Kabalevsky's *Sonatina* and things that felt kind of modern. I would just learn them, and it almost became automatic. I was pretty good, but I never felt great. I expected immediate physical access to music the way I wanted it. When I found out about theory, I felt like I could take care of things. I felt that I didn't have to deal with practicing all the time to try to make it perfect in front of people. That was too much pressure. I wrote this thing called "Peasant Song." What a bizarre thing! I think I had seen that name in a Bartók book that I used when I was playing piano. I wrote this little song that sounded like an Eastern European folk song. It was harmonized in this cool way, because I had learned harmony, secondary time, sliding chromatic chords—it was full of all of that. I showed that to Mr. Valentine and he said, "That's interesting." Little did I know, that was my first composition. I had never thought of it that way, but it turns out that it was.

After Choate I went down to Duke University for undergraduate study and without declaring a major. To be honest, I had no concept of education per se. I became really liberal about learning while I was at Choate Rosemary Hall. I learned to want to know stuff that I needed to know. I didn't learn on a track to get a good job or get a better job than this other guy; I didn't have that in me at all. Choate fostered a desire to know something. When I went to Duke, I knew that people went to college after high school, so I just applied, and I got in. It's not like I went to do anything specific, which was a different approach, compared with many of my classmates.

In my second year at Duke, I went to Vienna, Austria; it is always after I go to a foreign country, where language is arbitrary, that I come back and grow more rooted in music. When words become arbitrary I get really into instrumental expression. I took a trip to Europe, and when I came back I really wrote music. I went to Vienna with the Duke Wind Symphony; I was playing tuba with them, and I was also the equipment manager. That was my work-study job.

We had a great tour. I wrote a tuba piece there. It was so bad. When I brought it back, I had signed up for my first composition class with Robert Ward, my first composition teacher. It was a class with three or four of us who sat in with this Pulitzer Prize–winning composer. I brought in this tuba piece and his reaction was far from complimentary. I put the piece away. After that, I started writing pieces for piano. Ward took me under his wing; I started doing independent study with him from that point through the rest of my undergrad career. This was every semester during my third through last year of college. My very last semester, I finally declared music as my major. The thing I did most of at that point was writing music, but I didn't know exactly what I wanted to do with my life. I just happened to be writing tunes.

Ward sat me down on my last lesson with him—he retired after that, I was one of his last private students at Duke—and he said, "Even though everybody who is composing wants to do something great, don't forget there were composers out there like Edvard Grieg." I thought to myself, "What is he saying, that my music is second rate?" Then I realized he was saying that Grieg was a great composer but that doesn't mean he should be celebrated in the way that Beethoven is. I thought it was cool that you could just write and not worry about people. Those words totally made a difference. I decided to write.

I got out of school and, like any student who decides to be a music major, I didn't exactly move right into a fifty-thousand-dollar job. I worked in retail, I substitute-taught in elementary and junior high schools in my hometown. I moved back to Durham and worked in a store for a while. I sold rugs, lamps, luggage, and electronics for about two years. I was also writing tunes at the same time. I wrote a band piece and a flute piece and some pieces for piano.

I was in the store when one of my teachers came in and saw me. It was Stephen Jaffe, one of the composition teachers, who still is at Duke. He said, "Oh, you're still around." He said I should come and sit in on some of the seminar classes in grad school. To be honest, no one had talked about grad school to me. I wasn't around folks who were dealing with grad school; I had some free time on my hands, so I did it. I sat in, and I wrote a little paper, and he accepted me into the program the next year. I was the only graduate composer that year at Duke; they had a small beginning program, at least it was in a lull.

Jaffe took a sabbatical, and I started studying with Thomas Oboe Lee [American composer], who lives in Boston. Lee was a gigantic influence. He had played jazz when he was young, and he was really into the jazz composers, as well as into his own work. He can be pretty influential in and of himself. He kept saying, "You need to listen to Monk, you need to listen to Ellington, man."

I had never listened to any jazz guys, to be honest. All I knew was that I really liked Franz Liszt. Franz Liszt was my favorite composer; to this day, of all the European composers, his music still appeals to me the most. There is this concept of freedom in his music, but complete dedication of one's life to it at the same time. Where Brahms was trying to restrict people in their style, Liszt was able to achieve a broad range of expression. Liszt did really showy, virtuosic stuff as well as stark, cold music that no one could understand. He also wrote things in between that are "spiritually transcendental," to use one of his phrases. I really like the breadth of his expression. Here is a man who wrote seven or eight hundred pieces in his life. I don't know if we have many people who are as prolific as Liszt in terms of small note values. There is hardly a Liszt piece I don't know. I have spent many years listening to this man's music.

For me, music is a mode of communication. I am most intrigued by instrumental music, as was Liszt, generally speaking. I really believe that sometimes I am touched by actual thoughts I couldn't say again except with music. I believe that it is healthy to express things that way. It breaks you away from words, just like when you go to a foreign country; you need to break away from your own language sometimes. It is more than just the words, it is people touching each other with ideas. That is a really big deal; it is communication without words.

Q: What is your composition process?

A: My constructive process has changed over the years, since my earliest compositional years gave rise to my writing works in the abstract, based less on the occasion at hand than on a given whim or a desire to pay tribute to friends who happened to be performers. As I have enjoyed the good fortune of more or less regular commissions, I now have to start most often with a consideration of the circumstances of the commission, such as premiere venue, requested duration, and instrumentation of the commissioning performing force. Once all of these factors are in my scope of orientation, I imagine an appropriate general mood or tone to set for the occasion or specific performers' most acceptable points of capability and challenge. I also account for the same factors as I anticipate the points of pleasure, excitement, and tolerance of the probable audience that will receive the premiere. Thinking of one's listening audience is one of the most perplexing lacunae that I have observed in the field of "art music." What's the point of writing out a code to a language with no meaning or aspect of intent to communicate? And if one does finally decide to commit to conveying a set of new sounds to a set of listeners, doesn't that composer, like a good orator, want to consider the most effective way to communicate the ideas? If a physics lecturer had to do a talk on scientific aspects of agriculture at a farmers' convention, it would obviously be more effective for his speech to be tailored to the occasion and the audience of farmers rather than speaking completely in the rhetoric of the physics laboratory. Art music composers of today often lose the power of effective musical transmission by overly absorbing themselves in the aural rhetoric of the composers' laboratory without regard to their audiences. Fortunately, this is gradually changing, and the great rifts between listeners, performers, and composers have begun to mend.

Before beginning a work, I often take the time to digest possible smaller ideas that might serve as a basis for expansion. Sometimes these microthematic inspirations are drawn from musical devices themselves, such as specific sound sources in folk music. After deciding on a source for development, expansion, and reiteration, I try to visualize a suitable proportional space for the cohabitation of the sonic events. This means that I really *listen* for how much time should be occupied during sections of a work, accounting for the beginning, middle, and end of the piece. This is a valuable exercise, because feeling this temporal space occasionally gives rise to clear flashes of some of the truest musical units. By "true," I mean self-standing from my manipulation or construction. These flashes of more or less complete units of fresh music are the most magical, unexplainable products of the compositional process. They sometimes appear as sonic dreams that awaken me from sleep, and I have to get up from bed to transcribe my memory of them as quickly as possible, so that they will not be lost. These intuitive, inspired musical moments always reflect the core of my musical voice, which includes shades of African America and European America, with hints of many other eclectic sounds to which I've been exposed. With the patches of clear musical material before me, I begin to sew them together like a patchwork quilt, filling the squares with the thick, warm padding of culture and influence from my mentors, and using the precise, sturdy threads of my formal training to unify the patches into a single, larger, functional unit. Most often, I derive "contrasting" material by transforming the original sources of clear, "true" musical content.

Q: Give me some of your thoughts on American identity as an American composer being black?

A: I frequently celebrate the joys and bemoan the toils of American life in my music and in the discussions about my music. For instance, my grand rag fantasy for trumpet and piano, called *The New Ragtime* (1991), draws parallels between the bittersweet environment of America that gave rise to original ragtime style a century earlier. It was a period that celebrated America's liberation from the wretched practice of legal slavery, yet it was a period soiled with the horrors of the most severe, massive postslavery hate crimes and lynching, as a backlash to emancipation. In *The New Ragtime* I used and transformed the typical variable scale degrees, shifting rhythm, and arching melodic gestures of ragtime to cast a modern-day analogy to the contradictions of stability and instability in American culture. Another example might be found in my orchestral composition *The Breaks: Orchestral Homage to the American Maestros— Morton, Armstrong, Ellington, and Gillespie* (1998).

I should also mention that the eclectic, multicultural aspects of American society provide important portals for invigorating influence. For example, America's longstanding admiration of the European "masters" was a part of my own education. So, when I have been exposed to the "Three Bs" and the music of an amazingly prolific figure like Franz Liszt, the craft of that music is beyond reproach. It should be no surprise, then, that the high virtuosity of Liszt's music might be seen in combination with, or juxtaposition to, the spoken rhythm of a rapper in a single work by an American composer like me. Only my perspective considers both forces worthy of honor for their "mastery."

Black orchestral composers like William Grant Still, Duke Ellington, Ulysses Kay, Hale Smith, Olly Wilson, and T. J. Anderson are perhaps the most present forces of influence from the black music lineage, and I share them with honor. But it should also be noted that the multicultural nature of our society would necessitate my crediting some composers who are not African American but have thoroughly integrated African American–derived musical influences into their music to impressive effect. Some of these would be Gershwin, Andre Jolivet, Thomas Oboe Lee, and others.

I would be remiss if I neglected to mention the enduring influence of the popular music that I've heard, starting with the gentle, soulful sound of Bill Withers to the mind-expanding pyrotechnics of George Clinton and his bands Parliament and Funkadelic. Nile Rodgers and Bernard Edwards, of the group Chic, provided a basis upon which I began to understand the power of clean, precise understatement. The Motown and Quincy Jones production sounds opened doors of breadth and richness in orchestration. Rap grabbed my ear in the 1980s, and as in funk music, it expanded my interest in the rhythm and accent of black spoken dialect as well as my fascination with elaboration and layering over a repeated (or sampled) unit of music.

As I mentioned earlier, I owe a lot to my experiences as a young boy hearing black music in churches, especially those in the hometown of my grand-mother, who lived in a very rural, southern part of North Carolina. In these churches there would be spontaneous outbursts of spirituals and hymns. The squeaks, groans, creaks, and moans all serve as models for the shapes that I love to depict in my music. They also represent a part of black American cultural memory that I feel it is my duty to perpetuate and disseminate.

Jazz, as part of black music, is a world unto its own insofar as influence upon my style and place as a composer. I have found my most significant impro-vising hero in the pianist/composer Ahmad Jamal, who considers himself a pro-ponent not of "jazz" per se but rather "American classical" music. His music flexes the muscle of multiculturalism and eclecticism at every turn, yet never once can a listener lose sight of the fact that this is a unique performer with a voice all his own. Everything appears at once in even a fragment of Jamal's music: Liszt, Latin American, Ellington, Tatum, Africa, Europe, America, and more—all in a run of twenty or so notes. Wynton Marsalis's compositional explorations constantly inform my perspective on the potential of instrumental music to be both crystal clear and unbelievably dense and sophisticated, like much of the finest African traditional music. From Abdullah Ibrahim to Theloni-ous Monk, there are so many jazz performers who take me on important jour-neys toward my new compositional directions that I could not mention them in a short interview like this. Although I myself refrain from participation in jazz performance as such, I have enjoyed many hours of playing keyboard in a hybrid style of improvisation that I and my friends like to call "New Blues" style.

In recent days, my listening to old-time and folk blues recordings and performances has shed new light on the monumental presence of the authentic music outside the proscenium stage setting.

Jeffrey Mumford

Jeffrey Mumford was born in the nation's capital in 1955. Mumford, sometimes referred to as "a painter transformed into a painter of sounds, reflecting the inspiration of cloud imagery," received his training in composition from the University of California at Irvine, and further graduate studies at the University of California at San Diego. His teachers have included such greats as Bernard Rands, Peter Odegard, Lawrence Moss, and Elliott Carter. His works have been performed by such notable groups as the Atlanta Symphony, the National Symphony, the Minnesota Orchestra, the Los Angeles Philharmonic New Music Ensemble, the Roanoke Symphony, and the St. Paul Chamber Orchestra. Sources of his awards and commissions include the Guggenheim (1995–96), the American Music Center, an Aaron Copland scholarship, the Fromm Music Foundation, the Walter W. Naumburg Foundation, the American Composers Forum, and Meet the Composer. He was the winner of the 1995 National Black Arts Festival composer's competition with the Atlanta Symphony. His music has been heard around the world, including Aspen (Colorado), London, Finland, and Milan. His chamber works are recorded on CRI Records. Mr. Mumford holds teaching posts at the Washington Conservatory of Music; the Heights School in Potomac, Maryland; and the Oberlin Conservatory. Mr. Mumford currently serves as a visiting professor of music at Oberlin College. He lives in Oberlin, Ohio.

I try to be as passionate and direct with my music as possible. My music is based on cloud imagery, in terms of the layers that I try to construct. There are several things going on simultaneously. I am fascinated by the idea of suspended structure in music, several layers of activity moving simultaneously and referring oftentimes to a specific source chord or motif. I use a variation form, where there is a constant recycling of material. I use a tone row, which is the basis of a repository of thematic material from which I extract and develop my thematic and motific material. I am not at all rigorous about using the row, but I do find

using the row and rotating hexachords is a very effective way of arriving at the kind of harmonic language that I like.

Each piece uses a different row. I construct the row thematically with each work. It is a struggle each time, because each piece is different. Each piece will have different configurations, depending upon the instruments. Idiomatically, each piece is suited to a specific group or family of instruments or even a particular instrument, in the case of the concerto or a solo piece.

I am only in my forties, and I think I have found my style. One is always learning, however, and things change. My work has undergone a good deal of change over the last few years, specifically becoming more personal and lyrical. My earlier work was more harmonically severe, more rigorous in the treatment of the row. My later work is certainly a lot messier in the way that I use the row. If it doesn't suggest something that I want, I will just use something else. I am working toward the long line. I want my music to be as passionate as possible, as I said, and I am very concerned with counterpoint, with how things sound, and the isolations. Specifically, I am concerned with making the delineation of foreground and background materials as clear as possible.

Where I place myself as a composer in history, I really don't know yet. I suppose I would best describe my work as "lyrical atonality." I would say that is accurate. My work is not specifically twelve-tone. There are tendencies, which come and go, toward certain harmonic areas. My pieces, I hope, ebb and flow a great deal. Areas of tension release, periods of thicker and thinner texture—all of these things work to push the piece forward.

I was born in Washington, D.C. My brother, who is five years older, and I were given a record album. I was five, and he was ten. It was called *The Child's Introduction to the Symphony*. On this album were small excerpts from pieces from the repertoire. Bach was played by a huge orchestra—this is not authentic performance we are talking about! My brother and I used to play a little game associating these little snippets with football teams, because we watched football every Sunday. The swan from the *Carnival of Animals* was the Chicago Bears, the *l'Arlésienne Suite* was the New York Giants, another piece was associated with the Cleveland Browns. Those pieces would have significance for us. I don't know if it made sense to anyone else, but it made sense to us. We watched these games on a black-and-white television, and we could always tell the time of day of the game by the quality of light. Color and time of day mean a lot to me, the intensity and energy of light. Even back then, I could remember those elements having an effect on me, the sounds of these pieces and the degree of light, even while watching black-and-white television. I can look back now and see that it made some difference. Those pieces I can always remember.

Another formative experience happened in sixth grade. The public schools had an arrangement with the National Symphony to go to concerts at Constitution Hall. I can remember that the program was the *1812 Overture, The Sorcerer's Apprentice,* and the *New World Symphony* of Dvorak. That I remember this so vividly shows how strong and lasting was the impact of that experience. I think it is very important for these programs to continue, because they provide a wonderful opportunity for kids to hear a live orchestra and interact with it in a direct way. Those are two very powerful experiences that I can remember.

Also, growing up I played clarinet in the fourth grade, in the school orchestra. At home, when we trimmed our Christmas tree every year, we did it listening to Handel's *Messiah*. Again, we are not talking about a standard performance; it was played by the Philadelphia Orchestra and the Mormon Tabernacle Choir. We would do that every year. My father had a huge Count Basie collection as well. I also remember the first time I saw the name Clifford Curzon. My father had the performance of Curzon playing the *Emperor Concerto*. A lot of these things were very central to my experience.

When I was in high school, I was planning to be an art major. I spent a lot of time at the National Gallery doing style studies of old masters' paintings to develop technique. I was also interested in landscapes, as well as Italian and French Baroque paintings. I was particularly influenced by the Dutch landscape school of the seventeenth century, in terms of the clouds and the terrain. The sky takes up three-fourths of the vista. Those landscapes were accurate depiction's of what one saw. There were huge cloud formations in all the paintings, and that attracted me a great deal.

I went into college planning to be an art major, but the mood at the time was not conducive to painting at all. For example, a painting professor who was assigned to us came in the first day of class and said that he did not believe in the validity of painting as an expressive art form! So we were on our own, anyone who wanted to paint. Later on I did have a professor, named John Paul Jones, who was very encouraging. One of my works, a style study of François Boucher, a French baroque painter, was whitewashed, sabotaged. When I came in one day, it was covered in white paint. I was quite dismayed. At the time, I was practicing music on the piano in the music department. I was just hanging out there, and that's where I escaped for solace. They took me in, and I started taking composition classes and auditing music courses while I finished the art degree. More and more I saw that music was going to be the way that I expressed myself. So that was probably the best thing that happened to me.

I started organizing composers' concerts. I finished up the degree in painting and started to compose under the tutelage of a composer named Peter Odegard, who was himself a student of Roger Sessions [American composer]. He was quite helpful to me in a number of ways. Odegard taught me to play the viola, because he thought it was very important for a composer to have practical experience with a string instrument. I owe him a great deal for that. He said, "If you learn the viola, you learn three instruments for the price of one. It is tuned the same way a cello is and is fingered in the same way as a violin." I think that was a very important lesson for me. I have written a lot of string music, I like to write for strings a great deal, so having that knowledge has certainly been very helpful.

Early on I was doing style studies, like I did in painting, I suppose, to develop technique. I wrote a little piece in the style of Schumann, and I started working my way through the twentieth century. Les Six ["The Six," a group of six French composers in the 1920s] were very influential and still are, especially [Francis] Poulenc [French composer, one of Les Six]. I wrote a little suite for piano in the style of different members of Les Six—that's what I thought, anyway. Looking back, maybe the pieces tended toward certain ones and not toward others. I still love and listen to Poulenc's music and find it very affecting. I wrote a sonata for two pianos in the style of Stravinsky and then worked my way through the work of Elliott Carter [American composer].

I had the wonderful opportunity to work in a listening lab. I used to just camp out there with friends of mine. We would bring food in there and just listen and work our way through all the records. That is partly how I developed the knowledge of repertoire that I have, just by listening to records. I discovered cello and piano sonatas of Carter, and they both blew me away. This was someone I had to know more about. Later on I went to study with him. While I was studying privately with a composer named Lawrence Moss, a wonderful composer here at the University of Maryland, I was working on a string quartet. I told him how I was very interested in Carter's work, and he told me to call Carter up some time. Carter and Lawrence Moss had been colleagues at Yale back in the 1960s. I called Carter, and he said he was going to be in Aspen. I went up to New York for a couple of concerts and ran into Carter. I reminded him of our telephone conversation, and he said, "Why don't you come to Aspen? I'll see you there."

I was going to be in Aspen anyway, so I brought some scores and tapes and I scheduled a meeting with him. He was very gracious and told me to come and see him in the city library, where there was a listening facility. He listened to my stuff, and he agreed to teach me. I was blown away. At that time I played him a tape of the string quartet, which was going to be released on a record, and some other things. I studied with him for three years and it was great.

I worked on a piece for piano with him, and I reorchestrated my violin concerto with him. I found him to be a wealth of practical knowledge, even beyond the brilliance of his ideas. He speaks eight languages fluently. His sense of aesthetics is incredible, but in terms of practical knowledge, since his own music is very dense, he is keenly aware of orchestration and what needs to happen so that themes and lines can be heard.

My violin concerto was overorchestrated. It was my first large-scale work, and I made some calculation errors. We went through the orchestration measure by measure, cleaning up and taking things out so that the solo part could actually be heard. I had a lot of sustained chords in the background; he thought it would often be much more effective if instruments did not play at all. The contrast, the foreground and background, would not be as distinct if things had not been cleaned out and gotten out of the way of the solo. I keep that thought with me, no matter what I am writing. I still do that now for lines that I want to be heard. The idea is to keep things out of the way of whichever layer you want to be heard, so things come in and out. That was an important lesson. I found working with him, on a practical level as well as an aesthetic one, very, very helpful. He has been a great support for years, and he is still very supportive.

Music, for me, means everything. It is an environment, a sound environment, in which I live. I walk into it and keep it around me all the time. It is living energy. I hope that my music is affecting to people, that it moves them to some degree. I want my music to be a very compelling, direct experience for listeners. I used in the past the image of "grabbing you by the throat and throwing you across the room." I want the experience to be that visceral. I am keenly interested in music that is developmental in nature. I don't particularly care for static music. I think music moves you from one place to another.

I think my role in society is a great responsibility. In the community I have tried to help as many people as I can; help them get performances, etc. I think that it is important to be a role model as a black composer. I have taught black students, and I have encouraged many black students to get into music and to develop their skills and to take up their roles as artists in society. I try to encourage them to do anything that they want to do, even though some aspects of society will be very limiting—even, unfortunately, more and more, within our own community. We tell ourselves that we can only do this and not that. We don't allow ourselves permission to do what we want to do. Writing the music that we want to write [concert music traditions] has been attacked within our community as somehow foreign to what we are, but I think that the fact that we write it means that it cannot possibly be foreign; it is what we are. Any music we write is black music. I reject limitations, and I strive to help other people to reject them also. I encourage them to be who they are and to realize that in anything they write, in anything they do, they should do the best that they can possibly do, and that they should be celebrated for doing it.

Anything that is done sincerely and directly will be perceived as such by the audience. I think people can perceive game playing on any level. I give people credit for that, for being able to see through insincerity and half-hearted attempts.

All I can do is do what I do with as much passion, and as compellingly and as directly, as possible. I guess I would have to allow the power of whatever I do to communicate. As in anything else, it should be the force of the argument, whether it is verbal or artistic, that calls the tune. I would say, "This is something that comes from my heart. This is who I am. I am expressing this thought, this idea through this means. Other people express their ideas through other means, and all means are valid. The means I use is the means by which I can most powerfully say what I have to say."

The most subversive thing a black composer can do is to write art music, given the resistance in certain parts of our community—which fortunately I see changing, especially in the new guard of the NAACP, with Kweisi Mfume at the helm. I find there are signs of hope around. I had an interview with a local paper here [in Washington, D.C.] and suggested that we have a special burden, that we cannot know whether our music is being chosen, performed, or commissioned because we are black. That is a burden whites will never ever know. I would hope that the music is chosen because of its intrinsic interest and power, but the fact is that we never know. Someone may have had to fill a slot. There is always a question, and it seems as though this will always be with us, unfortunately, and that can be very debilitating if you allow it to be. I just write the music that I write, send it out, and do what I have to do. But these things can linger with you. Sometimes you look around the landscape and you see what is and isn't being played, and you wonder what is going on. You wonder how these decisions are being made.

I want my music to move people, to affect them. That is my ultimate goal, that people be able to listen to and experience the pieces that I have written, and afterward feel they have had a significant and positive experience in the space created by what I have done.

Gary Powell Nash

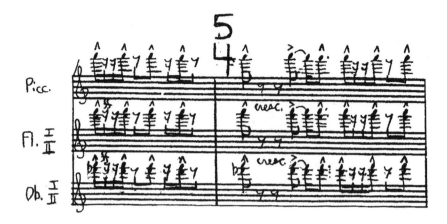

Gary Powell Nash has emerged as one of the successful composers of his generation. Before graduating from the Michigan State University, he had already been performed and recorded by the Czechoslovakia Bohuslav Martinu Philharmonic (*In Memoriam: Sojourner Truth*, Albany Records, Julius Williams conducting), and had a day in his hometown of Flint, Michigan, declared "Gary Powell Nash Day." Born in 1964, he completed his formal undergraduate and graduate studies at Michigan State and Western Michigan University, with further studies at the Aspen School of Music. Dr. Nash received his Ph.D. at Michigan State University; he is currently teaching composition and theory at Mississippi Valley State University. His teachers include an impressive list of contemporary composers, including Ramon Zupko, Charles Ruggiero, Mark Sullivan, Jacob Druckman, Bernard Rands, and George Tsontakis. His awards include a residency at the Virginia Center for the Creative Arts, National Black Arts Festival and ASCAP Young Composers Awards, the 1996 William Grant Still Emerging Composers Commission/Award, and a 2000 Fulbright scholarship. His works have been performed by orchestras of Baltimore, Atlanta, Chicago, Cincinnati, Detroit, and Flint. Dr. Nash currently lives in Itta-Bena, Mississippi and teaches at the Mississippi Valley State University.

Finding a teaching job has been the exclamation point to all the other activities that I have been involved in. There is a validation involved. I am looking forward to doing that job as professor of music for theory composition and clarinet to the best of my ability.

As far as composing goes, I have been able to meet people, and that is the thing that has helped me the most. I would go to a concert and hear an individual performer, and if I am impressed enough with the playing, I will say, "Would you like to perform this composition that I have written?" Or, if I have never written a piece, I would say, "I am interested in composing a piece for you." The reaction to that is usually positive.

My composition process, most of the time, is to start by looking at scores. The marimba piece I wrote, I researched by looking at scores of other marimba works and by listening to recordings. For my solo cello piece *Blues Impromptu*

for solo cello, because I was at an artists' colony [the Virginia Center for the Creative Arts], I was able to work simultaneously with a performer. I would write twenty or so measures and take it back to her and have her play through it and tell me what she thought. She even went as far as to say, "You write what you want; I'll let you know when I can't play it." As a result, I ended up with a virtuoso piece. If you have the opportunity to interact with a player, that is perhaps the best way to generate music. You need that constant feedback.

I use several types of process when I compose. I use a particular scale, and sometimes it is built on a combination of fourths, perfect and augmented fourths. I also like the minor/major seventh chord, and some of my harmonies are centered around that as well. Usually, though, I put the scale at the top of a blank piece of paper. My pieces are usually based on the same scale, or sometimes the piece will be based on a melody. From that melody I will extract notes and see if I can build a scale. I will compose a melody, but other than that, the process is intuitive. I make sure that the piece goes someplace—meaning that I will set up a climax and resolve that climax. I start at the beginning and work through. I know some people will write the ending first and the beginning last, but I start at the beginning. Most of the time I see the entire piece in my head first.

With *In Memoriam: Sojourner Truth,* I used a three-part form where the first section was slow, the next section was slightly faster, and the final, closing section was the fastest. I approached each one with a metric modulation. In fact, I did something similar in an earlier piece called *Mountain Rhapsody.* Sojourner was actually an extension of *Mountain Rhapsody.* I started with a slow metronome setting, quarter note equals sixty, and then used the metric modulation to get up to a quarter note equals eighty-eight, and another one to get up to a quarter note equals 132. There was that part of it, and then I also used two motifs. One was a bluesy, gospel-type melody that I created myself. There was a four-note rising and falling motif that suggests the name "Sojourner Truth."

I am interested in dense scoring, like in the work of Stravinski and Edgar Varèse. As far as my own personal style, I think Penderecki and the neo-Romantic influence can be seen in my work. Penderecki started the avant-garde, what they call the Polish Renaissance. Later on his works started getting tonal, but they still had those sliding glissandos and things. That is some of what I try to do. I don't use as many sliding glissandos as Penderecki, but I would definitely call it avant-garde, extending the orchestral range, using extended techniques to get as many sounds as possible but still with a tonal center—not necessarily triadic harmony. With *Sojourner Truth,* for example, the beginning section was in E-flat modality, the second was a C-minor modality, and the fast section was a D-minor modality.

In my freshman year at Michigan State University, the composer Carl Husa came to visit, and the band did a concert featuring all of his compositions. That was my first exposure to contemporary music, and I just thought it sounded interesting.

At first, when I decided I wanted to be a career musician, I thought I was going to be a jazz recording artist. When I heard Husa, though, I decided I would like to try to write music like that someday. At that point, I remember reading *Ebony;* someone had written the magazine saying that he wanted a career that no other black person had done before. I was thinking about that myself, about the fact that I didn't know many black composers. I was sure they existed, black composers in the Western European tradition, and thought it would be interesting to be one.

I began to find out about other black composers by talking to Ramon Zupko, who was my teacher at Western Michigan University. He had dropped some names, here and there, but none of them really stuck with me. Then I met Melvin Miles, who was the director of bands at Morgan State University and also the past president of Kappa Kappa Psi, the national honorary band fraternity; I met him at one of the Kappa Kappa Psi conventions. He told me about Dominique Delerma [musicologist]. He also told me about William Grant Still, and that name stuck with me. I did some research on Still and found out about his *Afro-American Symphony.* Miles told me about that piece, so I researched it. One of the two things that really educated me about black composers was the first year of my doctoral program, when we did a survey on composers. The teacher asked what composers we should study, and I said, "How about the music of William Grant Still?" He said "Okay" and introduced the class to the book *The Black Composer Speaks,* the first edition. That is when I learned about David Baker, T. J. Anderson, Hale Smith, and all the others who were in that book.

That book was very important for me. I discovered it in 1992, right before I attended the first Detroit Symphony African American Composers forum. I thought it was interesting to see that everyone in *The Black Composer Speaks* was asked the same questions, yet the answers were so diverse, especially the question asking for a definition of "black music."

I used to say there is no way to define black music. I used to think that music had no color. If you are talking about music that is done mostly by blacks, you say it is either jazz, pop, or soul, etc., but in actuality, white people do the same things. After further research—in fact, while I was studying for my comprehensive exam in music history—I realized that when you talk about the more popular forms of music, you can't help but say it was all black, because it actually originated in African American culture, everything but maybe folk and country/western. For the most part, if you ask "What is black music?" you are talking about *American* music. You need to use those terms synonymously.

One thing I discovered that I like the most about composing, other than just hearing my work reproduced by a major ensemble, is the human interaction. Even when I thought about why I wanted to be a college professor, the reason was human interaction. As long as I can continue to use my music to interact with people in any way, I will be happy.

Having entered contests since 1985, finally being selected in the Baltimore Symphony contest was a validating experience. My work was finally being judged and accepted as one of the best of a group. Also, I got the opportunity to hear an orchestra rehearse and perform, and I learned more about that process, dealing with professional musicians. They read [give orchestral performances of] Anthony Kelley, who is a year younger than I am; Ed Bland [black American composer], who has done a lot of commercial work with film scores but is now getting into classical work; and Raphael Aponte Ledée, who is from Puerto Rico. Ledée had a Latino influence in his work that I found interesting. Kelley considered himself a romanticist; it was interesting to see these three diverse backgrounds and approaches toward music.

The best thing about my experience at the Virginia Center, the artists' colony, was that all I had to do was compose. I was alone, to a certain degree, and I had the opportunity simply to compose. Artists' colonies are really for either visual artists and writers, so it was interesting to be able to interact with those types of people. There are usually twenty people at the Virginia Center, and there was maybe one other composer there, so it was even more isolated. It was a good experience, but at the same time, I missed being able to interact with other performers, as you get to do at a music festival. But when Tanya Anisimova [Russian cellist] came and I met her, I used that opportunity to the fullest extent.

I guess the best thing that came out of being at the colony for me was to be on my own and do what I could on my own without any other musicians around—the whole idea of isolation and solitude—not to mention the fact that they have only one telephone.

Q: Tell me about your experience recording *Sojourner* in Europe.

A: Unfortunately, I was not there for the actual recording of my *Sojourner Truth* piece. The major reason they used a European orchestra was that it was less expensive. From what I remember from Julius Williams [black conductor and composer], there was a language barrier, as well as cultural differences stemming from the fact that my piece was jazz oriented; there were problems of interpretation for an orchestra from the Czech Republic. Other than that, any time I can get a group from outside the United States to play my music, it is always a plus, simply because of the exposure. Also, there is, again, a sense of validation.

My ultimate goal is to win, one day, the Pulitzer Prize in musical composition. Other than that, I want to keep composing, keep meeting people, and keep taking advantage of the opportunities that I have—which, I guess, has been since 1991 the sum of my activities. When the contests come along, I want to submit works to them, making connections, and follow up.

Evelyn Simpson-Curenton

Evelyn Simpson-Curenton was born 1953 into the famous "Singing Simpsons" family of Philadelphia (her sisters are Joy and Marietta Simpson). She began piano at the age of two. Soon after her professional start, which was at age nine, Ms. Curenton became very serious about her desire to compose. A music graduate of Temple University, Ms. Curenton belongs to a unique group of composers who comfortably weave vernacular gospel and black church traditions with "classically bent" ensembles. She arranged seven works for Jessie Norman and Kathleen Battle for the critically acclaimed *Spiritual Collaborations,* recorded on Deutsche Grammophon and conducted by James Levine. She has accompanied and conducted on several occasions, including one of the last concerts of Mercer Ellington, in 1995, and she has been commissioned by such ensembles as the American Guild of Organists, the Philadelphia's National Opera Ebony, and Philip Brunelle and the Plymouth Music Series. Her symphonic works and settings have been performed by the National Symphony, the Minnesota Orchestra, the Philadelphia Symphony, and others. In addition to her work with her sisters, her arrangements include work for Howard University, the Smithsonian Institution, the renowned tenor George Shirley, and the late Duke Ellington. Ms. Curenton currently lives and works in Alexandria, Virginia.

I started playing piano at the age of two. I started out playing by ear, and then I think I started taking my first piano lesson at age five. This was at the Germantown Settlement Music School in Philadelphia, where I was on a scholarship, under a teacher named Melvina Leshock. I studied with her for about ten years. It was a really funny experience, because I did so many things by ear. I was a little lazy. Sometimes Ms. Leshock would play my lessons for me. She would stop me in the middle of a lesson and say, "Evelyn, where are you?"—and I would have been playing by ear. It got to the point where she stopped playing my pieces for me until I would learn them by note.

My writing ability became evident around the age of nine. However, my first signs of loving the intricacies of composition came at about age five. My mother said I used to get up faithfully every morning and put on the *Messiah* and play it all day and all night. I would have a fit if anybody turned it off. I just absorbed that music, and to this day it is so much a part of me. I know pretty much all of it by memory. I had no idea of the impact of that upon my ears as far as listening to instrumentation and voicing. I simply love the *Messiah;* it is very special to me. As far as writing, or having an ear for writing, I was about nine when a little chorale came to me; I played it for my piano teacher, and she

was so excited. At that time I didn't have any writing skills, but the more we listened to it, she said, "That sounds familiar, it sounds like one of those Chopin preludes." I forget which prelude it was, but sure enough, it was very similar, except the melody was just a little different. That was the first real sign of any skill in the area of writing.

My family began to sing together when I was eleven years of age. We belonged to different church choirs. We were asked to come together to do a concert, and so we did a program of spirituals, anthems, gospels, and even a madrigal. We also did some hymn arrangements. My sister Joy was then studying voice, and I remember I played for her Mozart's "Alleluia" by ear on the piano. She used to play it all the time around the house. Some years later I finally learned it by note. Joy and I did collaborations on hymns, spirituals, etc., together. I would play for her primarily, but my sister was the main one who played for us as a family. We did some things *a cappella* and some things accompanied.

There was an unusual situation in our home, in that we had all kinds of musicians coming in and out all of the time. We had gospel music; in fact, we had a neighbor who was a gospel artist. I would hear most of my music in church. Actually, we have had all kinds of different influences, because our family has gone to different denominations over the years. My first recollections of church music were at Grace Baptist Church in Philadelphia. In our church they would sing the anthems, they would sing oratorios. A piece from an oratorio on Queen Esther—I don't know who the composer was—was my first encounter with something operatic in the church. My sister played the part of Esther. I thought it was interesting to hear this dialogue going in the music between these two people. At the time I was really not up on my Bible; I was just really interested in the fact that my sister was standing there wearing a gown and singing this wonderful music. My mother and father were great lovers of the classics, and their interests were influential for me. My mother was a part of a women's chorale. I remember going to hear them and they had these beautiful first and second soprano and alto arrangements; they also sang some songs from Broadway. Additionally, along with hymns, my parents would sing songs like "He" and "Trees" [folk tunes] around the house.

My formal training did not come until much, much later, not until I was in my college years, but early on we had phenomenal choral directors who took us through all kinds of music. I would say that that experience played an integral part in opening my ears to good music. We were in something called the All Philadelphia Chorus, and I remember one composer who I really fell in love with there. We did a mass by Maurice Duruflé; it was my first encounter with Gregorian music. I just simply loved it, though it was very difficult to learn. We also did excerpts of Brahms's *Liebeslieden Waltzes*. When I went to Temple University as a composition major, I just could not get into atonal music.

A lot of things happened in junior high school. I stopped taking piano lessons, but I became like a sponge—I wanted to play and learn everything. That is where my greatest musical development happened. I had friends who would bring me recordings; in fact, my first recording of Quincy Jones, I will never forget, was called *Walking in Space*. I became completely absorbed in his chords and the voicings of his harmonies. Another thing that happened around that time was that I became interested in the music of Antonio Carlos Jobim. I had never heard this kind of music, because in my house we weren't allowed to listen to rock and roll and things like that. We had to sneak off to a neighbor's house to hear this music. I would say that it was in that era, the latter part of elementary school going into junior high school, that I began to listen to other music besides classical. I joined a jazz group in high school, and in college I started doing some other interesting things. Of course, I caught a little flack at home for that. but I was going through an interesting stage of development. I was playing music by Chic Corea, John Coltrane, and original music by John Blake, a jazz violinist, Leslie Burs [flautist and composer], and my own pieces.

As a result of the way my life has gone, I have always been sharing my gifts in the church. I think that knowing my music was a gift was the greatest thing my parents instilled in us. To share the music and to understand that you are just a vessel means, in essence, that you should not get caught up in your own self, as far as your gift is concerned, because musical ability is a gift from God. Because of that and because of my family's singing, I have always felt that music is something to be shared. Music can be shared either through teaching, which I have been doing—gospel music in particular, the music of the African American sacred experience—or though doing things like working with the Smithsonian on various projects, like my work on the music of the civil rights era of music and the early camp meeting era. I have been thrust into situations where I have had to learn about our music particularly, chorally as well as historically. I see myself, then, as a teacher and as, I hope, an inspiration to young people to further their studies and take our music more seriously. Our music is just as important as Bach and Beethoven, and we need to know its earliest forms.

I think that academicians do not treat African American music with the same respect as they do other music. I think part of the reason for that is because black gospel writers moved away from traditional gospel and to Hawkins [contemporary gospel writer, performer]; somewhere along the line we stopped writing the music down. Maybe it was because there were so many publishers among the early writers, like Sally Martin and various others. Additionally, when you go around to the schools, you see mainly student directors teaching gospel music. This has been a real concern of mine, because a lot of people in the academic world don't take it as seriously as they should—because we have not taken the music as seriously as *we* should. They take our classical artists more readily, but even there we are still not programmed along with the other mainstream composers—I feel we are *all* mainstream composers. In recent years I have had the opportunity to see my name listed among those of Gustav Mahler and folk like that, and that is a real treat, but more often black music tends to be programmed during Black History Month. What we as black composers have to do is be more aggressive in getting to orchestra conductors and showing them our music, ideally playing recordings, so that they can hear our work. I think that will help to get our music out there in the mainstream of repertoire.

Most of my orchestral or writing skills developed in college, but not under the tutelage of the composition department, which I had chosen as my major. When I came out of the composition department, I went on to study voice and music education. I do a lot of praying before I do my compositions. I ask for inspiration. That is part of the reason why I came out of the composition department; working on intervals and things like that is very mechanical, and I feel that music is inspired.

The first thing I usually do when I create is pray and ask what to write about. I will never forget my first encounter with this process, when my sister called on me to write for the National Symphony. I had transcribed things for small chamber groups before that time, but this was really frightening; I had never written something from my own spirit. When spirituals are involved, of course, I begin by looking at the lyrics, because the first challenge is to create music that depicts the words.

For instance, my inspiration for "Git on Board" was a black composer named Thomas Kerr. Sylvia Lee, a wonderful vocal coach, played Kerr's work for me, and I listened to how he portrayed the train spoken of in the lyrics. He moved sound about in a very interesting way. When I was trying to get ideas for my version of "Git on Board," the first sound I heard was a train whistle in the distance. I heard some overtones that sounded like brass to me. So I started my piece off with trumpets in thirds; then they fall off a little to give the effect of the harmonics in a train whistle. Sometimes you hear the echo of a whistle in the distance. I echoed that with trombones and French horns. I was trying to think of how a train would begin. The thought came to me to begin with an old locomotive, because that gives you more sounds with which to work. I began to talk with percussionists about what sounds would give me the choo-choo effects. We tried different sounds One of the percussionists said, "What about sound blocks?" We went with sound blocks, with a snare drum, to help give it the rumbling sound. We built up the sound slowly, and then the snare drums would give it the "engine." Then I began to start thinking about how street-car effects were orchestrated. Gershwin's *American in Paris* and Duke Ellington's *Harlem Suite* (I believe) give you the effect of city movement. This is where I came up with the strings. Then periodically the horns give the effect of the train engine huffing along, and trumpets simulate a train whistle blowing, as well as the flute and piccolo at intervals.

The lyrics have a lot to do with how to color the piece. The words in this particular piece are wonderful, because they talk about a train coming. The piccolo and flute give the effect of a little whistle. They also help to give the effect of brakes screeching, by overblowing [the mouthpiece]. The tubas have a repetitious melodic and rhythmic figure that creates tension with the piccolo and flute.

My whole concept in writing is to make any piece come alive and to let listeners feel like they are actually there, let them see and hear what I see and hear. I find that people will often write about a theme or lyrics that are moving emotionally, and yet the music seems to have nothing to do with the text or theme. I guess it is the child in me that makes me want people to see and feel what is going on.

I like for the music to be inspired. I think one of the reasons that I connect with Bach is that he did all of his music "to the glory of God." I personally believe—and if I am not mistaken, I think it was Ray Charles who said this—that there is soul in all music, you just have to find it. I feel there is a lot of soul in Bach's music. You can feel it as he works with those texts, as he builds to these wonderful climaxes. I find in the music that I borrow from these various composers whom I have admired, like Bach, Gershwin, Ellington, and various others, according to what the piece is and the instrumental colors that I want. I find that you give the essence of who you are in your music.

I have four kids, so I can definitely speak about popular music. As I was just telling my daughters today, I believe that whatever you absorb into your physical and mental being affects everything. A book that I read that talks about the secret power of music. It is a really interesting book, because it talks about how first of all music shows where society is at a particular point in time. If music disintegrates, so does that culture. In a lot of ways I see that happening with some of the rap music. There are some who are rapping about things that are really wonderful, things that have uplifting texts, but classical and other musics have become so mechanical and technical that they no longer speak to the person but rather to the intellect. I have found myself sometimes feeling nauseous hearing some of the music that is being written; maybe the frequencies and things they are working with just don't work with my body. I say the same thing about some of the popular music. Some of the instrumentation has a gnawing effect.

I have felt nausea particularly when the texts are vulgar. Some of these songs have a way of grinding at you. When you hear a beat booming so loud you feel the vibrations through the car, I feel as if I am having heart palpitations. I really do feel that music has a lot to do with the disintegration of a society. As it begins to lose the ability to inspire, to lose the quality of building one's spirit, it brings a form of decadence.

In my first writing experiences, when I was about seventeen or eighteen years old, I really didn't know much about how to get the music out there. I am learning how to disseminate the music, now that I am approaching my mid-forties. I hate to say this, but I think the only reason why symphonies have been turning to the black composer and other so-called minorities (I can't stand that word, because I don't think it is true) right now is because the concert hall is starting to become empty; people are tired of what they have been hearing. They have been playing a lot of the old masters, and people now need something that is new. It is a wonderful time right now for black composers to start taking themselves a whole lot more seriously, to get our music to as many conductors as possible. There is a real hunger for our repertoire right now, and I think that is a blessing.

The source of my musical inspiration has a lot to do with the fact that in my family we were taught to love the spirituals. I remember seeing the little books of spirituals; one of the first spirituals I had a little solo in was "Couldn't Hear Nobody Pray." At first I wasn't really crazy about the spirituals; I don't think I quite appreciated this music until I started arranging it, when I did the arrangements for the National Symphony. I began to see that there was a lot to this music. My sister Joy was a great lover of the spirituals, and she would bring them to life. My mother sang them around the house a lot, but Joy, who is now deceased, created many wonderful characters in the way she portrayed the spirituals. I remember she once did an *a cappella* piece called "Lord, How Come Me Here?" My love of the music of the black composer really started there.

I would do some transcriptions of the *Sacred Concerts,* Duke Ellington's music. I remember having the opportunity to sing with him, actually doing these pieces. This was before college. It was the most exciting experience to me, hearing a black composer. This man was writing music that was beyond anything that I had heard.

It was unbelievable to hear that band under his baton. I think it was his third sacred concert; there was this wonderful piece that he had written called "The Supreme Being," which portrayed the creation. I was astounded. I couldn't believe the band was playing all that I heard. I remember being so spellbound that I almost forgot to come in with the choral part. It was awesome to hear this man's music. Later on, after he died, I got a chance to transcribe some of his things, because I was working with Roscoe Gill, Ellington's choral director. I got a chance actually to look inside of his music, to see what he was doing. I think it was "Praise God and Dance" that I helped to transcribe. I said to myself, "When does he stop doing improvisation?" It seemed that every chorus was different. It just went on and on and on. It was so exciting to hear the band doing all of that. I got a chance to do an arrangement for him on one of his birthdays. It was a piece called "Jump for Joy," from a musical that he had written some years before. That was really exciting, and he gave me a great "thank you" for doing that arrangement for him. That was a real treat.

The Kathleen Battle/Jessye Norman project I did came up because of Mrs. Sylvia Lee, who had heard my work for the Urban League with the National Symphony. I told Sylvia that I was so excited that she would even ask me to do this. I had been looking at some expensive computer equipment. I had been praying, and I said, "Oh, I need a project so that I can get this equipment." Within months of that prayer I was told by Sylvia Lee that I was being discussed by Jessye Norman and Kathleen Battle. I said, "What?" I think it was Willis Patterson from the University of Michigan who told me about this first. He and Sylvia Lee had been talking about me, and he wanted me to submit some pieces to him. He wanted to see my work, because they were looking for some black composers to do arrangements of spirituals. I was so excited. I was thinking that with all of these wonderful black composers, surely they wouldn't consider me, because I was not renowned. Initially, I was asked to arrange three or four songs. They were having problems contacting the other composers. My list kept getting longer and longer until finally at one point I had to say, "That's enough. I can't do any more."

They were trying to find traditional spirituals, things that weren't too outlandish. They also had different concepts about the music. I know Jessye Norman wanted "Calvary" and "They Crucified My Lord" together as a medley. She wanted no strings; she wanted percussion and a TTBB (four parts—two tenor, two bass) arrangement. These songs were recorded on Deutsche Grammophon. It was a really interesting project, and it was kind of scary. I was thinking that these ladies had the best of everything, and I just felt like a little composer who was trying to do a few songs. But both of the women were in a jovial mood, which really helped to free me up, because I was wondering how I would be received.

My sister Joy was deceased at this time, but Kathleen had been to one of her concerts, so there was a connection between the two of them. I think she and my sister had lunch together, if I am not mistaken. After the project Kathleen requested some of my sister's albums. I thought that was really, really special. In fact, I brought one piece, "The Little David," which is based on a composition I did for my sister Joy. I used a good bit of that version in the arrangement that I did for Kathleen Battle.

Jessye Norman is very much a perfectionist about her work. My experience with her reminded me very much of Joy, in the way that she carried herself. Jessye was very direct. When Jessye looked at a piece, she knew what she wanted and what she didn't want. There were a couple of sections of "Calvary" that were cut out because they sounded too Hollywood to her, but I had written it so that the middle part could stay intact. I originally had written it to give the effect of Jesus in Pilate's hall. There were rumblings of the people. The piece begins with Pilate asking, "What then should I do with Jesus?" The crowd says, "Crucify him," and then it goes into Calvary. The piece ends with an orchestral interlude, which for this project I cut out.

My first project with the Smithsonian was based on the work of a wonderful black hymn writer, the Reverend Charles Tindley. A Howard University group was initially supposed to do this performance, and to this day I am really glad that I got a chance to do it with my own group, which was from Philadelphia. The project we did was like a docudrama, based on Tindley's hymns. This production featured Avery Brooks, who played the part of Tindley. The play encompassed Tindley's poetic, masterfully written sermons. Brooks brought Tindley to life in a unique way. My task was to train my group to portray the various groups who had performed Tindley's music. This concept was really fascinating. When I listened to the recording of the music, the task before me, I kept thinking, "I can't do this." Then I turned the tape on again and listened to the various male groups whose works I had listened to while growing up, like the Dixie Hummingbirds, the Caravans, and the Clara Ward Singers.

I decided to listen to these pieces because at that time I had worked as an arranger with a group at the Deliverance Evangelistic Center. My sister was the choral director, and I was her assistant. We were exploring various types of gospel music and quartets of that era, so I at least had my feet wet. At the beginning of the Smithsonian project the thought came to me, "Okay, listen to these kinds of pieces and see if you can hear some voices that you think can colorize these various eras." Then numerous things began to come to me; different people came to mind. I realized that we could do this project, so I called them back and said I would do it. It was fascinating, because it gave me the idea that this music could be researched and re-created.

I talked to people like Pearl Williams Jones, a wonderful gospel music historian, now deceased, who was responsible for me getting this engagement. She is the one who instilled in me the notion that gospel is a music that can be learned and should be taught. I think what I found so exciting about doing this Tindley program was that for the first time my dream about bringing forward research concerning the history of gospel was coming to fruition. As I began to work with these various eras of people who were doing Tindley's music outside of the hymn tradition, I found that I was learning so much about my heritage. That was one of my first projects.

I think because Dr. Bernice Johnson Reagan enjoyed my work, she brought me in on another project. She said I was like a guinea pig in the lab. I had to do some research on an 1801 hymnal that was compiled by Richard Allen of the African Methodist Episcopal Church. The hymnal was just text; what I had to do was to talk to some old-timers to see if they could recollect any tunes that might have been passed down orally. I met a group of people from choirs, and they began to sing some of these old melodies for me. My task then, after doing that research, was to put together a group of people who could do this music in the way these people described them and sang them to me. These projects were all recorded.

We knew we were going for an African type of harmony. At that particular time, when I interviewed my singers, there weren't a lot of them who could actually sing that type of harmony. There were just singing melodies. We started with having them singing in fourths; that gave us a semblance of what was supposed to happen. But I had a lot of old-timers and other people who were familiar with this music. They brought their knowledge of what this music sounded like, and that, combining with us singing in fourths, was really interesting. After a while we started calling ourselves "The Richard Allen Singers." The group later did other docudramas based on this music and gained a reputation. As a result, we are doing some of this music for the Wade in the Water Series that Dr. Reagan put together.

I was a great lover of Copland and also of Duke Ellington. I would say that as a composer, I would be somewhere in between the two of them, as far as the classics are concerned. Because of Duke Ellington's experiences with the big bands and some of his classically written things, I would say that I would be closer to Ellington than Copland. I would also tend to be closer to Ellington because most of my things tend to be very jazz oriented, with close harmony singing, as well as some more traditional gospel things. I call them gospel, but I guess what I do is not quite gospel; it is more inspirational, similar to Take Six's kind of writing. I love thick harmonies.

I hope that people will remember me as a prolific African American composer whose repertoire spans the varied repertoire of my people. I am trying to unearth as much material by African American choral writers as I can, the things that I don't see in print, especially the sacred literature. That is what I hope will be said about me, that I tried to bring the history of that music as much to the forefront as possible. I would consider that to be my most significant artistic achievement, to bring all of this music back to the public ear.

James Kimo Williams

James Kimo Williams, born 1950 on Long Island, New York, returned from the war in Vietnam with a creative desire to capture those experiences in art. *The Symphony for the Sons of Nam* has received numerous performances and rave reviews. This work and others have been performed by such orchestras as the Chicago Sinfonetta, the Savannah, Detroit, Lincoln, Sacramento, and Arkansas Symphonies, and the Czechoslovakia National Symphony. After returning from Vietnam, Kimo attended the Berklee School of Music, graduating as a composition major. He later decided to hone his business skills and earned a master's in management and human relations from Webster University. From 1987 to 1990 he served on the faculty at the Sherwood Conservatory of Music, Chicago, where he directed the program in commercial studies. He has served as artist in residence at Columbia College, Chicago. His awards and commissions include the 1992 ASOL African American Composers Competition, and he has received commissions from AT&T and the West Point Bicentennial, among others. He is a composer with multiple interests. His *War Stories* was an outgrowth of his record/recording/publishing company, Little Beck Music. His artwork and photography have been on display at the National Viet Nam Veterans Art Museum in Chicago. Mr. Williams lives and works in Chicago.

I grew up on my grandfather's [sharecropper] farm in North Carolina. At the age of fourteen my dad took me away from all of that. My dad was in the Air Force, and we did a lot of traveling, through Mississippi, through Louisiana, through Newfoundland, Seattle, Washington, and places like that. I was in all kinds of different places, because my parents divorced. I stayed with my dad, and my sister went with my mom. The family really split up. Being with my dad, I was really on my own a lot.

As a kid I was never really seriously influenced by any music per se. I did not go out to clubs, and no one in my family was musically inclined or anything like that. Most of the music that I got was in school. A rhythm and blues band came by once, and these guys were the coolest I had ever seen. Still, I just thought they were cool; I never said, "One day I want to play the guitar and be like that."

I think the first time I actually felt like music was the direction I wanted to go into was in high school. There were a lot of bands. I figured that if I played the guitar I would be able to get girls, I would be able to put on a show. I never, ever, was influenced by jazz, or rock, or pop, or anything like that. It wasn't around the house. I didn't see much music going on. The only exception I can

remember was once seeing Elvis Presley on TV doing "Blue Suede Shoes" or something, and I thought that was cool. But I never actually said, "I want to be like that, I want to play the guitar."

My becoming a musician was not from listening to Coltrane or anything of that nature; it was more because of the opportunity of being recognized as somebody who was unique or different. That has been the direction that I have always taken as an individual, with music as well as with anything else—to be as unique and individualistic and creative as possible. If somebody else was doing something, I made sure I wasn't doing the same thing. That was what happened in high school. Nobody else was playing the guitar, other than one or two people in the band, so I figured I would pick up that instrument for that particular reason. I wanted to be the only one in school at that point in time playing the guitar. The first time I actually had a guitar in my hand was down in Mississippi. It had one string on it. For years, or as long as I had the guitar, all I did was strum it, without touching the neck. One day I just happened to touch the neck and found out that the pitch changed. That discovery opened up a whole new world for me. From that point on, I was intrigued with music in general. But when I was in high school and playing the guitar, I wanted to learn more songs. I wanted to expand my repertoire so I could play more things sitting on the curb. You would play on the streets; people would gather around and think you were the greatest thing they ever heard, as long as you played the type of tunes they wanted to hear.

While I was in Mississippi—my dad was away in the Philippines or someplace—I was playing the guitar in downtown Biloxi. There were a bunch of guys hanging around a hotel, and we would see who could play the best song. I wasn't serious. It was fun, and I got a lot of attention. When I took my limited knowledge to Hawaii, I started to realize that if I wanted to learn any songs, I would have to do some type of practicing. I started picking out guitar books and started learning chords. I was still not very serious at this time. I hadn't decided this was what I was going to do with my life. Playing the guitar was more of a hobby. I never was good enough to put a band together and have a group that everybody got excited about until my senior year. Then I put a band together.

After I graduated from high school, I started playing with local groups around town for about a month or so. I was playing around with some friends and realized how good they were and how bad I was. I sort of backed off of the guitar thing.

The draft was on, and I knew I might get picked. This was 1969. I hoped that by joining the army I wouldn't be drafted and I wouldn't go to Vietnam. I joined, and they sent me to Vietnam anyway.

The two most significant things that got me seriously approaching the guitar happened when I was in Vietnam. I was a combat engineer, in the field most of the time, where people were shooting and being shot at. When you came back in from the field, you would come back to the home base, the safe area, where there wasn't any fighting. You go to these service clubs, where you could play the guitar, play pool, and watch movies. Groups would come by, major, major jazz groups. I can't remember any names. I started thinking, "Wait a minute, maybe I can do that." I put a band together while I was in one of the service clubs when I was back from the field. One of the Special Services people heard me and asked if I would like to put a group together and tour. I said,

"Tour where?" He said, "Tour Vietnam and go to these outlying locations where the soldiers are fighting and provide music." I said, "I'll do it." I listened to some other musicians who were around at the time, and we put a band together and toured Vietnam for about thirty days. It was then that I realized that perhaps this was the direction I should start to move in, because we were doing some pretty good things. I say good—it was really pretty bad, but for then and for where I was, it seemed pretty good.

Music may have saved my life, but it also put me in more danger. I had to do things that I did not have to do when I was with my regular unit. In my regular unit, my only job was to go out and clear land mines and trees and things like that. In a touring group, especially as a soldier as opposed to a civilian, we were dropped down into active zones, where there was actual fighting. The guys were taking breaks from the fighting, and we were providing them with music. One time we were performing a Hendrix tune—I can't remember if it was "Purple Haze" or "Fire"—and there was a sniper. Everybody in the entire place hit the ground, and when we got back up afterward, I swear there was a hole in my amp that wasn't there before. I always attribute that to a bad solo I was taking.

I think at this point I decided to be serious. I was influenced by a lot of musicians who were serious about what they were doing. If I wanted to play with them I had to understand them. There was one particular individual, Joe Cadera, who was on tour with a band called Poverty Train. They were in Hawaii. I went to the club and heard this guy. I thought he was a great guitar player. Afterward I went up and I met him. We hit it off, and I asked him if he could teach me and show me some things. This guy was a blues fanatic. He said, "Just listen to the blues, the blues, the blues." He started showing me some things, and I taped him. I actually have a tape of him and me during our lessons together. It is amazing, every once in a while I listen to it. This is when I realized that there was a serious aspect to music.

Symphony for the Sons of Nam, Quiet Shadows, and *War Stories* (which is a jazz/rock album) are all based on specific events that happened while I was in Vietnam. There are eight titles on *War Stories,* called "Ton Raw," "Bleath"— these titles were part of my creative aspirations. I made up words to represent specific things that were unique to me and my experience in Vietnam. "Fique," "Stolen Butterflies"—all of these have significance to my experience of Vietnam. Others are called "The Life and Death of Life," "Ask Me Not, for I Am but a Figment of My Imagination," and "Opizmes." These titles represent different things. One represents dope; another represents somebody crying when he realizes that here he was, a lawyer, emptying shit in a barrel; and so on and so on.

Symphony for the Sons of Nam is an orchestration of my string quartet, *Quartet for the Sons of Nam.* My wife and I went to see the movie *Platoon.* That was the first time I could talk to my wife about my experiences in Vietnam; we had been married for about fourteen years. Before that, I couldn't really talk about it. She would always ask me what I did in Vietnam, and I would say, "I don't know, just stuff." She never pressured me, and I never went any further with it. But after seeing *Platoon,* I realized that Oliver Stone was an artist, and if he couldn't talk to someone about his experiences in Vietnam, he was able to do it in his art. That is what I got from that movie. I decided I was ready to represent what I felt my experiences had been in Vietnam. This is when I really started working on my *War Stories* album, and I also started writing my string quartet.

I had started out in rock and moved to jazz. I had become interested in writing in the classical genre when I was exposed to it at the Berklee College of Music in 1976. So I decided to write a string quartet. I wanted to represent two specific things. The two things about Vietnam that had the most impact on me were going to Vietnam and coming back. This piece represents those experiences in two chapters. Chapter one represents soldiers, myself and all of the others, going to Vietnam and landing there. Chapter two represents leaving Vietnam and arriving back home. Chapters three and four have yet to be written, but they will represent actual events and situations that occurred while I was in Vietnam. *Symphony for the Sons of Nam"* is chapter one, and it is for full orchestra. I went to Vietnam in September 1997 to lecture at the Hanoi Conservatory and to complete my symphony.

What music does for me is to allow me to express feelings that I am unable to express verbally. Music provides me a paralanguage; intonations, dynamics, feelings that are indescribable in normal language are so easy for me through music. I can have conversations in music; I can say to someone, "I went to Vietnam in 1969, and then I came back twelve months later, and, boy, it was rough." Their response would be, "Yeah, sure was, Kimo, that's great." But with music, the words aren't even there. It is so expressive. Every time the music is performed, the things that come from it show me that the communication I am looking for can only be provided through music, at least for me. Mothers and fathers in the concert halls write to me or come to me and say, "Thank you"; that's important. If it were a verbal conversation, very seldom would you hear that type of emotional thanks. The thank you is for providing something special to them as they relate to their husbands or their sons who were in Vietnam. Vietnam veterans are also providing this type of feedback. So my purpose with music is solidified now. Nearly every time I compose, it is based on some emotional impact.

Every once and while I will get a call—"I need somebody to write music for this or for that." I always try to involve myself emotionally with the person or with the project. In fact, I turn down a lot of commercial ventures, when people say, "We don't care what you think, we just want you to write it." I try to stay away from that as much as possible by having interviews for major projects—films, or a theater piece. I tell them that it is very important for me to know who the director is, to explain how I involve myself through music. I got a commission two years ago, for example, to write a piece for a baptism; this again leads to my purpose as a composer and why it is so important to me. The family that commissioned me said, "Every time we have something special in our lives, we commission a string quartet." I said, "Let's meet and let's talk." We met and we talked, and we really hit it off.

I have found that American society has perpetuated the notion—of course, this is in general—that one must have expertise in one specific area. That is the American way—"You are an expert in this area or that area"—so you spend all of your time becoming the best in that particular area. At Columbia College, where I was teaching, the chair of the music program was insistent on my developing expertise in some preconceived area appropriate to his frame of reference. Creativity and curiosity can be hampered; my main motivation as an artist is to try everything, to know a little about a lot of things, as opposed to knowing a lot about one thing. You inevitably get the question, "Are you a jazzer, are you classical, or are you rock? What is it that you do?" Well, "I do music" is what I normally say. Right now I have an album out with jazz music, I have an album out with classical music, and I am working on a power trio [guitar, bass, drums] album of rock music. They are all my compositions. I write in all different types of genres.

In the negative sense, that has put me at a disadvantage with certain people. In the conservatory sense, composers who write very well in the classical music genre have backgrounds in that area. That is not to say that they started there, but their background for composing is based in learning, understanding, and gathering all the necessary knowledge to write in that field. My background is in rock and roll, then the jazz college band. Then on my own, through books and things, I learned and applied some of the understandings of the classical music, or European tradition of writing classical music. That has been a major disadvantage for me with regard to competitions and performances of my music, when they are looking for the standard approach to the composition of classical music. I don't usually win. I was very lucky with the Savannah and the Detroit competitions, at least I feel I was; I was a finalist in Detroit and did well in Savannah. I think that had to do with the adjudicators themselves. In a major contest, I don't have the academic, technical skill that makes people look at a score and say, "He has studied classical music, so therefore he should be considered."

From the jazz standpoint, because of my versatility, or because of my working in all types of music, it is very hard for me to establish a relationship with different clubs and groups. It is specifically difficult for groups to call me (I play the electric bass) and say, "I want Kimo Williams to play bass on this gig," because I don't spend the time learning standard repertoires that all jazz musicians who play out in clubs must know. This goes way back to the forties. Everybody who went into a club to play knew the tunes, knew the rhythm changes, it was automatic. Once you devote yourself to that style of music, to jazz music, those things become extremely necessary. I never did that, mainly because I am just looking at music from so many different angles.

I am overwhelmed by excitement about being that type of composer. It has given me opportunities in more areas, to do more things with more people with different types of music. I have more ways to express myself. I love playing rock and roll and banging out on the guitar or on the bass. I have written songs specifically in that genre. I am able to play in the jazz clubs or in the rock clubs, but not at the level where I could say I was a jazz musician or a rock musician, a classical musician. None of those labels will apply to me, because I don't devote enough time to any one area.

I have never actually done a commercial project that has started with me or that has come to a conclusion. A lot of them have been speculative—"Okay, we are not going to use that," or we get to one point and decide to pull back. I was once part of a production team to write commercials. I sat down to talk with a client about the music that he needed, I think it was Amoco; there was a specific sound that they were looking for. I said, "Okay, I'll temp it out, or spec it out [hire the musicians], and make a little demo for them." I made the demo and the person came over to the studio and took a listen to it. This is a nonmusician, a business guy. He sat down and said, "That's just not right." I asked him what he meant, and he said, "That doesn't sound like somebody is going to be pumping gas," or something like that. He said, "It doesn't sound like happiness." He was using all these adjectives to decide what the music should sound like. He said we needed to do the music over, and he gave me a deadline. The pressure was just amazing.

It was at that time that I knew this was not the direction I wanted to go. I had to have the freedom to write the music as I see it, with regard to the reason they want the music. I pulled back from writing commercial music, basically jingles for products or for advertisers, mainly because of the pressure of writing music not for the music itself but for the product. It just felt awful. I usually try to write music because it feels good.

As an African American, depending on who it is you are dealing with and who is around you, you are superior or inferior. You are either put on a pedestal, or you need to get where someone else is. That is how I have found it. The younger white society really looks up to you as an artist until you prove that there is a reason for them not to. The older white musicians, jazz musicians and so forth, look down upon you until you prove to them that they must look up to you. You have that kind of situation with white society, in my experience as a composer.

When I look at orchestras, I look at it from the standpoint of a composer, not an African American composer. February and January are times when we are able to have our music played more than usual; that is a negative, but it is also something to be taken advantage of. I think when we take advantage of it, things start to change. We have got to stop looking at African Americans as this outside force that wants to become an inside force. Art organizations must start looking at African Americans not as on the outside wanting to come in, but as a part of the community that they want to include. Once they start doing that, all of the barriers that hold back composers of African American descent will be broken down. Whether the music is programmed in November or January is not relevant. What is relevant is that it is a great composition. The clientele that visits the orchestra is not just going to come in January or February but year round.

Being labeled a "black composer," as opposed to a "composer," bothers me greatly. My wife is a phenomenal saxophone player. For her to get a review that says, "What a great saxophone player, for a woman," is the same thing as saying, "What a great composer, for a black person." That is totally ignorant. They advertise "music by an African American composer." They may be trying their best to bring in an African American community, but it also tells that white suburbanite, "you don't have to go that night, because it is an African American composer. That means it is for the African Americans." As soon as they stop doing that and say, "This is a concert with a new work, and here is the person's name," people are going to come with interest and curiosity to hear what the music sounds like, not prejudging it as being for a specific ethnicity.

I want to be able to leave my impressions of the world and the events that surrounded my life. That is what I want to do. I can only do that through music, writing, and art. I paint, and I also take pictures. I took hundreds of pictures while I was in Vietnam, and these photographs are on display at the National Vietnam Veteran's Arts Group here in Chicago, with a couple of my paintings.

My music has been recorded and will continue to be recorded. When I do a piece that represents a part of my life, it is a statement about my history. African American music has always been about oral history. It is talking to that daughter and that son and telling them, "This is what I did, that is exactly what I have done, and that is what I want to continue to do," to keep that history alive—my history, specifically. My daughter can always pull out one of my albums and say, "This was my dad." She can go to a gallery and see a photograph long after I am gone and say, "That was my dad." My great-great-great granddaughter or son can do the same thing. That is my ultimate goal, to leave as much about myself as I can, artistically and creatively.

Postlude: Extensions of the Tradition— Linkages and Canon

In discussing the work of black American composers, we have seen several examples of what may be called "extensions of traditions"—that is, legatees of American creative thinkers who are black, simultaneously vindicating past blocked voices and forging new musical paths in the twenty-first century. While the word "tradition" has been tossed around a lot, it is a concept that is increasingly complex in relation to musical experiences. Many American artists refine and create traditions. We take in and are informed by a great deal of musical information through technology, the media, new printed texts, and art that is performed. Our palettes are expanding, and as artists we respond. It is fair to say that the artists presented in this text are the result of these influences, traditions, and experiences, but it was their special "take," their perspective, that has been the main focus.

An industry that has been sleepwalking around and overlooking deserving black talent in concert music can no longer ignore the stream of black composers from at least three generations, especially since the national searches sponsored by the ASOL (American Symphony Orchestra League) for symphonic works by African American composers. As mentioned earlier, the 1996 Pulitzer Prize awarded to George Walker was the first for a black composer. Some say it was too late, too little; yet the landscape is beginning to look very colorful. But are the gatekeepers prepared for such eruptions from underfoot?

When I began my own search for historical linkages, this quest for traditions, I identified more easily with the procedures, creative products, rhythmic conceptions, tonal languages, sonorities, and motif interplay of black artists.

That was true not only because it was what I knew, from my surroundings, but also because much of this music reflected the contemporary "move" and music of the times. Even in the dense textures of some composers' works, I found the drumbeat, as it were, and I was taken "home." Equally important is a connection with an unspoken-of, yet present, host of ancestral muses. It should be evident that much of black musical tradition is ritualistic in some sense and that in small ways—and in some larger ways, too—black American composers are connected to ritual. From these perspectives and sharing came aesthetic, social, procedural, and stylistic commonalities—as well as vast differences in interpretation and opinions about "common" artistic experience, cultural significance, and the direction of contemporary music.

In the examination of the common linkages as well as differing vantage points, we can find a variety of opinions, backgrounds, and aesthetic positions as well as an understanding of how these artists view themselves and society. This brings to mind Amiri Baraka's prophetic remark (from his ground-breaking work) that any discussion of the art of black Americans gives a "real read" and understanding of America and its uniqueness.

The question of accepted and expected repertoire or canon is quite an issue but something that all sorts of contemporary artists face. The idea of contemporary music as a rallying point for change is a common belief of American composers. Not much is said of the uniqueness, profundity, or richness of black works, which are usually dismissed as "too vernacular" (William Grant Still) "unapproachable," or more abstract than the work of most accepted white avant-gardists.

The notion of a canon is very problematic. Yet there has existed in the minds of conductors, teachers, and arts administrators a well defined, locked-down canon, a "greatest list" of works that maintain popularity among audiences and are favorites of musicians. These works are maintained for some good reasons; other works, however, are left out for bad reasons. While no one has any special authority to add new works to the canon, casting the net more widely is something any wise, sensitive, and informed appreciator of music should do.

What about inventive, pioneering work by black composers? Does it exist? The wide variety of forms, styles, and procedures practiced and devised by black creators, not the least of which are improvisational, are not spoken of in any serious way in contemporary concert music circles. Long before Gershwin, Bliztstein, Bernstein, and Copland even began to explore the expressive possibilities of a black woman's bluesy groan, black creators were notating and practicing the popular aesthetic as art while keeping company with Varèse and other early avant-gardists.

Why is it, then, that when Steve Reich decides to be moved by the distillation of a syncopated pulse of African drumming, we have a movement called Minimalism? The eclectic voices of so many black composers who have fused European and black music structures as a cohesive language, as common practice, should be recognized before white composer colleagues are placed on public radio to discuss "their newly found freedoms" in such popular music forms as the blues or jazz, or even rap.

Innovation as trailblazing as that of Ives, Cowell, Varèse, or Cage was produced by early black voices: by Francis Johnson (1792–1849); by James Reese Europe (1881–1919), especially his experiments after 1910 with the All-

Black Clef Club Orchestra, over a hundred strong, with five pianos, ten drum sets, mandolins, harp-guitars, banjos, cello, and brass;, by Fletcher Henderson (1897–1952); by Florence Price (1888–1953); and by the Duke, in his evocative and innovative pairings, experimenting, voicings, and instrumentations.

When we speak of, in Adolphus Hailstork's "dream term," a black canon, we can cite works that probably will not explode into any recognizable "top ten" list in *Fanfare* magazine. However, those works—along with other compositions ranging in styles and forms from symphonies and opera and chamber works to extended jazz suites and adult contemporary grooves and ballads—are glowing testimonies to the uniqueness, musicality, and native profundity of black American composers. Look for these work on the composers' labels—CRI, New World Records, Tel Arc, Innova, Leonardo, Koch, Albany, GRP, EarthBeat, GramaVision, Columbia, Verve, Epic, Blue Note, and Atlantic. Updated listings of works, recordings by composers, and their publishers are available from the Center for Black Music Research (CBMR), Columbia College, 600 South Michigan Street, Chicago, Illinois, 60605, telephone (312) 663–1600.

While many important contemporary composers are "pushing the envelope" in interesting and needed ways, American music can no longer be defined simply by any one group of men and "their view" of art and practice, and their "his-stories." We must also include the pioneering work of persons and forces like Mary Lou Williams, Ornette Coleman, Anthony Braxton, Rashaand Roland-Kirk, Miles, Charles Mingus's experimental orchestras, George Russell's Lydian Chromatic, the Art Ensemble of Chicago, Jimmy Hendrix, George Clinton, Prince, Me'Shell Ndegeocello, and numerous other black American musical pioneers who continually stretch the limits of sound and creativity in theory, performance practice, and compositional structure.

Research, writing, and discussion in ethnomusicology and popular culture also provide extremely powerful questions, models, and paradigms, new ways to think about music performance creation and appreciation. The artists that emerge from this stirring will be American men and women whose craft, preparation, professional interests, competence, and creative ingenuity will define the twenty-first-century schools of American composition practice, pedagogy, and principle.

The broader connections for artists, as I see them, are to the whole of music making, the universality of life and expression in the world we share. Monteverdi, Bach, Beethoven, Clara Schuman, Wagner, Schoenberg, Debussy, the Boulanger sisters, Stravinsky, Cowell, Copland, Cage, Barber, Bernstein, Orrego-Salas, Argento, Joan Tower, John Corigliano, and Libby Larsen are all soul brothers and sisters by the virtue of their common linkages as artists born in the West.

As can be seen in these sharings, perspectives, and professional quests, "tradition" is a very complex and intricate concept, by the virtue of time, circumstance, and expanded boundaries. This book, however, is about black American artistic experience seen through the eyes and ears of composers. These creators—some through conscious choice, others by "hue association"—are, in Anthony Davis's words, "warriors," people who by their very presence constantly define American music, particularly in the concert arena. One of the most telling statements is that of Jeffrey Mumford, who said that being a black composer is a "subversive activity."

These composers bear the torch of American creativity and innovation, just as they are extensions of a rich cultural tradition. As represented by these tradition bearers, the work stretches across our West African encoding and Western European training, infused comfortably and compatibly with contemporary American experience and ethos. These are the traditions of which we are extensions, and the extensions are both seeds and by-products of the artistic and socially expressive experience that we call American music.

Taken as a whole, these landscapes form the musical expanse that define our contemporary culture and prepare us for musical art in the twenty-first century.

Index

About the Author

William C. Banfield is a composer and a frequent lecturer and composer in residence at college and university campuses across the country, including Harvard, Princeton, Duke, Morehouse, Bowling Green, Spelman, the University of Richmond, the University of Michigan, the University of Texas/Austin, and Carnegie Mellon. He hosted the nationally distributed program *Landscapes in Color: Conversations and Concerts of Black American Composers* on National Public Radio. He founded the Undine Smith Moore Collection of Scores by Black American Composers, an archive of significant original manuscripts at Indiana University in the Archives of Music and Culture. He has several published articles and essays on the role of black American artists.

A native Detroiter, Dr. Banfield received his bachelor of music degree from the New England Conservatory of Music in Boston, a master's of theological studies from Boston University, and the D.M.A. in composition from the University of Michigan. His symphonic, operatic, chamber, and jazz popular works have been performed by numerous orchestras, including the National Symphony and the symphonies of Dallas, Detroit, Indianapolis, Minnesota, and San Diego. Recordings of his works are on Collins Classics, Atlantic, Innova, Centaur, and Tel Arc.

Dr. Banfield currently holds the Endowed Chair in Humanities and Fine Arts at the University of St. Thomas, is director of the American Cultural Studies Program, and is associate professor of music, teaching composition and courses that examine popular music and culture. He also conducts his Bmagic Orchestra, a nationally recorded chamber jazz ensemble. Dr. Banfield resides in St. Paul, Minnesota.